THE NEW WORLD POLITICS OF THE INDO-PACIFIC

The book offers a vivid analysis of the new geopolitics in the Indo-Pacific in terms of big power rivalry between the US-China and country-wise perspectives situating largely within the late 2000s and culminates with the developments of the COVID-19 period. The great power shift, marked by the rise of China and the relative decline of the US, poses a serious challenge to the balance of power in the Indo-Pacific region and the world order in general. Ironically, the play of realism in the region is stymied by broad partnerships of key countries that utilise the liberal approaches of cooperation with both rivals – the US and China. The book captures the mosaic of stakeholders – rivals the US and China along with Russia; other QUAD members Australia, India, and Japan; key ASEAN members, Indonesia, Malaysia, Singapore, and Vietnam; vulnerable states in East Asia, viz. Taiwan and South Korea; and groupings including the ASEAN and QUAD – that constitute the new world politics of the Indo Pacific.

The volume will be of great interest to scholars and researchers of Indo-Pacific studies, global politics, and international relations.

Josukutty C A is Professor and Director in the School of Social Sciences, Department of Political Science at the University of Kerala, India. He was Fellow of the United States Institute on US Foreign Policy at the University of Florida in 2010 and awarded the Fulbright Nehru Academic and Professional Excellence Fellowship in 2015. In 2019, he was selected for the "Academic Excellence Award" by the University of Kerala. His areas of interest and research include International Relations, India's foreign policy, and electoral politics. He has published five books and many research articles in reputed peer-reviewed journals, which include *Maritime Affairs, Glocalism: Journal* *of Culture Politics and Innovation*, *Indian Journal of Asian Affairs*, *Gandhi Marg*, and *International Journal of South Asian Studies*.

Joyce Sabina Lobo is Assistant Professor at the Department of Political Science, St. Aloysius (Deemed to be University), Mangaluru, India. She has formerly worked with Manohar Parrikar Institute for Defence Studies and Analyses (formerly called Institute for Defence Studies and Analyses, IDSA), New Delhi, with the Eurasian Centre. She has completed her MA (Political Science) from the Centre for Political Studies; and MPhil and PhD (International Relations) from the Centre for Russian and Central Asian Studies, JNU, New Delhi. Currently her research interests are Russian cum Myanmar politics and foreign policy in which she has published, and at her hometown her research interests include study on the Beary Muslims in Dakshina Kannada.

Indo-Pacific in Context

This series brings together topical research on contemporary and long-standing issues encompassing the Asia-Pacific region.

With countries steeped in history, communities diverse in cultures, developing economies and emerging markets, Asia-Pacific has emerged as the key stakeholder in a world order in flux. The region has solidified its presence in the global political discourse through multilateral initiatives, defence agreements, and strategic partnerships. It has emerged as a zone of contestations, conflict, and cooperation.

The works published in this series showcase interdisciplinary research in the arts, the humanities, and the social sciences, including a range of subject areas such as politics and international relations, international economy, sociology and social anthropology, women, gender and sexuality studies, history, geo-politics, military studies, area studies, cultural studies, environment and sustainability, development studies, migration studies, urban development, digital humanities, and science and technology studies.

Works in the series are published simultaneously in UK/US and South Asia editions, as well as in e-book format. We welcome a range of books aimed at furthering scholarship and understanding of the Asia-Pacific region. Authors and researchers interested in contributing to this series may get in touch with rioeditorial@tandfindia.com

Handbook of Indo-Pacific Studies
Edited by Barbara Kratiuk, Jeroen J. J. Van den Bosch, Aleksandra Jaskólska and Yoichiro Sato

Japan and its Partners in the Indo-Pacific
Engagements and Alignment
Edited by Srabani Roy Choudhury

The New World Politics of the Indo-Pacific
Perceptions, Policies and Interests
Edited by Josukutty C A and Joyce Sabina Lobo

For more information about this series, please visit: www.routledge.com/Indo-Pacific-in-Context/book-series/IPC

THE NEW WORLD POLITICS OF THE INDO-PACIFIC

Perceptions, Policies and Interests

Edited by Josukutty C A and Joyce Sabina Lobo

LONDON AND NEW YORK

Designed cover image: Gettyimages

First published 2024

by Routledge
4 Park Square, Milton Park, Abingdon, Oxon OX14 4RN

and by Routledge

605 Third Avenue, New York, NY 10158

Routledge is an imprint of the Taylor & Francis Group, an informa business

© 2024 selection and editorial matter, Josukutty C A and Joyce Sabina Lobo; individual chapters, the contributors

The right of Josukutty C A and Joyce Sabina Lobo to be identified as the authors of the editorial material, and of the authors for their individual chapters, has been asserted in accordance with sections 77 and 78 of the Copyright, Designs and Patents Act 1988.

All rights reserved. No part of this book may be reprinted or reproduced or utilised in any form or by any electronic, mechanical, or other means, now known or hereafter invented, including photocopying and recording, or in any information storage or retrieval system, without permission in writing from the publishers.

Trademark notice: Product or corporate names may be trademarks or registered trademarks, and are used only for identification and explanation without intent to infringe.

British Library Cataloguing-in-Publication Data
A catalogue record for this book is available from the British Library

Library of Congress Cataloging-in-Publication Data
Names: C. A., Josukutty, editor. | Lobo, Joyce Sabina, editor.
Title: The new world politics of the Indo-Pacific: perceptions, policies and interests / edited by Josukutty C A and Joyce Sabina Lobo.
Description: Abingdon, Oxon; New York, NY, 2024. |
Series: Indo Pacific in context | Includes bibliographical references and index.
Identifiers: LCCN 2023056720 (print) | LCCN 2023056721 (ebook) |
ISBN 9781032638645 (hbk) | ISBN 9781032766393 (pbk) |
ISBN 9781003479307 (ebk)
Subjects: LCSH: Indo-Pacific Region–Foreign relations. | Indo-Pacific Region–Strategic aspects. | Geopolitics–Indo-Pacific Region. |
Indo-Pacific Region–Foreign relations–China. | Indo-Pacific Region–Foreign relations–United States. | China–Foreign relations–Indo-Pacific Region | China–Foreign relations–United States | United States–Foreign relations–China. | United States–Foreign relations–Indo-Pacific Region
Classification: LCC DS341 .N489 2024 (print) |
LCC DS341 (ebook) | DDC 320.954–dc23/eng/20240216
LC record available at https://lccn.loc.gov/2023056720
LC ebook record available at https://lccn.loc.gov/2023056721

ISBN: 978-1-032-63864-5 (hbk)
ISBN: 978-1-032-76639-3 (pbk)
ISBN: 978-1-003-47930-7 (ebk)

DOI: 10.4324/9781003479307

Typeset in Sabon
by Deanta Global Publishing Services, Chennai, India

CONTENTS

About the Editors	*x*
About the Contributors	*xi*
Acknowledgements	*xv*

SECTION A
The Indo-Pacific Construct   **1**

1 Introduction   3
  Josukutty C. A. and Joyce Sabina Lobo

2 The Geo-Politics of the Indo-Pacific: Perceptions,
  Opportunities, and Challenges   16
  Srikanth Kondapalli

3 The Indo-Pacific as the New Theatre of "Cold War"
  Politics: Challenges and Regional Responses   34
  Shankari Sundararaman

4 From Quad 1.0 to Quad 2.0: The Persisting Discourse   49
  S. Y. Surendra Kumar

viii Contents

SECTION B
China and the Quad Nation States   69

5 China in the Indo-Pacific: Perspectives and Interests   71
Huo Wenle

6 Russia in the Indo-Pacific through Multipolarity,
Eurasian Integration, and the RFE   89
Joyce Sabina Lobo

7 The US in the Indo-Pacific: Interests and Strategy   103
Nanda Kishor M. S.

8 Japan's Interests and Strategies in the Indo-Pacific   118
Anil Kumar P.

9 India's Interests and Strategies in the Indo-Pacific   133
Uma Purushothaman

10 Indo-Pacific: Australian Middle Power Ambitions and
Dilemmas   148
Madhusudhan. B

SECTION C
Key ASEAN Nation States and Vulnerable Neighbours
of China   165

11 Malaysia's Responses to the Indo-Pacific: Between
Trepidations and Aspirations   167
Ivy Kwek

12 Singapore's Strategy in the Indo-Pacific   182
Vignesh Ram

13 Indonesia in the Indo-Pacific: The Rise of a Strategic
Geopolitical Power   194
Vignesh Ram

14 Vietnam in the Changing Strategic Environment of
Indo-Pacific   207
Aswani R. S.

Contents **ix**

15 South Korea's Approach to Indo-Pacific 221
   Jojin V. John

16 Taiwan in the Indo-Pacific 236
   Suresh K.

17 Conclusion 250
   Joyce Sabina Lobo and Josukutty C. A.

Index 259

EDITORS

Josukutty C. A. is Professor and Director in the School of Social Sciences, Department of Political Science at the University of Kerala, India. He was a fellow of the United States Institute on US Foreign Policy at the University of Florida in 2010 and awarded the Fulbright Nehru Academic and Professional Excellence Fellowship in 2015. In 2019, he was selected for the "Academic Excellence Award" by the University of Kerala. His areas of interest and research include International Relations, India's foreign policy, and electoral politics. He has published five books and many research articles in reputed peer-reviewed journals, which include *Maritime Affairs, Glocalism: Journal of Culture Politics and Innovation*, *Indian Journal of Asian Affairs*, *Gandhi Marg*, and *International Journal of South Asian Studies*.

Joyce Sabina Lobo is Assistant Professor at the Department of Political Science, St. Aloysius (Deemed to be University), Mangaluru, India. She has formerly worked with Manohar Parrikar Institute for Defence Studies and Analyses (formerly called Institute for Defence Studies and Analyses, IDSA), New Delhi, with the Eurasian Centre. She has completed her MA (Political Science) from the Centre for Political Studies; and MPhil and PhD (International Relations) from the Centre for Russian and Central Asian Studies, JNU, New Delhi. Currently her research interests are Russian cum Myanmar politics and foreign policy in which she has published, and at her hometown her research interests include study on the Beary Muslims in Dakshina Kannada.

CONTRIBUTORS

Madhusudhan B. is Head of the Department at the PG & Research Department of Political Science, N.S.S Hindu College, Changanacherry, Kerala. He has received his PhD and MPhil from Mahatma Gandhi University, Kerala. He has a teaching career spanning 18 years and has held numerous administrative positions. He is an approved mentor in Political Science at Mahatma Gandhi University. He has published widely and has organised seminars and workshops of national stature. He is presently pursuing a Post-Doctoral Programme on "Transgender Policy of Kerala" at the Institute of Socio-Economic Change. His areas of interest are international relations, regional studies, and gender studies.

Jojin V. John is Assistant Professor in the School of International Relations and Politics at Mahatma Gandhi University, Kerala. Previously, he was Research Fellow for East Asia at the Indian Council of World Affairs on East Asia focusing on the Korean Peninsula and Japan. Before joining ICWA, he taught political science at Christ University, Bangalore. He has also held visiting research positions at Hankuk University of Foreign Studies, Seoul (July–September 2022); National Chengchi University, Taipei (2015); Institute of Chinese Studies, Delhi (2013–14); Seoul National University (2012); and Academy of Korean Studies, Korea (2010–11). Dr. John received his PhD from the School of International Studies, Jawaharlal Nehru University. He has several publications to his credit, including monographs, book chapters, and articles that have appeared in academic journals such as the *Copenhagen Journal of Asian Studies*, *China Report*, *The Journal of International Relations*, *Strategic Analysis*, *India Quarterly*, and *Area Studies*.

xii Contributors

Suresh K. is Assistant Professor at the Department of Political Science, Panampilly Memorial Government College, Chalakudy, Thrissur, Kerala. He received his MA, MPhil, and PhD degrees from the Department of Political Science, University of Kerala. His research interests include East Asian Politics, India-Japan relations, China-India, and US triangular relations, and international political economy. He has published a number of articles in edited books and journals related to East Asian politics and international political economy.

Srikanth Kondapalli is Dean of School of International Studies and Professor in Chinese Studies at Jawaharlal Nehru University. He is educated in Chinese Studies in India and China with a PhD in Chinese Studies. He was Visiting Professor at National Chengchi University and the China Institute of Contemporary International Relations, Honorary Professor at Shandong University, Jinan and Jilin University, Changchun, and Yunnan University of Finance and Economics, Kunming, and Non-Resident Senior Fellow at People's University since 2014. He has a number of books, articles, and monographs to his credit. He received the *K. Subramanyam Award* in 2010 for Excellence in Research in Strategic and Security Studies. He is Editor of JNU SIS *International Studies* Journal.

S. Y. Surendra Kumar is Professor and Chairperson at the Department of Political Science, Bangalore University, Bengaluru, India. He has 19 years of teaching experience in Political Science (PG) at Bangalore University. He earned his MPhil and PhD in South Asian Studies, School of International Studies, Jawaharlal Nehru University, New Delhi. He has received the Mahbubul-Haq Research Award as well as a Short Duration Fellowship. He has four books to his credit and his recent book is *Empowering the Marginalized Communities in India: The Impact of Higher Education* (2021). He has contributed over 23 chapters for various edited books and his latest one is "China-Pakistan Economic Corridor (CPEC): India's Conundrum and Policy Option" in *The Palgrave Handbook of Globalization with Chinese Characteristics* (2023) and has more than 40 research articles published in prestigious national and international publications. He is the Editor-in-Chief of *Journal of Contemporary Politics* (Quarterly) and E-Newsletter *Rajneeti* (Quarterly). His main areas of research are South-Asian security and Indian foreign policy in relation to the United States and China.

Ivy Kwek is a Malaysian scholar with a research focus on Southeast Asia's regional security and geopolitical dynamics. Previously, she served as Special Functions Officer to the Deputy Defence Minister of Malaysia (2018–2020) and has worked in advisory roles in various international organisations and diplomatic circles. She was also Visiting Scholar at the National ChengChi University, Taiwan from April 2021 to February 2022. She holds an MA in International Studies and Diplomacy from the School of Oriental and African Studies (SOAS), University of London.

Nanda Kishor M. S. is Associate Professor at the Department of Politics and International Studies, Pondicherry University, and formerly Head of the Department of Geopolitics and International Relations, Manipal Academy of Higher Education, Manipal. He holds an MPhil and PhD in Political Science from Hyderabad Central University (HCU), Hyderabad, India, and completed a postdoc at the University of Leiden, the Netherlands, with ERASMUS MUNDUS Fellowship from the European Union. He received the Short-Term JRF from UNHCR, Brookings, the Government of Finland, and MCRG (Kolkata). He visited Hochschule University of Applied Sciences, Bremen, Germany, on an SRF by the DAAD-sponsored programme of HS Bremen in 2012. He was part of the International Visitor Leadership Programme (IVLP) by the United States in 2013. He has published (2023) the book titled *Reimagining India in the Geopolitics of the 21st Century*.

Anil Kumar P is Associate Professor in the Department of International Relations and Director, Capital Centre, Central University of Kerala, India, and is also a member of the Academic Council of the Central University of Kerala. His areas of interest are US, China, and South Asian security. He was Visiting Fellow at the University of Florida under the US State Department-sponsored SUSI Programme in 2012. Dr. Anil is the recipient of the TV Paul Award in 2011 for the best PhD thesis in International Relations/Political Science and was a research affiliate at the Institute of Chinese Studies in the Centre for the Study of Developing Societies, New Delhi. He is also a member of the Indo-Pacific Circle. He has published research articles in reputed peer-reviewed journals and is a regular commentator on international affairs in the media.

Uma Purushothaman is Assistant Professor in the Department of International Relations & Politics, Central University of Kerala. She was previously associated with the Observer Research Foundation and the United Service Institution of India. She is Non-Resident Fellow at the Middle East Institute, New Delhi, and a member of the Indo Pacific Circle. An alumnus of JNU, her areas of interest include great power politics, Russian foreign policy, soft power, Middle East politics, and US domestic and foreign policies. She serves as a peer reviewer for many international and national journals. She has published in national and international journals and presented papers at national and international conferences. She serves on the Board of Studies at Goa University and Chinmaya Vishwavidyapeeth.

Aswani R. S., Assistant Professor, School of Liberal Studies, UPES, Dehradun, is an interdisciplinary scholar whose research interests lie at the intersection of security, strategy, and the environment. She has a PhD and MPhil from the University of Kerala in Maritime Security and a master's from the

University of Hyderabad. Her MPhil thesis on *India-Maldives Relations: A Geostrategic Perspective* received the Best Dissertation Award from T.V.Paul, McGill University, Canada. She has widely published in Scopus and WoS journals in the areas of Energy, Environment, and Security – a nexus that aligns with her research interests. She teaches undergraduate and graduate courses on Energy Policy, Contemporary South Asia, and Climate Politics. Apart from teaching and research, she spends time dream-weaving and leading a mindful – minimalist – sustainable life.

Vignesh Ram is Assistant Professor at the Department of Geopolitics and International Relations at Manipal Academy of Higher Education (MAHE), Manipal. He has multi-disciplinary experience in the field of research cutting across areas of government policy research, think tanks and academics, science and technology research, political consulting, geopolitics, and corporate global risk analysis. Prior to joining MAHE, he worked closely in setting up a division on political risk for a defence start-up in Bengaluru. His areas of research interest include the Geopolitics of Southeast Asia and the dynamics of the ASEAN organisation, Indo-Pacific strategies of major powers, Terrorism and Asymmetric conflicts, Soft power, Media, and Public Diplomacy.

Shankari Sundararaman is Professor of Southeast Asian Studies and former Chair at the Centre for Indo-Pacific Studies, School of International Studies, Jawaharlal Nehru University. Prior to this, she worked as Research Officer and Research Fellow at the Institute for Defence Studies and Analyses (1996 to 2003). She was Visiting Fellow at the Asia-Pacific College of Diplomacy, Australian National University, Canberra, from May to July 2005, where she worked on the trilateral relations between India, Indonesia, and Australia. She was awarded the ASIA Fellows Award 2005–2006 (Funded by Ford Foundation), and based as a Visiting Fellow at the Centre for Strategic and International Studies (CSIS), Jakarta, in 2006–2007. She has published extensively on Southeast Asia and the Indo-Pacific.

Huo Wenle is currently Assistant Professor at the Centre for South Asian Studies, School of Political Science and Public Administration, Shandong University, Jimo District, Qingdao City, China. He completed his PhD at the Centre for East Asian Studies, Jawaharlal Nehru University, New Delhi, India between 2015 and 2020. His PhD thesis title was "Sino-Indian Maritime Security Relations: A Case Study of the Indian Ocean, 2000–2016". His research interests include Sino-Indian maritime security, China-India relations, and Indian foreign policy.

ACKNOWLEDGEMENTS

We have been supported by institutions and people for the successful fruition of this book project. We acknowledge with gratitude all the contributors of this book for sharing their expertise and scholarship through their papers. We are particularly grateful to the Indian Council of World Affairs (ICWA), New Delhi, the Indian Council of Social Science Research (ICSSR), New Delhi, and the University of Kerala for the financial support in conducting the international seminar on the Indo-Pacific that enabled us to identify papers to be part of this edited book.

We are grateful to all the faculty members and students of the Department of Political Science, University of Kerala, who supported the conduct of the seminar. Gratitude is due to the management of St. Aloysius (Deemed to be University), Mangaluru, for the encouragement and its Department of Political Science for its unconditional support.

A special thanks to Dr. Surinder Mohan, Assistant Professor of International Relations in the Department of Strategic and Regional Studies (DSRS) at the University of Jammu for the moral and academic courage given to the realisation of this edited book.

No amount of gratitude is sufficient to our dear family members Tency – wife to Josukutty and children Nikitha and Nikhil, and Nigel Monteiro – husband to Joyce Lobo and children Sara and Mark for bearing the brunt of our absence from many family responsibilities. We thank you for your love, kindness, and generosity for the sacrifices you made during the period of this book project.

Our special thanks to Routledge India and its editorial team for all the support and guidance.

Josukutty C. A. and Joyce Sabina Lobo

SECTION A

The Indo-Pacific Construct

1

INTRODUCTION

Josukutty C. A. and Joyce Sabina Lobo

The term geopolitics suggests interstate conflicts from a geographic perspective, and in this context, a nation looks for alliances to balance power, build up military force, promote economic development, gain access to resources and goods, control maritime routes, and influence its spheres of interest. Most of the traditional approaches of geopolitics focused on the control of space and the position of the state, beginning with Alfred Thayer Mahan, Friedrich Ratzel, Rudolf Kjellen, and then followed by Halford J. Mackinder, Karl Haushofer, and others. The works of Nicholas Spykman blended with those of classical realist Hans J. Morganthau in terms of understanding competition between states, and here geopolitics became one of the conditions of such competition, while also being a factor of foreign policy. New geopolitics today moves further away from the world level analysis of a state-centric conception of who rules the world to understanding interactions between different centres of power, even at the regional and local levels (Legucka, 2013).

The present focus is more on the control of seas and sea routes in a democratic manner, utilising normative justifications for a "rules-based order". The control of seas and sea routes, as argued by Alfred Thayer Mahan in 1890, within the Indo-Pacific region by China brings the significance of geopolitics into the region (Kaplan, 2012). This, along with the wielding of undue influence on neighbouring states, characterises the behaviour of China, suggesting the unfolding of new geopolitics along with the play of balance of power between Beijing and the US. The US is challenging this emerging regional challenger, i.e., China in the Asia-Pacific, now renamed as Indo-Pacific. Utilising the normative justifications for a "rules-based order", the US intends to secure its interests in this region and,

DOI: 10.4324/9781003479307-2

meanwhile, prevent China from gaining regional supremacy or becoming a regional hegemon, like the manner in which it "prevented Imperial Japan, Imperial Germany, Nazi Germany, and the Soviet Union" (Mearsheimer, 2010: 238).

The rise of China and the tendency of the US to dominate world politics constitute the core of new geopolitics that give added meaning to the Indo-Pacific region. This may become the new arena for the new Cold War or a geographical expanse where new world politics might play out. The US attempt to strengthen its traditional alliances and partner with new friends is fundamental to the evolving new geopolitics in the Indo-Pacific. Chinese strategies of the Belt and Road Initiative (BRI), its territorial issues with neighbouring countries and those from the extended neighbourhood, the assertions over the South China Sea, the defiance to the rules-based international order and most importantly, the possibility of closing ranks with the US as an economic superpower have brought the former in conflict with the latter, giving rise to the US-China rivalry. More importantly, the concerns, dilemmas, and positions of other powers within the region and their attempts in balancing dynamics of the new developments are core to the shaping of the new geopolitics.

The search for partners by both sides of the Sino-US rivalry is more confusing due to the juxtaposition of balancing the power of these rival states while cooperating with them through economic-technological cooperation by the state actors within the Indo-Pacific region. The fact that China is one of the top US trade partners while the latter is one of the top trading partners of the former suggests a dilemma of sorts. Moreover, nations like Australia, Japan, South Korea, the Philippines, and Thailand have treaty alliances with the US while being acrimonious with an assertive China. These nations, along with other stakeholders, ironically have robust economic cooperation with China. The politics that is played over this vast expanse of geography called today the Indo-Pacific redefines the term geopolitics, which does not come close to the meaning given during the Cold War. The rise of China with its attempts at power projection, especially in the South China Sea and in the Taiwan Strait viz-a-viz the need for the US to contain its rise in becoming a regional power, redefines the geopolitics for every stakeholder within the Indo-Pacific region.

The Indo-Pacific is the most important economic and strategic site in world politics today. This region is a combination of the Pacific and Indian Oceans that includes countries located on and within the edges of both the oceans. Economically, the region is of central importance in terms of availability of natural resources, trade flow, and energy transportation. It has almost half of the world's population and a third of world exports. The Indo-Pacific region has two-thirds of global economic growth, 60% of global GDP, and about half of world population, making it the world's fastest growing region

(The White House, 2022). Apart from the US as a Pacific power, China, India, Japan, South Korea, and Australia are the region's largest economies.

By 2030, 65 percent of the world's middle class will reside in the Indo-Pacific, representing an unrivalled amount of purchasing power (US DoD, 2019). The increased economic and trade activities open avenues both for cooperation and competition, making it a highly contested terrain. The region hosts six of the world's nuclear weapon states with no consensus on arms control. Disputes over maritime territories and their militarisation, assertion of freedom of navigation, and the existence of live nuclear hot spots are serious security challenges. The region also faces security threats such as piracy, smuggling, susceptibility to terrorism, cybercrimes, and environmental degradation. Thus, the Indo-Pacific is geopolitically significant for the divergent and competing security interests of key countries. In this context, the most important challenge is to maintain a balance between the divergent and convergent interests of all stakeholders, particularly the US and China.

The region is notable for its evolution, from the colonial period to the present, into a unique regional construct with contested concepts and interpretations marked by divergence between the US and China and others over its very nomenclature. The challenge that the rise of China causes to the predominance of the US, the varied anxieties of powers such as India, Japan, Malaysia, South Korea, Taiwan, Australia, Indonesia, and other Indian Ocean littorals are the key drivers of the new geopolitics in the Indo-Pacific. The US and its traditional allies view it as a strategic site with a focus on security, whereas India and some South-East Asian countries like Indonesia perceive it more as a geographic condition focusing on trade and energy ties (Taylor, 2020).

The great power shift marked by the rise of China and the relative decline of the US adds an uncertain dynamic to the balance of power in the region. The US tries to maintain its position as the pre-eminent power in the region while China strives for recognition as the emerging great power. Countries such as India, Japan, Australia, Malaysia, Singapore, South Korea, Taiwan, Indonesia, South Korea, and Vietnam are important stakeholders in the balance of power in the region. These countries hold and advocate competing and converging perceptions regarding what should shape the geopolitics of the region. The American and Japanese idea of Free and Open Indo-Pacific (FOIP); China's view of peace, development, and win-win cooperation; India's vision of inclusiveness, openness, and multilateralism; Australia's vision centred around security, openness, prosperity, and rules-based order; Indonesia's idea of friendship with all; and ASEAN's emphasis on openness, transparency, inclusivity, and a rules-based framework with its own centrality in the Indo-Pacific all aim for new roles and practices in the region (Wei, 2020).

South Korea's "strategic ambiguity" born out of its security dependence on the US and its economic partnership with China, Singapore's cautious balancing with the players of the region, Taiwan's risky balancing of China and the US and Malaysia's usual non-aligned or "not choosing side" approach to the dynamics of the Indo-Pacific further points to the diverse interests of the countries and their plans to protect it through myriad ways. The US Department of Defense Strategic Guidance 2012 and the Indo-Pacific Strategy Report 2019 state that the US core economic and security interests lie in the arc extending from the Western Pacific and East Asia into the Indian Ocean region and South Asia (US DoD, 2019). While the US, India, Japan, and Australia have a somewhat common view of a "rules-based order in the Indo-Pacific", China views it as an essentially meaningless, attention-grabbing concept and prefers the term Asia-Pacific instead of the Indo-Pacific (Yang, 2016). The US considered China in its Indo-Pacific Strategy Report 2019 as trying to "reorder the region to its advantage" thus calling it a "revisionist power" noting its actions in the South and East China Seas as militarisation along with the use of non-military coercive tools including economic tools. It further adds to this argument (The White House, 2022) by stating that China remains one of the key challenges to the Indo-Pacific due to its aim to turn the region into its sphere of influence. Thus, US-China rivalry and strategic competition have become key new geopolitical features of the Indo-Pacific while the attempt of some stakeholders appear to ensure security guarantees viz., Australia, Singapore, or Taiwan while for others like India or South Korea, it's more of securing one's interests without upsetting bilateral relations with rival nations. This adds more to the dilemma of perceptions that are divergent and convergent on the Indo-Pacific region.

The divergent and convergent perceptions have created some broad partnerships of countries with competing views and schemes as to how to deal with the emerging situation. The US promoted Quadrilateral Security Dialogue (QUAD), India's "Act East Policy", and Japan's schemes of Partnership for Quality Infrastructure (PQI) and Asia-Africa Economic Corridor, Australia's 'dependent ally' relations with the US, and the tri-lateral Malabar naval exercise, among other things, are aimed at containing the growing Chinese influence. China's schemes for greater influence through the "Maritime Silk Road" challenge the conventional prominence of the US in the region. The "ASEAN Outlook on the Indo-Pacific" – document approved by the 34th summit of the Association of Southeast Asian Nations (ASEAN) in Bangkok in June 2019 emphasises an inclusive and rules-based Indo-Pacific (The ASEAN Outlook on the Indo-Pacific).

The balancing that is attempted by the US and its partners through the Quad does not reflect a full-fledged alliance. However, elements of realism are found through joint naval exercises, regularising of summits and meetings, through security pacts like AUKUS, etc. There is a greater emphasis on establishing and adhering to a "rules-based international order" that relies on liberalism to which the stakeholders of the Indo-Pacific region are more inclined. An open confrontational attitude has not been exhibited by any Asian power since Japan in the Second World War. The US, on the contrary, has postured a confrontational tone in its white papers – the 2017 National Security Strategy, the 2018 National Defence Strategy, 2019 IPR Strategic Report, and the 2022 Indo-Pacific Strategy of the United States – with a direct reference to China, along with Russia being called a "revisionist" power. Furthermore, it states that the aim of the US is "not to change the PRC [China] but to shape the strategic environment in which it operates, building a balance of influence in the world that is maximally favourable to the United States, our allies and partners, and the interests and values we share" (The White House, 2022). This confrontational tone is not present in the ASEAN policies, in the joint communiques of the Quad, or in any of the Asian nations.

The COVID-19 pandemic and the abrupt US withdrawal from Afghanistan saw an emboldened China asserting itself globally and regionally, picking up fights with the US and others as was evident in the WHO and in the South China Sea and Galwan with India. This has led India to shed its initial hesitations in order to strengthen participation within the Quad through naval exercises with other members. Additionally, the AUKUS defence and security pact and the adoption of the Build Back Better World (B3W) plan by the G7 to bolster the infrastructure needs (which are devastated further due to the pandemic) of low- and middle-income countries, the formation of the Indo-Pacific Economic Framework for Prosperity (IPEF), the Indo-Pacific Partnership for Maritime Domain Awareness (IPMDA), and the European Union's and G7's reiteration of support for Western perspectives on the Indo-Pacific in their recent meetings are developments to contain and balance Beijing and its Belt and Road Initiative (BRI). An emerging area is the forming of the Quad Critical and Emerging Technology Working Group (Ray, 2021), as a continuation of the strategic framework to balance China. The Russian-Ukraine crisis has demonstrated the global range of US-China rivalry, indicating more intensive eventualities in the Indo-Pacific centred around the Taiwan Strait. However, the edited volume also explores how the divergent perceptions have also created some broad partnerships of key countries, including ASEAN, within the Indo-Pacific that utilise the liberal approaches of cooperation with both the US and China. These need to be analysed for their short- and long-term effects. Through this discernment, a representation can be formed on how the alignment of nations will take place, or will these events really confirm the new Cold War phenomenon?

The new balance of power marked by competition and rivalry between the US and China poses a number of challenges for all the stakeholders in the region. The emerging scenario raises questions about rules-based regional order, freedom of navigation of the seas and skies, access to maritime resources, and above all, balance of power dynamics in Asia. How do other powers, including regional formations and understandings, respond to US-China strategic competition? How do the economic and security ties these countries have with China and the US are shaping? Do they have any alternative middle power strategy to balance against US-China to avoid taking sides? Do new technological developments enhance the Cold War mentality or counter it through high economic interdependence? What is the response of these countries to Free and Open Indo-Pacific, the Quad, the Maritime Silk Route, and middle power strategies? What has been the status of the area and changes in geopolitics since the global pandemic COVID-19 took place? These issues and challenges are both interstate and transnational in nature and include strategic rivalry and competition among the major stakeholders. The COVID-19 pandemic has accelerated and reconfirmed these anxieties and challenges. A country-specific narrative of the region would answer these questions.

Insights from realist and liberal approaches are used to make sense of the developments in the Indo-Pacific. The chief objective of major powers in the Indo-Pacific is to affect a favourable balance of power in the ensuing rivalry between the US and China. The US policies are aimed at containing China while maintaining its own hegemony. China, on the other hand, is trying to carve out a space for itself in the Indo-Pacific and beyond as an emerging great power. The Quad and AUKUS, along with many other schemes devised by the US, are attempts to contain the rise of China by bringing together like-minded countries under a strategic framework to balance against China. The BRI/Maritime Silk Route, with its geo-strategic and geo-economic dual objectives, aims to consolidate China as the pre-eminent power in the Indo-Pacific. The Global Security Initiative (GSI), along with the Belt and Road Initiative (BRI) and the Global Development Initiative (GDI), propose in Chinese interpretation to foster a new type of security that replaces confrontation, hegemony, alliance, and a zero-sum approach of the West with dialogue, partnership, and win-win results and thus to discredit US engagements in the Indo-Pacific (Kewalramani, 2023). However, this rivalry frame and balancing alone will not explain the new dynamics of the region. While aligning with the US in any attempt to contain China, the other countries utilise their own bilateral and multilateral mechanisms and designs to balance the rivalry of the two great powers and thereby protect their interests and ensure peace and stability in the region.

Most of the countries in the region do not want the ensuing rivalry between China and the US to spiral out to war and adversely affect their interests. Therefore, they have resorted to liberal economic investment, infrastructure development, and human security measures for a peaceful, orderly, and stable Indo-Pacific. Countries with an anti-China mode also focus on how they together can progress faster through an inclusive rather than an exclusive policy. India's Indo-Pacific inclusivity approach and emphasis on negotiations, transparency, and evasive balancing is averse to a direct and all-out China containment. The ASEAN Outlook on the Indo-Pacific 2019 also stands for regional cooperation over "rivalry" is an effort to neutralise great power rivalry. Japan's FOIP vision and Expanded Partnership for Quality Infrastructure (EPQI), apart from other objectives, want to avoid an intensive confrontation between the United States and China by developing regional rules and norms for peace and development. For Australia, too, bilateral relations with China are crucial for trade and investment. Countries like Indonesia and Malaysia do not want to derail their economic cooperation with Beijing (Smith, 2018). Vietnam and the Philippines, which have direct territorial disputes with China, have strong economic and diplomatic associations with China. Some of these countries, like India, Japan, and Australia, explore the prospects of middle power coalitions as parallel arrangements for mutual benefit and to mitigate the master rivalry of the big powers. The economic and trade ties of most of the countries in the region with China have grown in the recent past in the midst of growing security concerns. These countries want to avoid getting enmeshed in intense China-US rivalry. They opt for freedom and stability in the region through mutually beneficial economic and trade ties, taking advantage of mega projects, including the BRI/Maritime Silk Route, in the liberal framework (Keohane & Nye, 1977). They argue that economic interdependence, shared interests, and mutual benefits are motivations for international cooperation. They want to create new opportunities for mutual growth and development by defending the liberal worldview-free and rules-based world order as propounded by Michael Doyle (Doyle, 1997). He focuses on a rule-based order for trade and cooperation. Cooperative engagement between these countries is encouraged to attract large-scale investments. Fighting the non-conventional challenges of piracy, terrorism, climate change, energy security, and pandemic and to ensure technology cooperation for achieving better results, a liberal cooperative framework is imperative.

At the same time, the developments in the Indo-Pacific need to be delineated in the context of China's attempt to exploit the COVID-19 pandemic to promote its geopolitical objectives, the US withdrawal from Afghanistan, India-China border clashes, the strengthening of the Quad, and the formation of the AUKUS.

Therefore, the new dynamics in the Indo-Pacific need to be analysed through a vast spectrum that includes realism and liberalism. The countries are exploring both realist and liberal options for a stable and peaceful order in the region. But the leading framework of analysis is realist in nature as both big powers engage in realist balancing. However, individual countries exploit liberal means to protect their interests and promote peace and development in the region.

Thus, the template of the new dynamics in the Indo-Pacific is a combination of realist balancing and liberal mechanisms working side by side as enunciated by different countries. The focus on country-wise perspectives in the context of the big power rivalry adopted for the book captures the entirety of developments from a realist template with liberal insights superimposed on it.

The book is divided into three main sections depending on the theme that the authors focus on. In the first section, the construct of the Indo-Pacific is attempted vis-à-vis the main rivals, the new developments like BRI, Quad, AUKUS, Quad Plus, etc. To begin with, **Srikanth Kondapalli** explores the Indo-Pacific from the geopolitical context. The strategy and geographical spread indicate variance with key stakeholders like the US, Japan, and India on the idea of the Indo-Pacific, suggesting that the concept is in the fructification stages. However, the unfolding events – rechristening of the Pacific Command of the US towards the recent Indo-Pacific Command, statements in the Shangri-La meeting in June 2018, 2+2 dialogues, the US-Japan-India trilateral meeting, the naval exercises, etc. indicate the increasing activity in the region. Of these, Japan has upgraded from the Indo-Pacific idea to that of a vision. There are also the quiet counter-measures by China in recent times through not only its Belt and Road Initiative but also specific maritime and military moves. It is argued here that while the Indo-Pacific idea has not unfolded all the required elements, it is gaining ground substantially in recent times, as seen from the statements of ASEAN, the UK, and France. While Kondapalli is giving a wide perspective from the geopolitical context, **Shankari Sundaraman** examines through the theories of realism and constructivism whether the dynamics within the Indo-Pacific illustrate a New Cold War theatre given the fact that the idea of Indo-Pacific responds to a growing China. High levels of economic integration between the rivals and with the respective stakeholders are present, suggesting contrariness to this idea. Also, the US-China rivalry brings in a security dilemma that undermines the efforts of the ASEAN towards multilateralism and its centrality. ASEAN and many stakeholders of the Indo-Pacific like India prefer the normative approach to the challenges of interstate behaviour. Sundaraman predicts that the Indo-Pacific will strengthen such a web of arrangements at the security level – integrating both the economic and security aspects into a more complex regional architecture.

The second section deals with the rivals China, with Russia on its side, and the US along with the other three member states within the Quad. The Indo-Pacific idea has fired more or less the positions of key stakeholders vis-à-vis China. China's rise and assertion in the South China Sea is looked at from a variety of perspectives by the stakeholders, particularly after the former's adoption of the BRI. China's views on the Indo-Pacific appear divergent while other stakeholders have sufficient reasons to be concerned on the former's strategies. One of the strong responses to the BRI has been the Quad and particularly its re-emergence under Quad 2.0. When comparing the Quad 2.0 factors of revival with Quad 1.0, **S. Y. Surendra Kumar** singles out China as one of the common factors for both the creation and revival and hence the reasons for renaming the region from Asia-Pacific to the Indo-Pacific. Quad 2.0 shows better signs of institutionalisation wherein talks/summits have taken place at the level of the heads of the states more during COVID-19. The three members of the Quad rely unconditionally on the normative approach to the question of freedom of navigation by respecting the UNCLOS, while the US's postures are more belligerent in tone. The varying threat perceptions on China limit Quad's progress in balancing/containing Beijing while it ironically remains their largest trading partner.

The Chinese perspective on the Indo-Pacific is significant to complete the mosaic of understanding on the region. **Huo Wenle** examines the Chinese perspective on the Indo-Pacific from the government and academia angle wherein the former views it as one of many regional cooperation initiatives while objecting to any geopolitical and geo-economic arrangements; and while scholars hold an aggressive view of threatening China's peripheral security, economic development, and strategic space. Wenle's reasons for China's hesitations on the Indo-Pacific mirror some of the very reasons for the failure of Quad 1.0 and the challenges to Quad 2.0 as delineated by **S. Y. Surendra Kumar.** The reasons for China's response to the Indo-Pacific as "utopia" or "bubble" are expressed on the lines of the liberal and neo-liberal approach where cooperation and institutionalism impede balancing by the stakeholders. He asserts that China is the only major power yet to achieve reunification, claiming that the territorial claims by China are rightful, and suggests realpolitik along with cooperation between stakeholders.

Russia, along with China, defines the Indo-Pacific region by retaining the old nomenclature of "Asia Pacific", while dismissing the dominant use of the concept, as part of a continuation of Cold War efforts to contain (this time) China. **Joyce S. Lobo** points out the Russian idea to emerge as one of the poles in the multipolar world by establishing leadership within the Eurasian space. As a corollary, Russia therefore focuses on the integration process within this space, calling its sphere of influence, thereby making it convenient for it to support likewise China's claim over its sphere of influence in the Asia-Pacific. Hence, both diverge from the countries that are discussed in this book in terms of the nomenclature and also by defining the politics in the region away from the "rules-based order".

A change in the dynamics would have been possible if the Democrats had won the US presidential elections during Hillary Clinton, which would have witnessed the continuance of the Obama legacy of establishing cooperation over conflict. **Nanda Kishor M. S.** argues that since President Trump's administration has interpreted the Indo-Pacific less as the region for mere free navigation and more as a strategy and "priority theatre", the rivalry has intensified. The US was one of the first countries to come up with a posture on the Indo-Pacific region as a "strategy" by pointing to China and Russia as "revisionist" powers in its 2019 IP Strategic Report. Hence, he employs theories of realism, neo-realism, neo-liberal institutionalism, and constructivism to explain the perception of the US on Indo-Pacific. He points out that the success of the strategy depends on the "consistency, cooperation and conduciveness" that the US creates for its identified partners.

Anil Kumar P. suggests that the balancing act of Japan is to create a rules-based order through mini-lateral and multi-lateral frameworks in the Indo-Pacific region and beyond. He argues that while it is very clear that Japan's Indo-Pacific strategy will increase security risks to China's sea lanes of communication, at the same time, the free and open Indo-Pacific (FOIP) and Quad will allow Tokyo to hedge the risk from its alliance dilemma and be in line with its own security policy. Though the vision of FOIP composition may be unclear at this stage, it has already demonstrated promise as a means of developing mutually reinforcing if not identical approaches to various challenges in the Indo-Pacific. Kumar points out that FOIP is still abstract and developments in the region are the result of an order transition rather than a power transition, wherein Japan is attempting a rule-based order rather than a power-based order in the current liberal international political order.

India appears to be the loose chink in the Quad chain. However, **Uma Purushothaman** gives a nuanced meaning of India's understanding of the Indo-Pacific that portrays the awareness among erstwhile experts like Kalidas Nag and K. M. Pannikar. Hence, Purushothaman delineates the foreign policy of India in the context of the Indo-Pacific – the need to have a favourable balance of power in the region, its geo-economic interests, and the larger strategic goal to emerge as a great power. Her approach is largely liberal and based on the normative framework to build cooperation over competition between India and China. Of all the Quad members, Australia's tilt toward the US is more pronounced within the Indo-Pacific concept. **Madhusudhan B.** focuses on Australia's three policy postures that hold the key to this tilt – the US as a close ally, China as a threat and competitor, and assertion of Australia as a middle power. To this end, the Quad and particularly the security pact called AUKUS have been a game-changer that infuses a new meaning into the Indo-Pacific concept from the US prism. Australia's realism is also marked by pragmatism as it depends on both China and the US.

Apart from the Quad countries, the other stakeholders within the Indo-Pacific region are the key member states of the ASEAN – Singapore, Malaysia,

Indonesia, Thailand, Vietnam, along with East Asian countries – Taiwan and South Korea, which form the interest of the third section of the book. **Vignesh Ram** locates Singapore's Indo-Pacific policy and strategy within the changing regional security environment while drawing the perspective and perplexity of small states. His chapters, on Singapore and Indonesia, examine the former through its regional differences with Indonesia and Malaysia while fine balancing with China on economic cooperation and with the US militarily. Singapore depends on the US for security while balancing relations and not the power of China. While Indonesia continues to place itself at the "maritime fulcrum" and the centre of China's Maritime Silk Road, Singapore actively involves itself in joint military drills with the "Quad" and individually with its members. Ram suggests the contradictions in terms of how the two countries within the Indo-Pacific region and in particular the ASEAN dealt with the new conceptualisations. In contrast, **Ram** locates Indonesia's approach to the merging regional security scenario from an institutional approach driven by a multitude of powers. Malaysia's response towards the Indo-Pacific has been muted or lukewarm at best, writes **Ivy Kwek**. She suggests that to date, the closest document that can reflect Malaysia's stance on the Indo-Pacific would be the ASEAN Outlook on the Indo-Pacific (AOIP), which was spearheaded by Indonesia but supported by all member states including Malaysia. Kwek points out that outright embrace of the Indo-Pacific strategy or embracing-resisting strategies is avoided, reflecting the insecurity of a small state that prefers being non-aligned with a hedging approach. **Aswani R. S.** examines Vietnam's policy, interests, and approach to the developments in the Indo-Pacific and how it uses the prospects to secure its national interests against the fast-changing geopolitical situations in the Indo-Pacific. While securing its interests, Vietnam has to balance China's expansionist policies and America's Asia Pivot policies.

South Korea within the East Asia portrays a likewise reluctance to embrace the Indo-Pacific concept to which **Jojin V. John** refers to as "strategic ambiguity". This is so given Korea's security dependence on the US and its economic partnership with China – a situation in which several small and middle powers in the region find themselves in, points out John. As a safe bet it endorses the AOIP. He introduces Korea's "New Southern Policy" (NSP) as its pivot to Indo-Pacific which aligns much with the Indian position. The NSP is more of a bilateral than of a minilateral/multilateral engagement of Korea's policy on the Indo-Pacific. The COVID-19 pandemic saw South Korea as part of the Quad Plus grouping that took the safe stance of acting to stem the infectious disease along with cooperation on areas of climate change and supply chain issues. The "strategic ambiguity" as portrayed is largely driven by the need to survive as the geopolitical rivalry unfolds in its close neighbourhood. One of the small powers that seem to be directly threatened by China bringing the rivalry between the latter and the US to a brink is Taiwan. Its territorial integrity and diplomatic leverage are more challenged today by Beijing than ever before. Taiwan has tried to counter China's BRI with its 2016 New South Bound Policy that goes beyond the economic and trade relations to include its role as a global logistics centre. **Suresh K.** strikes a positive note that China has so far not stopped Taipei from contributing to the world where we can defend the liberal international order and universal values.

The book aims to understand the geopolitical and geo-economic concept of the Indo-Pacific through the lens of the rival powers (US-China), through the perception and interests of various stakeholders including the ASEAN member states and those states that are vulnerable within the region. This constitutes the central theme/query of the book. The attempts are to understand whether/how this region is the new theatre for New geopolitics/New Cold War. Whether this region will continue the dilemma of whether to align or cooperate with one of the rival states? Whether the ASEAN centrality will prevail over the dominance of the rival states? It needs to be seen what the impact of cooperation in technologies in terms of 5Gs, cooperation in artificial intelligence, critical inputs to technologies like rare earths, etc., would be, especially in relation to the new security pacts like the AUKUS in the Indo-Pacific region. Would these have an impact on the traditional way of looking at the Indo-Pacific as geopolitical and geo-economic concepts? These are the questions that would be examined within the scope of the book.

Hence, the realist-liberal approaches are employed to discern the emerging geopolitics of the region with the ensuing rivalry between the US and China (along with Russia) as the base upon which the perceptions, opportunities, and interests of various stakeholders are either interconnected or diverge, and where partnerships and cooperation are sought with these two rivals. These constitute different aspects of the new world politics of the Indo-Pacific. The focus of each book chapter is on key players of the Indo-Pacific region – rivals the US and China; other Quad members Australia, India, and Japan; key ASEAN members viz., Indonesia, Malaysia, Singapore, and Vietnam; vulnerable states in East Asia viz., Taiwan and South Korea; and groupings including ASEAN and Quad. The timeframe for the book ideally situates largely between the developments during the late 2000s and culminates with the developments during the COVID-19 period up to the recent times that include the Russian-Ukraine crisis.

References

ASEAN. (2019). *The ASEAN Outlook on the Indo-Pacific.* https://asean.org/asean2020/wp-content/uploads/2021/01/ASEAN-Outlook-on-the-Indo-Pacific_FINAL_22062019.pdf

Bhowmick, Soumya. (2021). The Indo-Pacific Economics: Inextricable Chinese Linkages and Indian Challenges. *ORF*. https://www.orfonline.org/expert-speak/the-indo-pacific-economics-inextricable-chinese-linkages-and-indian-challenges/

Doyle, Michael. (1997). *Ways of War and Peace: Realism, Liberalism and Peace*. Norton.

Kaplan, D. Robert. (2012). *The Revenge of Geography: What the Map Tells Us About Coming Conflicts and the Battle against Fate*. Random House.

Keohane, O. Robert., & Nye, S. Joseph. (1977). *Power and Interdependence: World Politics in Transition*. Boston: Little Brown.

Kewalramani, Manoj. (2023). *China's Global Security Initiative Undermining US Alliances or Quest for a New Security Architecture?* (Vol. 1). Takshashila Discussion Document 2023 –02.

Legucka, Agnieszka. (2013). New Geopolitics – What Is Actually New. *The Copernicus Journal of Political Studies*, 2(4), 5–19.

Mearsheimer, J. John. (2010). The Gathering Storm: China's Challenge to US Power in Asia. *The Chinese Journal of International Politics*, 3, 381–396.

Ray, Trisha. (2021). A Quad 2.0 Agenda for Critical and Emerging Technologies. *ORF*. https://www.orfonline.org/expert-speak/a-quad-2-0-agenda-for-critical-and-emerging-technologies/

Smith, M. Jeff. (2018). The Return of the QUAD . In Jeff M. Smith (Ed.), *Asia's Quest for Balance: China's Rise and Balancing in the Indo-Pacific* (pp. 208–224). Rowman & Littlefield.

Sun, Yang. (2010). Strategic Perspective in the Indo-Pacific Region: A Chinese Perspective. In Gurpreet S. Khurana & Antara Ghosal Singh (Eds.), *India and China: Constructing a Peaceful Order in the Indo-Pacific* (pp. 1–10). National Maritime Foundation.

Taylor, Brendan. (2020). Is Australia's Indo-Pacific Strategy an Illusion?. *International Affairs*, 96(1), 95–109.

US DoD. (2019). *Indo-Pacific Strategy Report, Preparedness, Partnerships and Promoting a Networked Region*. https://media.defense.gov/2019/Jul/01/2002152311/-1/-1/1/DEPARTMENT-OF-DEFENSE-INDO-PACIFIC-STRATEGY-REPORT-2019.PDF

The White House. (2022). *Indo-Pacific Strategy of the United States* https://www.whitehouse.gov/wp-content/uploads/2022/02/U.S.-Indo-Pacific-Strategy.pdf

Wei, Ling. (2020). Developmental Peace in East Asia and its Implications for the Indo-Pacific. *International Affairs*, 96(1), 189–209.

Yang, Sun. (2016). Strategic Perspective in the Indo-Pacific Region: A Chinese Perspective. In Gurpreet S. Khurana & Antara Ghosal Singh (Eds.), *India and China: Constructing a Peaceful Order in the Indo-Pacific* (pp. 1–9). National Maritime Foundation. https://maritimeindia.org/View%20Profile/63624526047062960.pdf

2

THE GEO-POLITICS OF THE INDO-PACIFIC

Perceptions, Opportunities, and Challenges

Srikanth Kondapalli

As economic, technological, and military developments in the eastern hemisphere are inexorably acquiring prominence, global attention is today focused on the region that is renamed as Indo-Pacific. Despite the continuing conflict in the Russia-Ukraine front, the fact that important signals are emanating in the Indo-Pacific suggests the resurgence of this idea. The idea for the Indo-Pacific was floated in the 2000s with the United States leaders suggesting alternatives to the Asia-Pacific as a concept as well as a security mechanism to manage regional tensions and provide security for the region in the light of the assertiveness of China. Ever since the Indo-Pacific idea gained traction formally in November 2017 between the medium-level officials of the United States, Japan, Australia, and India, several developments have unfolded to support this phenomenon. The concept of the Indo-Pacific, its strategy, policies, and programmes are still in the making – visible in the number of different statements made by several officials – in this regard. The US, Japan, and India's definitions, strategy, and geographical spread appear sometimes to be at variance with each other – indicating that due to difference, this idea is still in the stage of fructifying. On the other hand, a number of events have been unfolding in the region, including the rechristening of the Pacific Command of the US towards the recent Indo-Pacific Command, statements in the Shangri-La meeting in June 2018, 2+2 dialogues (between foreign and defence ministers), and the US-Japan-India trilateral meeting and the Quad naval exercises. Of these, Japan has upgraded the Indo-Pacific idea to that of a vision. The Southeast Asian grouping has also come out with the ASEAN outlook. India has created a territorial division in its foreign ministry at the Joint Secretary level. Viewing these developments as balancing at best and containment at worst, China quietly began countermeasures in recent times

DOI: 10.4324/9781003479307-3

through not only its Belt and Road Initiative but also specific maritime and military moves. It is argued here that while the Indo-Pacific idea has not unfolded all the required elements to become a full-fledged strategy, it is gaining ground substantially in recent times, as seen also from the statements of ASEAN, the UK, France, and others.

Indo-Pacific Region

Defining geographical regions is fraught with difficulties and most times historically too. Analysing the political relations, specifically power relations, behind the geographical entities is more arduous. However, the geographical entities and power relations do reflect the dominant themes of the times and a shift in power in the region and the world at large or power relations as such. One such region that has gone through various transformations in perceptions is Asia, which was configured as the Orient or, in the view of Rabindranath Tagore, calling for identity formation among Asian colonies. The 1950s was a formative period with the post-colonial states clubbing together under the Afro-Asian unity movement even as the then Superpowers were trying to carve their influence in the region. For instance, in 1954, the United States National Defence Education Act defined five major regions of Asia for better management of the resources and direction of policies. As one of the superpowers, the US had its way and the labels stuck in practice and in theory. Thus, the sub-regions of East Asia, Southeast Asia, South Asia, and the then Soviet-controlled Central Asia and the Middle East (or West Asia, as it is called in India) came into being. Containment of Soviet and Chinese communist expansion in East and Southeast Asian regions became the main policy thrust during this time, resulting in the alliances of the Southeast Asia Treaty Organisation in the 1950s and the formation of the Association of Southeast Asian Nations (ASEAN) grouping in the 1960s and alliances with Pakistan in South Asia. The Soviet bloc was also expanding first with the Communist International and then with active support to the revolutionary movements in the region. Thus, the Asian region – both in its continental and maritime areas – was carved out by the geo-political trends of the times, even as India was advocating "positive neutrality". Mao Zedong, at the founding of the People's Republic of China (PRC), wanted his country to be at the "centre of gravity" in Asia but his country was then hardly recognised in the international system. India at that time was an active member of the Non-Aligned Movement advocating positive neutrality between the then Superpowers or even aligning with the then Soviet Union in 1971. While the US built up relations with China to counter the then Soviet Union, it also expanded relations with Beijing in economic and technological spheres. It was during this period that the concept of Asia-Pacific became popular, mainly in the economic field, with the

Asia-Pacific Economic Cooperation (APEC) becoming a major driver in the regional economic integration. Despite being a large country, with a huge population and market, India was excluded from the APEC. India was also confined by both the US and China during the Cold War to the South Asia box. As India began to emerge in the comprehensive national power indices, the previous formulation of Asia-Pacific no longer became valid, also aided by China losing steam of late.

Four decades of reform and opening up in China had built substantial depth to the US-China relations, propelling China as the second largest economy in the world by 2010 and the largest high-tech exporting country by 2014, displacing Japan and Germany from these two positions. China soon became the largest trading partner for over 120 countries in the world and remained at the centre of the trade value chain. Simultaneously, with the new economic heft, Beijing began demanding respect for its expanding "core interests" from its neighbours and others. Bilateral trade with the US increased to over $700 billion with huge trade surpluses in favour of Beijing, investments increased with China investing $1.2 trillion in the US Treasury Securities. However, while "the US welcomed the rise of China" as successive Presidents of the US stated, China began encroaching on the US alliances or began militarily influencing regions such as South China Sea, East China Sea, and Pacific and Indian Oceans. China also began "setting up a different kitchen" through the Belt and Road Initiative since 2013 in the continental and maritime regions – chipping away at the US or the influence of its allies. The 19th Communist Party Congress (CCP) of China in October 2017 paved a road map for celebrating "two centennials" and building "socialist modernisation" by 2050 and occupying the "centre stage" in global and regional orders. This was followed by an ambitious policy of Made in China by 2025 for high-tech products. These are some of the changes in the region that set concerned countries rethinking on the overall strategic approach.[1]

For decades, the larger strategic idea that captivated the imagination of many a country was the Asia-Pacific region which in many ways benefited China's rise in the international system. Today, given the strategic landscape undergoing tectonic shifts in the region, and in the light of Chinese assertiveness in many regions, a new discourse became necessary to accommodate the rise of other countries and address their concerns. With the intensification of globalisation and its attendant challenges, many changes are unfolding that are triggering a realignment of not only borders and nations but also the larger entities and ideas (Buzan, 2012; Duara, 2010; Acharya, 2010). Increasingly, the Indo-Pacific strategy is gaining traction, although this was mentioned a decade ago. In both the previous Asia-Pacific and the current Indo-Pacific, the United States' role has been crucial in promoting the idea as well as providing the policy framework and programmatic wherewithal. In each case, the major beneficiary of the strategic idea was different, reflecting the ground realities of the times and changing power dynamics.

The Obama Administration and the Japanese leader Shinzo Abe rekindled the Indo-Pacific idea.[2] This region broadly refers to the maritime area between the east of Africa and the west of Oceania.[3] After the initial work by the then US Secretary of State Condoleezza Rice who proposed interaction between these four countries' navies to provide timely relief measures for Southeast Asian countries affected by the Tsunami disaster, in September 2007 they conducted a naval exercise in the Bay of Bengal. China saw this exercise as a part of an effort at potentially blocking its energy supplies – 80 percent of more than 500 million tonnes of its imports from West Asia and Africa passing through the Indian Ocean region. This was also the time when China's rhetoric and coercive diplomatic efforts against Taiwan President Chen Shuibian were becoming acute. China's subsequent demarche to Australia and Japan, change in government in the US, and President Obama's visit to China in 2009 changed the situation in favour of Beijing and the Indo-Pacific idea took a back seat (Nicholson, 2007; Madan, 2017). This suggests that China – with extensive economic and political relations with a number of states – could be an influential power in deciding outcomes in the Indo-Pacific region.

The idea of Indo-Pacific was referred to by the then US Secretary of State Hillary Clinton in 2010 obliquely but more extensively in 2011. Clinton stated:

> Stretching from the Indian subcontinent to the western shores of the Americas, the region spans two oceans — the Pacific and the Indian — that are increasingly linked by shipping and strategy. It boasts almost half the world's population. It includes many of the key engines of the global economy, as well as the largest emitters of greenhouse gases. It is home to several of our key allies and important emerging powers like China, India, and Indonesia.
>
> *(Clinton, 2011)[4]*

President Obama, in his speech to the Australian Parliament in November 2011, suggested a "rebalance" of the US from the Atlantic to the Asia-Pacific (Obama White House, 2011). The rebalance is aimed at rationalising US force structures in the trans-Atlantic and the Asia-Pacific to about 40:60 in favour of the Asia-Pacific, in addition to building a ballistic missile defence (BMD) shield; "strengthening alliances" with Australia, Japan, and South Korea, "deepening partnerships with emerging powers" like Singapore, Indonesia, Thailand, Vietnam, and India; "building stable, productive, and constructive relationships with China"; "empowering regional institutions" like the East Asian Summit; and "helping to build a regional economic architecture" in the form of the Trans-Pacific Partnership (TPP) and others.

Kurt Campbell, who served in the Obama Administration on East Asian affairs at the State Department and currently in the Biden Administration, argued that the "pivot" policy is not to contain China militarily but to reinforce the US influence through a combination of policies, including in the economic domain. The TPP of high-grade liberalisation and environmental standards was proposed as a way to reinforce the US economy as well as its allies (Campbell, 2016).

After President Donald Trump took over in January 2017, several changes took place. Increasingly, Trump used Indo-Pacific as a concept in his speeches and documents. During his speech at Da Nang in Vietnam in November 2017, Trump proposed the Indo-Pacific strategy. Trump mentioned that his strategy was "to strengthen America's alliances and economic partnerships in a free and open Indo-Pacific, made up of thriving, independent nations, respectful of other countries and their own citizens, and safe from foreign domination and economic servitude" (Trump White House, 2017).[5] According to Alex N. Wong, US Deputy Assistant Secretary, Bureau of East Asian and Pacific Affairs, the Indo-Pacific strategy has the following components:

> We want the nations of the Indo-Pacific to be free from coercion, that they can pursue in a sovereign manner the paths they choose in the region. … we want the societies of the various Indo-Pacific countries to become progressively more free – free in terms of good governance, in terms of fundamental rights, in terms of transparency and anti-corruption. [We want] open sea lines of communication and open airways. [We want] more open logistics – infrastructure [-] to encourage greater regional integration, encourage greater economic growth. [We want] more open investment [and] open trade. it acknowledges the historical reality and the current-day reality that South Asia, and in particular India, plays a key role in the Pacific and in East Asia and in Southeast Asia. That's been true for thousands of years and it's true today. Secondly, it is in our interest, the U.S. interest, as well as the interests of the region, that India play an increasingly weighty role in the region. India is a nation that is invested in a free and open order. It is a democracy. It is a nation that can bookend and anchor the free and open order in the Indo-Pacific region, and it's our policy to ensure that India does play that role, does become over time a more influential player in the region.
>
> *(US Department of State, 2018 and Senate*
> *Committee on Foreign Relations, 2018)*

The above conceptual proposals for the Indo-Pacific strategy were reiterated by the then Secretary of State Rex Tillerson in a speech to the CSIS in

October 2017. Tillerson stated the expanding relations with India in this speech and underlined that

> India and the United States must foster greater prosperity and security with the aim of a free and open Indo-Pacific. The Indo-Pacific, including the entire Indian Ocean, the Western Pacific and the nations that surround them, will be the most consequential part of the globe in the 21st century. Home to more than 3 billion people, this region is the focal point of the world's energy and trade routes. Forty percent of the world's oil supply criss-crosses the Indian Ocean every day, through critical points of transit like the Straits of Malacca and Hormuz…India can also serve as a clear example of a diverse, dynamic, and pluralistic country to others.
>
> *(CSIS, 2017)*

On November 11, 2018, officials of four democratic countries – the United States, Japan, India, and Australia got together in Manila to form a low-key grouping called the Quad- Quadrilateral Security Dialogue. They individually announced their support, in varying degrees, for the rule of law, freedom of navigation, maritime connectivity, maritime security, countering North Korean nuclear/ballistic missile proliferation, and other related aspects.

There has also been a change in terminology from Asia-Pacific to Indo-Pacific as an area of their collective cooperation (Auslin, 2018). It is likely that many countries in the region may find this initiative interesting and hence would like to join, while others like China have expressed concerns and may take measures to counter the Quad. For instance, China's foreign minister Wang Yi was critical of the idea of India-Pacific, suggesting that the current phase of international relations does not reflect a renewed cold war phase and that the Indo-Pacific strategy is basically an "attention-grabbing idea" that will "dissipate like ocean foam" (Birtles, 2018). A Chinese military commentary argued that "As the Indo-Pacific Strategy is in full swing, we cannot neglect it, but we also do not need to be inexplicably nervous." It further stated:

> The theoretical basis and behavioral models of the Indo-Pacific Strategy is a reflection of the Cold War mentality based on ideology and the demarcation of friend or enemy. This definitely goes against the economic globalization, cultural inclusion, political pluralism, shared interests and other requirements of our times.
>
> *(Wu, 2018)*

However, despite enunciating the strategy of the Indo-Pacific, a number of sinews of this strategy are not explained nor implemented so far (Sayers, 2018). The US, Japan, and India did discuss "economically sensible projects" though.[6] The US Department of Defence released a comprehensive report in June 2019 that sought to build linkages between economics, governance, and security (The Department of Defense, 2019). That the idea as such is of significance is reflected in the elevated meeting at the ministerial level in New York in September 2019 between the four countries (Scott & Reynolds, 2019). Later, senior officials of these four countries met in Bangkok on November 4, 2019, and reiterated ASEAN centrality (Economic Times, 2019).

Also, the US has sent the message that despite the change in the government with Joe Biden taking over the reins, there is no major shift in its policies on the Indo-Pacific. Indeed, in addition to the three summit meetings of the Quad leaders in February 2021, September 2021, and March 2022, the US released its updated Indo-Pacific Strategy in February 2022.[7]

With the US troops' withdrawal from Afghanistan since August 2021, it appeared that the US would focus mainly on the Indo-Pacific maritime regions. However, the Russian military actions on Ukraine in February 2022 appeared to have upset this calculation by bringing the Eurasian region into focus. Nevertheless, the fact that there has been an elevation from bureaucratic to ministerial to heads of state level discussions on the Quad and the Indo-Pacific suggests that the interest in the subject has not waned.

Japan's Role

The role of Japan in the Indo-Pacific has become crucial given its proximity to China and its recent marginalisation in the economic field and concern with the security of the Senkaku islands and the Air Defence Identification Zone (ADIZ) established by China. Japan was the earliest to have proposed the idea of the Indo-Pacific region in a speech by Prime Minister Shinzo Abe in New Delhi in 2007, referring to the confluence of the two oceans in an "arc of freedom and prosperity" (Abe, 2007). Japan has been making initiatives since the 1990s – constrained as it was by its Constitutional provisions as well as to counter an assertive China which began making inroads in the Japanese-administered Senkaku Islands. The 1997 treaty revisions with the US included provisions for acting in the "surrounding areas", although this has not been defined. With China increasing first its naval "research activities" and then transgressions in the Senkaku Islands through coastguard and air force intrusions, Tokyo began amending its constitutional provisions to include "collective self-defence", going beyond the 1,000 nautical mile limits (as in its non-combat role in Iraq and Afghan campaigns), increasing marginally the defence budget, and the like. Japan's dependence on the Indian Ocean through which an estimated 75 percent of its energy transits has become a main concern, partly due to a spike in piracy incidents in the Indian Ocean and Southeast Asia but also due to the militarisation of the

South China Sea by China in the recent past. China's "territorial sea" concept for the South China Sea and claiming of 80 percent of this sea territory could result in Japan losing its edge in the region at a minimum and depending on China for trade transit in the longer run. While much of the economic and technological aspects of Japan are still in China, the maritime dimensions are becoming a major constraint in the region. The proposed Code of Conduct by China for the concerned South East Asian countries places Japan and other countries utilising the waters of the South China Sea at a disadvantage. China's Coast Guard Law of 2021 and its survey ship's presence in the region, the Whitsun Reef incident when China mobilised several boats closer to the Philippines in April 2021, added further to the tensions.

Also, as the earliest state to modernise and democratise in Asia, Japan's "arc of freedom and prosperity" is a natural choice for the Indo-Pacific region. Support for this idea is also in Japan's interests in diversifying economic assets from an increasingly nationalist China towards the Southeast Asian states and India. This expands the role and leadership of Japan in the two oceans in the long run. The concept of "security diamond" further links up with major democracies in the region (Abe, 2012). Thus, Japan is at the forefront of the Bay of Bengal quadrilateral exercise in September 2007 with the US, India, and Australia, but also in the recent revival of the concept of the Indo-Pacific and joining the trilateral Malabar exercises with the US and India in the last few years and proposing the concept of the Asia-Africa Growth Corridor in 2017. According to Japan's Ministry of Foreign Affairs, "Japan will enhance "connectivity" between Asia and Africa through a free and open Indo-Pacific to promote the stability and prosperity of the regions" (Ministry of Foreign Affairs, 2017). Providing a robust role for Japan (as with the others) is the trilateral with the US and India, which is taking a more concrete shape recently, beginning with lower-level official interactions. Two summit level meetings between the three leaders of the US, Japan and India took place in December 2018 and June 2019. Several trilateral meetings between the US, Japan, and Indian officials took place, offering an elevated level of interactions. Also, a 2+2 dialogue began between the foreign and defence establishments, with the interoperable Malabar naval exercises accommodating Japan recently. Japan thus sees an opportunity in strengthening the Indo-Pacific regions, with guardrails built around Taiwan, the Senkaku Islands, and the South China Sea, preventing any Chinese misadventure.

India's Role

The idea of Indo-Pacific is attractive to India, even if entering uncharted waters, as it propels New Delhi's role beyond the Cold War confinement to South Asia.[8] The US and China during the Cold War had worked against

India, while this policy is currently continued by China, given the strengthening of its "all weather" relations with Pakistan but also expansion of the Belt and Road Initiative. Also, China had sent nearly 40 naval contingencies to the Indian Ocean to address piracy issues since 2008. While piracy incidents declined, due to the US International Task Force and Asian Naval Symposium efforts, China's naval contingencies continue to be deployed. China also had commissioned a naval base at Djibouti, in addition to building ports at Gwadhar and Hambantota. One of the other main considerations for India is the huge coastline of over 7500 km, having control and management of 1200 islands, and protection and development of an Exclusive Economic Zone of about 2,000,000 square km (Kumar, 2019). The Mumbai terror attacks a decade ago underlined the security of the coastline.

India had a set of policies even before the Indo-Pacific idea came into being (Saran & Singh, 2018). It began as Look East policy in 1991 which has been changed to Act East policy in 2015. The Act East policy coincides with the Indo-Pacific idea to a large extent. In India, the concept of the Indo-Pacific was first mentioned by a naval officer Gurpreet S. Khurana in an article on cooperation between Indian and Japanese navies (Khurana, 2007; Raghavan, 2018). The term was used by former PM Manmohan Singh at the India-ASEAN Summit in 2012. Later, Manmohan Singh used the term in May 2013 in an address to the Japan-India Association in Tokyo. India's rise in the recent times, its robust democratic processes and rule of law, geographical position in the Indian Ocean, rising middle class, sustainable economic growth rates with high domestic consumption, its integration process in the world and IT software and others have attracted global attention, specifically of the US and its allies in the recent times. India's Act East had expanded its interactions from South Asia to an extended format. The January 2015 Obama-Modi joint vision statement on the Indian Ocean and the South China Sea caught global attention although the Indian naval doctrine is based on the Indian Ocean as a primary area of responsibility and the South China Sea and the Persian Gulf as "secondary". Nevertheless, China's forays in the South China Sea alerted the Indian side which learnt through the INS Airavat incident in 2009 that freedom of navigation through the region is crucial for the protection of its more than half of global trade passing through these waters (Singh, 2017). India's alignment with the renewed Quad members is thus visible since November 2017.[9] There is also an unresolved territorial dispute for India in its northern borders with China, besides the Sino-Pakistan active military cooperation and China's entry into the Indian Ocean region to be considered.

The new government in New Delhi since 2014 has been attempting to introduce certain new policies. One of these includes the upgrade of the 1991 Look East policy into Act East policy, the latter formally announced by

Prime Minister Narendra Modi in his speeches at Naypyidaw in November 2014 (The Hindu, 2014). Although the Act East policy was mentioned by various others before, after the implementation of the Look East policy for over two decades, a mid-course correction towards an action-oriented outlook, regional demands and aspirations, and change in the context have all necessitated the new initiatives by India.[10] With over 7 percent economic growth rates (except during the pandemic years), and prospects for sustaining such growth rates, the new leadership had announced a change in policy from being reactive to one of aspiring to be the "leading power" in global affairs as India's then foreign secretary S. Jaishankar suggested in a speech at Singapore in 2015. This necessitates a shift in focus and policy to provide public goods and services to the neighbourhood and beyond. To cushion such a policy is to invoke the diplomatic, commercial, and military resources of the country in a coordinated manner. Many of the visits undertaken by PM Modi after assuming office since mid-2014 are towards the east and include visits to Japan in September 2014 and November 2016, Myanmar, Singapore, Fiji, South Korea, Mongolia, Vietnam, Australia, and others. During his second term, these visits only intensified, suggesting a renewed focus on the Indo-Pacific region but in the light of current ground realities in the region. In December 2015, Prime Ministers of India and Japan mentioned their effort to strive for "a peaceful, open, equitable, stable, and rule-based order in the Indo-Pacific region and beyond" (MEA, 2015). The June 1, 2018 speech by PM Modi at the Shangri-La dialogue was the first definitive Indian statement on the subject, referring to the word Indo-Pacific as many as 11 times when he suggested that India stands by "inclusive" architecture for the Indo-Pacific region with ASEAN "centrality" as its outlook. Unlike the US definitions of the Indo-Pacific that generally aligns with the previous Pacific Command of the US Navy, PM Modi included east of the African region in the Indian formulations (MEA, 2018a). A day earlier at Jakarta, PM Modi signed a maritime cooperation agreement with Indonesia to reinforce the Indo-Pacific construct (MEA, 2018b). A second major speech of "Indo-Pacific Oceans Initiative" is that of PM Modi at the East Asia Summit in Thailand in 2019 that had seven features, viz., maritime security, ecology and resources; capacity building; disaster risk reduction and management; science and technology and academic cooperation; trade, connectivity, and maritime transport. External Affairs Minister S. Jaishankar also clarified that the Indo-Pacific idea is not to contain any country but that it intends to take all countries together, even as it upholds the rule of law (MEA, 2019). A more concrete unfurling of the Indo-Pacific idea came up when India organised the first counter-terrorism tabletop exercise of the Quad countries in November 2019 – suggesting other priorities of India (The Hindu, 2019). Indian foreign secretary defined the geographical contours of the Indo-Pacific thus:

India's Indo-Pacific geography can perhaps be best described as a succession of semi-circles. The innermost semi-circle incorporates our closest neighbours, that share our civilizational and cultural heritage. The arc of the outer neighbourhood covers the Gulf states to our west and Southeast Asia and the ASEAN countries to our east. For India, the Horn of Africa, the western Indian Ocean and the Straits of Malacca are a seamless region.

(MEA, 2021)

More concrete steps were undertaken by India to further the Indo-Pacific idea. It had established a separate division in the Ministry of External Affairs in April 2019 under a Joint Secretary level official to focus on the subject. India also utilised the Indo-Pacific idea to further its connectivity between its northeast to the Southeast Asian countries and emphasised on the role of the BIMSTEC mechanism.[11] More concretely, at the September 2023 meeting in Jakarta, India's Prime Minister proposed building economic corridors between Southeast Asia and West Asia.

Others' Role

The other main country in the Indo-Pacific is Australia. It has been a founding member of the Quad in 2007. However, after the demarche from China for its participation in the Bay of Bengal multinational navies, Australia withdrew. This action has left concerns on the future orientation of Australia. However, the 2013 Australia's defence white paper considered the Indo-Pacific as its zone of strategic interest. Australia has also been a member of the Indian Ocean Rim Association for Regional Cooperation (renamed as IORA). The geographical limits of Indo-Pacific for Australia, according to its white paper on defence, are the regions between India and Japan, roughly coincides to the position its ally – the US – holds. While Australia toyed with a free trade agreement with China, and had also facilitated China's investments in crucial sectors of the Australian economy, it has become critical of Beijing's influence operations (Tyler, 2018). On the other hand, Australia's relations with India improved, elevating ties in the 2+2 dialogue format, joining the Quad, signing an interim trade agreement and maritime agreements (MEA, 2020).

For an idea to become popular, legitimate, and normative, it has to be adopted by several countries. While China had naturally shown its antipathy to the Indo-Pacific idea, others are increasingly reflecting on or even embracing the concept, suggesting its rise in the international system. The Southeast Asian grouping, ASEAN, has also been at the forefront of its position on the Indo-Pacific. Divided as it was on the South China Sea dispute since the Hanoi summit meeting of its members in 2010, and under pressure from

Beijing to conclude the Code of Conduct, ASEAN has, after a series of meetings, released an Outlook (ASEAN Outlook on the Indo-Pacific) (ASEAN Outlook, 2019).[12] As with many countries, the ASEAN also expressed concern about the rule of law situation and advocated an open international system conducive for trade, investments, and markets. It, of course, reiterated its mantra of neutrality and centrality of ASEAN in any new emerging architecture.

Others as well are quick to embrace the idea of the Indo-Pacific. France, which has seven overseas territories in the Indo-Pacific region, with over 1.6 million citizens, 20,000 expatriates, and covering 9 million square km, has released a position paper on the subject in May 2019 explaining its defence ministry's responsibilities in the region (France's Defence Strategy in the Indo-Pacific, 2019).[13] The United Kingdom, despite being busy with the Brexit events, was concerned about the rules-based order and sensed opportunities in maritime connectivity and security against instability in the region (Patalano, 2019).

Observations

The above brief overview suggests that the idea of the Indo-Pacific is of recent origin, although discussions about it are more than a decade old. The success or failure of the Indo-Pacific will be based on the ability of the members to institutionalise their efforts and expand to co-opt the regional states in ASEAN and others in the two oceans – an area increasingly seen as contested between China and other powers.[14] Since the Declaration of Conduct on the South China Sea in the early 2000s, the ASEAN had, for the first time, exhibited serious weaknesses in not coming out with a consensus statement on the islands dispute. Laos, Cambodia, Myanmar – the non-claimants – are seen closer to the Chinese position and reportedly blocked the consensus. Other states which are claimants to the dispute either remained powerless or were divided by China's charm offensive. Philippines' former President Duterte's visit to Beijing and the latter's announcement of largesse of over $24 billion in proposed investments in Mindanao and other areas have softened this country's position. Brunei, another claimant as well, has been making positive statements towards Beijing. Malaysian purchases of military weapons from Beijing are creating conditions of friendship with China. This leaves Vietnam, which fought historical wars against the Middle Kingdom, to oppose China's incursions in the South China Sea. This became more evident after the deployment of the Haiyang Shiyou rig by China in the Paracels since May 2014. A number of pitched battles both on the seas as well as in civil society ensued. Vietnam has also diversified relations with the US, Japan, and India in hopes of balancing China. Once again, in October 2019, China deployed Haiyang Dizhi closer to Malaysia,

Vietnamese, and the Philippines claimed reefs, thus raising further concerns in the maritime domains.

Secondly, the idea of the Indo-Pacific and the revised 2+2 dialogues at the moment, bilaterally, and the trilateral maritime Malabar exercises or the group sailing in the South China Sea by several naval forces recently is considered to be an answer to usher in security and stability in the region and to put China's unbridled assertiveness in its place. Of course, the revived Quad is straddled with several problems, suggesting China could wade through the Indo-Pacific waters.

The Indo-Pacific collective has not been able to make a joint statement of purpose and an institutional mechanism, but the US-India-Japan have organised "inter-operable" Malabar naval exercises since 2015 and the quadrilateral naval exercises in 2020, besides political coordination. The revived Quad could also address "low politics" for the moment by tackling piracy, humanitarian assistance during disasters and rescue missions, countering illegal fishing, etc., given China's active opposition and potential strengths.[15] The economic side of the Indo-Pacific is also weak with the Trans-Pacific Partnership revoked. On the other hand, the RCEP (Regional Comprehensive Economic Partnership) has gained momentum in 2021, though without India, the 5th largest economy in the grouping. While former Australian Prime Minister Turnbull, during a visit to the US, suggested to a joint regional economic block, this may take some time to fructify. In April 2019, US, Japan, and Indian business leaders and officials met in New Delhi to suggest a division of labour in constructing energy, ports, and industrial corridors in the Indo-Pacific region. Certain projects were identified, although the progress is at a snail's pace in comparison to the BRI projects.[16] Nevertheless, combined signalling – even in evolving norms and symbolic measures – itself could make the Indo-Pacific relevant for the evolving regional situation.

Moreover, China could deter the Quad once again by sending different signals to different actors and coercive measures. While at the official level it had exhibited confidence or even suggested that such initiatives could "destabilise" the region or as President Xi Jinping critiqued at the 20th party congress in 2022 and at the National People's Congress in March 2023, the formation of "small cliques", think-tanks, and others has also raised the bogey of "containment" of China, forgetting for the moment the complex interdependence in the region. More mature Chinese analysts see the Quad at most as a balancer to an unpredictable but rising China.

Notes

1 See Rory Medcalf (2020), *Contest for the Indo-Pacific: Why China Won't Map the Future*, La Trobe University Press.; Rory Medcalf (2018), *China and the Indo-Pacific: Multipolarity, Solidarity and Strategic Patience*, <https://nsc

.crawford.anu.edu.au/sites/default/files/publication/nsc_crawford_anu_edu_au /2018-04/rory_medcalf_sorbonne_indo-pacific_march_2018.pdf> and Brahma Chellaney (2019), Changes on the Indo-Pacific's Geopolitical Chessboard *The Japan Times*https://www.japantimes.co.jp/opinion/2019/09/02/commentary/ world-commentary/changes-indo-pacifics-geopolitical-chessboard/>

2 On the subject, see Rory Medcalf (2013), *The Indo-Pacific: What's in a Name?* The American Interest https://www.the-american-interest.com/2013/10/10/ the-indo-pacific-whats-in-a-name/>; Rory Medcalf (2015), *Reimagining Asia: From Asia-Pacific to Indo-Pacific*, http://www.theasanforum.org/reimagining -asia-from-asia-pacific-to-indo-pacific/>; and Premvir Das (2017), *India's 'Indo-Pacific' Challenges*, Business Standard <http://www.business-standard.com/ article/opinion/india-s-indo-pacific-challenges-117040100822_1.html>

3 Oceanic domains are a crucial aspect of the Indo-Pacific idea. The Indian Ocean has four of the six major choke points servicing global energy and other resources trade to India, China, Japan, South Korea, and Southeast Asia. While no major territorial dispute is visible in the region, citing piracy, China has expanded its influence in the region. The Pacific Ocean was under US control for decades, although emerging China and ensuing conflicts on the Senkaku islands, Taiwan, and South China Sea required the US to reorganise the Pacific Command. Essentially, the emerging focus of the Indo-Pacific is in the South China Sea, the Bay of Bengal, and partly in the Arabian Sea. China's militarisation of the South China Sea then becomes the central focus for the Indo-Pacific advocates as this has the potential to block maritime traffic in the region.

4 See also Hillary Clinton, (2012), Hillary Clinton Lauds India's Role in Indo-Pacific Region, Urges for Increased Participation, *India Today*, <https://www .indiatoday.in/world/rest-of-the-world/story/hillary-clinton-lauds-indias-role -indo-pacific-region-talks-china-breifly-in-australia-121455-2012-11-14>

5 See also Nikhil Sonnad (2017), *All about Indo-Pacific, the New Term Trump Is Using to Refer to Asia* <https://qz.com/1121336/trump-in-asia-all-about-indo -pacific-the-new-term-trump-is-using-to-refer-to-asia/>

6 *US wants to work on economically-sensible projects in Indo-Pacific*, says official (2018, April 20), *Financial Express*, <https://www.financialexpress.com/ india-news/us-wants-to-work-on-economically-sensible-projects-in-indo-pacific -says-official/1139157/>

7 Apart from the issues the US raised in the previous document on the free and open Indo-Pacific, it also wanted to expand the format to include countries outside the region such as European countries, in addition to emphasising the ASEAN. With the UK, Germany, and France expressing their Indo-Pacific strategies, the US idea is gaining traction. The US critique on China continued thus "The PRC is combining its economic, diplomatic, military, and technological might as it pursues a sphere of influence in the Indo-Pacific and seeks to become the world's most influential power. The PRC's coercion and aggression spans the globe, but it is most acute in the Indo-Pacific. From the economic coercion of Australia to the conflict along the Line of Actual Control with India to the growing pressure on Taiwan and bullying of neighbors in the East and South China Seas, our allies and partners in the region bear much of the cost of the PRC's harmful behavior. In the process, the PRC is also undermining human rights and international law, including freedom of navigation, as well as other principles that have brought stability and prosperity to the Indo-Pacific". See the White House, "Indo-Pacific Strategy of the United States" February 11, 2022 at <https://www.whitehouse .gov/wp-content/uploads/2022/02/U.S.-Indo-Pacific-Strategy.pdf>

8 See Satish Chandra & Baladas Ghoshal (Eds.) (2018), *The Indo-Pacific Axis – Peace and Prosperity or Conflict?*, Manohar.

9 See Rajiv Bhatia & Vijay Sakhuja (Eds.) (2014), *Indo Pacific Region: Political and Strategic Prospects*, Viji Books; Brahma Chellaney (2018), *A New Order for the Indo-Pacific*, <https://www.project-syndicate.org/commentary/china-indo-pacific-security-framework-by-brahma-chellaney-2018-03> and *India-Australia-Japan-U.S. Consultations on Indo-Pacific* (2017), <https://mea.gov.in/press-releases.htm?dtl/29110/IndiaAustraliaJapanUS_Consultations_on_IndoPacific_November_12_2017>

10 See Amitandu Palit (2016), India's Act East Policy and Implications for Southeast Asia, *Southeast Asian Studies*, pp. 81–91 Danielle Rajendram (2014), *India's New Asia-Pacific Strategy: Modi Acts East*, Lowy Institute, <https://www.lowyinstitute.org/sites/default/files/indias-new-asia-pacific-strategy-modi-acts-east_0.pdf>

11 Recurring themes in the Indian leader's observations on the Indo-Pacific include economic development, infrastructure, connectivity, digital transformation, climate change, biodiversity, health, multipolarity, multilateralism, plurilateralism and collective action, Coalition for Disaster Resilient Infrastructure, International Solar Alliance, and others.

12 Renato Cruz de Casro (2017), *How Indo-Pacific Geopolitics Affects Foreign Policy: The Case of the Philippines, 2010-2017*ResearchGate. https://www.researchgate.net/publication/330292511_How_IndoPacific_Geopolitics_Affects_Foreign_Policy_The_Case_of_the_Philippines_2010-2017.

13 See also Luis Simón & Ulrich Speck (Eds.) (2018), *Natural Partners? Europe, Japan and Security in the Indo-Pacific*, Real Instituto Elcano, <http://www.realinstitutoelcano.org/wps/wcm/connect/e1b07fbd-ac5f-4d8d-874c-1fe1b7ff1892/Policy-Paper-2018-Natural-Partners-Europe-Japan-security-Indo-Pacific.pdf?MOD=AJPERES&CACHEID=e1b07fbd-ac5f-4d8d-874c-1fe1b7ff1892>

14 *The Indo-Pacific- Defining a Region*, Stratfor, <https://worldview.stratfor.com/article/indo-pacific-defining-region>; See also Axel Berkofsky &Sergio Miracola (2019) *Geopolitics by Other Means- The Indo-Pacific Reality*, <https://www.ispionline.it/sites/default/files/pubblicazioni/indo-pacific_web_0.pdf>

15 For the focus on geo-economic and non-traditional security challenges in the region, see Christopher H. Lim & Tan Ming Hui (2018), *Indo-Pacific: The Next Growth Engine?*, RSIS Commentary, <https://www.rsis.edu.sg/wp-content/uploads/2018/08/CO18135.pdf>

16 See Kaewkamol Karen Pitakdumrongkit, *The Impact of the Trump Administration's Indo- Pacific Strategy on Regional Economic Governance*, <https://www.eastwestcenter.org/system/tdf/private/ewc_policy_studies_79_web.pdf?file=1&type=node&id=37123> John Hemmings (Ed.) *Infrastructure, Ideas; and Strategy in the Indo-Pacific*, Asia Studies Centre, <https://henryjacksonsociety.org/wp-content/uploads/2019/04/HJS-Infrastructure-Ideas-and-Strategy-in-Indo-Pacific-web.pdf>

References

Abe, Shinzo. (2007, August 22). *Confluence of the Two Seas*. Ministry of Foreign Affairs of Japan. <http://www.mofa.go.jp/region/asia-paci/pmv0708/speech-2.html>.

Abe, Shinzo. (2012, December 27). *Asia's Democratic Security Diamond*. Project Syndicate. <https://www.project-syndicate.org/commentary/a-strategic-alliance-for-japan-and-india-by-shinzo-abe?barrier=accessreg>.

Acharya, Amitav. (2010). Asia Is Not One. *Journal of Asian Studies*, 69(4), 1001–1013.

ASEAN. (2019). *ASEAN Outlook on the Indo-Pacific.* <https://asean.org/storage/2019/06/ASEAN-Outlook-on-the-Indo-Pacific_FINAL_22062019.pdf>.

Auslin, R. Michael. (2018). *The Question of American Strategy in the Indo-Pacific.* Hoover Institution. <https://www.hoover.org/sites/default/files/research/docs/auslin_webreadypdf.pdf>.

US Department of State. (2018)*"Briefing on The Indo-Pacific Strategy" Special Briefing by Alex N. Wong Deputy Assistant Secretary, Bureau of East Asian and Pacific Affairs on April 02, 2018.* Special Briefing by Alex N. Wong Deputy Assistant Secretary, Bureau of East Asian and Pacific Affairs on April 02, 2018 https://2017-2021.state.gov/briefing-on-the-indo-pacific-strategy/

Buzan, Barry. (2012). Asia: A Geopolitical Reconfiguration. *IFRI.* <https://www.ifri.org/sites/default/files/atoms/files/barrybuzanengpe22012.pdf>.

Campbell, M. Kurt. (2016). *The Pivot: The Future of American Statecraft in Asia.* Hachette Book Group.

Choudhury, R. D. (2018, April 04). India-US-Japan Discuss South China Sea Tensions; Indo-Pacific Region. *The Economic Times.* <https://economictimes.indiatimes.com/news/defence/india-us-japan-discuss-south-china-sea-tensions-indo-pacific-region/articleshow/63614072.cms>.

Clinton, Hillary. (2011, October 11). America's Pacific Century. *Foreign Policy.* <http://foreignpolicy.com/2011/10/11/americas-pacific-century>.

CSIS. (2017, October 18). *Defining Our Relationship with India for the Next Century: An Address by U.S. Secretary of State Rex Tillerson.* Downloaded from: https://csis-website-prod.s3.amazonaws.com/s3fs-public/publication/171018_An_Address_by_U.S._Secretary_of_State_Rex_Tillerson.pdf

DoD, France. (2019). *France's Defense Strategy in the Indo-Pacific.* <https://www.defense.gouv.fr>.

Duara, Prasenjit. (2010). Asia Redux: Conceptualizing a Region for Our Times. *The Journal of Asian Studies, 69*(4), 963–983. <https://www.researchgate.net/publication/231993775_Asia_Redux_Conceptualizing_a_Region_for_Our_Times>.

Khurana, S. G. (2007). Security of Sea Lines: Prospects for India–Japan Cooperation. *Strategic Analysis, 31*(1). <https://www.academia.edu/7710744/Security_of_Sea_Lines_Prospects_for_India-Japan_Cooperation>.

Kumar, Yogendra. (2019, October 18). *India's Maritime Diplomacy in the Indo-Pacific in Pursuit of its National Objectives.* MEA. <https://mea.gov.in/distinguished-lectures-detail.htm?852>.

Madan, Tanvi. (2017). The Rise, Fall, and Rebirth of the Quad. *War on the Rocks* November 16, 2017. https://warontherocks.com/2017/11/rise-fall-rebirth-quad/

MEA, India. (2015, December 12). *Joint Statement on India and Japan Vision 2025: Special Strategic and Global Partnership Working Together for Peace and Prosperity of the Indo-Pacific Region and the World.* Retrieved from: https://www.mea.gov.in/bilateral-documents.htm?dtl/26176/Joint_Statement_on_India_and_Japan_Vision_2025_Special_Strategic_and_Global_Partnership_Working_Together_for_Peace_and_Prosperity_of_the_IndoPacific_R

MEA, India. (2018a, June 01). *Prime Minister's Keynote Address at Shangri La Dialogue.* <https://www.mea.gov.in/Speeches-Statements.htm?dtl/29943/>.

MEA, India. (2018b, May 30). *Shared Vision of India-Indonesia Maritime Cooperation in the Indo-Pacific.* <https://www.mea.gov.in/bilateraldocuments.htm?dtl/29933/Shared_Vision_of_IndiaIndonesia_Maritime_Cooperation_in_the_IndoPacific>.

MEA, India. (2019, October 19). *External Affairs Minister's conversation with Valdai Discussion Club, Moscow on 27 August 2019.* Retrieved from: https://www.mea.gov.in/Speeches-Statements.htm?dtl/31957

MEA, India. (2020, June 04). *Joint Declaration on a Shared Vision for Maritime Cooperation in the Indo-Pacific between the Republic of India and the Government of Australia.* Retrieved from: https://www.mea.gov.in/bilateral -documents.htm?dtl/32730/Joint_Declaration_on_a_Shared_Vision_for_ Maritime_Cooperation_in_the_IndoPacific_Between_the_Republic_of_India _and_the_Government_of_Australia

MEA, India. (2021, December 02). *Foreign Secretary's Remarks on 'Quad and Future of the Indo-Pacific' at the 5th India-US Forum.* Retrieved from: https:// www.mea.gov.in/Speeches-Statements.htm?dtl/34571/Foreign+Secretarys +Remarks+on+Quad+and+Future+of+the+IndoPacific+at+the+5th+IndiaUS +Forum

Ministry of Foreign Affairs. (2017). *Priority Policy for Development Cooperation FY2017.* International Cooperation Bureau, Ministry of Foreign Affairs (MOFA) of Japan. <https://www.mofa.go.jp/files/000259285.pdf>.

MOFA, Japan. (2017). *Priority Policy for Development Cooperation FY2017.* <http://www.mofa.go.jp/files/000259285.pdf>.

Nicholson, Brendan. (2007). China warns Canberra on Security Pact. *The Age.* <https://www.theage.com.au/national/china-warns-canberra-on-security-pact -20070615-ge54v5.html>.

Obama White House. (2011, November 17). *Remarks By President Obama to the Australian Parliament.* National Archives and Records Administration (.gov). <https://obamawhitehouse.archives.gov/:https://obamawhitehouse .archives.gov/the-press-office/2011/11/17/remarks-president-obama-australian -parliament#>.

Patalano, Alessio. (2019). *UK Defence from the 'Far East' to the 'Indo-Pacific.* Policy Exchange. <https://policyexchange.org.uk/wp-content/uploads/2019/07 /UK-Defence-from-the-%E2%80%98Far-East%E2%80%99-to-the-%E2%80 %98Indo-Pacific%E2%80%99.pdf>.

Prime+Ministers+Keynote+Address+at+Shangri+La+Dialogue+June+01+2018.

Raghavan, A. (2018, March 31). What Indo-Pacific Means for India. *The Hindustan Times.* <https://www.hindustantimes.com/opinion/what-indo-pacific-means-for -india/story-VmLixgjeLnLKWV58i8e3yM.html>.

Rajendram, Danielle. (2014). *India's New Asia-Pacific Strategy: Modi acts East.* Lowy Institute. <https://www.lowyinstitute.org/sites/default/files/indias-new -asia-pacific-strategy-modi-acts-east_0.pdf>.

Saran, Samir, & Singh, Abhijit. (2018, May 03). *India's Struggle for the Soul of Indo-Pacific.* Lowy Institute. <https://www.lowyinstitute.org/the-interpreter/ india-struggle-soul-indo-pacific>.

Sayers, Eric. (2018 April 15). 15 Big Ideas to Operationalize America's Indo-Pacific Strategy. *War on the Rocks.* <https://warontherocks.com/2018/04/15-big-ideas -to-operationalize-americas-indo-pacific-strategy/>.

Scott, John, & Reynolds, Isabel. (2019, September 26). Indo-Pacific Ministers Elevate Security Talks That Irk China. *Bloomberg.* <https://www.bloomberg .com/news/articles/2019-09-26/-indo-pacific-ministers-elevate-security-talks -that-irk-china>.

Singh, Abhijit. (2017). *A 'Rules-Based' Maritime Order in the Indo-Pacific: Aligning the Building Blocks.* Regional Outlook Paper, 57. <https://www.griffith.edu.au/_ _data/assets/pdf_file/0019/108703/Regional-Outlook-Paper-57-web.pdf>.

The Department of Defense. (2019, June 1). *Department of Defense Indo-Pacific Strategy Report 2019.* <https://media.defense.gov/2019/Jul/01/2002152311/-1/ -1/1/department-of-defense-indo-pacific-strategy-report-2019.pdf>.

The Economic Times. (2019, November 04). *Quad' Reviews Situation in Indo-Pacific Region.* <https://economictimes.indiatimes.com/news/defence/quad

-reviews-situation-in-indo-pacific-region/articleshow/71906338.cms?from
=mdr>.

The Hindu. (2014, November 13). *Look East' Policy Now Turned Into 'Act East'
Policy: Modi.* Retrieved from: https://www.thehindu.com/news/national/look
-east-policy-now-turned-into-act-east-policy-modi/article6595186.ece>.

The Hindu. (2019, November 20). *NIA to Host Counter-Terrorism Exercise for
Quad Countries.* Retrieved from: https://www.thehindu.com/news/national/nia
-to-host-counter-terrorism-exercise-for-quad-countries/article30020447.ece

The US Department of Défense. (2019). *Indo-Pacific Strategic Report - Preparedness,
Partnerships, and Promoting a Networked Region.* <https://media.defense
.gov/2019/Jul/01/2002152311/-1/-1/1/DEPARTMENT-OF-DEFENSE-INDO
-PACIFIC-STRATEGY-REPORT-2019.PDF>.

The White House. (2011, November 17). *Remarks by President Obama to the
Australian Parliament.* <https://obamawhitehouse.archives.gov/the-press-office
/2011/11/17/remarks-president-obama-australian-parliament>.

The White House. (2017, November 15). *Remarks by President Trump on His Trip
to Asia.* <https://www.whitehouse.gov/briefings-statements/remarks-president
-trump-trip-asia/>.

Tyler, C. M. (2018). Australian Perceptions of the Indo-Pacific. Australian Institute
of International Affairs. <http://www.funag.gov.br/images/2018/Setembro/
Views_Asia/Australia-and-Indo-Pacific_M-Conley-Tyler.pdf>.

Birties, Bill. (2018 March 08). "China Mocks Australia Over 'Indo-Pacific' Concept
it Says Will 'Dissipate". *ABC News.*Retrieved from: https://www.abc.net.au/
news/2018-03-08/china-mocks-australia-over-indo-pacific-concept/9529548

Wu, Minwen. (2018 February 23). *Where Will the Indo-Pacific Strategy Go?.*
<http://english.chinamil.com.cn/view/2018-02/23/content_7949833.htm>.

3

THE INDO-PACIFIC AS THE NEW THEATRE OF "COLD WAR" POLITICS

Challenges and Regional Responses

Shankari Sundararaman

For over a decade now, the terminology of the Indo-Pacific has been gaining prominence, particularly in regards to its usage to address a wider regional perspective within foreign policy circles. Today as countries in the region are increasingly trying to address their own definitional conceptions of what constitutes the Indo-Pacific, it is worthwhile to focus briefly on how the Indo-Pacific is different from the Asia-Pacific. The use of these two terminologies interchangeably also gives emphasis to the huge transitions shaping the broader region. Any efforts to answer the question as to the kind of "regionalism" which is implied by the term Indo-Pacific is challenging, especially since the term indicates a region in which competing and contradictory visions of what this region actually represents are different for different countries. One of the simplest definitions of the Indo-Pacific is that it is a "security driven regional project", focused on retaining existing norms and rules of interstate behaviour, while simultaneously addressing shifting regional transitions, particularly structural changes in the regional and global order (Wilson, 2018). As compared to the Asia-Pacific, which was primarily based on economic integration as a means to promote security cooperation, the Indo-Pacific is mainly driven by security concerns. The Indo-Pacific as argued by Wilson, by its very terminology, "marks a contested period in Asia's international politics" where the varieties of purposes of "regional cooperation are being reoriented to focus on security challenges emanating from shifts in the global order, implicating both economic and security challenges" (Ibid). Significantly, to this contested landscape in Asian geopolitics, there are also "newer" players such as India which are moving the conceptual understanding from an Asia-Pacific to an Indo-Pacific region. The erstwhile understanding of the Asia-Pacific did not include India, and

DOI: 10.4324/9781003479307-4

this was "untenable". So Rory Medcalf argues that the Indo-Pacific was not just about placing India in its rightful place but must also be seen as a mental map within which regional and global states can also respond to the rise of China (Medcalf, 2019).

Is There a New Cold War in the Indo-Pacific?

This chapter looks at whether the Indo-Pacific is a new theatre of the cold war. Even as the shift from the Asia-Pacific to the Indo-Pacific is viewed by several as a change from an economically driven focus to a strategic one, the reassertion of geopolitics is not new. The works of Realist scholar Michael Leifer argue that the US-China rivalry in the region of East Asia has always been evident, even since the nineties. Leifer's argument on the salience of balance of power explains how the region of Southeast Asia addressed the nature of its growing ties between the US and China. Highlighting the irredentist claims of China in the region, particularly with regard to the South China Sea, Leifer was categorical about the ineffectiveness of mechanisms like the ASEAN Regional Forum as this lacked the means to address any kind of binding commitment to the preservation of a regional order in the Asia-Pacific. This period was seen as one of China's rise and the impact of that was assessed as the precursor to the geopolitical shifts that are more clearly evident today. Similarly, in the context of Europe, Russia has since 2008 systematically undermined the peace of Europe with its annexation of parts of Georgia in 2008, followed by the invasion and annexation of Crimea in 2014, and the current ongoing invasion in Ukraine. While this may seem critical in the context of Europe, it nevertheless constitutes a significant challenge for the Indo-Pacific too, especially as Russia is an important part of northeast Asia and the impact of the growing Sino-Russian ties will also have critical implications on the Indo-Pacific region. While at the end of the Cold War constructivist literature on the Asia-Pacific region clearly endorsed the space for the building of norms and ideas through socialisation between China and the ASEAN members, which are core to the Indo-Pacific region, the increasing challenges in the region are pointing towards the emergence of a security dilemma, rather than the move towards constructing a security community. This dilemma is critically based on the claims by China, which, with its rise, has begun to reshape the contours of the rules-based order that governed the global order since the end of the Second World War, particularly affecting the Indo-Pacific region.

While these issues clearly indicate the move towards a more intensified great power rivalry, this does not necessarily imply a move towards a cold war. Several factors actually account for this. First, the nature of the original cold war was far more exclusive in that it led to the establishment of two distinct blocs at the systemic level. This was most evident in the European context with NATO defining the Western allies and the Warsaw Pact accounting for the Soviet bloc. While the iron curtain significantly kept the European continent as two mutually exclusive zones, the Asian region already had a third systemic player – China. For East Asia and Southeast Asia, the cold war revolved around two key issues, peace on the Korean peninsula and the Vietnam war which extended to both Cambodia and Laos, which were the key flashpoints of the cold war conflict. Second, the former mechanisms of economic power have shifted critically since the economic liberalisation of China in the late seventies. While the Soviet Union relied on a state-driven economic model well until its collapse in 1991, the Chinese economy adopted an open door policy in the late seventies, ushering in a capitalist, market-driven economic focus that matched the economic options of several of the regional countries, bringing about the space for closer economic integration with the ASEAN, Japan, India, Australia, New Zealand, and the Pacific Islands. This shift in the Indo-Pacific also belies the notion of a new cold war, as the levels of integration economically are far more critical. As the rhetoric of the US-China rivalry increased during the Trump administration with the onset of the US-China Trade War, the actual notion of decoupling between the US and China will be difficult to achieve. According to Richard Bullock, in a study done on *Cold War 2.0: Geopolitical Dimensions and Market Implications*, there is a reference to the levels of integration that the United States and China enjoy in the economic realm (Bullock, 2020: 3). As explained in this analysis, the volume of two-way trade between the US and China in the year 2018 stood to the tune of US$670 billion. US investments in China were at the tune of US$120 billion and Chinese investments in the US were at the level of US$40 billion (Ibid). While the COVID-19 pandemic has had a negative impact on several economies, for the year 2020, the volume of US-China two-way trade, including both goods and services, amounted to US$615.2 billion, which was only marginally lower than the trade in 2018 (Office of the United States Trade Representative, 2022).

US-China Rivalry and Impact on Multilateralism

With the increasing US-China stand-off and the push forward towards the concept of a Free and Open Indo-Pacific (FOIP), the situation in the region has been difficult for regional groupings like ASEAN to address, even as there are several stresses on ASEAN unity. As the grouping deals with increasing major power rivalry in the region it is central to, the stresses on its unity and ability to be pivotal to the region are critical. The situation within the region reflects a security dilemma rather than any move towards a security community as envisioned by the constructivist approach.

Just prior to the 2012 ASEAN summit, the United States unveiled its "pivot to Asia" policy and its rebalance strategy for the Asia-Pacific region

– this emerged in the aftermath of a series of moves before the Obama administration took office in early 2009, basically focusing on what was termed as the "US return to the Asia-Pacific", which was in itself a debatable issue. This question of the US return to the region must be viewed within the context of the sub-regions of the Asia-Pacific rather than seeing the Asia-Pacific as a singular unit. The US had never been "absent" from its commitments to East Asia or the Pacific – both its relations with its Eastern allies – that is Japan and South Korea were continuing. Similarly, its ties with both Australia and New Zealand were still clearly continuing through the ANZUS treaty. So the debate on the US absence was once again defined in terms of the sub-region of Southeast Asia – particularly in the light of the withdrawal of its military bases from the Philippines.

The US rebalance strategy of the Obama administration was clearly articulated by US Secretary of State Hillary Clinton's words at the ARF meeting in 2009 when she stated "we are back" (ASEAN, 2010). This statement was a reaffirmation of strengthening the US-ASEAN relations and of the US commitment to strengthening the ASEAN framework for the region. During the 2010 lecture at the East West Centre, Secretary of State Hillary Clinton identified three clear indicators of the shift in US policy, which began to be visible – this was also reiterated in her article in Foreign Affairs on America's Pacific Century. First was the importance of maritime security in the Indo-Pacific; second was the focus on the South China Sea and the need to move towards a more binding code of conduct among the claimants to the conflict; and third, the reference to the increased focus on naval diplomacy. During the same year at the ARF summit in Hanoi, Secretary of State Hillary Clinton reiterated the emphasis on the maritime commons as being a critical part of the global commons, stressing the need for a normative order to prevail regarding the management of these maritime commons. Subsequently, the United States National Security Strategy papers for the years 2010 and 2015 reaffirmed the focus of the maritime commons and maritime security cooperation, with the US leading the security architecture in the Indo-Pacific (The White House, 2010 and 2015). Both these documents reiterated the importance of international norms, international law, and a rule-based order for the Indo-Pacific region.

In comparison to these two National Security Strategy papers, the NSS paper of 2017 had one clear shift under the Trump administration for the Indo-Pacific in general and the ASEAN in particular. The paper identified both China and Russia as rival countries emphasising the outbreak of a `new cold war' for the region with the US on one side of the spectrum and China and Russia on the opposite side of the polar spectrum. In terms of the competition within the global order, the NSS 2017 identified both China and Russia as the "competitors to American power, influence and interests" (The White House Office, 2017). Both the NSS 2017 and more recently in the Indo-Pacific Strategy Report of June 2019 from the US Department of Defence, the focus has been to identify China as a "revisionist" power (US Department of Defence , 2019:7). It clearly states that

> *the PRC (China) under the leadership of the CCP undermines the international system from within by exploiting its benefits while simultaneously eroding the values and principles of the rules based order.*
>
> (Ibid)

While both these papers clearly identify the rivalry between the US, China, and Russia, the attention given to the ASEAN states was different. In the NSS, the ASEAN is seen as the core of the institutional mechanism in the Asia-Pacific, with both Thailand and the Philippines identified as allies in the region. However, the Indo-Pacific Strategy Report of 2019 did greater damage to the ASEAN identity – it identified and divided ASEAN members into three distinct categories: friends, potential friends, and unfriendly states, particularly with an emphasis on their relations with both China and the US (Discussions with Siswo Pramono, Ministry of Foreign Affairs of the Republic of Indonesia). Moreover, the division of ASEAN members was also based on their individual responses to the US Free and Open Indo-Pacific Strategy that was unveiled by President Trump in 2017 at the APEC summit in Vietnam. This policy of differentiating the ASEAN members has been detrimental to the vision of ASEAN centrality and unity in the Indo-Pacific region. Several voices from within the ASEAN region have addressed this as the `*salami slicing'* of ASEAN into various layers through which the US will leverage its own role in the ensuing transitional shifts in the Indo-Pacific.

Limits of ASEAN Multilateralism in the Indo-Pacific

As the transition from the Asia-Pacific to the Indo-Pacific brings in the context of structural transitions in the regional and global order, it raises questions on the relevance of multilateralism. Given the nature of the power transitions shaping the wider Indo-Pacific, it becomes far more critical to evaluate how states are responding to multilateral institutions and using these as a mechanism for the promotion of regional peace and stability. In this context, as far as Southeast Asia is concerned, both the role played by ASEAN and the question of ASEAN centrality in the regional dynamics will be crucial to evaluate. How do major powers like the US and China address the significance of these multilateral institutions in the region? How have they addressed the question of ASEAN centrality in the region? As stability is dependent on regional peace and economic growth, how do the major powers allow for the priorities of smaller states to shape the regional agenda. Any effective multilateral mechanism needs to address these critical questions to achieve the stability that it seeks to impart. It is also imperative to understand how India responds to the challenges in the region and how it engages multilateralism as a means of achieving stability in the wider region? India's own approach to the regional balance is driven by the use of normative options to strengthen its role regionally and globally.

In terms of understanding the multilateral processes that shape the region, it becomes imperative to see how multilateralism in Southeast Asia has evolved from the time of its origins during the Cold War to the current regional environment in the Indo-Pacific. While the origins of the ASEAN take place in the Cold War, it remained critically focused on three core aspects of its objectives – cooperation on issues relating to insurgency at the domestic level; keeping the region free from external power interference, and economic cooperation. As the Cold War ended, it paved the way for ASEAN-driven or ASEAN-led multilateralism extending to the rest of the wider Asia-Pacific. Following the Cold War for nearly a period of two decades, the region, according to Marvin C. Ott, experienced a state of "strategic quiescence", a period during which there was growth of multilateralism in the region especially driven by the ASEAN (Ott, 2013). ASEAN's core principle from the time of its emergence in the 1960s was to ensure that the region was insulated from external power interference. Within this context, ASEAN used three basic frameworks to promote a regional cooperation model driven by what is called its adherence to the "intramural peace and stability principle" – basically meaning that there were certain commonalities that would bring the regional states together to address their security environment (Cabellero-Anthony, 1998). Broadening this argument further meant an adherence to two basic factors – first, interstate diversity was accepted as a given, as a result of which states agreed to accept this diversity focusing on areas of convergence on normative issues. Second, over a period of time, the logic of "intramural peace and stability" was extended outwards from the ASEAN core (original members) to integrate newer members as well as external players (Ibid.). In this process of endorsing its principle of "intramural peace and stability", the ASEAN's dialogue partnerships expanded to cover several countries such as China, Japan, and South Korea in East Asia, India in South Asia, and Australia and New Zealand in the Pacific. Using the core focus of "intramural peace and stability", the ASEAN advocated the principle of non-interference in internal affairs, which became the core pillar of the regional grouping. In addition to this, within each of the member states of the ASEAN, non-interference became further enshrined as a foreign policy objective towards other member countries. From its very inception, the objective of the ASEAN was to promote a norms-based regional order – which led to the advancement of concepts such as the Zone of Peace, Freedom, and Neutrality (ZOPFAN); the Treaty of Amity and Cooperation (TAC); and the Southeast Asia Nuclear Weapons Free Zone (SEANWFZ).

The core focus of evolving these principles at the regional level was clearly to address the ability of ASEAN to move beyond the issues of territorial conflicts and interstate rivalries based on historical claims prior to the advent of the colonial powers. This ability set the ASEAN apart from other regional groupings which seemed to remain embroiled in territorial conflicts. Apart from this, ASEAN also followed the core driving principles of consensus and consultation, which have been both critiqued and appreciated by its dialogue partners – those who looked at consensus and consultation as ineffective because it did not lead to significant outcomes and those who supported it on the grounds that ASEAN was a "process oriented initiative and not a progress oriented one" (Jones and Smith, 2007).

Through the two decades following the Cold War, ASEAN promoted regional multilateral initiatives such as the ASEAN Regional Forum (ARF); the East Asia Summit (EAS); the ADMM+ (Shangri La Dialogue); ASEAN Expanded Maritime Forum (AEMF), and several other initiatives that focused on building a regional security architecture that addresses normative interstate behaviour. Theoretical debates between realist and constructivist scholars placed Southeast Asian security studies into the binary schools of Realism and Constructivism. Realist scholars focused on the question of regional stability and order through the promotion of a balance of power. Constructivist scholars, on the other hand, argued on ASEAN's potential to push forward the logic of a Deutschian model of a security community. Proponents of the Constructivist school identified ideational factors pushed by the ASEAN processes as having the potential to "*socialise*" a diverse set of actors into the "ASEAN way" of interstate behaviour (Acharya, 1997: 3). However, Michael Leifer's work on the ASEAN Regional Forum argues the converse view. The ability of the ASEAN Regional Forum to maintain any form of regional order through a balance of power was seen as negligible by Leifer, especially since the ARF did not have any defence capabilities and given the nature of China's repeated irredentist claims to the South China Sea. Leifer's work on the ARF clearly highlighted the limits of ASEAN-driven mechanisms in the light of Chinese assertions that remained visible (Leifer, 1996: 52–59). This was a critical recognition of the limits of ASEAN's ability to steer the regional order through its mechanisms, even as it was able to promote a sustained process of dialogue.

Even as structural changes were shaping the region profoundly due to the rise of China, the committed ASEAN advocates focused on the ability to move forward the processes of regionalism as being so effective that in June 2011, former Thai foreign minister and former ASEAN secretary-general, Surin Pitsuwan in an article in the *Jakarta Post* referred to ASEAN as the "heart of Asia" referring to the multilateral processes as being core to the regional order and stability (Pitsuwan, 2011). By July 2012, the ASEAN was floundering in its inability to produce a joint communiqué on the issue of the

South China Sea. This brought the question of ASEAN unity and centrality to the forefront leading to the debates on the role of ASEAN as a normative regional grouping that was central to the regional mechanisms in the Asia-Pacific. Over the past few years, as great power rivalry emerged sharper in the region, the capacity of the ASEAN to direct the course of the regional security debates has consistently been challenged, endorsing Michael Leifer's argument on the limits of its mechanisms.

The emergence of the Quadrilateral Security Dialogue has also been a critical factor that is now pushing the limits of the erstwhile Asia-Pacific identity. As the Quad has emerged in the second phase as a more consultative mechanism, the focus of the ASEAN has been to take a neutral distance from the Quad, particularly as there is ambiguity over what exactly the Quad represents. What is increasingly obvious, however, is that the Quad does not seem to merit a cohesive ASEAN response, which is clearly articulated in the ASEAN Outlook for the Indo-Pacific (AOIP) wherein the ASEAN reiterates its centrality and states that no other mechanism is required for the region (Koga, 2023: 39). However, on the issue of the Quad individual responses indicates the divergences among the ASEAN members in how they approach or look at the Quad. Evan Laksmana argues that there is a difference between the individual ASEAN states and the ASEAN as a grouping, a difference that is not merely semantic, as he puts it (Laksmana, 2020: 106). He further states that the detractors of the Quad, such as Indonesia and Singapore, differed as to the reasons for their reticence towards the Quad, particularly as it affected the position Indonesia regards for itself within the region and the ASEAN (Ibid., 107). Simultaneously, countries such as the Philippines and Vietnam were more open to the idea of a Quad, especially as these countries were far more concerned about the South China Sea conflict, as argued by Laksmana. Another important factor that is critical in viewing the Quad is how it has evolved under the Biden administration. While the sense of continuity was evident, the Quad today has moved towards greater institutionalisation with the regular Quad leaders meeting as supported by the Foreign Ministers' consultative mechanism. In April 2021, France joined the Quad countries in the La Perouse naval exercises that were conducted in the Bay of Bengal to increase interoperability among the countries concerned. In the same month, the UK also brought out its review of its national security titled *"Global Britain in a Competitive Age: The Integrated Review of Security, Defence, Development and Foreign Policy"*, in which it clearly highlights the "tilt to the Indo-Pacific" (Sundararaman, 2021). In September 2021, the move towards the AUKUS was a further step in shifting the multilateral dynamics in the region as it brought together three key allies, the US, the UK, and Australia, into an agreement enhancing nuclear-powered submarine capabilities in the Indo-Pacific where the three countries would share and explore critical technologies and assistance to the maintenance of

China's Relations with Regional States

China's relations with Southeast Asia have dramatically shifted since the end of the cold war. Through the cold war years China and the ASEAN remained pretty much on opposite sides of the ideological spectrum, except for the Third Indo-China war, during which individual ASEAN members viewed China differently. However, over the three decades since the end of the cold war China's relations with Southeast Asia have grown tremendously, especially in the areas of economic integration, while simultaneously the growing concerns over the security impact of these ties are continuing to shape the regional thinking among Southeast Asian states. Over a period of three decades China's position vis-a-vis its territorial claims in the maritime regions of the South China Sea has shown a clear shift. In 1990, during Li Peng's visit to Southeast Asia, which was focused on normalising the ties with countries like Indonesia, both ASEAN and China focused on the possibility of joint cooperation and exploration of the resources of the South China Sea. From this period onwards, for about a decade, the foremost focus was placed on deepening economic ties between China and the ASEAN region, leading up to the signing of the China ASEAN Free Trade Agreement in 2002. This year also saw the agreement in principle on a move towards a Declaration on the Code of Conduct (DoC) on the Claimants to the South China Sea dispute. This DoC was to be evolved into a more binding Code of Conduct (CoC) within a decade. However, this has not yet come to a conclusion, and in 2012, during the ASEAN summit, the inability to finalise a joint communiqué was directly linked to the close association between China and Cambodia, which as Chair of the ASEAN for that year did not allow discussions on the South China Sea (Hunt, 2012). By 2012, China's inroads into the regional political dynamics within ASEAN and its economic assistance to some of the smaller and newer ASEAN members such as Laos and Cambodia had pulled the reins of ASEAN centrality, affecting regional cohesion within the ASEAN. From 2013 onwards China's move towards the Belt and Road Initiative (BRI) and the 21st Century Maritime Silk Route added the dimensions of geo-economic competition clearly into the geopolitical shifts shaping the region.

Another indication on the ineffectiveness of international opinion on China was evident following the ruling of the Permanent Court of Arbitration (PCA) in July 2016. In the face of the ruling, China did not back down and claimed that the PCA arbitration was not binding upon it (Glaser,, 2016). It looked at the ruling as *"null and void"* and continued to violate the principles enshrined in the United Nations Convention on Law of the Seas (UNCLOS) (Ibid). Moreover, the ASEAN countries themselves did not show any signs of assertion that the ruling went in favour of the Philippines – this was probably due to the fact that as a non-binding judgement, there was little space for the PCA ruling to be anything more than a "moral" judgement which was more likely to endorse normative interstate behaviour rather than have any legally binding implications for the region at large. In the aftermath of the PCA ruling, President Duterte also began to improve bilateral relations with the Chinese. As the US under the Obama administration began to be critical of Duterte's human rights record and the manner in which he handled the issues of the drug war within the country, these were clearly reasons that led to the shift in Duterte's policy with China (Calonzo and Jacob, 2017). Interestingly in the aftermath of the improvement of bilateral ties, President Duterte was open to receiving Chinese infrastructure aid to the tune of US$ 24 billion of which US$140 million had been given to implement Duterte's *"build build build"* programme which was a domestic infrastructure plan Duterte had promised in his election manifesto (McLaughlin, 2019).

Smaller countries such as Laos and Cambodia, even while reiterating a rules-based order in the maritime zones, are clearly caught in the grip of receiving Chinese economic loans and grants. Laos seems less focused on the larger issues relating to the US-China rivalry unfolding in the region and is more preoccupied with its immediate neighbourhood – particularly its relations with its three neighbours – Cambodia, Vietnam, and Thailand. As a country that received economic assistance from China, Laos is also expected to play a critical role in the Chinese BRI project with a railway link from Vientiane to Boten (Kunming) (LSE Ideas, 2018: 23). One of the major concerns regarding this initiative is that the debt trap for Laos in this case is likely to be very crucial. In 2016 itself Laos' debt was nearly 68% of its GDP. Moreover, in contravention to the "rules of the road" principles enshrined in the International Monetary Fund (IMF), Chinese loans are not clear in terms of their rules but are more individually tailored to suit the countries to which they are lending, causing greater debt-related liabilities for these countries (Ibid).

The context of Cambodia is different, even as it remains one of China's closest and most dependent "ally". There have been recent writings of China setting up a naval base in Ream which is located near the port of Sihanoukville. This, however, has been strongly contested by voices from within Cambodia, including a recent statement by Prime Minister Hun Sen (Panda, 2020). One of the arguments in Cambodia's favour relating to this issue is that offering a naval base to any country actually is in violation of the Cambodian Constitution, which prohibits any foreign country from buying land within Cambodia. But this does not cover areas that can be leased for a period of 99 years by Chinese companies. While the smaller countries have been grappling with these situations, the larger countries are better placed, especially as they have been able to recalibrate their approach to the question of Chinese infrastructural assistance and their links to the BRI. Countries like Malaysia and Indonesia are critical examples here – Malaysia had reviewed and withdrew from the Eastern Coast Rail Link project of the BRI, with Prime Minister Mahatir calling it "neo-colonialism" in 2018. However, in 2019, the proposed East Coast Rail Link has once again been reviewed, especially after the costs were significantly reduced to about US$11 billion. It was initially priced at approximately US$15.5 billion (Al Jazeera, 2019). With the reduction in costs, the project is once again in the offing. Indonesia has been more adept at diversifying its infrastructure needs across several programmes and is not limited to receiving aid from China alone (ADB Discussions, March 2019). As a larger and bigger economy, its reliance on China has not been as much as several of the smaller ASEAN members. More recently, its infrastructure project with India in Sabang is clearly an indicator of the measure of diversity it brings into its developmental projects where other countries are involved (Ibid).

India-ASEAN Convergences in the Indo-Pacific

It is within the backdrop of the US-China rivalry in the region that compels an understanding of the India-ASEAN dynamics in the Indo-Pacific. From the context of India-ASEAN relations and the role of multilateralism in the Indo-Pacific, there are several indicators of the broad convergences that India and ASEAN share in terms of regional security commonalities. At the Special Commemorative Summit of 2012, the focus was drawn to the question of maritime security, bringing the regions closer into areas of cooperation. India's naval diplomacy and the joint exercises with the ASEAN countries have been well in place and have been growing too, with the MILAN exercises expanding to cover almost all of the ASEAN, excluding Laos. From around 1995 till date, the MILAN exercises are the core naval focus where India and ASEAN members are involved along with other countries that are in the Indian and Pacific Oceans. The MILAN exercises that were scheduled for March 2020 had been postponed due to the outbreak of the COVID-19 pandemic and was to be rescheduled to a later date.

One of the important developments in the move towards evolving an understanding of the normative approaches to the Indo-Pacific shift is clearly enshrined in two specific indicators for India. First, the position reiterated by Indian Prime Minister Narendra Modi at the 2018 Shangri La Dialogue.

Second, the India-Indonesia Shared Vision for Maritime Cooperation in the Indo-Pacific. Both of these highlight certain core commonalities which bind India and Southeast Asia together. These are adherence to the United Nations Convention on the Law of the Seas and the Treaty of Amity and Cooperation; reiterating a free, open, and inclusive and rules-based order. In addition, there is a clear indication of growing convergence between India and Indonesia on two broad areas – India's Act East policy also finds resonance in Indonesia's *"dua samudera"* policy which is a reiteration of Indonesian commitment to a two-ocean strategy. Similarly, the focus on the Sagarmala project finds resonance in Indonesia's Global Maritime Fulcrum (*poros maritim dunia*) (Sundararaman, 2018).

It is within the backdrop of these developments that Indonesia drove the agenda for the ASEAN approach to the Indo-Pacific, which evolved as the ASEAN Outlook for the Indo-Pacific (AOIP). The AOIP of June 2019 focused on four key elements – first, the "integration of the Asia-Pacific with the Indian Ocean"; second, it emphasised the need for "dialogue instead of rivalry"; third, it reiterated the need for "development and prosperity for all"; and fourth, it gave critical focus to the maritime domain and the importance of the regional security architecture. In this regard, it clearly focuses on advancing "maritime cooperation, connectivity, sustainable development and economic growth" (ASEAN Secretariat, 2019). Prior to the release of the AOIP, there were divisions within the ASEAN states over the manner in which they would look at the Indo-Pacific both individually within the foreign policies of member states and collectively as a regional grouping. However, regardless of these distinctions within member states, the focus was on a consensus-driven approach to the Indo-Pacific idea, making the AOIP a "living document" that will evolve according to the changes shaping the regional environment. The most significant aspect of the AOIP is that it clearly reiterates the issue of ASEAN centrality in the region and how ASEAN will evolve a role for itself in the changing regional architecture (Sukma, 2019).

It is only at the ASEAN Summit meeting held on 26 June 2020 that the ASEAN, for the first time under the leadership of Vietnam as Chair of the ASEAN, has come out with a joint statement that the South China Sea must be settled on the basis of the principles enshrined in the United Nations Convention on the Law of the Seas (UNCLOS). This is a big step for the ten-member nation grouping which has often been at odds to project a united and cohesive picture when it comes to its stand on the South China Sea dispute. This Summit was focused on two issues of critical importance – the COVID-19 pandemic and the long-drawn conflict over the South China Sea. This kind of assertive stand by the ASEAN is critical as it poses a formal challenge to the historical claims of China's nine-dash line and puts the onus of resolving the contested claims firmly upon the normative principles within the UNCLOS (Gomez, The Diplomat, 29 June 2020).

Conclusion

The Indo-Pacific clearly represents the shifting power equations and structural shifts in the regional and global order. Even as the region goes through various transitions, the core focus on the normative order will remain critical as states vie and contend for a greater role. The distinctive shift that the Indo-Pacific brings is a strategic one, where the compulsions of geopolitics are driving the manner in which states arrange their responses both individually and collectively. This becomes even more critical as the structural shifts are also challenging the existing norms of interstate behaviour. The question of norms is critical as it defines the core processes through which states interact, and strengthening these has been the focus of multilateralism. Interestingly, as the "regional" dynamics of the Indo-Pacific evolve, there will be multiple forms of interaction at the bilateral, minilateral, and multilateral levels, which will all contribute to creating a web of security arrangements. Even as the Asia-Pacific endorsed a web of such arrangements at the economic level, the Indo-Pacific will strengthen such a web of arrangements at the security level by integrating both the economic and security aspects into a more complex regional architecture.

References

Acharya, Amitav. (1997). Ideas, Identity and Institution Building: From the ASEAN way to the Asia-Pacific Way, *The Pacific Review*, Vol. 10, No. 3, pp.319–346.
Al Jazeera.(2019, July 25). China, Malaysia restart Belt and Road rail project after hiccups. Al Jazeera. Retrieved from https://www.aljazeera.com/economy/2019/7/25/china-malaysia-restart-belt-and-road-rail-project-after-hiccups
ASEAN. (2019). ASEAN Outlook for the Indo-Pacific , Retrieved from https://asean.org/storage/2019/06/ASEAN-Outlook-on-the-Indo-Pacific_FINAL_22062019.pdf
Bullock, Richard. (2020, August). Cold War 2.0: Geopolitical Dimensions and Market Implications, *Investment Management*. Retrieved from www.mellon.com/insights/insights-article/-/asset_publisher/zOKIt5We8eAi/content/cold-war-2-geopolitical-dimensions-and-market-implications/264414+&cd=1&hl=en&ct=clnk&gl=in
Cabellero-Anthony, Mely, (1998). Mechanisms of Dispute Settlement: The ASEAN Experience, *Contemporary Southeast Asia*, Vol. 20, No. 1, pp. 38–66.ISEAS: Singapore, 1998. Retrieved from: https://www.jstor.org/stable/25798408
Calonzo, A. and Jacob J. (2017, November 13). Trump Bonds With Duterte Over Their Dislike of Obama, Avoids Human Rights, *Bloomberg*. Retrieved from https://www.bloomberg.com/news/articles/2017-11-13/trump-to-meet-duterte-as-ties-warm-a-year-after-obama-dust-up

LSE Ideas. (2018, October). China's Belt and Road Initiative (BRI) and Southeast Asia. *LSE Ideas and CARI CIMB ASEAN Research Institute*. Retrieved from http://www.lse.ac.uk/ideas/Assets/Documents/reports/LSE-IDEAS-China-SEA-BRI.pdf

Discussions with ADB experts in Manila in March 2020.

Glaser, Bonnie S. (2016, July 18). Shaping China's response to the PCA Ruling, *The Interpreter*, Retrieved from: https://www.lowyinstitute.org/the-interpreter/shaping-china-s-response-pca-ruling

Gomez, Jim. (2020). ASEAN Takes Position vs China's Vast Historical Sea Claims, *The Diplomat*, 29 June 2020, https://thediplomat.com/2020/06/asean-takes-position-vs-chinas-vast-historical-sea-claims/

Hunt, Luke. (2012. July 20) ASEAN Summit Fallout Continues. *The Diplomat*.Retrieved from: https://thediplomat.com/2012/07/asean-summit-fallout-continues-on/

Jones, D. M. and Smith, M. L. R. (2007). Making Process, Not Progress: ASEAN and the Evolving East Asian Regional Order. *International Security*, Vol. 32, No. 1, pp. 148–184.

Koga, Kei. 2023. Institutional Dilemma: Quad and ASEAN in the Indo-Pacific, *Asian Perspective*, Vol. 47, No. 1, pp. 27–48.

Laksmana, Evan. (2020). Whose Centrality? ASEAN and the Quad in the Indo-Pacific. *Journal of Indo-Pacific Affairs*. Special Issue, Vol 3 No 5 , pp. 106–117. Downloaded from: https://papers.ssrn.com/sol3/papers.cfm?abstract_id=3814082

Leifer, Michael. (1996) The ASEAN Regional Forum: Extending ASEAN's Model of Regional Security, *Adelphi Paper 302*. IISS: London.

McLaughlin, Timothy. (2019. May 8). A US Ally is Turning to China to Build. *The Atlantic*. Retrieved from https://www.theatlantic.com/international/archive/2019/05/philippines-us-ally-china-investment/588829/

Medcalf, Rory. (2019, December). Mapping a Multipolar Future: The Contest for the Indo-Pacific. *Global Asia*. . Retrieved from http://www.globalasia.org/v14no4/feature/mapping-a-multipolar-future-the-contest-for-the-indo-pacific_rory-medcalf Accessed on 30 January 2020

Office of the United States Trade Representative (2022) The People's Republic of China, US-China Trade Facts. *Executive Office of the President*, Retrieved from https://ustr.gov/countries-regions/china-mongolia-taiwan/peoples-republic-china

Ott, Martin C. (2013, February). The Geo-Political Transformation of Southeast Asia. *Foreign Policy Research Institute*.Retrieved from http://www.fpri.org/articles/2013/02/geopolitical-transformation-southeast asia

Panda, Ankit. (2020, June 2). Cambodia's Hun Sen Denies Chinese Naval Base Again – But What's Really Happening? *The Diplomat*. Retrieved from https://thediplomat.com/2020/06/cambodias-hun-sen-denies-chinese-naval-base-again-but-whats-really-happening/

Sukma, Rizal, (2019). Indonesia, ASEAN and Shaping the Indo-Pacific Idea, *East Asia Forum*, 19 November 2019. Retrieved from: https://www.eastasiaforum.org/2019/11/19/indonesia-asean-and-shaping-the-indo-pacific-idea/

Sundararaman, Shankari. (2021, April 9). China Piqued as More Adopt Indo-Pacific Framework. *The New Indian Express*.Retrieved from https://www.newindianexpress.com/opinions/2021/apr/09/china-piqued-as-more-adopt-indo-pacific-framework-2287735.html

Sundararaman, Shankari. (2018). Understanding the Indo-Pacific: Why Indonesia Will Be Critical?, in Satish Chandra and Baladas Ghoshal (eds), *The Indo-Pacific Axis: Peace and Prosperity or Conflict*, Routledge, 2018. pp. 177–196.

Pitsuwan, Surin. (2011, June 15). The ASEAN Heart of Asia, *The Jakarta Post.* Retrieved from https://www.thejakartapost.com/news/2011/06/15/the-asean-heart-asia.html

US Department of Defence, (2019). *The Department of Defence: Indo-Pacific Strategic Report: Preparedness, Partnerships and Promoting a Networked Region*, June 1 2019, Downloaded from: https://media.defense.gov/2019/Jul/01/2002152311/-1/-1/1/DEPARTMENT-OF-DEFENSE-INDO-PACIFIC-STRATEGY-REPORT-2019.PDF

The White House. (2010).National Security Strategy 2010. *The White House*, Retrieved from https://obamawhitehouse.archives.gov/sites/default/files/rss_viewer/national_security_strategy.pdf, p. 50. See Also United States National Security Strategy 2015, Office of the President of the United States of America, *The White House*, 2015, https://obamawhitehouse.archives.gov/sites/default/files/docs/2015_national_security_strategy_2.pdf

The White House Office (2017). *National Security Strategy of the United States of America*. Homeland Security Digital Library Retrieved from https://www.hsdl.org/?abstract&did=806478

ASEAN (2010), US Here to Stay, Says Clinton Ha Noi, 23 July 2010Retrieved from https://asean.org/us-here-to-stay-says-clinton-ha-noi-23-july-2010/

Wilson, J.D. (2018). Rescaling to the Indo-Pacific: From Economic to Security-Driven Regionalism in Asia. *East Asia*, Vol. 35, No. 2, 2018, pp. 177–196, https://doi.org/10.1007/s12140-018-9285-6Accessed on 22 January 2020.

4

FROM QUAD 1.0 TO QUAD 2.0

The Persisting Discourse

S. Y. Surendra Kumar

Quadrilateral Security Dialogue (Quad)

The United States (US) proposed the Quad in 2006, asserting that the four democracies – the US, Japan, Australia, and India – had significant naval capabilities and maritime interests in the Asia-Pacific region, and as a result, they felt there was a need for a consultative regional forum to deal with "maritime emergencies and security threats such as piracy and so on" (Saran, 2017:11). The idea of Quad was taken forward in December 2006, with the visit of former Indian Prime Minister Manmohan Singh to Tokyo, Japan, where the two leaders held a formal discussion to further the idea of Quad. In addition, during Japanese Prime Minister Shinzo Abe's visit to New Delhi, India (August 2007), he mentioned while addressing the Parliament that the "confluence of two seas called for a border Asia with the cooperation of Japan and India, as well as the US and Australia in the entirety of the Pacific Ocean" (Panda, 2018a.85). This idea or proposal, however, was vehemently opposed by both China and Russia, who dubbed the Quad initiative as "Asian NATO".

The shared interest of Japan and India in the Quad was endorsed by US Vice President Dick Cheney during his February 2007 visit to Japan and Australia, where he stated that the US was open to forming a Quad alliance. In addition to the support of the leaders (three countries), the formation of the "Regional Core Group" by the US, Japan, Australia, and India to carry out relief work in the aftermath of the Indian Ocean Tsunami (December 2004) laid the foundations for the emergence of the Quad (Kumar, 2012). Thus, it was argued that because the four countries had successfully handled

DOI: 10.4324/9781003479307-5

the post-tsunami crisis, they could aim to achieve shared strategic interests in the Asia-Pacific region.

Although the idea of the Quad emerged in 2006 as an ad hoc coordinating mechanism, the unpublicised first meeting took place in April 2007 on the sidelines of the Association of Southeast Asian Nations (ASEAN) Regional Forum (ARF) in Manila, Philippines, at the rank of Assistant Secretary of four countries (*Ibid*). This was followed by the Malabar 07 multilateral military exercise, which had previously been US-India bilateral exercises (since 1994), was expanded to include Japan and was held off the coast of Okinawa, Japan. In the process, the second round of exercises in the Bay of Bengal, India, in September 2007, included Australia and Singapore, along with over 20,000 personnel, 28 ships, 150 aircraft, and three aircraft carriers (Hawk, 2007). All of these developments suggested the possibility of a formal Quad establishment; however, the initiative was not formally institutionalised due to India, Japan, and Australia's lukewarm and ambiguous responses. Before delving into the reasons for Quad's failure to take off, it's critical to understand the factors that shaped Quad 1.0.

Quad 1.0: *The Guiding Factors*

The Indo-Pacific region is strategically important for the US, Japan, Australia, India, and China because it contains half of the world's population, six of its ten largest countries, two of the world's most critical cases of nuclear proliferation (North Korea and Pakistan), and the world's three most populous Muslim states (Indonesia, Pakistan, and India); and it increasingly dominates US and Chinese trade (Armacost and Roy, 2008). As a result, the Asia-Pacific region was of critical strategic importance to both major and emerging powers. Aside from that, there are other reasons for the formation of Quad 1.0, such as the following.

Shared Values

The US, Japan, Australia, and India are democratic countries that share common values such as freedom, respect for human rights, and the rule of law. Following that, the Quad was to focus on promoting peace, democracy, counter-terrorism, economic freedom, development, and humanitarian and disaster relief in the Asia-Pacific region. Besides that, it was presumed that the alliance would go a long way forward in addressing the major irritants in the four countries' bilateral relations.

Shared Security Objectives

The Quad would aid in addressing the region's shared security objectives, such as the rivalry between China and Japan, tension between India and

China, North Korea's nuclear programme, tension in the Taiwan Straits, increasing competition for energy resources, and instability and unrest in Myanmar and Thailand. Aside from that, combating sea piracy, terrorism, preventing drug and material trafficking, illegal migration of people, and the proliferation of weapons of mass destruction, particularly in the maritime waters surrounding Southeast Asia, were guiding factors for the four countries to form the Quad.

Further to that, the Indian Ocean is one of the busiest trade routes for supplying oil and gas around the world, and the Malacca Straits alone accounts for more than 25 percent of global maritime trade, and terrorist groups such as the Abu Sayyaf, Jemaah Islamiy, and Laskare-e-Jihad had also reportedly planned terrorist attacks to disrupt the global supply chain system (Mohanty, 2007). In this regard, Japan advocated for a "Naval Ocean Peacekeeping Force," and India and other Southeast Asian countries conducted frequent joint naval exercises to safeguard their maritime interests. Following that, many countries welcomed the establishment of the Regional Cooperation Agreement on Combating Piracy and Armed Robbery Against Ships in Asia (ReCCAP). As a result, it is believed that the Quad could create a collective and effective maritime cooperative security system to protect the Indian and Pacific Oceans.

Rise of China

The international security environment was witnessing a power shift from the West to the East, led by China's and India's rapid rise. More than India, the rise of China was a major concern for the US, Japan, Australia, and India. Although these countries have not formally expressed their concern, their trilateral strategic dialogue and Quad efforts have clearly indicated the growing threat from China. For example, China has successfully increased its engagements in the Asia-Pacific region through trade and economic integration, most notably through the Free Trade Agreement (FTA). China's strong diplomatic initiatives, manifested in the East Asia Summit (EAS), ASEAN+3 (China, Japan, and the Republic of Korea), and the Shanghai Cooperation Organization (SCO), have been interpreted as an attempt to create an alternative security group.

Furthermore, to address its energy security needs, it had established a significant naval presence along vital maritime chokepoints, popularly known as China's "String of Pearls," a plan to acquire several strategically located ports, naval bases, and posts in friendly countries such as Gwadar (Pakistan), Hambantota (Sri Lanka), Sittwe (Myanmar), and Chittagong (Bangladesh). This is in order to safeguard the billions of dollars in trade that pass through strategically significant sea lanes such as the Strait of Hormuz and the Malacca Straits to the Middle East, Africa, and Latin America (Prabhakar,

2009:44; and Ladwig III, 2009). This string of pearls also enabled China to gain access to a number of preferential resources as well as market access on highly subsidised terms (Layton, 2009). There were no parallel strategies by the US, Japan, or any other power. As a result, China's rise remained a major concern for the Quad's emergence. This concern was expressed by US Deputy Secretary of State Robert Zoellick in September 2005, who stated that the "US was in fact hedging against China by reinforcing diplomatic and military ties with Japan, particularly with India" (Xue Fukang, 2005). As a result of China's growing economic, diplomatic, and military power, countries such as the US, India, Japan, and Australia have been compelled to reconsider existing security arrangements and take preliminary steps that may lead to the formation of regional groups of nations, or Quad, with common interests and values.

Regional Forums Not Effective

Although regional initiatives such as the ARF, EAS, and APEC forums exist to help the four countries achieve their strategic goals, these forums are too large and unwieldy to produce long-term results on their own. The APEC, for example, was primarily concerned with trade liberalisation, whereas the ARF was concerned with confidence-building measures and preventive diplomacy. The ASEAN+3 and EAS processes overlap in membership, and their explicit roles have yet to be clearly defined. This was later articulated by Australian Prime Minister Kevin Rudd at the Shangri-la Dialogue in Singapore in May 2009, while advocating for the formation of an "Asian-Pacific Community" (APC). He said "none of the existing regional mechanisms as currently configured were capable of engaging in the full spectrum of dialogue, cooperation and action on economic and political matters and future challenges to security" (Thayer, 2009). The countries, on the other hand, had varied feelings about the APC (first proposed in June 2008). As a result, it was claimed that a smaller initiative, such as the Quad, comprising major powers, would go a long way towards attaining the geopolitical interests of Asia-Pacific countries.

Decline of Quad 1.0

Although all four countries initially agreed on the necessity for a Quad, it could not be fully institutionalised for a variety of reasons, including:

Lack of Unanimity

Initially, the US, Australia, and Japan were all eager to form Quad alliances; but, due to India's reluctance to join the group and regime changes in the US (2008), particularly in Australia and Japan in 2007, the Quad took a back seat. In an Asia-Pacific security setting, the new governments were more inclined to consider such democratic coalitions as overly provocative and unproductive. Quad 1.0 hence declined as a result of the regime transition.

US: From Pro-active to Soft Peddling

To achieve US strategic interests in the Asia-Pacific region, the Bush administration was proactive in forming trilateral and even Quad security arrangements. The main goals of the grouping were to prevent any single power or coalition of powers, such as China or its allies, from dominating Asia; to maintain an alliance system to facilitate American power projection; to secure sea lanes of communication to facilitate American commercial access and the free flow of trade in the region; and to promote American values such as democracy, humanitarian aid, and disaster relief (Avery and Vaughn, 2008:2). President Bush even advocated for the formation of an "Asia-Pacific Democracy Partnership" in September 2007 to promote democratic values and build democratic institutions in the area. Overall, the Bush administration believed that collaborating with countries that share common principles, such as Japan, Australia, and India, would benefit US interests.

The Quad project did not take off during the Bush administration due to the three countries' lacklustre reception. Although President Barack Obama initially had said that "a more effective structure in Asia is required that goes beyond bilateral accords, sporadic summits, and ad hoc arrangements, highlighted this new policy orientation" (Lampton, 2009; Obama, 2007:12; Tow and Loke, 2009), but did not make enough efforts to advance the Quad idea, despite the fact that the administration was fully aware that it needs China's help to guide the global governance process and settle transnational concerns. As a result, the Obama administration did not make any major meaningful steps to formalise Quad.

Australia: From Quadrilateral to Asia-Pacific Community

Initially, Australian Prime Minister John Howard, as well as the US and Japan, overwhelmingly favoured the formation of a Quad grouping with India as a member. However, Howard's administration suffered a major blow in November 2007, when his party lost the election and he lost his own parliamentary seat in Bennelong. As a result of the election, Kevin Rudd, the leader of the Labour Party, was elected Prime Minister, despite his opposition to the Quad grouping. The cause for this reaction was Bush's unpopularity in Australia as a result of unilateral measures, notably in Iraq (2003). It was also a verdict against the Howard administration's unwavering support for US policies such as the deployment of specialist Australian Defence

Force (ADF) in Afghanistan (2001) and Iraq (2003) (Jain, 2006). As a result, the Kevin government did not place the Quad grouping as a top priority.

At the same time, Australia did not want to antagonise China because the former was profiting from exports and the latter was seeking a Free Trade Agreement (FTA), and Australia believed it was in its best interests to engage rather than oppose China. "We do not intend to establish an official quadrilateral strategic conversation in defence and security areas... we do not want to do anything that... may otherwise raise alarm in the region, notably China," Australian Minister for Defence Brendon Nelson stated in July 2007 (Nelson, 2007:11). He also stressed that the Quad talks can focus on trade, economics, and culture rather than defence and security.

Apart from that, Prime Minister Kevin was attempting to create his own independent ties with Asian nations such as China, India, Japan, Singapore, and others, without appearing to be merely an American ally in the region (Vaughn, 2008:15). Surprisingly, he advocated for a multi-layered Asia Pacific Community (APC) initiative, which included all countries, including major powers such as the US, Japan, India, and Indonesia, participating in the emerging regional architecture of Asia. The APC's main goal was to break down the compartmentalisation of current regional organisations, develop effective leadership, and address political, economic, and security challenges holistically rather than piecemeal. Thus, the Kevin government was uninterested in moving the Quad further.

Japan: Proactive to Lukewarm

Although Prime Minister Abe was instrumental in forming the Quad alliance, however, with his departure from the office, the successive Prime Ministers restrained towards the alliance due to domestic compulsions like the growing public pacifist sentiments towards Japan's overwhelming support to the US's unilateral policies in Afghanistan and Iraq. Moreover, successive governments worked on strengthening relations with China. Even the then Prime Minister Yukio Hatoyama had emphasised a greater willingness to engage Beijing and the rest of Asia to achieve Japan's strategic interests in the Asia-Pacific region. He was also proposing the possibility of an East Asia Community (EAC) without the US, which China would welcome. Furthermore, Japan was fully aware that its economic future was becoming increasingly dependent on China, which had already eclipsed the US as its top trading partner (Fackler, 2010:11). Hence, the Quad grouping was placed on hold, with Japan wanting to promote good relations with China.

India: Principle Acceptance to Non-committal

With the US, Japan, and Australia, India has many shared ideals and strategic interests. As a result, India was concerned about China's growing economic and military prowess, as well as its growing influence in the Asia-Pacific region, particularly in South Asia. However, New Delhi had shown little interest in joining the Quad group from the start, owing to strong resistance from both leftists and rightists in India, who feared that joining any defence grouping with the US would turn India into the US's "Asian Israel." Furthermore, India refused to "choose sides" and was opposed to any formal regional defence alliance that targeted China. India, like Australia and Japan, preferred to strengthen rather than antagonise its relations with China. Rather than joining these organisations, India focused on improving bilateral ties with the three nations through the Indo-US strategic partnership, the India-Japan Action Plan 2009, and the Australia-India joint declaration on security cooperation, all of which were signed in November 2009. Overall, India was balancing its stance and responding to Quad initiatives with a tepid attitude.

China's Unease

China has always been critical of Quad groupings; for example, in response to the first informal meeting between the four countries in Manila, Philippines in May 2007, China's foreign affairs department dispatched individuals to each country to enquire about the motivations for floating such an idea. Following the Malabar naval drill in September 2007, China made a formal diplomatic complaint to Australia, India, and Japan over their decision to build a security alliance with the US against China. At the same time, China saw these developments as an indication of their probable desire to constrain China's growing naval and military cooperation with Bangladesh, Myanmar, and Sri Lanka in South Asia in general, and to send a strong signal to India in particular (Xia, 2007). Many Chinese commentators have nicknamed the Quad group "Asian NATO," "Asian Arc of Democracy," and the US' attempt to construct an anti-China axis in Asia. Russia expressed its concerns as well, stating that Asia should avoid "exclusive formations" (Varadarajan, 2008:10). As a result of China's vehement rejection, the Quad initiative was never taken forward or institutionalised.

QUAD 2.0: *From Asia-Pacific to Indo-Pacific*

Although Quad 1.0 was regarded as a forgotten chapter in the Asia-Pacific region, the concept was revived in December 2012, when Shinzo Abe was re-elected as Prime Minister of Japan and advocated for an "Asian Democratic Security Diamond," stating that "I envision a strategy whereby Australia, India, Japan, and the US should safeguard the maritime common stretching from the Indian Ocean region to the western Pacific" (Panda, 2018a:88). He went one step further and proposed the European Maritime Association, with Britain and France joining in the near future (Mohan, 2017:3).

Following that, India hosted the first-ever high-level trilateral dialogue between Australia, Japan, and India in New Delhi in June 2015. Maritime security, particularly freedom of navigation patrols, was one of the subjects discussed, and they urged restarting Quad between India, Japan, Australia, and the US (Chaudhury, 2016:11).

According to reports, US Admiral Harry B. Harris Jr., chief of the US Pacific Command (PACOM), formally proposed the Quad 2.0 in March 2016 when addressing an International Security Conference in New Delhi. Moreover, the return of Shinzo Abe as Japan's Prime Minister and the successful bilateral ties among the four countries, as well as the trilateral talks for collective exercises between the US-Japan-India, the US-Australia-Japan, and India-Japan-Australia, propelled the establishment of Quad 2.0 forward. In addition, the Quad 2.0 was shaped by Japan's participation in the Malabar exercise (2015), which included the US, India, and Australia.

Against this background, the inaugural meeting of Quad 2.0 took place in November 2017, with little fanfare and in a low-key manner. Only senior officials from the four countries met in Manila, Philippines, to discuss and address the seven core themes: rules-based order in Asia; maritime freedom of navigation and overflight; respect for international law; enhancing connectivity, maritime security, the North Korean threat and non-proliferation; and terrorism (Gale and Shearer, 2018:4). On the fringes of the East Asia Summit (EAS), the second Quad meeting was held in Singapore (November 2018). They highlighted opportunities for cooperation among the alliance/grouping in order to create a "Free and Open Indo-Pacific" (FOIP).

Nevertheless, the first official Foreign Ministers meeting in New York on the sidelines of the United Nations General Assembly (UNGA) meeting in September 2019, gave Quad 2.0 a huge boost. All four foreign ministers – Marise Payne (Australia), S. Jaishankar (India), Toshimitsu Motegi (Japan), and Mike Pompeo (US) – attended the Quad. However, no joint press statement was published; instead, a separate statement was issued, which indicated that the meeting was a "major elevation in the level of...dialogue", according to Alice Wells, US State Department's Acting Assistant Secretary for South and Central Asia. The four countries "reaffirmed their commitment to shared principles and cooperation on marine security, infrastructure, and connectivity in support of rules-based frameworks", according to Australian Foreign Minister Marise Payne in an email to the media. She also added that they discussed "efforts to maintain and promote an open, prosperous, and inclusive Indo-Pacific".[1]

Revival of Quad: *The Factors*

After a decade, the Quad resurfaced as the four countries' top priority, with two factors (Indo-Pacific and China) boosting Quad 2.0. The Asia-Pacific was the emphasis of the Quad 1.0, while the Indo-Pacific was the focus of the Quad 2.0. In 2016, for example, Japanese Prime Minister Shinzo Abe began advocating for a "Free and Open Indo-Pacific" (FOIP), claiming that Quad members played a critical role in ensuring FOIP, which he defined as a "value freedom, the rule of law, market economies" (Szechenyi and Hosoya, 2019:1). This was approved by the Trump administration in 2017, with US Secretary of State Rex Tillerson noting that FOIP is vital and that China is a regional threat. The "geostrategic confrontation with China as a battle between free and repressive conceptions of the world in the Indo-Pacific" was emphasised in both the December 2017, US National Security Strategy and the December 2018 National Defense Strategy (Ibid:2).

Overall, the US's twin objectives were to prevent China's aggressive actions in Taiwan, the East and South China Seas, and to counter China's increasing espionage operations, unfair trade, and alleged intellectual property and technology theft by China. Aside from the China issue, the US was also intrigued in investing in the development, energy, infrastructure, and technology in the Indo-Pacific. Similarly, Japan also intends to prevent China's attempts to alter the status quo in the East China Sea and unbalanced bilateral trade. For India, China's increasing and aggressive efforts to unilaterally alter the Line of Actual Control (LAC) and the deepening of bilateral ties between China and Pakistan through the Belt Road Initiative (BRI). Australia's need to counter China was more guided by economic – uneven trade balance and economic coercion, rather than security. Thus, the China factor pushed the revival of Quad (Lee, 2023:4).

The Indo-Pacific has been a focus of the Australian White Paper on Foreign Policy since 2013, and it formally defined the Indo-Pacific as stretching from the US Pacific coast to the India-Pakistan border (Grahann, 2018:5). India pledged to connect with four countries in order to secure FOIP as part of its "Act East Policy". Furthermore, India and Japan's ambitious cooperative relationship in pursuing the Asia-Africa Growth Corridor (AAGC), which intends to enhance development and connectivity between the two massive regions in order to ensure a FOIP (Gale and Shearer, 2018:2). In the process, in November 2020, the four navies engaged in their first joint exercise in over a decade, and India officially approved Australia's participation in the Malabar drills in the Bay of Bengal and the Arabian Sea.

Against this background, the year 2021 turned out to be an ideal year for Quad's growth since it hosted a virtual meeting (March 2021) of the leaders of the four countries, which was hosted by the US. Three Indo-Pacific countries were also represented at the meeting: New Zealand, South Korea, and Vietnam. All seven countries reaffirmed their commitment to promoting a free, open rules-based order, peaceful resolution of disputes, democratic values, and territorial integrity, and promised to respond to COVID-19's economic and health impacts, cyberspace, critical technologies, counterterrorism, quality infrastructure investment, humanitarian aid and disaster relief, as well as maritime domains (The White House, 2021; Ambrogio, 2021:12).

Another notable step was the Quad's first-ever in-person Leaders' Summit in September 2021, at the White House, which was attended by all four Heads of State – US President Joe Biden, Australian Prime Minister Scott Morrison, Indian Prime Minister Narendra Modi, and Japanese Prime Minister Yoshihide Suga. They retreated once more to strengthen bilateral ties and enhance practical cooperation on 21st-century issues (Ministry of External Affairs, 2021). The second phase of Malabar naval drills in the Bay of Bengal began in October 2021 and focused on advanced surface and anti-submarine warfare exercises, seamanship evolution, and weapon firings, in addition to the first phase, which was held in August 2021. Keeping the momentum, the foreign ministers of Quad convened for the fourth time in February 2022 in Melbourne, Australia, and resolved to speed up the delivery of COVID-19 vaccinations (worth billions of dollars) and agree to organise a special meeting on climate and to bolster their efforts to secure maritime security in the region (Haidar, 2022:11). More recently, the Quad leaders – President Joseph Biden, Prime Minister Anthony Albanese (Australia), Prime Minister Kishida Fumio (Japan), and Prime Minister Narendra Modi (India) on 20th May 2023 met at Hiroshima for the Quad Leaders' Summit and came up with a joint statement and vision statement focusing on critical issues concerning the Indo-Pacific and expressed their commitment to meet in India (2024).

Quad 1.0's emergence was aided by the China factor, and Quad 2.0's rebirth has been aided by the same cause. With China's growing political, economic, and military might in the Indo-Pacific region, the power balance is shifting in China's favour. Despite resistance from Southeast Asian countries and major powers, China is aggressively building artificial islands, conducting military exercises, and continuing to defy the judgement of the Permanent Court of Arbitration (PCA) at The Hague in 2016. As a result of China's maximalist stance on the South China Sea, the four countries were forced to take Quad seriously. Although the March 2021 leaders' meeting joint statement did not name China, observers believe that the inclusion of New Zealand, South Korea, and Vietnam suggests that this group might be a future "Quad plus", influenced by the China factor.

At the same time, China's ambitious BRI, which includes the Maritime Silk Route (MSR), has succeeded in improving ties with Indian Ocean Rim Association (IORA) countries to some extent. As a result, China's trade with IORA is far higher than that of the Quad members, such that China is the major importing partner for more than 24 countries and the top exporting partner for more than 13 countries from the Indian Ocean region (Baruah et al, 2023). China's increased engagement with countries in the Indo-Pacific region, including through infrastructure projects and loans, as well as strategic/military ambitions, has alarmed Quad members such as the US and Japan. Also, China's growing ties with Southeast and South Asian countries pose a clear threat to India's regional clout. Despite its excellent ties with China, Australia's defence White Paper (since 2009) reinforces China's growing military capability and aggressiveness in the Indo-Pacific area as a key aspect in the country's future defence plans (Byrne, 2019). In addition, in a joint statement (February 2022), four foreign ministers made a veiled allusion to China's aggressive actions in the SCS and the East China Sea, while reaffirming their commitment to a free and open Indo-Pacific "in which states attempt to safeguard their most vulnerable citizens from coercion" (Haidar, 2022:11).

The Quad 1.0 was also a result of common security concerns in the Asia-Pacific, as well as bilateral conflicts between the US, Japan, India, and Australia. As a result, these variables continue to bind them in the Quad 2.0's establishment. Overall, the Quad members believe China's rise threatens regional order and stability in the Indo-Pacific, but they continue to communicate their concerns in a circumspect manner, avoiding direct references to China.

Quad 2.0: The Challenges

The reasons for Quad 1.0's decline have not vanished; rather, they have become more pronounced as territorial disputes, economic dependency, and China's growing power in the Indo-Pacific continue. The following are some of the other issues that Quad 2.0 faces.

Divided House to a United House?

The inaugural Quad summit, held in Manila in November 2017, was noteworthy, although the four countries issued separate declarations, concentrating on "supporting peace, stability, and prosperity in the interconnected region and agreeing for a free, open, prosperous, and inclusive Indo-Pacific region". The Quad was sarcastically portrayed as a divided home in four countries' media releases. India's statement, for example, made no mention of freedom of navigation and overflight, respect for international law, or maritime security. Only Australia and the US mentioned "Quad" in their respective news announcements, while Japan's announcement made no reference of "connectivity" (Gale and Shearer, 2018). In September 2019, at the Quad's Foreign Ministers meeting, a similar scenario arose, with no joint press release or press conference. Since 2020, however, this tendency has reversed, with Quad's foreign ministers and leaders meeting on a regular basis and undertaking joint naval exercises regularly.

60 S. Y. Surendra Kumar

Despite this, there are several points of contention, such as although all four Quad members agree on the importance of ensuring FOIP in the region, India, Australia, and Japan insist that it must be based on a legal framework to ensure freedom of navigation, which includes strict adherence to the United Nations Convention on the Law of the Sea, 1982 (UNCLOS,), which all three have ratified. Ironically, the US, which is not a signatory to UNCLOS, likewise emphasises the rule of law, but it is unclear which rule. Furthermore, unlike the other three countries (India, Japan, and Australia), the US regards FOIP as a strategy. Furthermore, the full scope of Quad's intentions is unknown. Similarly, on defence strategy, Japan's strategy is moulded by its defence Self-Defense Force, Australia intends to ensure immediate regional security, and India is largely focused on defending LAC, and the US is "built to defend through power projection" (Diehl, 2021:2).

Moreover, with regard to the ongoing Russia-Ukraine War (since February 2022), unlike the US, Australia, and Japan, which responded critically and imposed sanctions on Russia and gave much-needed political and arms support to Ukraine to resist the Russian invasion. But, India continues to resist pressure from its fellow Quad members and is following its strategic autonomy and abstained at successive UN and United Nations Human Rights Council (UNHRC) voting on the Russia-Ukraine War. This uncertainty sends the wrong signal in the political arena. As a result, the Quad's growth may be hampered by a lack of consensus among its members.

Perceptions of China as a Danger

In terms of China's rise in the Indo-Pacific, the four countries do not have a unified danger perspective. For example, for the US, China's dominance in global political and economic structures, such as the China-led financial institution Asia Infrastructure Investment Bank (AIIB), the National Development Bank (NDB), and the BRI without the US, is posing a challenge to US supremacy. As a result, US policymakers believe (as represented in the NSS and NDS) that China is attempting to displace the US in the Indo-Pacific. In October 2019, US Secretary of State Mike Pompeo expressed his concerns that "we have reconvened the Quad... this will prove very important in the efforts ahead, ensuring that China retains only its proper place in the world" (Henry, 2019).

In the case of Japan, it is suggested that China's rise and dominance in the Indo-Pacific has come at the expense of Japan's regional and global significance as an emerging power. As a result, China's considerable military capabilities (maritime) pose a threat to Japanese security and maritime interests, as the country's trade is 80 percent seaborne. China's growing military and economic power in the Indo-Pacific, the lingering border dispute at Ladakh,

China's unwavering support for Pakistan, and its bold claim over Arunachal Pradesh are all important issues for India. Despite political and military tensions, India and China, bilateral trade is increasing and by the end of 2022, it stood at US$135 billion, and with both countries cooperating in counter-piracy operations in the Indian Ocean region and holding common viewpoints on global issues such as climate change.

On the other hand, Australia did not initially regard China as a threat, preferring to maintain strong economic connections and participate in the BRI and AIIB. However, in recent times (post-COVID-19 period), bilateral tensions have risen, with Australia demanding an independent investigation into the origins of COVID-19 in China, a strong critique of China's actions in Hong Kong, Taiwan, and the South China Sea, as well as a diplomatic boycott of the Beijing Winter Olympics (February 2022) along with the US. The trade war has become more intense. As a result, the Quad members' perceptions of the threat vary, impeding the Quad's progress in containing/balancing China. At the same time, all four Quad members have strong economic relations with China, such that China remains the Quad's largest trading partner. Thus, Quad members have a stronger relationship with China than they do with one another.

Is India a Leading Player in Indo-Pacific?

The US, Japan, and Australia have all argued that India may be an important participant in the Indo-Pacific area at various times. Prime Minister Shinzo Abe of Japan, for example, declared that "a powerful Japan and a powerful India can protect each other's interests in the Indo-Pacific" (Panda, 2018b). In its December 2017 National Security Strategy report, the US stated that it would support India's status as a prominent global force in the area (*Ibid*). Australia views India as a "major strategic partner" in the region, as evidenced by the fact that India was referenced 64 times in 2017 Foreign Policy White Paper of Australia , compared to only six times in 2003 (Eisentraut and Gaens, 2018:4). As a result, the big question is whether India can take on the leadership role or the obligations that the other Quad members have envisioned.

India initially refused to join the Quad, claiming that "it was willing to join Quad on its own terms or an agenda that is relevant to us, and the process should begin with officials rather than ministers" (Mohan, 2017:3). Despite being part of Quad 2.0, it is attempting to balance its relations with China while also advocating for a stronger Quad in the region. For example, India's Minister of External Affairs, S. Jaishankar, stated in November 2017 that the Quad is "a reflection of the evolving character of diplomacy where diverse actors engage in advancing and configuring their national interests" (Panda, 2018b). Following that, Prime Minister Modi stated at the

62 S. Y. Surendra Kumar

Shangri-La Dialogue in Singapore (June 2018) that ""India's strategic alliance with the US is a new foundation of our shared vision of an open, stable, safe, and prosperous Indo-Pacific" ... Modi also stated that India's relationship with China "has many dimensions", and that it is "critical for global peace and growth" (*Ibid*). Added to this is India's neutral position on the Russia-Ukraine war, hence, in the Indo-Pacific, India is attempting to strike a balance between the Beijing Consensus and the Washington Consensus.

Furthermore, rather than being China-centric, Quad 2.0 has chosen a pragmatic and uniting focus on urgent global commons, indicating India's reluctance to offend China, especially while its border conflict remains unresolved. At the same time, India is not interested in discussing a leading role in Quad 2.0, as India prefers inclusive growth (including China and other powers) in the Indo-Pacific, and India is well aware that the other Quad members are balancing their respective ties with China and are also participating in BRI. Following that, during the Doklam standoff in 2017 (a 70-day standoff between India, China, and Bhutan), the three countries (the US, Japan, and Australia) took a neutral stance and adopted a similar position during the Galwan Clashes in Ladakh (June 2020). At the same time, India continues to be sceptical of Australia's and the US' commitment to the Quad, believing that if the government changes in the near future, both will retreat like they did in 2007. Overall, India wants China confined, but does not want to be the one to contain China.

China's Opposition

Since the inception of Quad 1.0, China has been outspoken in its opposition to the formation of Quad and has expressed its concerns on several occasions. As it sees the Quad as merely a containment measure against it and a step towards an Asian NATO. "We have no problem with relevant countries' normal collaboration", Chinese Foreign Ministry spokesman Hong Lei stated in March 2016, "but we feel that relevant cooperation should not be targeted against a third party".[2] Simultaneously, they prefer to argue that Quad will not exist long due to the members' various interests. For example, Chinese Foreign Minister Wang Yi compared the "concept of recreating the Quad to sea foam, destined to dissolve soon", emphasising that it was nothing more than a "headline-grabbing idea", even an "exclusive clique" (Eisentraut and Gaens, 2018b; Scott and Reynolds, 2019). As a result, the Quad continues to be opposed by China.

China's ambassador to Tokyo (October 2021) publicly chastised former Prime Minister Suga, alleging that the new Quad diplomacy is "100% outmoded" and shows a "Cold War mentality" (Smith, 2021). Chinese President Xi Jinping went one step further to propose the "Global Security Initiative" in April 2022, which he envisions as a "common, comprehensive, cooperative and sustainable security, that opposes unilateralism, group politics and bloc confrontation" (Krishnan, 2022:11). Thus, many analysts regard this initiative as counter to Quad. Apart from expressing dissatisfaction, China has used economic coercion against Australia and Europe, military coercion against India, and heightened regional concern through heightened sovereignty claims, frequently far from established borders, since 2020. All of these hostile acts are part of China's overall strategy against the Quad nations.

Quad Plus: Is It 3.0?

Generally, Quad Plus currently refers to a mini-lateral engagement in the Indo-Pacific that is primarily focused on developing a cooperative framework to address common international difficulties such as pandemic-related economic and public health concerns. The participation of representatives from New Zealand, South Korea, and Vietnam at the virtual Quad summit (March 2021) signalled that Quad is on the verge of expanding its membership. In a similar vein, the US sponsored a summit of the Quad nations in May 2021, which also comprised Brazil, Israel, and South Korea, to consider a global reaction to COVID-19 (Panda, 2022). As a result, many analysts and policymakers fear that it may weaken Quad's influence in the Indo-Pacific region and further antagonise China. However, it appears that the leaders' aim is not to expand the number of Quad members, and neither country is eager to join at the expense of their ties with China. Bangladesh, for example, reacted angrily (May 2021) to China's pre-emptive warning that it should not join Quad. The Bangladesh foreign minister suggested that the country does not wish to participate in the initiative, stating that "Dhaka maintains a non-aligned and balanced foreign policy and it will decide what to do according to those principles".[3] Overall, whether or not countries will join Quad if and when it is expanded at the expense of bilateral ties with China remains to be seen. The speculation for security dimension of Quad plus arose at the 15–17 May 2023, senior level military commanders meeting held at Sunnylands in California before the Quad leader's summit in Hiroshima. This meeting was hosted by the Commander of the US Indo-Pacific Command and was attended by Japan's Chief of Staff, Australia's Chief of Defence Force, India's Chief of Defence Staff, and the UK's Vice-Admiral rank representative (Saha and Mishra, 2023). Thus, the presence of the UK at the meeting, despite it being part of AUKUS, gives an impression that the UK might be part of Quad plus in the near future.

AUKUS

The AUKUS is a security alliance formed by Australia, the United Kingdom, and the US that focuses on defence, scientific, and technology collaboration.

This emphasis underscores Washington's real intention to collaborate with allies to achieve a favourable balance of power to deter Beijing, as evidenced by the US and UK assistance to Australia in the deployment of nuclear-powered submarines in the Pacific. It benefits Australia since it will be able to develop nuclear-powered submarines for the first time, thanks to US technology, and the agreement also covers Artificial Intelligence (AI) and other technologies. China had denounced the pact as "very irresponsible". The Chinese embassy in Washington accused the two countries of having a "Cold War attitude and ideological bias", according to the embassy.[4] The 13th March 2023 was a landmark for Australia and the AUKUS partnership, as its leaders announced an arrangement for Australia to acquire conventionally armed nuclear-powered submarines (SSN-AUKUS).

On the other hand, former Indian Foreign Secretary Harsh Vardhan Shringla reacted to the news by saying the agreement was "neither relevant to the Quad nor will it have any impact on its functioning".[5] However, Japan's equivalent has expressed his willingness to collaborate with the three on AUKUS-related issues. Members of ASEAN, who had previously indicated support for the Quad, have expressed concern over the risk of a nuclear weapons race erupting in the Indo-Pacific area. France emerged very critical among the EU nations, and it even summoned its ambassadors to Canberra and Washington, D.C., noting its anger with Australia's termination of a US$90 billion bilateral submarine contract without prior notice that it would be buying nuclear submarines from the US after entering the accord.[6] As a result, while AUKUS has major consequences for the credibility and growth of Quad 2.0, it remains to be seen how its members will handle the negative impact of AUKUS on Quad.

The Way Forward

Quad 2.0 has made significant progress in contrast to Quad 1.0, but it still has to be strengthened further, namely: (a) constructing and maintaining marine infrastructure, such as ports and harbours, is critical for keeping Quad alive. (b) Improving regional joint intelligence sharing, consultations, and naval exercises, and including other countries in Malabar naval drills. (c) Quad should concentrate solely on issues or areas that cannot be resolved through bilateral or trilateral discussions. (d) Quad should be mindful of ASEAN interests, as they are also important participants in the Indo-Pacific and FOIP. Singapore Prime Minister Lee Hsien Loong in the year 2018 expressed worry in this regard, "indicating ASEAN's embrace of the Indo-Pacific, provided the end outcome is an open and inclusive regional architecture, where ASEAN member nations are not pushed to take sides" (Byrne, 2019:32). (e) While there is a drive to expand the membership of Quad 2.0 to include Vietnam and other Southeast Asian countries, it is far

From Quad 1.0 to Quad 2.0 **65**

too early to consider doing so. Instead, the focus should be on strengthening the Quad and increasing member consensus on crucial issues. (f) While Quad 2.0 does not need to be institutionalised, it can operate to ensure coordinated results in areas such as counter-terrorism, cybersecurity, and disaster relief. As a result, certain measures are required to move Quad forward.

In a nutshell, a Quad with common ideals, high-end capabilities, and complementary geography, can contribute to FOIP if China factor/pressure, as well as regional and economic pushbacks, can be avoided in the near future. If not, Quad 2.0 will follow in the footsteps of Quad 1.0.

Notes

1 "Quad gets an upgrade as foreign ministers of India, Japan, Australia and US meet", 27 September 2019 [Online]. Available at https://thewire.in/diplomacy/quad-gets-an-upgrade-as-foreign-ministers-of-india-japan-australia-us-meet
2 "Security Grouping proposed for India, Japan, Australia and US", *Indo Asia-Pacific Defense Forum*, 25 March 2016 [online]. Available at http://apdf-magazine.com/security-grouping-proposed-for-india-japan-australia-and-u-s/
3 "We decide on foreign policy: Bangladesh reacts to Chinese warning over joining quad", 11 May 2021 [online] Available at https://timesofindia.indiatimes.com/world/south-asia/we-decide-our-foreign-policy-bangladesh-reacts-to-chinese-warning-over-joining-quad/articleshow/82548632.cms
4 China's embassy in Washington accused the countries of a "Cold War mentality and ideological prejudice", *The New Indian Express*, 21 September 2021, p. 1
5 Ibid.
6 "A critical component for global and strategic policy frameworks", 22 September 2021 [online]. Available at https://www.atlanticcouncil.org/uncategorized/experts-react-the-september-2021-white-house-quad-meeting/

References

Ambrogio, Enrico D. (2021) *The Quad: An Emerging Multilateral Security Framework of Democracies in the Indo-Pacific Region*, European Parliamentary Research Service, pp. 1–12{Online} Available at https://www.europarl.europa.eu/thinktank/en/document/EPRS_BRI(2021)690513
Armacost, Michael H. and Roy, Stapleton (2008) "American Overview: Asian Policy Challenges for the Next President", in Asia Foundation (ed.), *America's Role in Asia: Asian and American Views*, San Francisco: The Asia Foundation, pp. 73–100.
Avery, Emma Chanlett and Vaughn, Bruce (2008) "Emerging Trends in the Security Architecture in Asia: Bilateral and Multilateral Ties among the US, Japan, Australia, and India", *CRS Report for Congress*, 7 January, pp. 1–20[Online], Available at https://www.everycrsreport.com/reports/RL34312.html.
Baruah, Darshana, Labh, Nitya and Greely, Jessica (2023) *Mapping Indian Ocean Region*, Carnegie Endowment for International Peace, 15 June [Online]. Available at https://carnegieendowment.org/2023/06/15/mapping-indian-ocean-region-pub-89971
Byrne, Caitlin (2019) "Can the Quad Navigate the Complexities of a Dynamic Indo-Pacific?" 01 November [Online]. Available at https://www.orfonline.org/

expert-speak/can-the-quad-navigate-the-complexities-of-a-dynamic-indo-pacific-55716/

Chaudhury, Dipanjan Roy (2016) "US Pushes for Naval Quadrilateral between India, US, Japan and Australia to edge out China in Indo-Asia-Pacific region" *The Economic Times*, 2 March, p. 11.

Diehl, Justin L. (2021) "Indo-Pacific Deterrence and QUAD in 2030", *Journal of Indo-Pacific Affair*, Spring, pp. 1–26[Online] : Available at https://www.europarl.europa.eu/thinktank/en/document/EPRS_BRI(2021)690513 .

Eisentraut, Sophie and Gaens, Bart (2018) "The US-Japan-India-Australia Quadrilateral Security Dialogue", *FIIA Briefing Paper*, May, pp. 1–8.

Fackler, Martin (2010) "US Frets as Japan Inches Closer to China", *Deccan Herald*, 24 February, p. 11.

Fukang, Xue (2005) "Hedging Strategy Won't Do Relationship Goo", *Chain Daily*, 21 November [Online]. Available at http://www.chinadaily.com.cn/english/doc/2005-11/21/content_496508.htm

Gale, Jesse Barker and Shearer, Andrew (2018) *The Quadrilateral Security Dialogue and the Maritime Silk Route Initiative*, Centre for Strategic and International Studies, March [Online]. Available at https://csis-prod.s3.amazonaws.com/s3fs-public/publication/180717_GaleShearer_QuadSecurityDialogue.pdf

Grahann, Euan (2018) "The Quad Deserves its Second Chance", in Euan Graham, et al (eds.), *Debating eh Quad*, Canberra: ANU Strategic and Defence Studies Centre, pp. 1–28.

Haidar, Suhasini (2022) "Quad Meet Focuses on Indo-Pacific Cooperation", *The Hindu*, 12 February p. 11.

Hawk, Kitty (2007) "Allies Complete Malabar Exercise", *US Navy Press Release*, 10 September [Online]. Available at https://www.navy.mil/submit/display.asp?story_id=31737

Henry, Iain (2019) "Finally, Some Plain Talk on the Quad", 23 October [Online]. Available at https://www.lowyinstitute.org/the-interpreter/finally-some-plain-talk-quad

Jain, Purnendra (2006) "Japan-Australia Security ties and the US: The Evolution of the Trilateral Dialogue Process and its Challenges", *Australian Journal of International Affairs*, 60(4), December, pp. 521–535.

Krishnan, Ananth (2022) "Xi's Global Security Initiative Looks to Counter Quad Grouping", *The Hindu*, 29 April, p. 11.

Kumar, S Y Surendra (2012) "US-Japan-Australia-India Quadrilateral Initiative: Opportunities and Challenges", in Yagama Reddy (ed.), *India-Australia towards Sustainable Relationship in 21st Century*, New Delhi: Akansha Publishing House, pp.134-145.

Ladwig III, Walter (2009) "Delhi's Pacific ambition: Naval Power, Look East and India's Emerging influence in the Asia Pacific", *Asian Security*, 5(2), pp. 87–113.

Lampton, David M. (2009) "The US and China in the Age of Obama: Looking Each Other Straight in the Eyes", *Journal of Contemporary China*, 18(62), November, pp. 703–727.

Layton, Kimberley (2009) "India-Australia Ties: Times for More Than Cricket", 22 April [Online]. Available at www.ipcs.org/article/india-the-world/india-australia-ties-time-for-more-than-cricket-2850.html

Lee, Sheryn (2023) *Prospects and Limitations for a Quad Plus Europe*, Policy Brief, Stockholm: Swedish Institute of International Affairs, pp. 1–16.

Ministry of External Affairs, Government of India (2021) "Fact Sheet: Quad Leaders' Summit", 21 September [Online]. Available at https://www.mea.gov.in/bilateral-documents.htm?dtl/34319/Fact_Sheet_Quad_Leaders_Summit

Mohan, C. Raja (2017) *India and the Resurrection of the Quad*, ISAS Brief, Singapore: Institute of South Asian Studies No. 525, November, pp. 1–6.

Mohanty, Satyajit (2007) "Indo-Japan relations and the Asian Security System", 25 July [Online]. Available at www.ipcs.org/article/india/indo-japan-relations-and-the-asian-security-system-2340.html

Nelson, Brendan (2007) "There is Nothing But Goodwill Towards India", *The Hindu*, 23 July, p. 11.

Obama, Barack (2007) "Renewing American Leadership", *Foreign Affairs*, 86(4), p. 12.

Panda, Jagannath P. (2018a) "India's Call on China in the Quad: A Strategic Arch between Liberal and Alternative Structures", *Rising Power Quarterly*, 3(3), pp. 83–111.

Panda, Jagannath P. (2018b) "India, the Quad and the China Question", 24 December [Online]. Available at https://idsa.in/idsanews/india-quad-china-question

Panda, Jagannath P. (2022) "Making 'Quad Plus' a Reality", 13 January [Online]. Available at https://thediplomat.com/2022/01/making-quad-plus-a-reality/

Prabhakar, Lawrence S. (2009) "China's String of Pearls in Southern Asia-Indian Ocean: Implication for India and Taiwan", in M. J. Vinod, Yeong-Kuang Ger and S. Y. Surendra Kumar (eds.), *Security challenges in the Asia-Pacific Region*, New Delhi: Viva Books, pp.39–60

Saha, Premesha and Mishra, Vivek (2023) "Quad 3.0: A Security-Oriented Reincarnation?", 9 June [Online]. Available at https://www.orfonline.org/expert-speak/quad-3-0-a-security-oriented-reincarnation/

Saran, Shyam (2017) "The Quadrilateral: Is it an Alliance or an Alignment", *The Hindustan Times*, 25 November, p. 11.

Smith, Sheila A. (2021) "The Quad in the Indo-Pacific: What to Know CFR Report", 27 May [Online]. Available at https://www.cfr.org/article/quad-aukus-and-indias-dilemmas

Szechenyi, Nicholas and Hosoya, Yuichi (2019) *Working Towards a Free and Open Indo-pacific*, Carnegie Alliance Policy Coordination Brief, Washington: Carnegie Endowment for international Peace, pp. 1–5.

Thayer, Carlyle A. (2009) "Kevin Rudd's Multi-Layered Asia Pacific Community Initiative", 22 June [Online]. Available at www.eastasiaforum.org/2009/06/22/kevin-rudds-multi-layered-asia-pacific-community-initiative

The White House, Quad Leaders' Joint Statement (2021) "The Spirit of the Quad", 12 March [Online]. Available at https://www.whitehouse.gov/briefing-room/statements-releases/2021/03/12/quad-leaders-joint-statement-the-spirit-of-the-quad/

Tow, William and Loke, Beverley (2009) "Rules of Engagement: American's Asia-Pacific Security Policy under an Obama Administration", *Australian Journal of International Affairs*, 64(4), December, pp. 443–457.

Varadarajan, Siddharth (2008) "India, Japan Say New Security Ties not Directed Against China", *The Hindu*, 23 October, p. 10.

Vaughn, Bruce (2008) "Australia: Background and US Relations", *CRS Report for Congress*, 8 August.

Xia, Liping (2007) "Ex Malabar: China not Keen on a 'Democratic' Alliance", *Opinion Asia*, 18 September [Online]. Available at www.opinionasia.com/Chinanotkeenonademocraticalliance

SECTION B

China and the Quad Nation States

5

CHINA IN THE INDO-PACIFIC

Perspectives and Interests

Huo Wenle[1]

In the last few years, the Indo-Pacific has been widely discussed among a growing number of countries and seems to emerge as a new geopolitical framework in the foreseeable future. In fact, the term Indo-Pacific is hardly new because it has a long-standing acceptance as a distinct bio-geographic region or has been used in ethnography since the 1850s. In the early and mid-20th century, the Indo-Pacific as a geopolitical term was occasionally used but soon was neglected for decades. In early 2007, Gurpreet S. Khurana, a research fellow at the Institute for Defence Studies and Analyses based in New Delhi, was the first scholar to use the term Indo-Pacific in a journal since the 21st century. During his speech in the Indian parliament in August 2007, the former Japanese Prime Minister Shinzo Abe elaborated on the Indo-Pacific vision and called for close cooperation between the US, Japan, India, and Australia in the Indo-Pacific region. However, the concept of Indo-Pacific did not have substantial progress until almost a decade later. In November 2017, during his trip to five Asian countries, the then US President Donald Trump laid out his vision for a free and open Indo-Pacific, which was followed by a series of Quad meetings between the US, Japan, India, and Australia. In 2021, the Quad mechanism has been upgraded from the foreign minister level to the summit level. In February 2022, the Biden administration released the new Indo-Pacific Strategy document following the Trump administration's Indo-Pacific Strategy Report released in June 2019.

Compared with countries mentioned above, China's attention to the Indo-Pacific started relatively late. In 2013, Zhao Qinghai, an associate research fellow from the China Institute of International Studies, first elaborated on the concept of Indo-Pacific and its implications in a journal article. Since

DOI: 10.4324/9781003479307-7

November 2017, when the Quad was resumed, the Indo-Pacific has aroused widespread attention and discussions in Chinese academic circles. The Chinese government, however, is still hesitant to formally adopt the term Indo-Pacific, not to mention policymaking for the forthcoming Indo-Pacific epoch. The article begins by briefly reviewing Chinese perspectives on the Indo-Pacific from the aspects of government and academia. It then examines China's geo-security, geo-economy, and geopolitical interests in the Indo-Pacific region. It also stresses how the Chinese government promotes and protects its strategic interests in this region. The article concludes that China is an indisputable stakeholder in the Indo-Pacific region, and the Chinese government should take a more positive attitude towards the Indo-Pacific.

Chinese Perspectives on the Indo-Pacific

For a long time, the term Indo-Pacific has not attracted much attention from the Chinese government, although it has been widely discussed and accepted by many other countries. It was not until November 2017 that Chinese officials started to respond to issues regarding Indo-Pacific. Generally speaking, the Chinese government has not explicitly expressed support or opposition to the Indo-Pacific. In other words, the Chinese government shows a cautious and sceptical attitude towards the Indo-Pacific. The traditional term Asia-Pacific seems more comfortable to Chinese officials, and the term Indo-Pacific has rarely been mentioned by them on different occasions. Otherwise, it would give the public the impression of Chinese endorsement of the term Indo-Pacific.

Chinese government views the Indo-Pacific as one of many regional cooperation initiatives. Beijing supports any constructive regional cooperation vision or strategy but objects any geopolitical and geo-economic arrangements designed to contain China. Since November 2017, Chinese Foreign Ministry spokespersons have expressed China's perspectives on the Indo-Pacific. They claimed that the Indo-Pacific strategy should conform to the trend of the times characterised by "peace, development and win-win cooperation" and help to "uphold and promote regional peace, stability and prosperity" (Ministry of Foreign Affairs, 2017a). It also should be "open and inclusive", and avoid "politicization and exclusiveness" and "against the third party" (Ministry of Foreign Affairs, 2017b). In October 2017, the Chinese ambassador to the United States Cui Tiankai stressed that any attempt to form exclusive clubs in the region [Indo-Pacific] following a so-called zero-sum approach will not help anybody, and China cannot be contained by any country (India Today, 2017). In March 2018, in response to a question whether the Indo-Pacific strategy is to contain China, the Chinese Foreign Minister Wang Yi expressed that the term Indo-Pacific strategy is "like the foam on the sea, and gets attention but will soon dissipate", "nowadays stroking a new Cold War is out of sync with the times and inciting confrontation will find no market" (Times of India, 2018). In July 2021, he repeated his ideas at the ninth World Peace Forum that "the implementation of the 'Indo-Pacific strategy' aimed at group confrontation is to create a 'small circle' of geographical competition, a restoration of the Cold War mentality, and a historical regression" (Ministry of Foreign Affairs, 2021). In March 2022, Wang Yi accused the US of trying to build an "Indo-Pacific NATO", which runs counter to the common vision of peace, development, cooperation, and a win-win situation within regional countries and is destined to have no future (Ministry of Foreign Affairs, 2022).

There are several reasons for the Chinese government taking a hesitating attitude towards the concept of the Indo-Pacific. Firstly, the Indo-Pacific framework is still in the initial phase and faces some uncertainties in the near future. Nowadays, there are different versions of regional cooperation initiatives in the Asia-Pacific region, and they differ from each other in terms of names, geographical ranges, principles, and approaches. Given the differences between the US, Japan, India, Australia, and other countries towards the Indo-Pacific, it is too early to conclude that the Indo-Pacific will replace the Asia-Pacific framework where China is enjoying a growing role. Secondly, the Indo-Pacific, to some extent, has been viewed by the Chinese government as a geopolitical arrangement to contain China. Although the Indo-Pacific has been declared by the US, India, Japan, and Australia as a free, open, and inclusive region, Beijing is still suspicious of their intention to propose a new geopolitical framework. Thirdly, the Indo-Pacific strategy proposed by the US, India, Japan, and Australia does not consider other players in this region, such as the ASEAN states, South Korea, and so on. China always expresses its support for the centrality of ASEAN in various regional cooperation mechanisms. Thus, China would prefer a real open and inclusive Indo-Pacific framework in which many other players should also join.

By contrast with Beijing's cautious and hesitating attitude, most Chinese scholars view the Indo-Pacific as a product against China and a threat to China's peripheral security, economic development, and strategic space. They pay more attention to the definition of the Indo-Pacific concept, the elaboration of major powers' Indo-Pacific strategy, and their strategic dynamics in the Indo-Pacific region, and prospective of the coming Indo-Pacific epoch. In addition, many Chinese analysts also propose a series of countermeasures that China can implement to respond to the adverse impact of the Indo-Pacific on China.

Most Chinese experts believe that the Indo-Pacific has evolved from a geographical terminology to a geostrategic one, and the Indo-Pacific is the reflection of some geo-economic and geopolitical developments in this region (Wu, 2014: 29–40). However, there is no consensus in the Chinese academic circle about its geographical range. Roughly speaking, there are four different geographical scopes about the Indo-Pacific region: the Western Pacific Ocean plus the Eastern Indian Ocean; the Western Pacific Ocean plus the entire Indian Ocean; the entire Pacific Ocean plus the Eastern Indian Ocean; and the entire Pacific and Indian oceans. China and India seem to accept the Indo-Pacific as a region that covers the Western Pacific and the entire Indian Ocean, while the US government supports that the geographic range includes the entire Pacific and Eastern Indian Ocean Region (IOR). In May 2018, the US Pacific Command was officially renamed as the Indo-Pacific Command, whose responsibility area still remains in the entire Pacific and Eastern Indian Ocean. The ambiguity in concept definition provides "space for power game" in concept construction process (Lin, 2018: 16–35). This will also allow as many countries as possible to participate in the discussion and construction of the Indo-Pacific framework.

Most Chinese scholars believe a complete Indo-Pacific strategy system has not been formed yet. However, in the Chinese academic circle, scholars often use "Indo-Pacific Strategy" to refer to different powers' Indo-Pacific policies. Generally speaking, they pay more attention to major powers' Indo-Pacific strategies, the US in particular. Most of the Chinese scholars realise the dual purpose of American Indo-Pacific strategy. On the one hand, the Indo-Pacific strategy is designed to maintain, secure, and consolidate the dominant role of the US in the Indo-Pacific region through comprehensive approaches including politics, diplomacy, and military. On the other hand, the Indo-Pacific strategy is certainly directed at China and aimed at containing or balancing China's rise through both geo-economic and geopolitical means. Liang Fang (2017), professor from China's People's Liberation Army (PLA) National Defense University, argues that the intentions of the Indo-Pacific strategy proposed by the US are to prevent the extension of China's Belt and Road Initiative through the Indian Ocean; hope India will increase containment of China's sea lines of communication (SLoCs) in the Indian Ocean; and avoid direct confrontation with China.

Chinese experts are paying close attention to the impact of Indo-Pacific on China's peripheral security including land and sea directions (Wei, 2022). Professor Xie Guiping (2018: 56–70) from Sichuan University and Professor Zhang Genhai (2022: 133–155) from Hebei University of Science & Technology believe that Indo-Pacific will threaten China's maritime security in the South China Sea, East China Sea and Taiwan Strait, and deteriorate China's peace and stability in Tibet, Xinjiang, and Northeast China Region close to North Korea. The Indo-Pacific strategy may deteriorate China's relations with neighbouring countries such as India, Japan, and ASEAN states. The Indo-Pacific strategy proposed by the Trump administration will expose Sino-Indian relations to greater uncertainty and intensify competition between China and Japan in Africa and other regions (Mei, 2017).

Professor Zhu Cuiping (2018: 1–17) and Wu Huaizhong (2018: 13–21) examine Indo-Pacific's impact on China's economy in their articles. They argue that the Indo-Pacific strategy will have a direct impact on China's Belt and Road Initiative and impede China's promotion of regional economic integration. In addition, many scholars also note that Indo-Pacific will influence China's rise in the strategic level. Ye Hailin (2018: 1–14), director of the Center for South Asian Studies from the Chinese Academy of Social Sciences, argues that strengthening strategic cooperation between the US, Japan, Australia, and India under the concept of the Indo-Pacific will not only complicate China's major power diplomacy and peripheral diplomacy but also make it more difficult for China to maintain strategic coordination between its major and minor strategic directions. Professor Zhang Jiadong (2018: 1–26) from Fudan University is one of the few Chinese scholars who realise the positive implications of Indo-Pacific on China. From his perspective, the term Indo-Pacific can strengthen China's validity and rationality in the Indian Ocean Region, and China should positively reflect on the rational contents of the Indo-Pacific proposal. Wang Lina (2023: 116–131) from Peking University argues that while the American "Indo-Pacific Strategy" poses a strategic threat to China and undermines China's surrounding security environment, it will also promote the strategic awakening of the region.

Although the huge potential threats and challenges to China, most of the Chinese scholars hold a negative or pessimistic attitude towards the implementation of the Indo-Pacific strategy and believe that containment of China in the Indo-Pacific region through the Quad security dialogue is bound to fail as a "utopia" or "bubble". Firstly, the Indo-Pacific region is too broad to be a coherent strategic region, and it is extremely difficult for the Quad to take joint measures and even build a powerful alliance to balance or contain China. Secondly, the Indo-Pacific Strategy led by the US is facing internal difficulties, namely that not only is there a serious mismatch between the cost the US can use for the "Indo-Pacific Strategy" and its expected benefits, but the overall strength of the US at this stage and the amount of money that can be used for the "Indo-Pacific Strategy" are seriously incompatible (Xie and Du, 2022; Ye, 2022). Thirdly, the Quad mechanism is still facing some uncertainties. The Quad lacks a strong economic structure like the Trans-Pacific Partnership Agreement and ignores other middle powers' role in this region. Although President Joe Biden and other 12 countries initiated the Indo-Pacific Economic Framework in May 2022, many commentators describe this initiative as "hollow" or "meaningless". Fourthly, inside the Quad, the US, India, Japan, and Australia have differences and contradictions about the Indo-Pacific framework. Fifthly, the growing interdependence among countries in the economic globalisation times has made it difficult for any country or group to isolate or contain China. Many other countries in the Indo-Pacific region are reluctant to get involved in the power struggle between China and the US at the cost of economic benefits. All four countries of the US, Japan, Australia, and India are closely trading partners with China, and China is the largest trading partner of each of them. Lastly, the China factor also works. With the development of China's comprehensive national power in every aspect, many regional and global issues cannot be resolved without China's participation. The US and the international community also need to cooperate with China on common significant security issues, such as climate change, counter-proliferation, and counter-terrorism. In addition, the improvement of bilateral relations between China and other states such as India, Japan, and ASEAN states will also help the collapse of the Indo-Pacific strategy against China.

Different scholars have proposed different suggestions for China to respond to the Indo-Pacific strategy. Some people argue that China should, to some extent, ignore the Indo-Pacific concept because they believe that if Beijing takes a strong reaction to Indo-Pacific, the US, Japan, India, and Australia will actively promote cooperation to contain China (Zhou, 2018: 29–39). The mainstream opinion in Chinese academia is that China should take comprehensive measures to offset the negative impact of Indo-Pacific. These measures include insisting on the moral orientation of Chinese foreign strategy and promoting its new security concept; maintaining stable relations with the US, Japan, India, and Australia; strengthening security, political, and economic cooperation with ASEAN states and South Asian countries; adopting a more positive foreign policy to provide leading values, international norms, and institutional arrangements for regional countries, and so on (Wu, 2014: 29–40; Wu, 2018: 13–21; Li, 2022). Additionally, a few scholars claim that China should participate in shaping and adjusting the regional security and economic order in the Indo-Pacific region (Zhang, 2019: 1–7). He Kai (2019: 13–21), chair professor from Nankai University, suggests that China should unite some ASEAN countries to join the Quad mechanism and expand its influence in Indo-Pacific framework. Chen Bangyu and Wei Hong (2015: 51–65) in their article suggest that China should propose its own strategic vision for the Indo-Pacific region and try to play a crucial role in the coming Indo-Pacific epoch.

China's Interests in the Indo-Pacific Region

Chinese government may be reluctant to officially adopt the Indo-Pacific strategy in the near future. China's decision-makers, however, have had one kind of Indo-Pacific vision for a long time. Geographically, China is not only a Western Pacific power, but also a near Indian Ocean state or Indian Ocean stakeholder. In other words, China is an undoubted Indo-Pacific power and enjoys a wide range of strategic interests in this region. Generally speaking, China's strategic interests in the Indo-Pacific region include three aspects: safeguarding national sovereignty and territorial integrity; ensuring the safety and security of energy and trade sea lines of communication; and maintaining stable strategic space in the Indo-Pacific.

China is the only major power in the world that has not achieved national reunification. It also has a number of territorial and maritime disputes with its neighbouring countries in the South China Sea and East China Sea. Therefore, safeguarding national sovereignty and territorial integrity has been listed as China's core interests. Since Tsai Ing-wen became the so-called Taiwan President in May 2016, relations across the Taiwan Straits have experienced a major setback. The Democratic Progressive Party under the leadership of Tsai Ing-wen not only refuses to recognise the 1992 Consensus which refers to the one China policy, but also attempts to promote the so-called Taiwan Independence Movement. In addition, during the last decade, China's territorial disputes with Japan, Vietnam, and the Philippines in the East China Sea and South China Sea have intensified, posing a threat to regional stability and China's core interests in the Indo-Pacific region.

China is keeping a close watch on the role that the US has played near the China seas. On one hand, the US is trying to balance the growing asymmetric power between Mainland and Taiwan through playing the Taiwan card. For a long time, the US government has continuously updated Taiwan's military forces through military trade. In 2018, the US Congress passed the Taiwan Travel Act, which is aimed at promoting the official exchange level between the US and Taiwan. In March 2020, American President Trump signed the Taipei Act to deter countries who build diplomatic relations with mainland China. In order to show its support to the Tsai Ing-wen administration, the US Navy and Coast Guard have regularly dispatched their warships through the Taiwan Strait. In June 2023, the Biden administration has approved two potential arms sales totalling 440 million US Dollars to Taiwan (Callahan, 2023). On the other hand, the US attempts to challenge China's territorial claims in the South China Sea. The US has changed its neutralising attitude towards South China Sea disputes. From the political level, the US encourages some ASEAN states to challenge China's claim and influence in the South China Sea. From the military level, the US military force has increased its presence in this region through ship visits, naval exercises, reconnaissance missions, etc. During the last few years, the US Navy has regularly dispatched its warships to China's exclusive economic zone and even territorial waters in the South China Sea to challenge China's maritime claim. More importantly, the US Navy also has plans to invite Japan, India, and other partners for conducting joint patrols in the South China Sea.

China is currently the second largest economy and largest trading country in the world. The total value of imports and exports of goods in 2022 reached 42,067.8 billion yuan, up by 7.7 percent over that of the previous year. Of this total, the value of goods exported was 23,965.4 billion yuan, up by 10.5 percent; the value of goods imported was 18,102.4 billion yuan, up by 4.3 percent (National Bureau of Statistics of China, 2023). With the long-term rapid development, China's consumption of crude oil and natural gas is growing year by year. After becoming the world's largest importer of crude oil in 2017, China surpassed Japan as the world's largest importer of natural gas in 2018. In 2021, China's crude oil and natural gas imports stood at 512.98 million tons and 121.36 million tonnes, and their external dependence rose to 71.9 percent and 43 percent, respectively (National Bureau of Statistics of China, 2022). More importantly, most China's oil imports are conducted by sea. It is reported that around 10,000 Chinese large merchant ships pass the Indian Ocean Region each year (Takungpao, 2017). Therefore, China's national security and sustainable development, to a large extent, heavily relying on the safety and security of SLoCs spanning from the Western Pacific to the Indian Ocean Region.

China's sea lines of communication are facing a series of threats and challenges. Firstly, China's energy and trade SLoCs security is facing a wide range of non-traditional threats, including piracy and maritime terrorism. Chinese merchant vessels are facing pirate attacks and armed robberies in the North Indian Ocean and the South China Sea. Thanks to the joint endeavours taken by the international community, the piracy threat in the Indian Ocean Region is decreasing. Secondly, continuous regional armed conflict in the Middle East and intensifying maritime disputes in the South China Sea pose threat to China's trade and energy SLoCs in the Indo-Pacific. The turmoil in the Middle East will have a huge impact on the international oil market. In the last few years, partly due to energy resources, the South China Sea disputes intensified between China and some ASEAN states, which not only influences normal oil production in this region but also poses potential threats to energy transportation through this region from the Indian Ocean. Thirdly, the Malacca Dilemma has played a significant factor in China's energy security strategy. The concept of the Malacca Dilemma first discussed by scholars after the address of the former Chinese President Hu Jintao at a conference on economic work in November 2003. He mentioned that about four-fifths of the transportation of the China's imported oil takes place by sea through the Malacca Strait and implied that the US and other powers have the capability and intention to contain China by cutting off the Malacca Strait. Similarly, if the Malacca Strait is at risk, China's trade transportation security will also be definitely in danger.

In addition, China's interests also include maintaining stable strategic space in the Indo-Pacific region. The Western Pacific and the North Indian Ocean Region provide strategic space for China's rise as a global political, economic and military power. With the expansion of China's overseas interests, China, a traditional major power in the Western Pacific, is projecting its power and influence to the Indian Ocean Region. In order to maintain a peaceful and favourable strategic space in the Indo-Pacific, it is significant for China to sustain or improve relations with neighbouring countries and major powers in and beyond this region, and also take a positive role in the regional multilateral cooperation mechanisms. China and the US are facing structural contradiction in the Indo-Pacific and beyond, which makes China's strategic space more uncertain. At the end of 2017, the Trump administration showed its enthusiasm for the Indo-Pacific and describes China as a strategic competitor in National Security Strategy. This is not surprising that the Chinese government and scholars doubt the true intention of the Indo-Pacific strategy proposed by the US. During the last few years, the US has significantly strengthened its strategic partnership with Japan, Australia, India, and the UK in the Indo-Pacific through the Quad, Indo-Pacific Economic Framework, AUKUS, etc.

China's Measures to Protect Its Strategic Interests in the Indo-Pacific Region

In order to deal with potential threats and challenges, Beijing has taken a combination of measures to protect its strategic interests in the Indo-Pacific region. Generally speaking, these measures include maintaining China's sovereignty and maritime interests, implementing the Belt and Road Initiative, and improving relations with its neighbours and major powers.

The Taiwan issue has always been a priority of China's national strategy. Since May 2016, mainland China has taken a series of measures in response to Tsai Ing-wen's authority and independent movement. By the end of June 2023, the number of countries which have established formal diplomatic relations with Taiwan decreased from 22 to 13, which was interpreted that mainland China is trying to narrow Taiwan's international space and force Tsai Ing-wen to acknowledge the 1992 Consensus (The Paper, 2023). In addition, the Chinese People's Liberation Army (PLA) has also sent clear signals to the Taiwan authorities through frequent training and exercises near Taiwan Island. According to the report published by the Taiwan authorities, the aircraft and warships of PLA conducted 25 operations near Taiwan Island between August 2016 and December 2017 (Taiwan Defense & National Security, 2017). It was reported that more than 940 military aircraft from the mainland have flown in Taiwan's so-called "airspace" in 2021, double the total for 2019 and 2020 (Ministry of National Defence, 2021). There are signs that the PLA will take more decisive measures in response to tensions across the Taiwan Strait. In the last one or two years, PLA aircraft flew across the median line in the Taiwan Strait. In early August 2022, in response to the speaker of the US House of Representatives Nancy Pelosi's travel to Taiwan, the PLA had conducted large-scale joint naval and air force exercises in areas north, southwest, and southeast of Taiwan.

Regarding China's territorial integrity, Beijing established a series of government agencies to consolidate its claims in the South China Sea. Since 2012, the prefecture-level Sansha City and various other government institutions have been announced and established. In order to improve the need of people's livelihood and basic military defence and maintaining territorial rights and interests in the Nansha Islands, China has started expansion projects on its controlled islands since the end of 2013. After the land reclamation activities, China has conducted a series of facilities construction on the reefs of the Nansha Islands, such as lighthouse, airport, hospital, maritime observation centre, automatic meteorological station, ocean scientific and research facility, etc. In addition to civil facilities, China has been reported to build military facilities on the islands and reefs in the SCS, which include outposts, ports, runways, helipads, radar facilities, barracks, communication facilities, solar arrays, berthing facilities, resupply facilities, and so on. China has also established a joint military-police-civilian defence mechanism to safeguard maritime rights and interests in the SCS. With the growing tensions in the South China Sea, China's military, law enforcement force, and fishermen have actively participated in maritime rights and interests protection activities. In addition, China also maintains maritime rights and interests through other methods, such as energy exploration, scientific investigation, and developing tourism.

Similar to the South China Sea, China has taken a combination of diplomatic, policy, economic, administrative, military, and social measures to safeguard its maritime rights and interests in the East China Sea. From the diplomatic level, the Chinese government has taken a series of active and forceful measures to state China's consistent proposition and position, such as "issuing diplomatic statements, making serious representations with Japan, and submitting notes of protest to the United Nations" (The State Council Information Office, 2012). In April 2023, China and Japan held the 15th round of maritime affairs consultations and reached multiple consensuses in the field of maritime security and cooperation. From the policy and legislative aspect, the Chinese government announced the standard names, the baselines, and geographical coordinates of the territorial sea of Diaoyu Island and its affiliated islands in 2012. From the economic aspect, China has started exploration and development activities at China's side close to the middle line of the ECS. From the administrative jurisdiction level, China's coast guard vessels and aircraft have conducted regular law enforcement patrols in the waters of Diaoyu Island since 2012 when the Japanese government announced the nationalisation of Diaoyu Island. In July 2023, it was reported that China Coast Guard drove away a Japanese fishing boat from the waters surrounding Diaoyu Island. From the military level, PLA Naval warships, including submarines and aircraft, increased presence in the waters of Diaoyu Island. On 23 November 2013, China established the

ECS Air Defence Identification Zone in order to identify, monitor, regulate, and deal with aircraft in the region and make sure air defence security. China's ADIZ in the ECS covered its claimed Diaoyu Islands and Suyan Rock, which are also claimed by Japan and South Korea, respectively. China also regularly dispatches scientific investigation ships and survey vessels to the ECS, including the Diaoyu Island and Okinotorishima, for scientific and research work. In addition, fishermen and compatriots from Hong Kong, Macao, Taiwan, and also overseas Chinese have also played an important role in China's maritime rights and interests maintenance.

In October 2013, Chinese President Xi Jinping proposed the 21st-Century Maritime Silk Road (MSR) initiative. As a core branch of the Belt and Road Initiative, the MSR initiative, spanning from China's coast to the SCS and further to the IOR through the Malacca Strait, has received wide attention and success. Firstly, in the political and diplomatic aspects, the MSR initiative has entered into the comprehensive implementation stage and got support not only from the central and local governments in China but also from other countries and international organisations. Secondly, in the financial and economic aspect, a series of financial mechanisms, Free Trade Areas, and overseas economic and trade cooperation zones have been established, and China's trade with countries along the MSR has improved. Thirdly, in the aspect of infrastructure, many of China's infrastructural projects, including port, railway, and energy pipeline construction, have achieved significant progress, such as the China-Pakistan Economic Corridor, Hambantota port, and Sino-Myanmar Oil and Natural Gas Pipelines.

With the expansion of China's overseas interests, PLA has also projected its maritime power beyond the Western Pacific. For a long time, China has maintained limited presence in the Indian Ocean Region. There is no continuous PLA naval presence in the Indian Ocean region until December 2008. Since then, the Chinese government has dispatched over 40 naval task forces to conduct escort operations in the Gulf of Aden and waters off Somalia. Chinese maritime presence in the Northwestern Indian Ocean provides an opportunity for the establishment of China's first overseas military base and a network of replenishment sites, which will improve China's power projection capability to maintain stability in the IOR. Chinese regular patrols of nuclear or conventional submarines also help PLA Navy to maintain strategic deterrence and contribute to the stability in the IOR. To a large extent, China's contributions to the stability in the Indian Ocean region are through the PLA Navy task forces. Firstly, they conduct anti-piracy operations and maintain the security of SLoCs. By the end of 2021, the PLA Navy has sent 39 naval contingents to carry out 1,460 batches of escort missions, safely escorting more than 7,000 Chinese and foreign vessels (Guangming Wang, 2021). Chinese task groups also enhance exchanges and cooperation with naval task forces of other countries such as Russia, India, Japan, and South Korea, and jointly secure international SLoCs. In the past 13 years, the Chinese naval escort taskforce has also established an information sharing mechanism and a commander meeting system with the fleets of many countries and conducted more than 140 joint escort and joint exercises (Guangming Wang, 2021). Secondly, they carry out naval diplomacy. During the ship visits, Chinese task forces will also conduct bilateral or multilateral naval exercises or training with Indian Ocean states such as Pakistan, India, Sri Lanka, Bangladesh, South Africa, and Tanzania. Lastly, they conduct Humanitarian Assistance and Disaster Relief operations. For example, Chinese naval ships from the 7th,17th, 19th, and 43rd task forces participated in the Libya evacuation in 2011, the search for Malaysian Airlines Flight MH370 in 2014, the Yemen evacuation in 2015, and the Sudan evacuation in 2023. In addition to the PLA naval task forces, China also provides medical services to the states in the Indo-Pacific. Since December 2008, the Chinese naval hospital ship Ark Peace has carried out seven Harmonious Missions and visited 43 countries and provided free medical services for more than 250,000 people, among which more than half of the countries are located in the Indo-Pacific region (Ministry of National Defence, 2023).

The basic characteristics of the current international situation are world multipolarisation, economic globalisation, cultural diversity, and social informationisation. Under this background, the Chinese government has put forward the idea of a community of shared future for mankind, with the aim to build a new framework of international relations and promote global governance. The concept of a community of shared future for mankind was delivered by former Chinese President Hu Jintao and advocated by current President Xi Jinping. According to Qu Xing (2013: 53–55), director of the China Institute of International Relations, the interdependent values of international power, common interests, sustainable development, and global governance provide a foundation of values for building a community of shared future for mankind. According to the idea of a community of shared future for mankind, the Chinese government has improved and promoted its relations with countries in the Indo-Pacific region, such as ASEAN states, Japan, and India.

In the last few years, China has proposed a dual-track approach to resolving the SCS issues, namely, sovereign states directly concerned in the issues resolve relevant disputes in the SCS through negotiations and consultations, and China and the ASEAN countries jointly maintain peace and stability of the SCS (Ministry of Foreign Affairs, 2015). In September 2013, China and ASEAN formally conducted specific consultations on the Code of Conduct in the South China Sea (COC). During the 21st China-ASEAN Summit in November 2018, China and ASEAN agreed to complete the first reading of the Single Draught COC Negotiating Text by 2019. In the China-ASEAN foreign ministers' meeting in July 2023, they completed the second reading of the draught. In order to strengthen strategic mutual trust, China and ASEAN conducted their first military exercise in the SCS in October 2018. Except for warships from Singapore, Brunei, Thailand, Vietnam, and the Philippines, three Chinese warships including one destroyer Guangzhou, one frigate Huangshan, and one supply ship Junshan Hu participated in this exercise. It is reported that the China-ASEAN naval exercise will be institutionalised in the future. In May 2023, the Chinese military workgroup engaged with five ASEAN states including Cambodia, Laos, Malaysia, Thailand, and Vietnam to conduct a multilateral exercise at the end of the year. In addition to the consultation on the Code of Conduct and the conduct of multilateral maritime exercise, Beijing also improved its relationship with the Philippines. China-Philippines relations experienced a serious setback between 2013 and 2016 due to the South China Sea Arbitration. After Duterte became the new Philippines president, China and the Philippines set up a bilateral consultation mechanism on the SCS in January 2017, which will become a platform for building conference measures and promoting maritime cooperation and security. During the visit of Philippines President Rodrigo Duterte to China in October 2016, the two sides signed an MoU to establish a Joint Coast Guard Committee on Maritime Cooperation. In November 2018, Chinese President Xi Jinping paid a state visit to the Philippines, they signed an MoU on cooperation in oil and gas development. However, since President Marcos was sworn in the new president on 30 June 2022, China-Philippine relations have deteriorated significantly due to the maritime dispute in the SCS.

China also promoted its relationship with Japan in the last few years. Generally, China's cooperation with Japan focuses on the CBMs such as the maritime and aerial communication mechanism and the establishment of the China-Japan High-level Consultation on Maritime Affairs, and also joint development of energies in the ECS. In May 2018, during Chinese Premier Li Keqiang's visit to Japan, the defence departments from both sides signed an MoU on setting up a maritime and aerial communication mechanism. In December 2018, the first annual meeting of China and Japan's maritime and aerial communication mechanism between their defence departments was held in Beijing. By April 2023, China and Japan have held 15 rounds of China-Japan High-level Consultation on Maritime Affairs. However, the China-Japan high-level consultation mechanism does not eliminate the confrontation and differences between China and Japan on the resource development in the ECS and the Diaoyu Islands issue, because these key issues have not been included in the scope of the consultation mechanism. In October 2018, during the visit of Japanese Prime Minister Shinzo Abe to China, the two sides signed an agreement on maritime search and rescue. On September 29, 2022, President Xi Jinping and Prime Minister Li Keqiang were congratulated on the 50th anniversary of the normalisation of Sino-Japanese diplomatic relations by the Japanese Prime Minister Fumio Kishida, respectively. In July 2023, China, Japan, and South Korea held the 2023 International Forum for Trilateral Cooperation to revitalise trilateral cooperation in the post-COVID era.

The Sino-Indian relationship has also experienced fluctuations during the last several years. During 2014 and 2015, Chinese President Xi Jinping and the Indian Prime Minister conducted exchange visits. However, divergences between China and India on the Nuclear Suppliers Group, anti-terrorism, and border standoff heavily weakened their strategic mutual trust. In 2017, the 73-day Doklam standoff happened in the border area close to China, India, and Nepal became the worst border incident in the last several decades. Thanks to the strategic guidance from Xi Jinping and Narendra Modi, China and India have established an Informal Meeting Mechanism. By the end of 2019, two rounds of the China-India Informal Meeting Mechanism have been held in April 2018 and October 2019, respectively. The China-India Informal Meeting Mechanism plays a significant role in the improvement of Sino-Indian relations. However, China-Indian relations had fallen into the bottom of the valley due to the 2020 conflict in the border area. As the two largest developing countries, their influences are expanding from the Western Pacific and Indian Ocean to the broader Indo-Pacific region. In order to maintain a stable and peaceful Indo-Pacific region, it is necessary to keep Sino-Indian relations sustainable in the long term.

Conclusion

Although the Indo-Pacific has been widely discussed among a growing number of countries in the last few years, the Chinese government shows a cautious and sceptical attitude towards the Indo-Pacific. Most Chinese scholars view the Indo-Pacific as a product against China and a threat to China's peripheral security, economic development, and strategic space. As an undoubted Indo-Pacific power, China's strategic interests in the Indo-Pacific region include three aspects: safeguarding national sovereignty and territorial integrity; ensuring the safety and security of energy and trade sea lines of communication; and maintaining stable strategic space in the Indo-Pacific. In order to promote China's strategic interests in this region, Beijing has taken a combination of measures to protect its strategic interests in the Indo-Pacific region, including maintaining China's sovereignty and maritime interests, implementing the Belt and Road Initiative, and improving relations with its neighbours and major powers.

Chinese government should take a more active stance towards the Indo-Pacific. Although some Chinese experts are worried that the Indo-Pacific will introduce more powers to the Western Pacific to involve China's maritime and territorial disputes with its neighbours, the Indo-Pacific will also justify

China's increasing maritime activities in the Indian Ocean and beyond. With China's rapid rise as a naval power in the last one or two decades, China's increasing maritime activities have always been exaggerated by some major powers in the Indo-Pacific region, especially in the Indian Ocean Region. The adoption of the Indo-Pacific strategy can help China view the Pacific Ocean and Indian Ocean as a unified strategic framework. More importantly, the Indo-Pacific will provide China's rise as a maritime power in a bigger theatre compared to East Asia or the Asia-Pacific. Just as Rory Medcalf (2012) argues, as a "quintessential Indo-Pacific power", although Chinese influence is "more diluted" in the Indo-Pacific region than in an exclusively East Asia setting, the Indo-Pacific can also "be the wider regional context in which China is rising".

Note

1 The article has been supported by "The Fundamental Research Funds of Shandong University".

References

Callahan, Michael (2023) "Biden Administration Approves Potential $440 Million Arms Sales to Taiwan", *CNN*, June 30 [Online]. Available at https://edition.cnn.com/2023/06/30/politics/us-arms-sales-taiwan/index.html

Chen, Bangyu and Wei, Hong (2015) "'The Era of the Indo-Pacific' and the Correspondent Strategy of China" [试论"印太时代"及中国的战略应对], *Indian Ocean Political and Economic Review* [印度洋经济体研究], no. 2, pp. 51–65.

Guangming, Wang (2021) "Reviewing the 'Firsts' of the Chinese Naval Escort Formations" [回顾中国海军护航编队那些"首次"], December 26 [Online], Available at https://m.gmw.cn/baijia/2021-12/26/1302737538.html

He, Kai (2019) "The Nature of American Indo-Pacific Strategy and China's Institutional Balancing" [美国印太战略实质与中国的制度制衡], *Contemporary Institutional Relations* [现代国际关系], no. 1, pp. 13–21.

India Today (2017) "No One Can Contain China: Beijing Envoy on US' Decision to Sell Weapons to India", October 31 [Online]. Available at https://www.indiatoday.in/india/story/no-one-can-contain-china-chinese-envoy-1078996-2017-10-31

Li, Jiasheng (2022) "The U.S. Indo-Pacific Strategy and Regional Bipolarization" [美国"印太战略"与地区两极化], *Indian Ocean Economic and Political Review* [印度洋经济体研究], no. 3, pp. 22–42.

Liang, Fang (2017) "The United States Pushes the "Indo-Pacific" concept, What does the US want to do?" [美国推"印太"构想，到底想干什么], *Huanqiu* [环球], November 28 [Online]. Available at http://opinion.huanqiu.com/hqpl/2017-11/11405093.html

Lin, Minwang (2018) "The Construction of 'Indo-Pacific' and the Tension of Asian Geopolitics" ["印太"的建构与亚洲地缘政治的张力], *Foreign Affairs Review* [外交评论], no. 1, pp. 16–35.

Medcalf, Rory (2012) "A Term Whose Time Has Come: The Indo-Pacific", *The Diplomat*, December 4 [Online]. Available at https://thediplomat.com/2012/12/a-term-whose-time-has-come-the-indo-pacific/

Mei, Xiouting (2017) "'Indo-Pacific Strategy': The Essence of Shinzo Abe's New Diplomatic Strategy" ["印太战略": 安倍晋三新外交战略的实质], *Qiushi* [求是], February 20 [Online]. Available at http://www.qstheory.cn/international/2017-02/20/c_1120496115.htm

Ministry of Foreign Affairs, the People's Republic of China (2015) "Li Keqiang Expounds on China's Principled Stance on South China Sea Issue at East Asia Summit", November 22 [Online], Available at https://www.fmprc.gov.cn/mfa_eng/zxxx_662805/t1318291.shtml

Ministry of Foreign Affairs, the People's Republic of China (2017a) "Foreign Ministry Spokesperson Hua Chunying's Regular Press Conference on November 7, 2017", November 7 [Online]. Available at http://www.fmprc.gov.cn/mfa_eng/xwfw_665399/s2510_665401/t1508304.shtml

Ministry of Foreign Affairs, the People's Republic of China (2017b) "Foreign Ministry Spokesperson Geng Shuang's Regular Press Conference on November 13, 2017", November 14 [Online]. Available at http://www.fmprc.gov.cn/ce/cemd/eng/fyrth/t1510216.htm

Ministry of Foreign Affairs, the People's Republic of China (2021) "Wang Yi: Indo-Pacific, a Restoration of the Cold War Mentality, and a Historical Regression" [王毅: "印太战略"是冷战思维的复辟，是历史的倒退], 3 July [Online]. Available at https://www.mfa.gov.cn/web/wjbzhd/202107/t20210703_9137570.shtml

Ministry of Foreign Affairs, the People's Republic of China (2022) "Wang Yi: The 'Indo-Pacific Strategy' Is Trying to Build an 'Indo-Pacific NATO'" [王毅: "印太战略"是企图搞印太版"北约"], March 7 [Online]. Available at https://www.mfa.gov.cn/web/wjbzhd/202203/t20220307_10648866.shtml

Ministry of National Defence, the People's Republic of China (2021) "Defense Ministry: The PLA Sorties than the DPP Authorities Hyped the Number of Only Many More" [国防部：解放军出动飞机架次比民进党当局炒作数量只多不少], December 30 [Online]. Available at http://www.mod.gov.cn/jzhzt/2021-12/30/content_4902035.htm

Ministry of National Defence, the People's Republic of China (2023) "Peace Ark Hospital Ship Sailing to Perform the 'Harmonious Mission-2023' Task" [和平方舟医院船起航执行"和谐使命-2023"任务], July 4 [Onine]. Available at http://www.mod.gov.cn/gfbw/jsxd/16234883.html.

National Bureau of Statistics of China (2022) "Statistical Communiqué of the People's Republic of China on the 2021 National Economic and Social Development", February 28 [Online]. Available at https://www.stats.gov.cn/english/PressRelease/202202/t20220227_1827963.html

National Bureau of Statistics of China (2023) "Statistical Communiqué of the People's Republic of China on the 2022 National Economic and Social Development", February 28, [Online]. Available at http://www.stats.gov.cn/english/PressRelease/202302/t20230227_1918979.html

Qu, Xing (2013) "Values Foundation for a Community of Shared Future for Mankind " [人类命运共同体的价值观基础], *Qiushi* [求是], no. 4, pp. 53–55.

Takungpao (2017) "China also Belongs to South Asian State and Has Core Interests in the Indian Ocean Region" [中国也属南亚国家，印度洋存核心利益], September 7 [Online]. Available at http://news.takungpao.com/society/topnews/2017-09/3491143.html

Taiwan Defense & National Security (2017) "National Defense Report" [国防报告书], December [Online]. Available at https://www.ustaiwandefense.com/tdnswp/wp-content/uploads/2020/02/Taiwan-National-Defense-Report-2017.pdf

The Paper (2023) "China and Honduras Establish Diplomatic Relations! Only 13 Countries Left Which Keep Diplomatic Relations with Taiwan" [中国和洪都拉斯建交！台"邦交国"仅剩13个], *The Paper* [澎湃新闻], March 27 [Online]. Available at https://www.thepaper.cn/newsDetail_forward_22460535

The State Council Information Office, the People's Republic of China (2012) "Diaoyu Dao, an Inherent Territory of China", September [Online]. Available at http://www.scio.gov.cn/zfbps/ndhf/2012/Document/1225271/1225271_2.htm

Times of India (2018) "'Quad' Move Will DissipateLiike Sea Foam: China", March 8 [Online]. Available at https://timesofindia.indiatimes.com/world/china/quad-move-will-dissipate-like-sea-foam-china/articleshow/63221055.cms

Wang, Lina (2023) "The Biden Administration's 'Indo-Pacific Strategy' Review" [拜登政府"印太战略"评析], *Contemporary International Relations* [现代国际关系], no. 4, pp. 116–131.

Wei, Zongyou (2022) "The Biden Administration's Indo-Pacific Strategy and Its Impacts on China" [拜登政府"印太战略"及对中国的影响], *International Studies*, [国际问题研究], no. 3, pp. 29–46.

Wu, Huaizhong (2018) "Japan's Indo-Pacific Strategy and China's Response" [安倍政府印太战略及中国的应对], *Contemporary International Relations* [现代国际关系], no. 1, pp. 13–21.

Wu, Zhaoli (2014) "Indo-Pacific: Origins and Multinational Strategy Game" ["印太"的缘起与多国战略博弈], *Pacific Journal* [太平洋学报], vol. 22, no. 1, pp. 29–40.

Xie, Guiping (2018) "Deal with the Indo-Pacific Strategy's Threat to China" [印太战略对中国的威胁及应对思路], *Frontiers* [学术前沿], no. 8, pp. 56–70.

Xie, Xiaoguang and Du, Dongguang (2022) "Transformation of the U.S. Indo-Pacific Alliance System: Measures, Characteristics, and Limits" [美国"印太"联盟体系转型：措施、特征与限度], *Northeast Asia Forum*, [东北亚论坛], no. 6, pp. 54–71.

Ye, Hailin (2018) "The Prospects of 'Indo-Pacific' Concept and China's Countermeasures" ["印太"概念的前景与中国的应当对策略], *Indian Ocean Economic and Political Review* [印度洋经济体研究], no. 2, pp. 1–14.

Ye, Hailin (2022) "The Logical Flaws of the U.S. 'Indo-Pacific Strategy' and China's Countermeasures" [美国"印太战略"的逻辑缺陷与中国的应对], *Indian Ocean Economic and Political Review* [印度洋经济体研究], no. 5, pp. 1–14.

Zhang, Genhai (2022) "New Tendency in Quadrilateral Cooperation among the U.S., Japan, India and Australia and Impacts on Security in the South China Sea against the Backdrop of the 'Indo-Pacific'" ["印太"背景下美日印澳"四边

机制"新动向及对南海安全的影响], *South Asian Studies* [南亚研究], no. 2, pp. 133–155.

Zhang, Jiadong (2018) "The US's 'Indo-Pacific' Proposal and Its Impacts on China" [美国"印太"倡议及其对中国的影响], *Indian Ocean Economic and Political Review* [印度洋经济体研究], no. 3, pp. 1–26.

Zhang, Li (2019) "Indo-Pacific Strategy: Determinants, Future Prospects and China's Response" ["印太"战略的决定因素、发展趋势及中国应对], *South Asian Studies Quarterly* [南亚研究季刊], no. 1, pp. 1–7.

Zhou, Fangyin (2018) "Indo-Pacific Strategy from Australian Perspective and China's Countermeasures" [澳大利亚视角下的印太战略及中国的应对], *Contemporary International Relations* [现代国际关系], no. 1, pp. 29–39.

Zhu, Cuiping (2018) "The Trump Administration's Indo-Pacific Strategy and Its Impact on China" [特朗普政府"印太"战略及其对中国安全的影响], *South Asian Studies* [南亚研究], no. 4, pp. 1–17.

6

RUSSIA IN THE INDO-PACIFIC THROUGH MULTIPOLARITY, EURASIAN INTEGRATION, AND THE RFE

Joyce Sabina Lobo

The end of the Cold War shifted the geopolitical focus, along with its share of connections and rivalries, towards nations in the Indo-Pacific Region (IPR) and West Asia, replacing ideological struggle with control of the seas and its resources. The US and China, closely competing global economies, find themselves in a new geopolitical and geo-economic rivalry, especially in the IPR. Russian perception of the IPR is in variance with key actors in the region, thus calling it the Asia-Pacific Region (APR). The IPR is observed by Russia as divisive – an attempt to contain China and divide nations into blocs, given the perception of the US and its allies towards both nations as "revisionist powers". Russia seeks to rebound to its former USSR status as an influential global power. The scant response from the West in the post-Cold War economic crises, events of 2014, and consequent sanctions, including in 2018, has led Russia to shift to the Asia pivot while tightening its embrace with Beijing. The Russian invasion of Ukraine in early 2022 has further reinforced relations with China and North Korea. Apart from this forced yet pragmatic move, Russia's objective of developing the Asiatic regions of Siberia and particularly the Russian Far East (RFE) gets bolstered. Russia's strategy in the IPR, by tilting to Beijing, its second power status, and its late entry into the region, particularly its late focus on RFE, add more to its dilemmas than clarity. Russia's diminished power both in the West and East, low economic growth, declining and ageing population, underdevelopment of regions in Siberia and Russian Far East, etc., lead to dilemma over reasserting as a great power of the past and an influential power at the present. The Russian challenges curtail its influence to introduce multipolarity in general and its late entrance into the Indo-Pacific region sans a strategy poses, at least from the short to medium term, a dilemma.

DOI: 10.4324/9781003479307-8

90 Joyce Sabina Lobo

Russia's participation with the IPR should be understood in three areas: first, its use of Asia-Pacific with reference to the region instead of Indo-Pacific as it aligns with its idea of Eurasia. As a strategy, it enables Russia to build a narrative as a Eurasian power. The chapter examines the rivalries in the context of Euro-Atlantic powers versus what the US refers to as the Revisionist powers like China and Russia at the global level and the counter-narrative of Russia in terms of multipolarity,[1] especially in the framework of IPR. Second, from the regional perspective, forging relations through the processes of integration and cooperation between Russia and neighbouring countries in Eurasia becomes important, with special focus on strengthening Sino-Russian relations. Third, from the national perspective, the development of Siberia and the Far East, which forms its two thirds of the Asian geographical space, is important.

Russian Variant of the Indo-Pacific Construct: Multipolarity, Eurasia, and Asia-Pacific

Russia considers itself as a Eurasian and Euro-Pacific power. The attitudes and national interests of Russia have to be understood in terms of how it views the international structure and what role it carves for itself within the post-Soviet space. This is today understood in terms of multipolarity and neo-Eurasianism that have their bearings on its understanding of the IPR.

Chebankova delineates the origins of Russia's idea of the multipolar world order or its desire to carve a separate identity, unlike the western Europe model, from the 19th century onwards beginning with the Slavophiles like Kireyevsky, Samarin, Danilevskii, etc. The Russian grassroots intellectuals like Nikolai Strakhov, Nikolai Danilevskii, and Konstantin Leont'ev did civilisational analysis of the world's geographic areas to argue that Russians could organise its civilization alongside other existing forms. In the 1920s and 1930s, pioneer scholars of Eurasianism N. M. Trubetskoi and Peter Savitskii gave effect to the theory that different civilisations and cultural diversity brings out its own value systems, traditions, economic models, and political forms (Chebankova, 2017).

The post-Cold War led Russia to opt for either of the two ways. At the onset, joining the new world order or what Alexander Lukin calls "West's united world project" or joining the "emerging multipolar world" (Lukin, 2016: 455). After its brief flirtations with the West, Russia abandoned its Atlantist policy or what was Mikail Gorbachev's idea of "common European home" it embraced the former Prime Minister Primakov doctrine steering the political administration to follow an independent path from the West and move in favour of multipolarity. This would become a sore point in future relations between Russia and the West.

The Primakov doctrine guides Russian policy since 1996 to follow an independent foreign policy, promote a multipolar world, establish primacy in the post-Soviet space and build Eurasian integration, oppose North Atlantic Treaty Organization (NATO) expansion, and build partnership with China (Rumer, 2019). This has resulted in the Russia, India, China (RIC) grouping (1998) and the Brazil, Russia, India, China and South Africa (BRICS) (2009) and later the Shanghai Cooperation Organization (SCO) (2001). Contemporary Russian intellectuals such as Alexander Panarin, Aleksandr Dugin, Andrei Fursov, Mikhail Delyagin, etc. theorized "pluralism of civilizations" (Chebankova, 2017: 7) to understand international relations. Prominent among them is Dugin, who gave the idea of Eurasian Union in 2001 which the President Vladimir Putin's administration has come close to emulating. He called for creating Eurasia as one of the poles (Dugin, 2012) so that Russia could take its rightful place in the world order. His theory of neo-Eurasianism is formulated from the perspective of geopolitics. This theory has been instrumental in shaping an ideocratic state within Russia heading towards a totalitarian system headed by Vladimir Putin and his United Russia party and to establish its dominance in the Eurasian region in which it wants to emerge as one of the poles in a multipolar world. A point in the case is Russian claims over parts of Ukraine belonging to the Eurasian heartland (Shekhovtsov, 2017).

Indo-Pacific Region (IPR), i.e., Indian Ocean and the Pacific Ocean, accommodates area between the eastern shores of Africa to the western coast of the US. The US considers the region to span from its Pacific coastline to the Indian Ocean. The ASEAN Outlook on the Indo-Pacific, 2019 includes the Asia-Pacific and Indian Ocean regions as part of IPR. Russia and China have preferred the old name of Asia-Pacific and consider the new terminology manifesting Cold War mentality. China, in its Policies on Asia-Pacific Security Cooperation (PRC, 2017) accepts the centrality of Association of Southeast Asian Nations (ASEAN) within the region. While it seeks an international system based on "mutually beneficial cooperation", Russia pursues a multipolar world. Both mean to challenge the hegemonic attitudes of any country in any part of the world, the IPR included. China calls the IPR as a creation of the US to contain China by including new entrants such as India (Krishnan, 2022). Put simply, Medcalf says that Indo-Pacific is not a replacement term for Asia-Pacific but a reflection of "changes in economics, strategic behaviour, and diplomatic institutions that are having real consequences regardless of who utters the words" (Medcalf, 2013). However, unanimous clarity on the concept is yet to emerge amongst different actors, while its significance is not lost. Moreover, the West led by the US along with the members of the Quad, AUKUS, ASEAN, and others in the region insists that all those states engaged in the region must adhere to a rules-based order, to which China and Russia have their objections. This is where Russia diverges to follow its own civilisational path in terms of dealing with any region globally.

The NATO expansion into the post-Soviet space that includes countries from the Baltics and all the members of the Warsaw Pact, USA's unilateral actions through its pullout from the Anti-Ballistic Missile (ABM) treaty in 2002 and its subsequent construction of the National Missile Defence over the Strategic Defense Initiative (SDI) have been considered as ways of containing Russia. It is considered that the international structure has been dominated by the West under the US that uses unilateral military solutions to key issues in world politics in circumvention of the fundamental rules of international law (Gazeta, 2000). This idea has long been with Russia, that this liberal order threatens security in general and leads to containment in regions like IPR. It's understanding of the importance of the IPR took place in the context of the changing of the international system that is in terms of the shift from the West to the East which it calls the "Asia-Pacific region" (APR) which is reflected in the "Concept of the Foreign Policy of the Russian Federation" (Russian Embassy in China, 2013). Here it carved a role for itself as a transit country for trade and economic relations between Europe and the APR.

What jeopardises the security in IPR is the Sino-American rivalry. China's military modernisation took off post 1996, especially after the missile crisis in Taiwan Straits. Claims over South China Sea and rejection of US claims of national interest in the region have irked the US. The actions of China within its neighbourhood and in the South China Sea go against the IPR idea of the US on IPR as "free and open". China refuses to accept the presence of the US navy in the Western Pacific (Auslin, 2011). The US is of the perception that a rising China competes for influence with its allies and partners in IPR, and hence its alliances with Japan, Republic of Korea, Thailand, and the Philippines in Asia "serve a very paramount role in both providing reassurances against aggressive and unproductive behaviour" of China (US Government Publishing Office, 2015). Chinese scholars understand that the IPR strategy of former US President Donald Trump has been built over his predecessor Barack Obama's "rebalance". Chinese actions then in 2017 were called assertive, while President Joe Biden's administration pronounces more deeply on the challenges to the region, particularly by China. While unveiling the Pentagon's 2018 National Defense Strategy of the US, former Defence Secretary James Mattis pointed to this new turn "Great Power competition, not terrorism, is now the primary focus of U.S. national security" (US DoD, 2018b). Therefore the US utilises the balance of power theory to retaliate against forces in regions like IPR that threaten its security.

The 2018 National Defense Strategy of the US has specified Russia and China as revisionist powers – posing a central challenge to its security and prosperity, wherein it suggests that "China is a strategic competitor using predatory economics to intimidate its neighbors while militarizing features in the South China Sea. Russia has violated the borders of nearby nations and pursues veto power over the economic, diplomatic, and security decisions of its neighbors" (US DoD, 2018a). Bobo Lo points out that Russia under Putin will look at IPR from a global perspective, as it has become central to the world order where geopolitical rivalries between the US and China will be played (Lo, 2019). President Joe Biden's administration has built on the understandings of his predecessor, George Bush Jr., to Donald Trump. China is considered to combine its "economic, diplomatic, military and technological might as it pursues a sphere of influence in the Indo-Pacific and seeks to become the world's most influential power" (The White House, 2022). However, the document has commitments to the climate change agreement and to get countries within the region to commit to limits, end the COVID-19 pandemic, lead investments in global health security, prepare regional platforms to detect biological threats, etc., and be less belligerent than under Trump.

Russia and China refuse to act as per the international order that the West, led by the US, imposes. Beijing has refused to adhere to the open and rules-based order, particularly in the South China Sea, against the claims by countries like Brunei, Indonesia, the Philippines, Taiwan, Malaysia, and Vietnam. This rules-based order is challenged by China questioning "the sources of authority" behind the interpretations, rather than the "legitimacy of the rules themselves" (Hall and Heazle, 2017). Like China, Russia questions as to who decides the rules in a way of challenging the authority. Russians actually point to the NATO's bombing of Yugoslavia in 1999, as well as the US-led invasion of Iraq in 2003, the elimination of Gaddafi from Libya, etc., as instances of the US flouting the international rules-based order while redrawing the rules as per convenience.

Added to the stance of the US in its security and military doctrines, the reactions and sanctions of the West to the events of 2014, i.e., annexation of Crimea by Russia and the conflicts in the Donbas and Luhansk regions of Ukraine, further alienated Moscow from the West and brought it closer to China. The former enemies during the Cold War today are forced to be partners. China was brought into the international order by the US in the 1970s to balance the power of the Soviet Union. China disappointed the US by not joining the liberal order while enjoying access to Western technology, capital and markets. Putin claimed in 2014 that "Russian-Chinese relations have reached an unprecedentedly high level of comprehensive partnership and strategic interaction" (Kremlin.ru, 2014). In his congratulatory message to President Xi Jinping on the occasion of the 65th anniversary of the founding of the People's Republic of China suggested that the reactions of the West have led to the current state of affairs. Therefore, any confrontation in the Indo-Pacific region would pit the US and its traditional allies against China and Russia.

Multipolarity gives centrality to civilisations in international politics, as suggested by Eurasian philosophers, where each state can follow its distinct identity without succumbing to the universality of values. Hence, Russia utilises multipolarity as a counter-narrative to the Euro-Atlantic order that claims universality in terms of values and justifies its imposition on other nations. How does the Euro-Atlantic/rules-based order versus multipolarity confrontation affect perceptions in the IPR region? Countries like Australia, South Korea, Japan, New Zealand, the Philippines, Thailand, etc. support the US as allies and partners who adhere to the "open and rules-based international order" in IPR. Multipolarity enables Russia to justify its actions in the post-Soviet space and China in South China Sea and East China Sea. By this, it backs the position of Beijing in IPR. Hence, it considers IPR as a strategy of containment towards Beijing. Russia questions the rationale for renaming the APR as IPR. Foreign Minister Sergei Lavrov said the concept of IPR "is an attempt, I think, to reconfigure the existing structures of the APR and to move from ASEAN-centred consensus-seeking forms of interaction to something that would be divisive" while the need to call the region IPR "is to contain China" (MFA Russia, 2020).

IPR and Eurasia as Part of Russia's Integration Process

Russia's foreign policy decisions have become more centralised since Putin took over as President in March 2000. This has also led Russian research organisations or think tanks to suggest policies that speak the language of the administration, wherein it refers to the region strictly as the Asia-Pacific Region (APR). Since 2000, the concept of Russian foreign policy calls Russia as "one of the largest Eurasian Powers" (FAS, 2000). When it comes to its neighbourhood and its idea of being a leader within the Eurasian space, its strategy includes promoting the process of regional and interregional economic integration through the concept of the Greater Eurasian Partnership (GEP), and organizations such as the Eurasian Economic Union (EAEU), Commonwealth of Independent States (CIS), Shanghai Cooperation Organisation (SCO), BRICS, and ASEAN are included within this idea. The idea of GEP has been in use since 2016 and has been used subsequently at meetings of the St. Petersburg Economic Forums and Eastern Economic Forums (Köstem, 2019). Lavrov explained the focus of Russia on the Eurasian region that embraces the entire space from Lisbon to Jakarta (Lukyanov, 2010) while referring to Putin's preference for integrating structures such as ASEAN and SCO, Eurasian Economic Union (EAEU), and ASEAN (Kremlin.ru, 2016b).

Foreign policy was then termed as "multi-vectored" in an attempt to boost its image in West and East countries, keeping in mind its great power ambitions. This saw Russia joining the ASEAN dialogue in 1996 as a participant, a member of Asia-Pacific Economic Cooperation (APEC) in 1997; brought Russia into the Korean Six-Party talks; and engaged actively in the ASEAN-plus dialogue and the East Asia Summit (EAS). Since 2007, Russia started to assert its leadership role to maintain strategic stability in Eurasia (Lukyanov, 2010) and also started its move to the east, especially after the global financial crisis of 2008–09, with an aim to attract investments to Siberia and the Russian Far East and also strengthen its relations with China and the Asia-Pacific (Köstem, 2019). Russia forged relations with China, Japan, the Koreas, and the ASEAN. However, Russia's trade with ASEAN was dismally low in 2018 (US\$19.9 billion) and has reduced to US\$15.5 billion in 2022 (Asean.org, 2023).

What started as a customs union in the mid-1990s culminated into the EAEU in 2015 on the lines of the European Union. However, this includes members such as Armenia, Belarus, Kazakhstan, Kyrgyzstan, and Russia. The only Asian countries to sign the Free Trade Agreement (FTA) are Vietnam, a former ally, and China (non-preferential FTA). China has built the linking of the Belt and Road Initiative (BRI) into the EAEU-FTA negotiations. This could be a game changer if more countries join, especially from Asia.

American military presence in the region, the conduct of joint US–South Korea military exercises, and Seoul's deployment of THAAD (Terminal High Altitude Area Defense) missile system, defence postures with Japan, Australia, and other allies in IPR have been common sources of hegemonic assertions by the US in their respective backyards. As part of the multipolar order, Russia accepts China as one of the poles and its position in the South China Sea, East China Sea, North Korea, BRI, among others. This is in lieu of Chinese acceptance of Russia's positions in the post-Soviet space.

Russia is one of China's top sources for energy imports (crude oil, coal briquettes, metals, etc.) while the latter exports finished products such as telephones, computers, cars, motor vehicles, etc., amounting to more than US\$190.271 billion. This has surged to US\$134.1 billion for the first seven months this year (Global Times, 2023). Bilateral trade amounted to US\$110.79 billion in 2019 with Chinese exports to Russia increasing to 3.6% and US\$49.7 billion, while imports from Russia increased by 3.2% to total US\$61.05 billion.[2] This trade surged due to the fresh sanctions and the Ukrainian invasion by Russia. The latter was forced to forge greater economic ties with China. Moreover, when it comes to the energy trade, Russia is a greater beneficiary as it exports to China, the Republic of Korea, Japan, Singapore, Taiwan, India, Malaysia, the Philippines, Vietnam, Hong Kong (China), Indonesia, Pakistan, Bangladesh, Democratic People's Republic of Korea, Myanmar, Sri Lanka, Cambodia, Nepal, the Maldives, and Timor-Leste. Out of these, China, India, Japan, the Republic of Korea, and Indonesia are its largest energy consumers (Taghizadeh-Hesary et al., 2021). The two countries participate in bilateral and multilateral military exercises together, including China's participation in Russia's annual strategic command and staff exercise – VOSTOK (meaning East) 2018. They jointly oppose US-sponsored measures at the United Nations Security Council quite often. Hence, both cooperate at various levels to counter the US through the multipolar world order.

However, the Sino-Russian relations do have challenges that undermine the role of Russia both at the global and regional (IPR) level. Russia becomes a secondary nation when it comes to power within the international system. Its economy is 8 to 11 times smaller compared to China.[3] China's top trading partners are the US, Hong Kong, Japan, South Korea, etc. (4.4 percent).[4] Russia's top trading partner is China and therefore suggests its economic dependence as it exports largely primary products. Many experts have pointed out that if the relations between China and the US become stable, then Russia will not be able to counter the West. Bobo Lo's calls the coming together of two former enemies as a "partnership of convenience". This alliance will be short-lived if one of the sides comes closer to the US as China's global ambitions and Russian pride cannot meet the twain. Lo claims that any "practical cooperation" between the two is constrained by "historical suspicions, cultural prejudices, geopolitical rivalry, and competing priorities" (Lo, 2008). The actual strategic component for the IPR region is missing between the two states. The West and NATO stances against Moscow and Beijing make the relations strategic at least for some years to come. Russia is forced to depend on China for investments and markets for its primary goods that the West has denied through sanctions.

One of the interesting relations that is emerging is between Russia and North Korea, which has not been a consistent one. Since Russia's invasion of Ukraine in 2022, there is greater understanding between both countries. North Korea has recognised the independence of breakaway regions of Ukraine. Against the backdrop of the Ukraine invasion and severe sanctions on Russia, the latter is believed to have established military cooperation with North Korea in lieu of an exchange of ammunition to use in the war.

Connecting the Russian Far East (RFE) with the APR/IPR

The third area where the IPR interests Russia is its link with Siberia and the Far East, or in short called the Russian Far East (RFE). This region is more connected with Asia as two-thirds of Russian territory lies here. Asia or the East did not receive much attention in the erstwhile USSR or present Russia's foreign policy. Joseph Stalin's "Pivot to Asia" (Lunev and Shavlay, 2018) was merely an initiative to set forced labour camps which became a source of economic development in Siberia and the Far East. Later, some of the cities became important military facilities. Leonid Brezhnev and particularly Mikhail Gorbachev in his speech at Vladivostok in 1986 indicated the need for a security system in APR and the development of RFE (Lukyanov, 2010).

The development and economic growth of RFE is a cause of concern that is reflected in the Russian white papers since Putin took over in 2000. However, the linking of this region with the acknowledgement of the fact that APR is where global economy and politics would shift was officially acknowledged in 2013 (Russian Embassy in China, 2013). The RFE occupies a third of Russia's territory with a population of more than 6 million (more than 5% of the total population). It gives access to the APR as it intersects northeast China, Japan, and the Korean Peninsula. The macro-region extracts 98 percent of Russian diamonds, 80 percent of stannary, 90 percent of borax materials, 50 percent of gold, 14 percent of tungsten, and has 40 percent of fish and seafood, one-third of all coal reserves, and hydro-engineering resources with 30 percent of the forest area.[5] Mining is the largest (more than 28%) sector of RFE economy, and manufacturing sector is low (around 5%). Otherwise, this region remains underdeveloped.

The initial thoughts on APR and connecting it to RFE were laid in the Pacific Strategy of Russia in 2010. Hence, the Ministry for Development of the Russian Far East (MINVR) in 2012 and in 2015, the Eastern Economic Forum (EEF) were established to attract investment into the RFE and integrate with East Asian economies. Russia aspires to turn RFE into a transport and trading hub. Russia's 2015 Maritime Doctrine recognised the need to develop the Pacific Ocean region and integrate it to the APR region "with the simultaneous restoration and development of regular passenger maritime transportation in the Far Eastern seas" (Studies Institute, Russia Maritime and Davis, A, 2015). The government under Putin introduced 20 advanced special economic zones (ASEZs) (Min, J. and Kang, B., 2017) and five free ports to sustain development and build entrepreneurship within the region. ASEZs are created so that investors implementing projects establish secondary industries to free RFE from being a producer-exporter of primary commodities to becoming a secondary commodity exporter to the APR. Keeping in mind the dwindling and outgoing population, the administration has tried to stem this by providing free land which is not devoid of problems (Troyakova, 2018). The investments have declined and projects have not taken off given the effects of post-2014 sanctions despite the pivot to Asia being considered seriously from economic and trade aspects.

The Eastern Economic Forum (EEF) is a key element in Russia's APR strategy, and hence, the refocus on its Far East regions for sake of bringing domestic economic development. The EEF was established in 2015 to bring foreign investments to the region. The sanctions that have continued since 2018 and 2022 bring Russia to Pivot 2.0 to build closer ties with East in terms of economic and trade ties. This is for reasons to avoid relations that are less susceptible to sanctions (Likhacheva, 2023). Presently, the only Asian economies that have laid sanctions, albeit on a moderate basis are Japan and South Korea. China, Japan, and South Korea have been significant partners to Russia in its RFE for exports and imports. Two major drawbacks in the region are lack of technical capacities and a low population, says Timofei Bordachev (2023). However, since European oil supplies have been closed, the East, particularly China, is the largest beneficiary of oil and other projects from the RFE. The Khabarovsk Krai province particularly has witnessed investments from China for cross border logistics and energy hub projects that Chris Devonshire-Ellis (2023) claims are part of the Belt Road Initiative (BRI). Chinese investments in transport, mining, and port development in the RFE have steadily increased since the war in Ukraine. China recently has bagged the huge energy logistics hub in Russia's Far Eastern Amur region that adjoins the Heilongjiang Province.

The concern for Russia being a petro-dollar state has not diversified its economy in general nor accelerated development in the RFE in terms of manufacturing. Though connecting RFE to APR is a good economic strategy, it will remain unfulfilled for a long time as growth is slackened due to sanctions. The positive aspects are that Russia has tried to bring in tax cuts, preferential laws, and simplified administrative procedures to make the investments in ASEZs more attractive than other SEZs in the world. Given the asymmetrical relations between Russia and China and the professing of a strategic partnership, the former has its own fears of the latter.

Conclusion

Russia therefore looks at the region as a rules-based order (led by US) versus a multipolar order (led by Russia) and as a geopolitical rivalry between the US and its allies versus Russia and China. When it comes to an independent policy, Russia looks through multi-vector diplomacy externally, which is largely compromised by being an appendage to Chinese interests, and internally as a need to develop its Russian Far East (RFE) to link it to the APR. China is today the top trading partner of Russia, while the US was one of the top five in Moscow's list in pre-war times.

Russia has not been able to convince the multipolar order to its partners in the IPR who prefer to adhere to the rules-based order, or the ASEAN which prefers ASEAN-led mechanisms, such as the East Asia Summit (EAS), as platforms for dialogue and implementation of Indo-Pacific cooperation. The Russian people today have an anti-West attitude, but more than two-thirds of the population live on the European continent. If a rapprochement is to take place between Russia and the liberal West, then the dilemma of whether Russians are Europeans or Asians will continue. Russia today is drawn more towards Asia because of its trade and economic necessities. Hence, this has put an end to the dilemma of whether it should turn to the West or East. Destiny in the form of the Ukraine war and the subsequent isolation of Russia has made the latter more than ever pivot to the East.

The massive military presence of the US in the IPR region through its powerful system of strategic and tactical missile defence systems checks Russia and China. These tensions affect the countries in the region. Many Asian countries welcome the presence of the US to provide security cover and balance China. Though Russia has attempted bilateral relations with economies such as Japan, South Korea, and Southeast nations, it cannot influence their foreign policies. So, relations remain purely economic and in Vietnam through military trade. Russia's defence posturing in the Pacific and particularly in the Sea of Okhotsk inconveniences partners such as Japan (along with non-settlement of disputes in the Kurile Islands) and the Koreas.

Most of the relations of Russia with states in IPR are bilateral and most of these perceive Moscow as a secondary power. It has been able to maintain great power status only as a nuclear-military power. China remains both an economic powerhouse cum military power in IPR. In the meanwhile, the US counts amongst its allies – South Korea, Japan, Australia, New Zealand, India, the Philippines, Thailand, Vietnam, Indonesia, Malaysia, and Singapore – and has pulled many of these into its recently launched Indo-Pacific Economic Framework (IPEF). It maintains defence postures with Japan, South Korea, and Australia in particular. Therefore, Russian influence in the IPR is limited in comparison to the US and China. Russia is not able to bring any kind of regionalisation into the IPR given its late interest, though there may be some hope in the future concerning EAEU and the EEF. Russia looks at the IPR more as a geopolitical reality and looks at the RFE from the lenses of geo-economics. It has been a late entrant into the region which is proved by the fact that its RFE has remained underdeveloped and hence its non-integration into the APR.

Without resetting ties with the West and enhancing ties with the East, Russia cannot emerge from its quagmire. Again, diversifying its economy can help it to secure its status in IPR, as its current status of being a primary commodity exporter, including in RFE, can push it to the periphery of the world economic order. Appending its interests to China not only makes Russia less of an influencer in IPR, but also puts great distance between it and the Asian economies. Asian states, particularly those in ASEAN, do not want to be caught in zero-sum games, nor do they want to be dominated by any power; the rise of new states is to be understood in this sense. Russia and China have become subjects of West's condemnation related to human rights. Second, the US's support to the Philippines and Vietnam in terms of territorial disputes with China in South China Sea, the US's support to Japan in the East China Sea, and US's support to Ukraine against Russia have led the two partners to build stronger relations. These actions by the West and particularly by the US for the short run will ensure the tight embrace between China and Russia. However, not for a long time, as rapprochements and resets can bring change in equations.

Notes

1 Fyodor Lukyanov explains, "Multipolarity may now be understood as a way of structuring the global international system where the basic constituent parts are no longer individual states but instead conglomerations of economic interests, united around the most powerful centers of attraction and economic growth." See Fyodor Lukyanov, "Russian Dilemmas in a Multipolar World", *Journal of International Affairs*, Vol. 63, No. 2 (Spring/Summer 2010), p. 24. URL: http://www.jstor.org/stable/24384332
2 As quoted from the Chinese Administration of Customs in Russia Briefing, Russia-China Bilateral Trade Hit US$110 Billion in 2019 – What Is China Buying? January 14, 2020. URL: https://www.russia-briefing.com/news/russia-china-bilateral-trade-hit-us-110-billion-2019-china-buying.html/
3 World Population Review, "GDP Ranked by Country 2023", http://worldpopulationreview.com/countries/countries-by-gdp/
4 See OEC, 2023, URL: https://oec.world/en/profile/country/chn#:~:text=Destinations%20In%20August%202023%2C%20China,and%20Brazil%20(%2412.2B).
5 Eastern Economic Forum, About the Far East, URL: https://forumvostok.ru/en/about/ Also see Huang, Jing and Korolev, Alexander (2017), *The Political Economy of Pacific Russia. Regional Developments in East Asia*, Palgrave Macmillan.

References

Asean.org. (2023). *The Twelfth AEM-Russia Consultation. 21 August 2023, Semarang, Indonesia. Joint Media Statement*. Retrieved from ASEAN: https://asean.org/wp-content/uploads/2023/08/ADOPTED-Joint-Media-Statement-AEM-Russia-12-.pdf

Auslin, M. (2011). *Tipping Point in the Indo-Pacific*. Retrieved from The American Interest: https://www.the-american-interest.com/2011/03/01/tipping-point-in-the-indo-pacific/

FAS. (2000*The Foreign Policy Concept of the Russian Federation Approved by the President of the Russian Federation V.Putin June 28, 2000*. Retrieved from Federation of American Scientists: : https://nuke.fas.org/guide/russia/doctrine/econcept.htm

Bordachev, T. (2023, September 13). *Pivot to the East at a New Stage: EEF Assesses Relations Between Russia and Asia*. Retrieved from Valdai Discussion Club: https://valdaiclub.com/a/highlights/pivot-to-the-east-at-a-new-stage-eef-assesses/

Chebankova, E. (2017). Russia's Idea of the Multipolar World Order: Origins and Main Dimensions. *Post-Soviet Affairs Vol 33(3)*, 217-234.https://doi.org/10.1080/1060586X.2017.1293394

Devonshire-Ellis, C. (2023, September 17). *China Announces Massive Cross-Border Logistics and Energy Hub Project in Russian Far East*. Retrieved from Silk Raod Briefing: https://www.silkroadbriefing.com/news/2023/09/17/china-announces-massive-cross-border-logistics-and-energy-hub-project-in-russian-far-east/

US DoD. (2018a, January 19). *Summary of the 2018 National Defense Strategy of the United States of America*. Retrieved from US Dept of Defense: https://dod.defense.gov/Portals/1/Documents/pubs/2018-National-Defense-Strategy-Summary.pdf

US DoD. (2018b, January 18). *Remarks by Secretary Mattis on the National Defense Strategy*. Retrieved from US Dept of Defense (US DoD): https://www

.defense.gov/Newsroom/Transcripts/Transcript/Article/1420042/remarks-by -secretary-mattis-on-the-national

Dugin, A. (2012). *The Fourth Political Theory*. Moscow: Eurasian Movement.

Gazeta, R. (2000, January 18). National Security Concept of the Russian Federation,Approved by Presidential Decree No. 1300 of 17 December 1999 (given in the wording of Presidential Decree No. 24 of 10 January 2000). *Rossiiskaya Gazeta*.

US Government Publishing Office. (2015, July 15). *U.S. Economic and Military Alliances in Asia, Hearing before the Subcommittee on Asia And the Pacific Of the Committee on Foreign Affairs House Of Representatives, One Hundred Fourteenth Congress First Session*. Retrieved from GovInfo: https://www.govinfo .gov/content/pkg/CHRG-114hhrg95515/html/CHRG-114hhrg95515.htm

Hall, Ian and Heazle, Michael. (2017). *The Rules-Based Order in The Indo-Pacific: Opportunities and Challenges for Australia, India and Japan*. India and Japan Policy Brief, Regional Outlook Paper: No. 50, pp. 1–16. Retrieved from https:// www.griffith.edu.au/__data/assets/pdf_file/0023/108716/Regional-Outlook -Paper-50-Hall-Heazle-web.pdf

Ionin, A. (2015). A Technological Alliance: New Ways to Respond to Strategic Challenges. *Russia in Global Affairs*, January/March.

Karaganov, S. (2016). Global Challenges and Russia's Foreign Policy. *Strategic Analysis*, Vol 40(6), pp. 461–473.

Köstem, S. (2019, February). *Russia's Search for a Greater Eurasia: Origins, Promises, and Prospects*. Retrieved from Wilson Center, Kennan Cable, No. 40: https://www.wilsoncenter.org/sites/default/files/media/documents/publication/ kennan_cable_no._40.pdf

Kremlin.ru. (2014, October 1). *Congratulations to President of the People's Republic of China Xi Jinping on the 65th Anniversary of the Founding of the People's Republic of China*. Retrieved from President of Russia: http://en.kremlin .ru/catalog/persons/351/events/46705/print

Kremlin.ru. (2016a, June 17). *Plenary Session of St. Petersburg International Economic Forum*. Retrieved from President of Russia: http://en.kremlin.ru/ events/president/news/52178

Kremlin.ru. (2016b, May 11). *President's Address to the Russia-ASEAN Summit Participants*. Retrieved from President of Russia: http://en.kremlin.ru/events/ president/news/51899

Krishnan, A. (2022, December 15). *U.S. Created Indo-Pacific Concept to Bring in India to Contain China, Says Chinese Official*. Retrieved from The Hindu: https://www.thehindu.com/news/international/us-created-indo-pacific-concept -to-bring-in-india-to-contain china says chinese-official/article66266771.ece

Likhacheva, A. (2023, September 25). *Nets Over Ropes, or the New Priorities of the Pivot to the East 2.0*. Retrieved from Valdai Discussion Club: https://valdaiclub .com/a/highlights/nets-over-ropes-or-the-new-priorities-of-the-pivot/

Lo, B. (2008). *Axis of Convienence: Moscow, Beijing, and the New Geopolitics*. London: Chatham House.

Lo, B. (2019, August 20). *Once More with Feeling: Russia and the APR*. Retrieved from Analyses in Lowy Institute: https://www.lowyinstitute.org/publications/ once-more-feeling-russia-asia-pacific

Lukin, A. (2016). Guest Editor's Introduction. *Strategic Analysis*, Vol 40(6), pp. 455–457.

Lukyanov, F. (2010). Russian Dilemmas in a Multipolar World. *Journal of International Affairs*, 63(2), 19–32. http://www.jstor.org/stable/24384332.

Medcalf, R. (2013, November–December). *The Indo-Pacific: What's in a Name?* Retrieved from The American Interest: www.the-american-interest.com

102 Joyce Sabina Lobo

Min, J and Kang, B. (2017) (Open access). Promoting New Growth: 'Advanced Special Economic Zones' in the Russian Far East. In Helge Blakkisrud and Elana W Rowe (eds.), Russia's Turn to the East-Domestic policy making and regional cooperation(pp. 51–74). Palgrave Macmillan, London and Chamhttps://link .springer.com/chapter/10.1007/978-3-319-69790-1_4

MOFA. (2007, August 22). "Confluence of the Two Seas", Speech by H.E.Mr. Shinzo Abe, Prime Minister of Japan. Retrieved from Ministry of Foreign Affairs of Japan: https://www.mofa.go.jp/region/asia-paci/pmv0708/speech-2.html

Russian Embassy in China. (2013). Concept of the Foreign Policy of the Russian Federation Approved by President of the Russian Federation V. Putin 12 February 2013. Retrieved from Russian Embassy in China: https://beijing.mid .ru/en/countries/rossiya/kontseptsiya_vneshney_politiki_rossii/

PRCTS. (2017, January). The State Council Information Office of the People's Republic of China. Retrieved from China's Policies on Asia-Pacific Security Cooperation: ttps://english.www.gov.cn/archive/white_paper/2017/01/11/ content_281475539078636.htm

Rumer, E. (2019). The Primakov (Not Gerasimov) Doctrine in Action. Retrieved from Carnegie Endowment for International Peace: https://carnegieendowment .org/files/Rumer_PrimakovDoctrine_final1.pdf

MFA Russia, (2020, January 15). Foreign Minister Sergey Lavrov's Remarks and Answers to Questions at a Plenary Session of the Raisina Dialogue International Conference. Retrieved from Ministry of Foreign Affairs of the Russian Federation: https://www.mid.ru/en/foreign_policy/news/-/asset_publisher/cKNonkJE02Bw/ content/id/3994885

Lunev, Sergey and Shavlay, Ellina. (2018). Russia and India in the IPR. Asian Politics & Policy, 10(4), 713–731.

Shekhovtsov, A. (2017). Aleksandr Dugin's Neo-Eurasianism and the Russian-Ukrainian War. In M. Bassin (ed.), The Politics of Eurasianism: Identity, Popular Culture and Russia's Foreign Policy (pp. 185–204). MD: Rowman and Littlefield, Maryland.

Studies Institute, Russia Maritime and Davis, Anna. (2015). The 2015 Maritime Doctrine of the Russian Federation (Vol. 3). Retrieved from RMSI Research: https://digital-commons.usnwc.edu/rmsi_research/3

Taghizadeh-Hesary et al, (2021). Determinants of the Russia and Asia–Pacific Energy Trade. Energy Strategy Reviews, Vol 38.

Global, Times (2023. China's Trade with Russia Surges 36.5% from Jan-Jul, Despite Global Downturn. 09 August 2023. Retrieved from Gloabal Times: https://www.globaltimes.cn/page/202308/1295937.shtml

Troyakova, T. (2018). Russia'sPrimorskii Krai and Russia's 'Turn to the East': A Regional View. In H. B. Rowe (ed.), Russia's Turn to the East-Domestic policy making and regional cooperation (pp. 31–49). Palgrave Macmillan, London and Cham. https://link.springer.com/chapter/10.1007/978-3-319-69790-1_3

The White House. (2022, February). Indo-Pacific Strategy of the United States. Retrieved from The White House (.gov): www.whitehouse.gov

7

THE US IN THE INDO-PACIFIC

Interests and Strategy

Nanda Kishor M. S.

With the advent of globalisation, across the spectrum from laypeople to scholars in academic circles, most were under the impression that the world would become flat and there would be no relevance of geography. Several even thought that globalisation would be a tailor-made solution to several ills of the world. There were sceptics of globalisation who were vehement in negating globalisation as the new tool for creating a digital divide among people. Geography seems to have risen above both of these arguments and made itself relevant by appearing as a newly imagined space in several parts of the world. Geography was a cause of wars and conflicts in the world and would probably continue to be that way in the world. It is for the world to decide whether this phenomenon would be considered as the revenge of geography, relevance, or resurgence of geography or reverence to geography. To reassert the arguments made above, Robert Kaplan too reiterates that the end of the Cold War led to a mistaken view that globalisation and economic interdependence would inevitably lead to the end of geographical rivalries among great powers and the emergence of a more enlightened liberal order. Despite the trendy talk of a "borderless world", the control of territory is still fundamental to world politics (Dibb, 2018). It is in this context that the new energised discussions among policymakers and strategic thinkers alike have been discussing the new buzzword Indo-Pacific.

Indo-Pacific in US Understanding

Some scholars seem to believe that 'Indo-Pacific' is yet another attempt by the US to use India as a lynchpin against China after its failed attempt through the Asia Pivot strategy. Some opine of the genuine interest of the US

DOI: 10.4324/9781003479307-9

in keeping the region close to its heart due to its allies. There are also arguments by scholars on how the US is trying to contain China in the region by redefining itself much more vigorously to come out of the much spoken 'shift of gravity from West to the East' statement during the Obama administration for two consecutive terms. The US in the Obama era was seen as a weaker power, and there were talks about the shift of gravity from West to East. This statement is no more a regularly spoken topic since Trump took over the administration, but the US seems to be under stress since Biden has taken over.

The emerging Asian strategic system that encompasses both the Pacific and Indian Ocean is being defined in part by the geographically expanding interests and reach of countries such as China and India, but also by the continued strategic role and presence of the US and its like-minded allies Japan and Australia. These two countries that conceive themselves as regional security architects. Why states and diplomats indulge in creating these new spheres of understanding needs to be analysed. A brutal way of putting it across through rhetoric and challenging China without a new construct would probably sound like an invitation to *Thucydides Trap* what Graham Allison brings as an analogy from history more to avoid conflict and war rather than suggesting there would be a war. Rory Medcalf explains this behaviour of the leaders and diplomats meticulously:

> The mental maps of regions that leaders and diplomats use have material effects. These maps help define where nations prioritise their diplomatic attentions, the power projection capabilities they develop for their militaries, the strategic problems they must attend to or can afford to ignore, the partners and rivals they identify, and the regional organisations they prefer – including the lists of who is in and who is out.
>
> *(Medcalf, 2018)*

Indo-Pacific Construct – the USA and China

The uneasiness of the existing Superpower to accommodate a newer power challenging its status has been observed in international politics. This is what happened between France and Great Britain, France and Russia, Germany and Great Britain, Great Britain and the US. Challenging by no way means that the challenging newer power can match in its military and economic might along with other components of the comprehensive national power of the existing power, but signals the possibilities of reaching through steady progress and marked credentials. The uneasiness could lead to war before the advent of nuclear weapons. The nuclear weapons have brought Mutually Assured Destruction (MAD) in place, but uneasiness has to be vented out in one or the other form. The reaction would lead to escalation through conflict, but a response would lead to strategy. Perhaps, Indo-Pacific can be envisaged as one such strategy. The complex interdependence in the contemporary world knitted through economic interdependence has pushed states to think beyond confrontations and conflicts instead of aligning with like-minded nations to pursue strategies that would hurt the adversary economically.

The comprehensive national power pursued by China seems to have upset the US from the beginning. Comprehensive National Power (CNP) has been popularised by 20th-century political thought in China and is presumed to be the roadmap given by Deng Xiaoping in which he asserted that "in measuring a country's national power, one must look at it comprehensively and from all sides". From then on, with the rise of China, it has been widely discussed and accepted. From German geopolitics to modern-day political thought, invariably, CNP has come as part and parcel of every power-aspiring nation in its assessment but was not codified as CNP. It is referred to as the combined strengths and conditions of a country measured, keeping in mind both the qualitative and quantitative techniques. Michael Pillsbury, in his work *China Debates the Future Security Environment*, states, as stated by Wang Songfen and others on CNP:

We believe that Comprehensive National Power is the organic sum of the different powers of a sovereign state during a certain period of time, it is the base which all countries rely on for existence and development, and it is the foundation on which world powers establish their international position and give full play to their influence and roles. Specifically, it is the condensed sum of the entire calculations of societies' various existence and development factors at a certain time, space, and under certain conditions.

(Pillsbury, 2000)

As there were no visible outcomes until the advent of the 21st century, the US seems to have taken it lightly as the collapse of the Soviet Union in 1991 allowed it to become the sole superpower. It was only somewhere around 2008 that China was seen becoming more aggressive in its region, and it also started talking about the peaceful rise, which subsequently led to the confrontation with the seizure of Scarborough Shoal in 2012. It was during this time there was another major development took place in the form of the Chinese Communist Party's 18th Party Congress in 2012, electing its new leader in China. In 2013, Xi famously pronounced the "Chinese Dream" (Dream-Meng), which perhaps had not been one phrase used by any Chinese leader since 1949. Chinese scholars, unlike the scholars who are suspicious of China's rise, have given a philosophical foundation to the idea of "Dream" by citing some of their philosophers. Confucius stands tall among them, and it is his terminology of "Ba Dao" (use of force) and "Ren Dao" (harmony) that has been used to substantiate it. This is evident in the works of Winberg Chai and May-lee Chai:

> One of the best examples of practicing "Ren Dao" is to be found under Ming Emperor Yongle), who sent his Admiral Zheng He (also commonly spelled Cheng Ho in English) on seven expeditions to explore the world. Admiral Zheng commanded 250 ships with 27,000 crew members and sailed from southern China throughout Southeast Asia, eventually reaching the Persian Gulf and East Africa. Zheng did not establish colonies in these lands, nor did he and his crew kidnap natives as slaves for trade. Instead, Zheng was ordered by the Ming Emperor to dispense gifts where his fleet landed in order to establish peaceful relations for China and to establish China as a powerful nation whose friendship should be valued. The current Chinese central government has sought to use these peaceful expeditions as contemporary metaphors for China's current rise, as shown most noticeably in the Opening Ceremony spectacle before the 2008 Beijing Olympics.
>
> *(Chai & Chai, 2013)*

The Chinese are not new to slogans or phrases coming from the Chinese President. This, on the one hand, is to make sure that they leave behind a legacy and on the other to keep the nation and its spirit together. For Jiang Zemin, it was the "theory of the three represents- Advanced productive forces, advanced culture and interest of the broad masses and finally the relative prosperous society". For President Hu Jintao, it was a harmonious society and the scientific concept of development. Some have interpreted it as a call to implement an ambitious programme, set by the just-ended party congress to realise the goals of "completing the building of a moderately prosperous society when the party celebrates its 100th birthday in 2021, and the building of a prosperous, strong, democratic, culturally advanced, harmonious and modernised socialist country when the new China marks its 100th anniversary in 2049" (Huang, 2013). Xi in the 19th National Congress of the Communist Party of China in 2017 asserted that China has a goal of becoming moderately prosperous society by 2021, a global technology leader by 2035, and a "strong, democratic, civilized, harmonious, and modern socialist country" by 2049 (Jinping, 2017). This essentially is being echoed again in China's assertiveness in the region, keeping in mind the requirements and the challenges it has till 2049.

There seems to be a dominant opinion on China's aggressive yet defensive strategy laced in its Deng style pragmatism when it comes to some of the most spoken programmes. For instance, the Belt and Road Initiative (BRI) is justified to be arriving from China's *Malacca dilemma*. This has led China to propose a geopolitical alternative solely to secure its economic interests in the Indian Ocean, Central Asia, to avoid strategic logjams in Southeast Asia. The US superiority in every region across the world is a frustrating factor, and to break this hegemony, China needs to engage with the world using its economic clout creatively. China needs western markets as it needs to go beyond its Southeast Asia realm. However, powerful China is in Southeast Asia; the ASEAN states collectively can face it if not individually.

US Interests and Strategy in the Indo-Pacific

The US being the sole Superpower in the world, naturally is uneasy about the fact that China is a potential challenger in the Indo-Pacific. For the US, challenging China in the Indo-Pacific is much more important than challenging it in Africa or Europe. With President Trump taking office in 2017, no challenge anticipated from the US towards China. The way the elections were and subsequently, the media coverage led China to think that it would be able to take forward the agenda it had during the Obama administration. The region was always a priority during the Obama administration too. As Hillary Clinton opined "for America, the Asia-Pacific is geo-economically, geostrategically and geopolitically vital, and the future of politics will be decided in Asia, not Afghanistan or Iraq, and the United States will be right at the centre of the action" (Saeed, 2017). The only difference between the approach of the Obama administration and that of the Trump administration is the language and the strategy being employed. The Obama administration looked more like a power that was ready to accept the rise of China and the inevitability of cooperation as the only way forward. This might have emerged as the Democrats did not think that there would be any competition for the post of the President of the United States from the Republicans and more so from someone like Trump. The Democrats almost wrote him off in the race, and the probability of having Hillary Clinton as the next President sounded more than obvious. Hillary Clinton wrote that

> we all know that fears and misperceptions linger on both sides of the Pacific. Some in our country see China's progress as a threat to the United States; some in China worry that America seeks to constrain China's growth. We reject both those views. The fact is that a thriving America is good for China, and a thriving China is good for America. We both have much more to gain from cooperation than from conflict.
>
> *(Saeed, 2017)*

The very first shock came in the form of the US National Security Strategy (NSS) of 2017. It states that a geopolitical competition between free and repressive visions of world order is taking place in the Indo-Pacific region. The region, which stretches from the west coast of India to the western shores of the United States, represents the most populous and economically dynamic part of the world. The U.S. interest in a free and open Indo-Pacific extends back to the earliest days of our republic.

(The White House, 2017)

The Free and Open Indo-Pacific Strategy (FOIP), as expressed by President Trump at the APEC summit of 2017 held in Vietnam, was unfolding. The expression from the US was to make it clear that the sole purpose of the FOIP was not only to counter China, but to use it as a response to China's aggressive posturing in the region and threatening the US allies. This indirectly meant to retell the American hegemony and its relevance in the 21st century. Unlike the NSS 2017, the Indo-Pacific Strategy Report was much more forceful in its hermeneutics. The opening remarks from the Indo-Pacific Strategy Report 2019 were black and white. There was no mincing of words or reconciliation, unlike the Obama administration. The document emphatically stated the Indo-Pacific as a priority theatre and called itself as a Pacific nation. It strongly stated that

We have an enduring commitment to uphold a free and open Indo-Pacific in which all nations, large and small, are secure in their sovereignty and able to pursue economic growth consistent with accepted international rules, norms, and principles of fair competition.

(US Department of Defense, 2019)

The unpredictability in Trump's behaviour engaged several countries to invest heavily in understanding him. On the other side, several US experts believe that for a successful Indo-Pacific strategy to be implemented in the region, there is a necessity to have the continuation of certain people in office holding important positions, including the defense secretary. This is a traditional understanding arising from the bureaucratic model of administration, whereas Trump moved beyond the bureaucratic model and believed only in the dictum "perform or perish" like that of a commercial establishment. His strategy might have sounded erratic like that of his behaviour, but eventually, it fetched benefits for the US. The current Biden administration pronounced its long-term position in and commitment to the Indo-Pacific region by focusing on Northeast Asia and Southeast Asia, South Asia, and Oceania, including the Pacific Islands. It further spoke about support for regional connectivity, trade and investment, and deepening bilateral and multilateral partnerships.

Given all this and several reports and scholarly writing on the Indo-Pacific, what are the ways one can analyse the operationalising of the Indo-Pacific strategy? Can international relations theory explain to us the behaviour, approach, and what would be the outcome in a diagnostic manner that would be examined in the course of this paper? There are three ways of looking at the Indo-Pacific construct and the US plan: through the prism of realism and Neo-realism, Neo-liberal Institutionalism, and Constructivism. The Realist theory is the most dominating theory to construct and understand US behaviour. Realism rests on their understanding and reiterates that states live in a context of anarchy – that is, in the absence of anyone being in charge internationally. In Morgenthau's account, every political action is directed towards keeping, increasing, or demonstrating power. The thinking is that policies based on morality or idealism can lead to weakness – and possibly the destruction or domination of a state by a competitor. In this sense, pursuing the national interest is "amoral" – meaning that it is not subject to calculations of morality (Antunes & Camisão, 2018). Given this premise and the pursuit of national interest by the state without being hounded by morality, the US in the Indo-Pacific very much suits the realist prism. The US may choose to go it alone if the perceived friends and allies of it do not support it. Mearsheimer believes that the concern for relative gain predicts that states will prefer a balance of power over collective security because the latter requires that states trust one another enough to entirely forgo relative gain through unilateral disarmament, which is inherently at odds with the idea of having a positional advantage for self-defence. The problem with the friends and allies the US has chosen for this action is that other than Japan, the remaining two are not entirely clear. Japan is clear about its motives and would want the US to play an active and decisive role in the region. Japan also expects the US to halt the aggressive posture of China in the South and the East China Sea. The other two, India and Australia, are still not clear, and they do not seem to have the same intensity as Japan and the US. If Japan and the US are for relative gain, India and Australia are for absolute gain. If we examine what the Prime Minister of India Modi said, it would be clear that in none of his statements, he goes as a confrontationist. Recently he proposed an "Indo-Pacific Oceans Initiative" for the safe, secure, and stable maritime domain. The focus areas include creating partnerships among interested states in enhancing maritime security; sustainably using marine resources; disaster prevention and management (Chaudhury, 2019). Analysing this statement, one can feel that Modi is not aggressive nor is ready to be adventurous militarily. Modi stressed that India and the US shared a vision of an "open, stable, secure and prosperous Indo-Pacific Region". Modi defined this region as stretching from the shores of Africa to that of the Americas, thereby incorporating the Gulf region and Indian Ocean island states left out of popular definitions. As this is to be a "free, open, inclusive region" in pursuit of progress and prosperity, the use of the term is not "directed against any country", nor is it to be seen as a "grouping that seeks to dominate". In this context, Modi deliberately did not use the word "Quad", the grouping of the US, India, Japan, and Australia (Roy-Chaudhury, 2018). India has never used the term ally in the past except for a recent usage by Prime Minister Modi in France. Addressing a gathering of the Indian community at the UNESCO (United Nations Educational, Scientific and Cultural Organization) office in Paris, PM Modi said in the 21st century, people talk of "INFRA". PM Modi said that for him "Infra"=In (India)+Fra (France). He said that this means the alliance between India and France (Sinha, 2019). However, everyone is aware of the fact that this probably might have happened as Modi is fond of creating acronyms for sloganeering. There are several other scholars of the opinion that this might be a signal at India's change in behaviour in the international setting and France might have filled the vacuum created by Russia (Rajagopalan, 2019).

Australia seems to be in a more significant confusion than that of India. Australia recognises the Indo-Pacific as an essential region and values the relationship it shares with the US, but at the same time, it wants to understand the region in which it lives and survives in the presence of China. It feels that it is not so capable of taking on China in the Indo-Pacific, but at the same time, it would want to be considered a formidable power in the Indian Ocean region when it comes to the relationship with India. The below statement summarises the position of Australia in an aptly articulated manner:

> At the core of Australia's 2016 Defence and 2017, Foreign Policy White Papers is the need to strengthen the traditional Australia-US alliance system. Arguably, Australia remedies the US' relative decline in the Indo-Pacific. Amidst China's assertive economic and strategic ascendance, Canberra does its share to assuage an inert friction between "two of Australia's most important partners – the United States and China". The white papers underscore the call for the US to retain its leadership role in the region, as Australia acknowledges that it "does not have the capacity to unilaterally protect and further our global interests". As such, Canberra has wittingly sided with a rules-based global order that protects its interests, ensures prosperity and protects global stability. Since free trade and military alliances are vital to its future, Australia deems it has the responsibility to remind its traditional partner of these alliance pillars.
>
> *(Adducul, 2018)*

This unique scenario comes up with two different scenarios. Firstly, though there can be the usage of the Balance of Power concept, the US is a preponderant power and there is no parity between its friends to come up with a strategy based on military cooperation as India does not want to be part of the military pact and Australia is hesitant. Secondly, if there has to be the use of Balance of Threat, the US has to agree that China is a threat rather than just uttering that China is aggressive in the region.

Neo-liberal institutionalism accepts two essential aspects of the Realists. Firstly, the system is anarchic, and secondly, the behaviour of states is driven by rational calculations of their national interest. They also recognise that cooperation is not harmony. Cooperation requires compromise and/or mediation. Cooperation is possible when there is a conflict. Harmony is the absence of all conflict, which is impossible. Cooperation is nonetheless possible through international regimes and institutions, and it is rational to focus on long-term benefits instead of short-term goals (collective goods). So far, the states which are actively interested in pursuing the Indo-Pacific strategy, leaving out China and propagated by the US, have not specifically drawn a road map to create an institution. Though economic cooperation is the primary agenda, so far, there seems to be no such move by any of the states, and instead, they appear to be more interested in insisting on a free and open Indo-Pacific for navigation. This is a deficiency, but at the same time, if the Indo-Pacific strategy takes a proper shape, there are possibilities of creating neoliberal institutions.

The central issue in constructivism is identities and interests. Constructivists argue that states can have multiple identities that are socially constructed through interaction with other actors. Identities are representations of an actor's understanding of who they are, which in turn signals their interests. They are essential to constructivists as they argue that identities constitute interests and actions (Theys, 2018). Probably democracy, freedom, and global commons can be seen as social constructs and identities. Perhaps this is one of the best formulations as all four countries – the US, Japan, Australia, and India – have been practising democracies. This was mooted as early as 2012 by Shinzo Abe. He stressed that

> Japan is a mature maritime democracy, and its choice of close partners should reflect that fact. I envisage a strategy whereby Australia, India, Japan, and the US state of Hawaii form a diamond to safeguard the maritime commons stretching from the Indian Ocean region to the western Pacific. I am prepared to invest, to the greatest possible extent, Japan's capabilities in this security diamond.
>
> *(Abe, 2012)*

Another significant contribution from Australia is in the form of being a "norm entrepreneur". Andrew Carr and Daniel Baldino opine that

> Given the scale of pressing challenges, and to make the concept of an Indo-Pacific community a reality in national security orientations, Australia will need to go beyond platitudes about ideal types of regional

cooperation and consider how it might best act as an agent of change as a norm entrepreneur to address dynamic security problems. In addition, Australia is still a comparatively small country that needs to be attuned to the realities of power and its relative position and profile. As a starting point, strengthening relevant and representative multilateral institutions will be essential. India will also be indispensable to any processes directed towards shared regional responsibility and security construction.

(Carr & Baldino, 2015)

Though all of the above sounds very constructive, there are specific prerequisites for the constructivist idea to be fulfilled. Though there is no immediate threat to democracy, at least in the core countries aspiring to be part of the Indo-Pacific strategy. If there has to be an effective Indo-Pacific strategy, then there is a necessity to include ASEAN. It is in ASEAN, China has a greater stake, and without ASEAN standing up to the perceived China threat, there is no possibility of the Indo-Pacific strategy becoming a success in the future. The democracies in India and the US are put to the test of lately in 2019, and there have been apprehensions in the media about the quality of democracy in these nations. Democracy's dependence on the democratic principle to animate institutions fatally undermines it because, paradoxically, democracy is eroded by the very politics it countenances (Datta-Ray, 2018). To substantiate this, Larry Diamond, in his work democracy in decline, opines that in the decade following the Cold War, democracy flourished around the world as never before. In recent years, however, much of this progress has steadily eroded. Between 2000 and 2015, democracy broke down in 27 countries, among them Kenya, Russia, Thailand, and Turkey. Around the same time, several other global "swing states" – countries that, thanks to their large populations and economies, could have an outsize impact on the future of global democracy – also took a turn for the worse. In nearly half of them, political liberties, as measured by the US non-profit Freedom House, contracted (Diamond, 2016). This, perhaps, is a significant factor that needs to be kept in mind while going overboard on democracy as a binding factor. Several nations in the Indo-Pacific still suffer from a democratic deficit. The other remaining options are limited concerning the constructivist idea of the Indo-Pacific at this juncture.

The Biden administration's Indo-Pacific strategy of 2022 outlines China's threat as a primary component but seems to accept China as "the" challenge for the US. The document outlines economic, military, diplomatic, and technological challenges as the primary concerns with regard to China. At the same time, it also sees windows of cooperation in the areas of climate change, international institutions, energy security, and technology (Saha & Mishra, 2022). The Biden administration is stressed in terms of how to manage the threat to Taiwan from China, the threat to Ukraine from Russia, and then how to manage the remaining friends like India, Australia, and France who have been crucial in taking forward the US's Indo-Pacific strategy.

The current strategy needs rigour in the wake of the Russia-Ukraine war. There are several questions that arise out of the geopolitical compulsion the US is going through since 2022–23. The involvement of the US in the Russia-Ukraine war has slowed down the resources utilised in the Indo-Pacific. It could suffer a major delay, as has happened previously during the Iraq and Afghanistan situation. There are issues about where the Quad is heading. What does it want to achieve? As much as the Americans would want to engage in the Indo-Pacific, foreign policies are always associated with "outputs" and "outcomes". In this scenario, is the US doing enough to ensure the confidence of its friends in the Indo-Pacific, or will it be concluded by the domestic audience in the US as another China containment strategy? Several scholars believe that if the Quad takes the Indo-Pacific strategy forward based on democracy as a common factor, how will the region's smaller nations be accommodated to make it an open, free, and inclusive Indo-Pacific? This is a very important question that needs a formidable answer from the Biden administration. One of the ways, perhaps, the Biden administration can turn its strategy in the Indo-Pacific to go beyond the China conundrum is to concentrate on non-traditional securities affecting day-to-day lives in the region. This includes climate change, sustainable development, refugees, and requirements of the smaller islands and nations in the region. It is high time that the US gets into action than still being worried about the hermeneutics regarding its engagement.

The COVID-19 pandemic has jostled the US and all the nations across the world. All the nation-states were exposed to the vulnerabilities of their respective public healthcare systems. The world GDP suffered a major setback from which several states are yet to recover. Many nation-states need handholding in dealing with economic conditions and living standards. The US can fill the vacuum created in the world order through its Indo-Pacific strategy by making it inclusive in all fields. This will elevate the Indo-Pacific strategy from being an anti-China strategy to a world leader's vision for the region. The pandemic has pushed states worldwide to look beyond their narrow national interests and move towards enlightened national interest. This is an opportunity for the US to change its image from being a hegemon.

The Limitations of the Strategy

The Indo-Pacific strategy, as proposed by the US, has its limitations. It can be categorised under leadership crisis, institutional crisis, and action plan deficit crisis. Under the leadership crisis, unlike Obama, a reasonable leader, Trump was no comparison. This does not mean that Trump was less in calibre. His ability to threaten the Chinese had been a moderate success.

The Chinese have felt the heat since the tariff regime to a full position and had almost led to a trade war. On the other hand, Trump was unable to take everyone along with him in a task he thought was of greater importance to the US and its like-minded friends. Joshua Kurlantzick opined that the Trump administration's actions at home, which are covered extensively in the Asian press – attacking US media outlets, publicly blasting judges and law enforcement agencies, and other actions – make Asian leaders wonder how Trump can claim to be an advocate for free and open politics, for playing by the rules, anywhere in the world. Trump's increasingly belligerent rhetoric towards North Korea, too, made Asian leaders wonder whether, in a crisis, Trump would work with any of the United States' Asian partners, whether or not they subscribed to his "Free and Open Indo-Pacific Idea". Instead, they worried, the White House might attack North Korea unilaterally, creating chaos in Northeast Asia (Kurlantzick, 2018). Trump praised a nation one's and then reversed the statement later. This unpredictability did not bring trust among partners of the strategy. Secondly, there was no institutionalised mechanism on the Indo-Pacific strategy. From the definition of what constitutes Indo-Pacific to how to go about it, different voices were being heard. The US was unable to keep all its like-minded friends in the same spirit. The case is not different under Biden's administration. It almost is a continuation of the previous era except for threatening China like Trump did previously. India has a different definition, and the US has a different definition of what constitutes the Indo-Pacific; this probably should not lead to some great powers messing up the region. It has not moved from strategy to institution and does not seem to be moving towards that direction. Thirdly, there was an evident deficit of an action plan. As previously discussed, India wants a free Indo-Pacific for navigation and commercial purposes; in contrast, Japan and the US want security architecture along with freedom of navigation and economics, Australia wants to play the normative role to avoid conflict but does not want to confront China being in the forefront. From the NSS 2017 to so far, there seems to be no significant progress, and it all has remained in rhetoric. If China feels deterred, it is due to the unilateral actions of the US related to trade tariffs rather than the efforts of the other three core members. The US has to define and take smaller and bigger powers of the region to make the Indo-Pacific strategy a success. If it remains an elite grouping, there would not be the expected outcome in the region. It should define whose interest it serves. In action to curb China's rise, the US should not end up undermining its long-conserved position of being a Superpower. The Trump administration had conceived a threefold strategy of Preparedness, Partnerships, and Promotion of a Networked Region was a welcome move. Its open challenge to China by asserting that the US has many belts and many roads displayed its primacy as a Superpower, which none other than the US could assert given the clout China continues to enjoy in world politics.

The latest Indo-Pacific strategy released by the Biden administration doesn't seem to have brought out great enthusiasm among leaders and scholars alike across the world. The expectations from the general public in the US to break the Trump era politics have not gone great, at least in world politics. Domestically, the US citizens feel Biden can deliver, but on the international relations front, Biden seems to be struggling. Be it Afghanistan or the ongoing Ukraine crisis. Biden's soft approach towards China and targeting Russia sounds like he has not come out of the Cold War politics. Jeff Smith opines that Biden's strategy says virtually nothing about the military competition with China or the steps necessary to roll back its intimidation of allies and partners. The document is too vague, too indirect, too diplomatic, and nearly silent on critical defence and military aspects of US strategy in the Indo-Pacific (Smith, 2022). Mattoo too feels that Biden's Indo-Pacific strategy seems long on attitude yet disappointingly understated in terms of policy prescriptions (Mattoo, 2022). The document seems to highlight a strategy already clearly laid out during the Trump administration, and this administration seems to be doing some sort of ritual rather than ushering clear commitment and confidence. The leadership crisis in the US is yet again visible in this document, as there are no fresh ideas in the strategy.

What defines the success of US strategy in the Indo-Pacific would be the "consistency, cooperation, and conduciveness" it creates for its partners through the praxis of its ideas. Nevertheless, China would not give up the grand strategies it has been harnessing for decades. It would be curious to see how things unfold in this highly unpredictable theatre with the new vigour and robustness the US has been displaying. A word of caution the US and its like-minded friends in the Indo-Pacific strategy should remember is from Karl Haushofer who asserted that "If an empire could arise with Japan's soul in China's body that would be a power which would put even the empires of Russia and the United States in the shade".

References

Abe, S. (2012, December 31). Shinzo Abe: Asia's Democratic security diamond. *Mint*. Retrieved April 29, 2022, from https://www.livemint.com/Opinion/viqg2XC8fhRfjTUIcctk0M/Asias-democratic-security-diamond.html

Adducul, L. A. M. (2018). The Indo-Pacific Construct in Australia's White Papers: Reflections for ASEAN-Australia Future Strategic Partnership. *CIRSS Commentaries, Center for International Relations and Strategic Studies (CIRSS)*, Vol. 6.

Antunes, S., & Camisão, I. (2018, August 5). Introducing realism in international relations theory. *E-International Relations*. Retrieved April 28, 2022, from https://www.e-ir.info/2018/02/27/introducing-realism-in-international-relations-theory/

Carr, A., & Baldino, D. (2015). An Indo-Pacific norm entrepreneur? Australia and defence diplomacy. *Journal of the Indian Ocean Region, 11*(1), 30–47. https://doi.org/10.1080/19480881.2015.1018500

Chai, W., & Chai, M.-L. (2013). The meaning of Xi Jinping's Chinese dream. *American Journal of Chinese Studies, 20*(2), 95–97.

Chaudhury, D. R. (2019, November 5). PM Modi proposes Indo-pacific oceans initiative. *The Economic Times.* Retrieved April 28, 2022, from https://economictimes.indiatimes.com/news/politics-and-nation/pm-modi-proposes-indo-pacific-oceans-initiative/articleshow/71915838.cms?from=mdr

Datta-Ray, D. K. (2018)As India proves, democracy is no longer fit for purpose. *South China Morning Post, May 29, 2018,.* Retrieved April 29, 2022, from https://www.scmp.com/comment/insight-opinion/article/2148249/india-proves-democracy-no-longer-fit-purpose-while-chinas

Diamond, L. (2016). Democracy in decline: How Washington can reverse the tide. *Foreign Affairs, 95*(4), 151–159.

Dibb, P. (2018). The return of geography. In R. W. Glenn (Ed.), *New directions in strategic thinking 2.0* (pp. 91–104). ANU Press.

Huang, C. (2013, February 6). Just what is Xi Jinping's 'chinese dream' and 'chinese Renaissance'? *South China Morning Post.* Retrieved April 28, 2022, from https://www.scmp.com/news/china/article/1143954/just-what-xi-jinpings-chinese-dream-and-chinese-renaissance

Jinping, X. (2017, October 18). Secure a decisive victory in building a moderately prosperous society in all respects and strive for the great success of socialism with Chinese characteristics for a NewEra. Delivered at the 19th National Congress of the Communist Party of China. Retrieved April 29, 2022, from http://www.xinhuanet.com/english/download/Xi_Jinpings_report_at_19th_CPC_National_Congress.pdf

Kurlantzick, J. (2018, February 21). *The trump administration's "Free and open indo-pacific": A solid idea, but difficult to pull off.* Council on Foreign Relations. Retrieved April 29, 2022, from https://www.cfr.org/blog/trump-administrations-free-and-open-indo-pacific-solid-idea-difficult-pull

Mattoo, S. (2022, February 19). Biden's Indo-Pacific strategy is high on attitude but is it enough to contain China? *News18.* Retrieved April 29, 2022, from https://www.news18.com/news/opinion/bidens-indo-pacific-strategy-is-high-on-attitude-but-is-it-enough-to-contain-china-4790333.html

Medcalf, R. (2018, July 20). China may not like it, but it already has an Indo-Pacific strategy. *South China Morning Post.* Retrieved April 28, 2022, from https://www.scmp.com/week-asia/geopolitics/article/2126210/goodbye-asia-pacific-why-sudden-buzz-over-indo-pacific

Pillsbury, M. (2000). *China debates the future security environment* (p. 219). Retrieved April 28, 2022, from https://nuke.fas.org/guide/china/doctrine/pills2/index.html

Rajagopalan, R. P. (2019, September 5). A new India-france alliance? *ORF.* Retrieved April 29, 2022, from https://www.orfonline.org/research/a-new-india-france-alliance-55143/

Roy-Chaudhury, R. (2018)Modi's vision for the Indo-Pacific region. June 02, 2018, *IISS.* Retrieved April 29, 2022, from https://www.iiss.org/blogs/analysis/2018/06/modi-vision-indo-pacific

Saeed, M. (2017). From the Asia-Pacific to the Indo-Pacific: Expanding Sino-u.s. strategic competition. *China Quarterly of International Strategic Studies, 3*(4), 499–512. https://doi.org/10.1142/s2377740017500324

Saha, P., & Mishra, V. (2022, February 19). Decoding the Biden administration's Indo-Pacific strategy. *ORF.* Retrieved April 29, 2022, from https://www.orfonline.org/expert-speak/decoding-the-biden-administrations-indo-pacific-strategy/

Scott, D. (2012). The "indo-pacific"—New regional formulations and new maritime frameworks for US-india strategic convergence. *Asia-Pacific Review, 19*(2), 85–109. https://doi.org/10.1080/13439006.2012.738115

Sinha, D. (2019, August 23). PM Narendra Modi coins new acronym 'infra' at UNESCO in Paris! Check meaning, significance. *The Financial Express.* Retrieved April 29, 2022, from https://www.financialexpress.com/infrastructure/pm-narendra-modi-coins-new-acronym-infra-at-unesco-in-paris-check-meaning-significance/1684264/

Smith, J. M. (2022, February 15). The Indo-Pacific strategy needs Indo-specifics. *Defense One.* Retrieved April 29, 2022, from https://www.defenseone.com/ideas/2022/02/indo-pacific-strategy-needs-indo-specifics/362022/

US Department of Defense. (2019)*The Department of Defense Indo-Pacific Strategy Report, June 01, 2019.* Retrieved April 28, 2022, from https://media.defense.gov/2019/Jul/01/2002152311/-1/-1/1/department-of-defense-indo-pacific-strategy-report-2019.pdf

Theys, S. (2018, February 23). Introducing constructivism in international relations theory. *E-International Relations.* Retrieved April 29, 2022, from https://www.e-ir.info/2018/02/23/introducing-constructivism-in-international-relations-theory/

The White House. (2017)*National Security Strategy of the United States of America, December 01, 2017.* . Retrieved , from https://trumpwhitehouse.archives.gov/wp-content/uploads/2017/12/NSS-Final-12-18-2017-0905.pdf

8
JAPAN'S INTERESTS AND STRATEGIES IN THE INDO-PACIFIC

Anil Kumar P.

Any theoretical attempt to understand Japan's interests and strategies in the Indo-Pacific theatre will reflect its realist balancing strategy in the liberal international dynamics coupled with the rise of China and its conflicting and competing strategic interests with the United States. Japan's *Free and Open Indo-Pacific* strategy is the best testimonial for this argument. Free and Open Indo-Pacific (FOIP) is the major policy of Japan towards the Indo-Pacific, which is considering the Indian and Pacific Oceans as a significant geostrategic arena. This policy is basically a threat-driven economic and strategic cooperation of different maritime powers whose interests are converging to promote a rules-based regional order in reaction to the emerging politico-strategic changes structured and characterised by China's rise and the potential strategic threat it is posing in the region. While the Japanese government has stressed that FOIP is not intended to contain China's rise, the Abe administration striked a delicate balance between cooperation and competition with Beijing and encouraged other regional stakeholders to embrace rules and norms presumably aimed at shaping China's behaviour. Tokyo's FOIP is complemented by the *Quad*, which promotes engagements in economic and strategic affairs, including maritime freedom and security. The Asia Reassurance Initiative Act of 2018 also documents US support for FOIP and the rules-based international order. But Trump's absence from the East Asia Summit and Asia-Pacific Economic Cooperation (APEC) Forum in November 2018 raised questions about the US commitment to regional institutions as a platform for shaping diplomatic engagement on rules and norms under FOIP. In the case of Beijing also, both have contrasting views. Japan is interested in creating stability with China and now highlighting Free and Open Indo-Pacific as a "vision" rather than a "strategy" to encompass

DOI: 10.4324/9781003479307-10

the interests of the excluded too. Contrary to this, the US and the Trump administration are emphasising the potential strategic threat competition with China. But it is very clear that Japan's Indo-Pacific strategy will generate more security challenges to Beijing's sea lanes of communication. It will also put pressure on China on its assertive behavioural pattern because more countries feel cautious about this nature of China. At the same time Japan's Indo-Pacific strategy and the Quad will help it to manage its complex relations in tune with its strategic interests. This strategy of Japan is the result of their realist balancing strategy in the liberal international dynamics for a rule-based international order to protect its long-term security and interests.

Though the vision of FOIP composition is abstract at this level, it has illuminated its strength as a potential cooperative mechanism to the various challenges posed in the Indo-Pacific region. Critics argued that Japan's Indo-Pacific strategy is still abstract and developments in the region are the result of an *order transition* rather than a *power transition.*

Japan's *Indo-Pacific* Policy: From *Tactical Hedging* to a *Realist Strategic Vision*

The Indo-Pacific concept was first used by Shinzo Abe in a speech during the summer of 2007 in which he referred to the "confluence of the two seas" (Sahashi, 2019: 2). In the speech, Abe pointed out that the Indian Ocean and Pacific Ocean are creating the threads for cooperation as the seas of freedom and prosperity. He also pointed out that a broader Asia is in the making in its distinct form, which is now divided on the basis of different aspects (Sahashi, 2019). Abe also highlighted the significance of universal values in the foreign policy of Japan. He also imagined a broader Asia connecting to the network spreading from the Pacific Ocean and incorporating the US and Australia. He also anchored strategic and maritime security aspects to justify the incorporation of the regions under one umbrella and explained that powers like Japan and India have converging interests in the sea lines of communication and security (Sahashi, 2018: 151).

In the beginning of 2010, former US president Barack Obama declared his Asia Pivot policy as a response to China's increasing strategic threat and competition. His policy was a comprehensive strategy involving the Asia-Pacific and aimed to integrate it into the strategic political and economic aspects. In reaction to this, Chinese President Xi Jinping declared peripheral diplomacy and the "One Belt, One Road (OBOR)" initiative. OBOR is considered as Xi Jingping's pivot to Eurasia and for the making of a Sino-centric Asia (Ishida, 2018: 159–160). The Japanese Prime Minister Shinzo narrated and practised the Abe Doctrine in the context of China's strategic threat and competition. He developed the strategy of building partnerships with India, Australia, and the Association of Southeast Asian Nations (ASEAN).

He also followed the Partnership for Quality Infrastructure (PQI) and Free and Open Indo-Pacific Strategy as a response to China's One Belt One Road initiative (OBOR) (Ishida, 2018: 160). India, the US, and Australia are key players in Japan's FOIP Strategy, intending for a free, open, and rules-based international order. India's look east policy and Japan's Indo-Pacific policy converge the strategic interests of both nations in the 21st century.

In his November 2017 visit to Japan, the US President highlighted the term *Indo-Pacific* (Ibid) and at the summit both Abe and Trump agreed to cooperate on Japan's Free and Open Indo-Pacific Strategy. The Quadrilateral Security Dialogue (Quad) supported the Indo-Pacific Strategy of Japan in the Manila meeting (Ibid). Zhang Jun, the Director General of the Department of International Economic Affairs of China's Foreign Ministry, stated that "there had not been a lot of discussion on the topic, but China needed to understand the idea of the *Indo-Pacific* better" (Ibid). After the Manila summit Geng Shuang (Chinese Foreign Ministry Spokesperson) remarked that "The US, Japan, India and Australia should not target Beijing. Indo-Pacific... should avoid politicising or excluding some relevant parties" (Ibid). Media in China raised eyebrows in the security agenda of the Quad and doubted that it has the potential to develop into an Asian NATO (Focus, 2017). In response to this, the media in Japan reported that "Its Indo-Pacific Strategy is not to check China, and Abe seems to decide to foster Japan-China cooperation for Japan's security and economic interests" (Ishida, 2018: 160).

Through FOIPS, Japan is addressing two important aspects related to its foreign policy – that is, engaging in *tactical hedging* to counter the uncertain strategic threats posed by the rising China's political and economic power in Asia and the US's uncertain policy towards the Asia-Pacific region (Koga, 2019: 286). Tactical hedging is "a declaratory policy doctrine that aims to utilize temporal strategic ambiguity to understand and determine whether any long-term strategy shift is necessary or possible" (Ibid). Japan has done proper analysis and homework to understand the strategic trends and principles with its partners like the US and AEAN and nurtured the concept of FOIP since 2016 (Ibid). The US's hardline policy towards China and ASEAN and Japan's strategic cooperation with them provide contrasting perceptions signalling the diminishing benefits of tactical hedging. If Japan wants to make FOIP a dynamic functioning concept, it must be clear in its political and strategic position towards China and ASEAN.

Japan took a positive approach and made efforts for improving its ties with India from the initial period of Narendra Modi's administration. They realised that strengthening the bilateral relationship between India and Japan is crucial for the Indo-Pacific region and its future. Japanese Foreign Minister Fumio Kishida stated that the partnership between Japan and India is a special one. It is a partnership that should drive the advent of the new era; an era when the Indo-Pacific region becomes the epicenter of global prosperity...the region still faces security vulnerabilities.

(Kishida, 2015)

It is very interesting to note that in 2016 at the VIth Tokyo International Conference on African Development (TICAD VI), Abe extended the geographical limit of the FOIP. He visualised the Indo-Pacific as a link between Japan and Africa (Abe, 2016). The focus was shifted to financial assistance, and he announced various projects and plans for Africa, including a 30 billion dollar infrastructure investment. Abe also highlighted the significance of international rules and norms as the bedrock of the Free and Open Indo-Pacific. He also stated that

When you cross the seas of Asia and the Indian Ocean and come to Nairobi, you then understand very well that what connects Asia and Africa is the sea lanes... Japan bears the responsibility of fostering the confluence of the Pacific and Indian Oceans and of Asia and Africa into a place that values freedom, the rule of law, and the market economy, free from force or coercion, and making it prosperous. Japan wants to work together with you in Africa in order to make the seas that connect the two continents into peaceful seas that are governed by the rule of law.

(Abe, 2016)

In the beginning, India and the Indian Ocean placed in Japan's foreign policy in the form of universal values. But Abe extended the scope and meaning of it by including many other purposes during his second term. The Indo-Pacific concept is still abstract in many ways. But it is very clear that this concept is leading Japan's approach to the Asian region, including South Asia, the Pacific, and Africa (Sahashi, 2019: 3). The Indo-Pacific approach of Japan sharpened their strategic thinking and diplomacy. In the context of China's rise they reflected a realist foreign policy and made efforts for the balance of power in Asia. They believed that the Indo-Pacific region is crucial for their economic growth and protecting common rules and norms, which are essential for their development. For Japan, the Indo-Pacific structure will build an order in the region protecting their interests (Ibid: 4).

There are different perceptions on Abe's FOIP. Those people who view China as a threat to the regional order and development consider it an exclusive concept. They consider FOIP a countering strategy against Chinese influence and power through the creation of a maritime network with regional powers through alliances like QUAD (Satake, 2019). They also view it as a response and alternative to China's One Belt One Road Initiative.

To some experts, FOIP is an inclusive concept that ultimately aims to incorporate China and other powers into an inclusive political and economic system in the Indo-Pacific (Satake, 2019). For them, Free and Open Indo-Pacific is a vision for development and progress through the network and development of maritime powers. It is a Japanese vision for regional development and connectivity. They are rejecting the idea that it is a counter-China strategy. Instead, they point out that as a long-term strategy in the context of shifting the centre of the global economy from Western Europe to the Indo-Pacific regions. Here Japan reflects their realist balancing strategy within the liberal international mechanism to establish a rule-based order for their long-term interests and benefits.

Japan's Geo-Strategic Interests in Indo-Pacific Reflect Realism

As mentioned earlier, Japan's "Free and Open Indo-Pacific" (FOIP) is the major policy of it towards the Indo-Pacific. The concept of FOIP includes three major aspects: "1) promotion and establishment of rule of law, freedom of navigation, free trade, etc.; 2) pursuit of economic prosperity (improving connectivity and strengthening economic partnerships) and 3) Commitment for peace and stability (capacity building on maritime law enforcement)" (Sahashi, 2019: 4). All the above aspects are significant, but they place the economic aspect before stability and peace. The abovementioned first principle of the Quad tells that it does not contain democracy, human rights, or even the Sustainable Development Goals (SDGs), but rather emphasises the rule of law in general, such as freedom of navigation and free trade (Ibid: 4).

Japan's national interests always go beyond its territories and the region. Over 90 percent of Japan's trade comes from sea lines of communication, and it depends on crude oil and natural gas mostly from the Middle East. A proposal from the Japan Institute of International Affairs (JIIA) asks Japan to allocate its resources to the Indo-Pacific as a priority. It suggests

> Japan should improve the security environment in Japan's vicinity and contributions to security in the Indo-Pacific region and ensure sufficient resources are allocated for Japan's defense and enhanced cooperation with other countries to improve the security environment in the Indo-Pacific region and secure the safety of sea lanes.
>
> *(Affairs, 2018)*

Rule-making and order-building are major strategies of Japan's foreign policy in the contemporary world order, especially in the Asian region. When international competition is intense, China and other emerging economies do not necessarily respect the rules-based international order. Issues like the South China Sea and other territorial disputes prioritise domestic politics over international stability. In the context of emerging comprehensive security threats like climate change, piracy, diseases, natural disasters, and human trafficking, migration, ethnic violence, etc., require a cooperative security mechanism to settle the issues. Hence, Japan needs to play a crucial role in rule-making and compliance (Sahashi, 2019: 4–5).

Strategic analysts argued that FOIP is the product of the geopolitical concerns of Japan in the context of rising China. Its actualisation is depicted as a "regional order-building strategy", rather than a mere geopolitical or geo-economic strategy, aimed at establishing a pluralistic and inclusive order incorporating various regional countries under common rules and norms. This order-building strategy highlights three important aspects: i) creating a stable (and multiple) power balance; (ii) promoting regional resilience, development, and connectivity; and (iii) rule-making and norm-setting – that Japan has pursued under the name of FOIPs (Ibid: 5). It is also interesting to note that Japan's cooperation with ASEAN will complement and play a critical role in the success of FOIPs as a regional order-building strategy in order to avoid the emergence of a "new Cold War" in the region. There is a developing consensus among Japan's governmental agencies that the Indo-Pacific is an arena for power politics, and FOIP as a foreign policy tool defines the Indo-Pacific as a place where diplomatic efforts, including security partnerships, should take place (Ibid).

In the midst of the "US-led Asian security system" and the "China-driven Asian economic system" new questions also emerged. This Asian system is in the process of excluding China in many ways. In this situation, countries like Japan and India have crucial roles in framing the security architecture of the region (Ishida, 2018: 163).

Free and Open Indo-Pacific: Japan's Balancing and Big Power Rivalry

Japan has a unique foreign policy based on the experience of feudalism and realism. It is determining the nature of its foreign policy on the basis of what is happening in international politics at that time. Rather than making changes in its course, it is more adapting to the situations and making benefits out of it (Pyle, 2007). After 2015, China's anti-Japan stand was very visible in the international political scenario. Shinzo Abe, Taro Aso, and Yasuo Fukuda – the three Liberal Democratic Party (LDP) cabinets faced the question of how to handle an assertive China in rise. Shinzo Abe and Taro Aso responded to the situation by following a policy of anti-China and containing it through an assertive Japan. But Yasuo Fukuda took a stand of strategic partnership and cooperation with China. From the Kozumi administration onwards, there was a clear attempt from the part of Japan to incorporate India and Australia into the diplomatic efforts of Japan as a balancer against the potential challenger China. From 2009 to December 2011, with a vision and strong political commitment, the Democratic Party of Japan changed the diplomatic approaches from the traditional pattern and thinking. Prime Minister Yukio Hotoyama adopted an East Asian Community approach, Prime Minister Yoshiko Noda's policy of the nationalisation of the Seneku Islands and Prime Minister Naoto Kan's Trans-Pacific Partnership are the major changes from the conventional approach. But their alternative attempts have not produced any serious results (Ishida, 2018: 170).

Issues over the Senkaku Islands in 2010 and 2012 had frozen the relationship between China and Japan. Leaders from both Japan and China met in 2014 at the meeting of the Asia Pacific Economic Cooperation (APEC), but it has not made any significant progress. From 2017 onwards, progress was visible in their relationship. Japan's surprise decision to attend the One Belt One Road Initiative conference through the participation of Toshihiro Nikai, Secretary General of Japan's ruling Liberal Democratic Party (LDP), and Takaya Imai, the Prime Minister's Secretary for Political Affairs, signalled its willingness to co-operate with China in many economic affairs. Nikai carried the direct message of Abe to Xi in the meeting and clearly stated that Japan would participate in the China-led Asian Infrastructure Investment Bank (AIIB). Abe undoubtedly cleared that it will participate in the OBOR and will cooperate with China in many economic and infrastructure projects (Sahashi, 2017).

Chinese Premier Li Keqiang made a successful visit to Japan in May 2018. Subsequently Shinzo Abe made a historic return visit to China in October 2018. It was a first meeting by a Japanese Prime Minister in China in seven years. During the visit, both countries signed on three important aspects: *to change from strategic competition to cooperation, avoid mutual threats, and to promote a mutually beneficial fair global trade* (Sahashi, 2019: 6). US President Trump had taken a tough stand against North Korea in 2017. Many people believed that this situation would create hostility between Japan and China. So, the Chinese government made various efforts to strengthen their relationship and to hedge against America. A professor of Chinese politics at the University of Tokyo – Shin Kawashima stated that "the Chinese leadership expressed their hope that Japan and China could combine forces to take the United States head on. But the likelihood of such a joint Japan–China pushback against the United States is slim" (Kawashima, 2018). Even though Japan and China made some progress in their relationship, subsequent incidents tell us the fact that the progress was not substantial. In the East China Sea problem and the food security issue, it was very visible. But the attempts of both nations revealed a fact that both nations want to improve their relations on economic and bureaucratic affairs.

The Japanese government has taken a lot of initiatives to balance and counter China's strategic Belt and Road Initiatives and periphery diplomacy. The Abe administration declared a Development Co-operation charter in 2015 and revised the previous name of the Official Development Assistance (ODI), which was declared in 1992 and revised in 2003. Japan started to cooperate with many international organisations and other countries on many quality infrastructure investment projects. They collaborated with the Asian Development Bank (ADB). In the area of quality infrastructure investment in Asia, they spend approximately US$110 billion in five years. This has improved the financial ties and cooperation with the private sector in the region and the world (Abe, 2015).

The Indo-Pacific strategy of Japan is a culmination of linkages between two continents and two free and open seas. The basic intention behind the linkages and connectedness is stability and development of the region. This Free and Open Indo-Pacific strategy will increase the linkages and cooperation between Asia, the Middle East and Africa. It will create stability and peace in the region as a whole. In Asia, Japan will engage with infrastructure development and trade. But in the case of Africa, it will help the process of development, politics, and governance of the region. Japan never involves and engage through a hegemonic nature; instead, it will join together for mutual trust and engagement. Japan's strategy is now expanded through strengthening ties with the QUAD (MFOA, 2017).

The Free and Open Indo-Pacific strategy of Japan is a geostrategy basically against China's maritime interests and objectives. But this policy never directly contains the OBOR initiative of China. However, it demands and promotes China's creative role as a responsible player in the rules-based Indo-Pacific region. It also invites US presence and participation in the Asian region. This is relevant in the context of the US Asia Pivot policy. The FOIP policy also ensures the participation of India, the US, and Australia and a strategic partnership with all these nations through various efforts.

The US and Japan have conflicting views regarding China which shapes the FOIP. The US considers China as a strategic competitor. Trump administration's National Security Strategy Report and Mike Pence's Hudson Institute lecture on 4 October 2018 justify this argument. So from the US perspective, Freedom of Open and Indo Pacific is also an effort to counter China in the strategic-political and economic realms. All approaches of the US towards the Indo-Pacific are constructs to strategically contain the expansionist and assertive ambitions of China (Sahashi, 2019: 7). Japanese diplomacy in the contemporary period aims to maintain the US-led, post-war international order in the Asia-Pacific as the balance of power shifts. More than its ties and friendship with the US, "Japan's Asia diplomacy has been securitized through sustained efforts to build and enhance both bilateral and multilateral security partnerships in the region" (Sahashi, 2018).

It is very interesting to note that the United States' diplomatic efforts and commitment to the Indo-Pacific region accelerated the speed and density of the cooperation between the US and Japan in the region and ensured more presence of the US in the region. By combining the theatres of East Asia, South Asia, the Indian Ocean, and the Western Pacific, Washington has created the Indo-Pacific framework. This framework envisions cooperating with like-minded nations to sustain a regional order based on rules. A comprehensive, context-specific assessment of the larger region is also constrained by the US's lack of attention to the Indian Ocean under the Indo-Pacific strategy. Pushing the Indian Ocean to become merely an appendix to the Pacific Ocean could endanger long-term US national interests in the face of growing Chinese presence and influence in the region (Saha, 2023).

The shared interest between the US and Japan ensures support for FOIP in the Indo-Pacific region. However, Japan is more concerned about US-China policy due to several reasons. *First*, they fear the unstable Trump policy towards China (Barnes, 2019). *Second*, US external economic ambitions are always driven by "US first" policy. But Japan's interests lie with a rule-based order for fair trade in matters of subsidies, support for State-Owned Enterprises (SOEs). US interests in trade with Beijing always prioritise the issue of trade deficit and its reduction. Their interest is not to satisfy Japan or other developed/developing economies. *Third*, Japan fears the US policy of control in FDI (Foreign Direct Investment) and its control over technology. However, US strategic concerns about China compel them for the control of International student visas, the Export Control Reform Act (ECRA), cooperative research projects, and technologies through legislation to strengthen the Committee on Foreign Investment in the United States (CFIUS) (Sahashi, 2019: 8). Japan also fears whether the US will make unilateral decisions and restrictions against foreign companies engaged in transnational trade and business. If the US does so, it will affect Japan's developmental interests in the region. However, Japan needed a partnership with a hegemonic maritime power – the US – as a trading nation far from the sources of energy and natural resources, dependent on exporting manufactured goods for economic growth, and dependent on the security of the sea lanes for trade. This alliance ensured that the Western Pacific and Indian Oceans were connected, bringing Japan's economic survival and defending its territorial integrity from outside threats (Sato, 2019: 109).

Japan is always interested in promoting a more open and inclusive world under the Free and Open Indo Pacific for its economic interests. They always reject a China centric world order. Instead, they promote their security interests for their own development and economic progress. They are also negating the United States's unilateral strategies to counter China. Instead, they are following a multi-lateral rule making strategy to counter China.

President of the National Graduate Institute for Policy Studies, Akihiko Tanaka, stated that

> Japan's goals in the era of U.S.-China competition [New Cold War] should not be metamorphosed into a hot war and Japan should make efforts not only for strengthening the U.S.-Japan alliance for deterrence but also for enlarging a sphere for *peaceful co-existence* with China... Japan should not give up shaping Chinese models of development and political reforms in the future.
>
> *(Tanaka, 2018: 37)*

Japan undoubtedly has declared that FOIP's intention is not to contain China in the world order. Instead, it is trying to bring a balance between cooperation and competition with Beijing. They also want to encourage the regional players to follow the rules and norms shaping China's response in the world order. Japan's Freedom of Indo Pacific strategy aligns with the interests of Quadrilateral Security Dialogue (Quad) and the security dialogue between Japan, Australia, India, and the United States. Quad aims for strategic cooperation in the areas of maritime security, terrorism, and freedom of navigation. Japan's FOIP's interests also converge with the interests of the Quad in these matters. The Asia Reassurance Initiative Act of 2018 enables US support for FOIP and a rules-based international order. But the US attitude many times raised doubts regarding its commitment towards regional organisations and institutions as a space for diplomatic engagement on rules and norms under FOIP. The best examples are Trump's absence from the East Asia Summit and Asia-Pacific Economic Cooperation (APEC) Forum in November 2018 (Szechenyi and Hosoya, 2019). Japan also fears US competition and strategic conflict with China on many matters because they fear that it will also affect their long-term economic and strategic interests in the region.

Now Japan's policy-making regarding China and the Indo-Pacific region is more challenging in nature. Because Japan wants to cooperate with China on many fronts. They want to establish stability in its relationship with Beijing. That is why they are changing their perceptions regarding FOIP and considering them as a *concept* rather than a *strategy*. This change from *concept* to *strategy* tells us the fact that they are interested in bringing many players to the region and cooperating with them including South East Asian nations. But contrary to the Japanese position, the Trump administration wants to engage in strategic competition with China with strong containment policies. This brings challenges to Japan in policy making.

In order to shape the strategic and developmental aspects of the Indo-Pacific region, it needs both Japan and the US to adopt a comprehensive security strategy that is more inclusive and open in character. It must preserve regional diversity and be able to manage China's rise and competition. The alliances and cooperation need to provide deterrence and reassurance, offering both risks and opportunities for their allies. Shinzo Abe declared FOIP as a framework for their regional strategy that respects the values of freedom, rule of law, and fair trade. Sometimes Japan clearly states that FOIP is not for containing China's strategic inroads or infrastructure development.

From all the above analysis, it is very clear that the US-Japan interests are not perfectly matching in all perspectives and interests. But the engagement between the two will help them to identify the areas of cooperation and conflict. It will enable them to engage in novel ways with the nations whose interests are converging on FOIP and in many other areas of development. The change in perception of FOIP from a *strategy* to the *concept* is giving great flexibility to Japan to develop a balancing strategy against China without hurting both nations' cooperative interests. Thus, the ambiguity of FOIP is also a strength for Japan in this context. Even though the ultimate objective and structure of FOIP are vague in nature, it will give ample space, framework, and imagination to work Japan in a multilateral world order by facing the challenges posing from the Indo-Pacific.

Japan and the Quad for a *Rules-Based* Order

The Quad was revived in 2017 with the purpose to create a rules-based order in the Indo-Pacific. Initially, it was started as an alliance of India, Japan, the US, and Australia in response to the Tsunami in the Indian Ocean (Envall, 2019: 1). After its formation, it quickly engaged in strategic competition in the Asian region and collapsed in 2008. Even though the interests of the Quad nations are diverging in many aspects, the revival of it in 2017 highlights the converging interests in economic development and strategic challenges in the changing context. In the current regional dynamics, Japan's strategy demonstrates internal and external balancing by reframing the pacifist nature on the one hand and reinforcing its alliance with the US and building a universal value-based network of maritime powers in the Indo-Pacific on the other (Basu, 2019: 1). In this regard, the US-Japan Security Consultative Committee is pursuing the common strategic objective of building partnerships within trilateral and quadrilateral frameworks with India (Ibid). Policies are pushing for constructing "multi-layered cooperative relationships with allies and partners, with the Japan-US alliance as the cornerstone" (Ibid).

Australia is also interested in constructing a multipolar rules-based order not only with other Quad nations but also with China and other Southeast Asian Nations. India is already dissatisfied with the existing alignments and rules. Its strategic engagement with China and Russo-Sino-Indian trilateral framework is a kind of system based on soft balancing in international relations. India's security and strategic cooperation with the US and Japan have resulted from India's feelings of insecurity and security mismatch with Chinese power (Hanada, 2018: 16). Hence, the Quad is considered as a framework for the existing rules-based order led by the US.

Japan's interest to pursue the Quad is the result of China's assertive rise and dominance in the region. Its concern is increasing in the context of the territorial dispute over a set of islands in the East China Sea (Senkakus in Japan and the Diaoyutai in China). This is compelling Japan to adopt a regional order which is promoting the economic and strategic interest of it in many ways. In order to balance the security threats from China, Japan is interested in following a maritime periphery, particularly with India. Defence White Paper of Japan in 2009 has also mentioned the expansion of China's defence capabilities in space, cyberspace, and the electromagnetic spectrum, and increased military activities in the Indo-Pacific region (Mehra, 2020). Japan's Official Development Assistance policy has also significantly attached the Indo-Pacific as a priority region.

There are many ambiguities regarding Quad in its present form. But it reflects the interest of big powers in the Indo-Pacific region. ASEAN also emphasises the significance of regional connectivity and the importance of economic interdependence for regional stability and peace (Saha, 2018). Regarding China's trade 75 percent crude oil going through the Indian Ocean and the Strait of Malacca on maritime transportation. Japan's Policy of Indo-Pacific and Quad will definitely increase security threats to China's sea lanes of communication.

Japan's multilateral initiatives and efforts are bringing new challenges and pressures to China. At the same time, the Indo-Pacific strategy and Quad will allow Japan to face its security risks and sharpen its diplomatic framework in line with its own national security interests.

When the strategic competition and conflict are increasing in the Indo-Pacific region, Japan and the US are furthering the vision of FOIP. In this context, strategic experts are evaluating the FOIP and developments in the region as the result of an *order* transition rather than a *power* transition.

At the time of the COVID-19 pandemic, the Quad also engaged in soft security aspects such as vaccine development and distribution. This highlighted the Quad's position as first movers in the areas of specific functional challenges. In the perspective of health diplomacy in the region as a soft power tool, expanding global vaccine supply is an example of reaching out to low- and middle-income countries and also to countries with smaller economies. Strengthening such cooperative efforts and soft power mechanisms will allow the Quad to balance its cooperative and competitive outlook in the region, linking its security with prosperity and development objectives (Upadhyay, 2021). The COVID-19 pandemic has changed the nature of the international political economy and market. It has increased the pressures on the structure of international trade and economic integration. It has also strengthened the political will for the reconfiguration, rebalancing, and resilience of supply chains. This Quad grouping has changed the landscape of Asian regional politics and has woven a concrete vision for the future of the Indo-Pacific that will also include the participation of more non-Quad members. Japan basically intends this aspect through a rules-based order rather than a power-based one.

Conclusion

The post-Cold War landscape of international politics is moving towards a cooperative multilateral security framework in the context of comprehensive security threats and economic integration. The transformation from a hegemonic US-led world order to a multipolar world order with the rise of China is more complicated in nature. The geo-strategic compulsions, economic factors, and an emerging multipolar system are driving Japan from tactical hedging to its strategic vision. From a theoretical perspective, Japan's vision is the result of the realist balancing strategy in the liberal international mechanism to achieve its long-term interests and goals in the context of the complex international situation coupled with China's rise and its strategic competition and conflict with the US. Japanese firms have established a strong presence in the Chinese economy. These firms' economic engagements are being threatened directly and indirectly by the ongoing trade war between the US and China (Sato, 2019: 115). In this context, Japan following a realist hedging strategy which will enable it to continue to enjoy the economic benefits of engaging both the US and China on most-favourable terms under multilateral liberal economic rules. At the same time, they are also trying to minimise the cost of collective defence with the US and seeking diversified security partnerships to possibly supplement the declining US credibility in countering the Chinese threats and encouraging key states in the Indo-Pacific region not to bandwagon with China.

In the Indo-Pacific, Japan's strategic interests lie in the concept of the Free and Open Indo-Pacific, but Japan wants to maintain a "rule-based" order rather than a "power-based" one. Japan's Indo-Pacific concept clearly looks towards the west for an integrated regional economic sphere beyond East Asia. The US–Japan Strategic alliance is the major springboard for Japan in its policy towards the Indo-Pacific region. A multipolar world order, maritime security, cooperation, freedom of navigation, commerce, and naval operability are in Japan's interests in the region. US engagement in the region is critical for maintaining this multilateral rule-based order. Japan's foreign policy emphasises its security interests and rejects a global order that is Sino-centric in nature. However, it simultaneously continues to seek a more open and inclusive region under FOIP for its own realist strategic interest and economic survival. It is also promoting multilateral rule-making to counter American unilateral policies against China. This reflects Japan's realist balancing strategy in the liberal international dynamics. Japan's emphasis on multilateral rules shows its status-quo orientation, which intends to bind not only China's military and economic manoeuvring in the region but also the US tendency to resort to nationalistic economic policy towards the region (Ibid: 116). In the current regional dynamics, Japan's strategy demonstrates internal and external realist balancing by reorienting the pacifist posture on the one hand and reinforcing its alliance with the US and building a universal value-based network of allies in the Indo-Pacific on the other. The success of Japan's strategy lies in the extension of regional economic integration, assisted by its infrastructure aid and private investments, soliciting partnerships of other Quad members and offering alternatives to the Chinese-led BRI projects. In the context of the converging geo-strategic interests of the US, ASEAN, and the Quad, Japan's attempt at a rule-based order depends upon its ability to balance the big power rivalry in the Indo-Pacific region through strong leadership and strategic vision.

References

Abe, S. (2015). The Future of Asia: Be Innovative. Retrieved April 21, 2018, from http://japan.kantei.go.jp/97_abe/statement/201505/0521foaspeech.html

Abe, S. (2016). Sixth Tokyo International Conference on African Development (TICAD VI). Retrieved Novemebr 24, 2019, from http://www.mofa.go.jp/afr/af2/page4e_000496.html

Affairs, T. J. (2018). A New Security Strategy for Addressing the Challenges in the Turbulent International Order: 11 Recommendations for the Defense of Japan. Retrieved December 30, 2019, from https://www2.jiia.or.jp/en/pdf/recommendations/A_New_Security_Strategy_for_Addressing_the_Challenges_in_the_Turbulent_International_Order.pdf

Barnes, J. E., and Satariano, S. (2019, March 17). U.S. Campaign to Ban Huawei Overseas Stumbles as Allies Resist. *The NewYork Times.*

Basu, T. (2019). *QUAD and India's Multi Alignment.* New Delhi: Institue of Defence Studies and Analysis.

Envall, H. D. (2019). *The Quadrilateral Security Dialogue: Towards an Indo-Pacific Order.* Singapore: Rajaratanam School of International Studies, Nanyang Technological University.

Focus, C.-U. (2017). China-US Focus. Retrieved December 22, 2019, from https://www.chinausfocus.com/foreign-policy/china-this-week-the-indo-pacific-a-new-american-strategy-for-asia

Hanada, R. (2018). The Role of U.S.-Japan-Australia-India Cooperation, or the "Quad" in FOIP: A Policy Coordination Mechanism for a Rules-Based Order. Centre for Strategic International Studies.

Ishida, Y. (2018). China's OBOR Initiative and Japan's Response: The Abe Doctrine, Free and Open Indo-Pacific Strategy and Japan-India Strategic Partnership. In T. B. Jagannath & P. Panda (Eds.), *China-India-Japan in the Indo-Pacific: Ideas, Interests and Infrastructure* (pp. 159–188). New Delhi: Pentagon Press.

Kawashima, S. (2018, November 1). A New Norm in China–Japan Relations? Retrieved December 22, 2019, from https://www.eastasiaforum.org/2018/11/01/a-new-norm-in-china-japan-relations/

Kishida, F. (2015). Special Partnership for the Era of the Indo-Pacific. Retrieved Novemebr 22, 2019, from http://www.mofa.go.jp/s_sa/sw/in/page3e_000291.html

Koga, K. (2019). Japan's Free and Open Indo-Pacific Strategy: Tokiyo's Tacticcal Hedging and the implications for ASEAN. *Contemporary Southeast Asia*, 41(2), 286–313.

Mehra, J. (2020). *The Australia-India-Japan-US Quadrilateral: Dissecting the China Factor*. New Delhi: Observer Research Foundation.

MFOA. (2017). Diplomatic Blue Book 2017. Retrieved June 21, 2020, from https://www.mofa.go.jp/files/000290287.pdf

Pyle, K. (2007). *Japan Rising – The Resurgence of Japanese Power and Purpose*. New York: Public Affairs TM.

Saha, P. (2018). *The Quad in the Indo-Pacific: Why ASEAN Remains Cautious*. New Delhi: Observer Research Foundation.

Saha, R. (2023, February 3). Prioritizing the Indian Ocean in US Indo-Pacific Strategy. Retrieved July 17, 2023, from Stimson: https://www.stimson.org/2023/prioritizing-the-indian-ocean-in-us-indo-pacific-strategy/

Sahashi, R. (2017). East Asia Forum. Retrieved January 15, 2020, from https://www.eastasiaforum.org/2017/06/06/japans-strategic-hedging-under-trump/

Sahashi, R. (2018). American Power in Japanese Security Strategy. In M. H. Andrew O'Neil (Ed.), *China's Rise and Australia–Japan–US Relations Primacy and Leadership in East Asia* (pp. 143–166). London: Edward Elger.

Sahashi, R. (2019). The Indo-Pacific in Japan's Foreign Policy. Retrieved December 29, 2019, from http://csis-website-prod.s3.amazonaws.com/s3fs-public/FINAL_Working%20Paper_Ryo%20Sahashi.pdf

Satake, T. (2019). Japan's "Free and Open Indo-Pacific Strategy" and Its Implication for ASEAN. In M. C. Daljit Singh (Ed.), *Southeast Asian Affairs 2019* (pp. 69–82). Singaopore: ISEAS–Yusof Ishak Institute.

Sato, Y. (2019, Winter). Japan's Indo-Pacific Strategy: The Old Geography and the New Strategic Reality. *Journal of Indo-Pacific Affairs*, 2(4), 107–119.

Szechenyi, N. and Hosoya, Y. (2019, October, 10). Working Toward a Free and Open Indo-Pacific. (C. E. Peace, Producer) Retrieved March 11, 2020, from https://carnegieendowment.org/2019/10/10/working-toward-free-and-open-indo-pacific-pub-80023

Tanaka, A. (2018, November). From Trade War to 'A New Cold War'. *Chuo Koron*, pp. 36–37.

Upadhyay, S. (2021). Covid-19 and Quad's "Soft" Reorientation. *Research in Globalization*, 3, pp. 1-6. https://www.sciencedirect.com/journal/research-in-globalization/special-issue/106G09N4486

9

INDIA'S INTERESTS AND STRATEGIES IN THE INDO-PACIFIC

Uma Purushothaman

The term the "Indo-Pacific" has today become a virtual catchphrase in understanding contemporary geopolitics and geo-economics. It reflects the shift of economic and political influence to this region, substituting the term the "Asia-Pacific".

While the origins of the phrase as a strategic concept have been attributed to many, including the German geopolitician, Karl Haushofer, in the 1920s and 1930s (Sempa, 2015), the Indian historian Kalidas Nag in 1941, and then reused by Indian naval analyst Captain Gurpreet Khurana in 2007 in an article in IDSA's journal *Strategic Analyses*, the term gained strategic currency after Japanese Prime Minister Shinzo Abe's now famous speech in the Indian Parliament titled "Confluence of the Two Seas" in 2007 (Oak, 2019). It became an essential phrase in academic discourse after the publication of its Defence White Paper in 2013 by Australia. The final stamp of legitimacy was conferred on the term when the Trump administration started referring to the "Indo-Pacific region" during President Donald Trump's first tour to Asia in November 2017, using it instead of the "Asia-Pacific" in official documents and renaming its oldest and largest military command – the Hawaii-based Pacific Command or PACOM – in June 2018 to the Indo-Pacific Command. The US NSS 2017 describes the Indo-Pacific as a priority area. Regional countries too have accepted the concept with the East Asia Summit (EAS) of 2018 discussing the concept.

However, awareness in India about the importance of the Indo-Pacific to India's maritime security environment is not new. Nehru in his *Discovery of India* had written that the Pacific would replace the Atlantic as the centre of geopolitics:

DOI: 10.4324/9781003479307-11

The Pacific is likely to take the place of the Atlantic in the future as a nerve centre of the world. Though not directly a Pacific state, India will inevitably exercise an important influence there. India will also develop as the centre of economic and political activity in the Indian Ocean area, in south-east Asia and right up to the Middle East. Her position gives an economic and strategic importance in a part of the world which is going to develop rapidly in the future.

(Nehru, 1985: 536)

The diplomat and historian K.M. Panikkar, too, had emphasised on the need to engage with the littoral states of the Indo-Pacific and argued that "India never lost her independence till she lost the command of the sea in the first decade of the sixteenth century" (1945: 7). In fact, Panikkar strongly decried the neglect of maritime power in India's defence, arguing that the assumption that the "security of India is a matter exclusively of the North-West Frontier and of a strong enough army to resist any aggression across the Hindu Khush" is a one-sided view (Ibid.). He further argued that since the 16th century, India's future has been determined not by "on the oceanic expanse which washes the three sides of India" but by land frontiers. Writing in 1945, Panikkar could not have foreseen the four and a half wars that India fought, which were mostly on land. Panikkar in his conclusion writes that unlike other countries, India is entirely dependent on the Indian Ocean and that its national interests have been in the Indian Ocean because trade was conducted over the Indian Ocean. He warns, "a true appreciation of Indian historical forces will show beyond doubt that whoever controls the Indian Ocean has India at his mercy" (Ibid., p. 83). Therefore, the Indian Ocean must remain "truly Indian" as "India cannot exist without the Indian Ocean being free" (Ibid., p. 84).

Both Nehru and Panikkar were remarkably prescient in understanding the role of the seas in determining India's future as a major power. Despite Nehru and despite Panikkar, however, India's security orientation till the 2000s remained mostly a continental one. India saw itself as a continental power and pumped in resources to its army and air force, often to the neglect of the Indian Navy, which became the Cinderella of the three wings of the armed forces.

But today, there seems to be a fresh rethinking of this approach. What is new is the fact that today the narratives around the Indo-Pacific are driven by the West thanks to the rise of China, the consequent anxieties of regional states as well as that of the West and the region's geo-economic and geo-strategic importance. So, the West, which historically controls all strategic narratives globally, is now more accepting of India's centrality in this particular geography. On its part, India itself has woken up to the potential and challenges that the Indo-Pacific offers and is beginning to see itself as a maritime power and is rediscovering and reasserting its old maritime traditions and links. India's geographical positioning, long coastlines, status as an emerging power, and blue water naval capabilities make India the most significant stakeholder in the idea of the Indo-Pacific. India began to officially use the term in official communiques after Prime Minister Narendra Modi took office in 2014. Modi put forth India's vision of the Indo-Pacific at the Shangri La dialogue in 2018. India's vision, as articulated by the Prime Minister, was in tune with the general norms articulated by regional powers like the US, Japan, Australia, and Indonesia and placed ASEAN at the heart of the Indo-Pacific.

India's Interests in the Indo-Pacific

India has three major foreign policy interests in the Indo-Pacific: 1) the need to have a favourable balance of power in the region; 2) geo-economic interests, i.e. to protect and promote its trade in the Indo-Pacific; 3) both of these goals build into the third one, i.e. India's larger strategic goal which is to emerge as a great power and to be able to project power abroad.

The first goal is a euphemism to refer to the need to manage China's rise as India does not want a hegemon in the region. Their border issue remains unresolved. The Doklam crisis in 2017 and the Galwan standoff in 2020 have made the China threat more real and dimmed hopes in India of a bonhomie between the two Asian neighbours. But the issues between India and China go beyond just the contestation over their borders. As Nehru himself had said, the rivalry between the two neighbours is not just about territory, it is about who would have a more dominating position than the other on the border and in Asia itself (quoted in Mohan, 2013, p. 24). As India and China rise and begin to look beyond their traditional maritime spaces, China in the Indian Ocean and India in the Pacific Ocean, both are wary of the expanding naval profile of the other in waters close to their territories (Ibid: 4–5). Beijing's forays into India's neighbourhood, in Sri Lanka and Pakistan, and its increasing influence in the Indian subcontinent have led to concerns about India being surrounded by China (China's assets around India were described as a "string of pearls" by analysts) and India's exercises with the US, Japan, and regional powers in the Western Pacific and its expanding ties with Vietnam are watched with deep suspicion in China. India and China have also been competing for influence in the Indian Ocean Region – India because it sees itself as the legitimate power based on its physical presence and China to protect its SLOCS (Sea Lines of Communication) that are key to its energy imports and trade routes. New Delhi's Indian Ocean strategy is therefore "meant to compensate for continental power inadequacies in any border conflict by taking action against Chinese interests in the Indian Ocean" (Brewster, 2015: 57). Another cause of the competition is India's perception that China is unwilling to allow India to become the leading power in the region (Brewster, 2014: 143). As a result, both countries have been expanding their naval capabilities in order to project more power into the Indian Ocean region and to build economic and political influence in the littoral states. Thus, the rivalry is developing into one for influence across regions.

The second goal, in the context of the Indo-Pacific, refers to the need to protect the Sea Lanes of Communication, or (SLOCs), and to develop trade relations with the countries of the Indo-Pacific. As a country which follows the liberal international order, India wants freedom of navigation and the rule of law to be followed by all states for unfettered trade. 95% of India's international trade by volume and over 70% by value is carried over the seas (Singh, 2024). This is particularly true of energy trade. "Taking into account the total oil imports by sea, offshore oil production and petroleum exports, the country's cumulative 'sea dependence' for oil is estimated to be about 93%" (Indian Navy, 2015: 26). As one of the fastest-growing economies, India needs a steady supply of oil and gas for which it depends on imports transported over the seas. Moreover, New Delhi is greatly dependent on the Indian Ocean's resources, like fishing resources and mineral resources. The former President of India, Mr Ram Nath Kovind, stated in December 2017 that "Today, our maritime interests are directly linked to India's economy and security, and to the well-being of our people" (Kovind, 2017). Though the Indian shipping industry is growing, given the pace and needs of national development, its dependence on foreign shipping will continue (Ibid.). As the Indian Maritime strategy published in 2015 says (Ibid.),

> There is also a significant presence of Indian nationals in the international seafaring community, operating on both Indian and foreign ships, with approximately 6.6% of the world's merchant mariners being Indian. The overall safety and security of Indian seaborne trade and seafarers, on both Indian and foreign ships, require that international shipping and sea routes remain safe, secure and free for navigation and legitimate uses.
> *(Kovind, 2018)*

Therefore, "given the size of their economies, rapid growth and the expanding international component of their economic activity" post globalisation, "protecting seaborne trade has become an important justification" for both India and China for their investments in naval modernisation (Mohan, 2013: 41) leading to the classic security dilemma at sea. Both countries see their dependence on imported natural resources as a strategic vulnerability (Ibid: 43) as it is related to domestic tranquillity and growth rates and as each seeks to decrease this vulnerability, the other feels threatened.

Finally, as India's geostrategic frontier vis-à-vis China is slowly expanding eastwards from the Indian Ocean, New Delhi wants to develop a credible strategic deterrence against China (quoted in Kuo, 2018). The "Indo-Pacific" construct provides India with a valuable opportunity to partner with the resident countries and major stakeholder powers of the Indo-Pacific, with whom its interests converge (Ibid.). The Indo-Pacific construct thus gives centrality to India, allowing it to project power and become a norm shaper.

The normalisation of the Indo-Pacific construct has benefited India in many ways (Oak, 2019). First, India has received due recognition as a responsible regional player capable of acting as a net security provider. This allows it to rationalise and justify its interest and presence in Southeast Asia and East Asia. Second, it allows India to expand its partnership with the US and its allies, which in turn, gives India access to advanced technology, critical resources, and military hardware that were absent earlier. Third, as an integral part of the regional architecture, India has had the opportunity to not only follow the norms but also set them and increase its influence in international affairs. Finally, the construct has given India an additional lever to deal with China.

India's Strategies

India has put in place several tactics and strategies to achieve its objectives in the Indo-Pacific. India is slowly becoming a net security provider and a first responder in the Indo-Pacific because of this. Most of these tactics and strategies were initiated by New Delhi on its own, but some were initiated by others, to which India joined.

The most talked about strategy is the Quad or the Quadrilateral of the US, Australia, Japan, and India, a "concert of democracies" perhaps. An informal strategic dialogue among these countries, the Quad has long been thought of as the most effective multilateral strategy to manage China's rise given the presence of the US, its treaty allies, Australia and Japan, as well as India, the only credible regional challenger to China. India had reservations about the idea initially due to concern over China's sensitivities but is no longer shy of calling the Quad by its name, partly due to the downturn in India-China relations. In fact, the Quad has now been elevated to the political level with the foreign ministers of the member states meeting three times already. The members of the Quad have also conducted joint military exercises and pledged to work together to promote a free and open Indo-Pacific. The Quad leaders have already had three in-person summits. The Quad leaders agreed on principles for critical technology, secure software, and clean energy and pledged $50 billion in aid to the Indo-Pacific region over five years. All of these are steps towards institutionalising the Quad.

At its most fundamental level, the Quad stands for a free, inclusive, and open Indo-Pacific and freedom of the seas and traces its origins to the

138 Uma Purushothaman

collaborative humanitarian and disaster relief efforts by the four countries after the Tsunami in 2004. While the members have conducted some military activities together, what it does is to serve the "limited purpose of political signalling and improve coordination among a set of like-minded and capable maritime powers in the Indo-Pacific" (Jaishankar, 2018). Moreover, "these four countries enjoy unprecedented levels of information and intelligence exchanges, personnel interactions, interoperable equipment and habits of cooperation" (Ibid.). More than quadrilateral relations, the members of the Quad have a matrix of strong bilateral and trilateral relations and political, military, and economic relations with each other, and this is what makes it unique, particularly since it has not yet been institutionalised.

However, one must keep in mind that all three of India's partners in the Quad have deeper ties at least economically with China than with India. Also, the ASEAN is wary of the Indo-Pacific concept, as it fears that it will undermine ASEAN's centrality in developing a regional security architecture in Asia and push them, with the concept's seemingly anti-Chinese thrust, to choose between the US and China, which they have so far been reluctant to do (Sibal, 2019). Moreover, related to this is the US's unwillingness to extend to India the same kind of trust it has for its Anglo-Saxon allies. For instance, the announcement of the AUKUS (Australia, the UK, the US) security pact in 2021 again kindled fears in India about how serious the US is in actually thwarting China with India in the lead and how much India can trust the US when even a NATO ally, France, was not informed about the AUKUS. There is worry whether AUKUS will upstage or dilute the Quad or complement the Quad. Finally, there appears to be some divergence of opinion about the Quad's purpose. After the COVID-19 pandemic, India wants the Quad to concentrate on development issues rather than military issues only as the US wants. Hence, there has been more emphasis on initiatives such as vaccine production and delivery. It has donated 79 million doses of vaccines so far. COVID-19 has also made militaries less prepared as they are not able to undertake large-scale exercises and there is an argument that post COVID-19, states will take pathogenic security more seriously in the long-term (Kim et al., 2020). Then there is the question of the US' priorities and how invested it will be in the Indo-Pacific. With the Russian invasion of Ukraine, it looks likely that US attention will shift to European security rather than the security of the Indo-Pacific. The US withdrawal from Afghanistan also leaves the US much less invested in the Indo-Pacific.

Act East Policy

As Prime Minister Modi has said, "India's Act East Policy is an important part of our Indo-Pacific vision" (Modi, 2019). So, the Act East Policy and India's Indo-Pacific vision have dovetailed now. The Act East policy was essentially meant to intensify India's interactions with the countries of Southeast Asia. This was to be done by drawing on the historical links between landlocked and underdeveloped north East region and South East Asia and deepening connectivity with them. The idea was to help the North East to develop and to prevent it from becoming an arena for insurgents and Chinese influence. The Act East Policy now has a security orientation as well with India stepping up its military, particularly naval ties, with the countries of the region. In tandem with Act East, in 2015, the Indian Navy promulgated its new maritime security strategy, which expanded India's "areas of maritime interest" to the entire western and southwestern Pacific Ocean (Kuo, 2018). India's status as a strategic partner of ASEAN and its membership in the EAS further enhance India's role in the region.

The Indo-Pacific Division

At the structural level, the Ministry of External Affairs created a new Indo-Pacific division in 2019. The division describes its remit as being two-fold: "to help consolidate India's vision of the Indo-Pacific across Government of India...and to provide substantive policy elements and programmes to that vision" (MEA, 2020: 1). It brings together the multilateral elements of the erstwhile Indian Ocean and ASEAN Multilateral divisions and includes groupings like the Indian Ocean Rim Association, the East Asia Summit, the Forum for India-Pacific Island Cooperation (FIPIC), and certain political-military functions, showing India's intention to bring a renewed focus on the region.

Regionalism

India has been focusing on cooperating with the smaller countries in the region to deepen maritime cooperation. It has been playing an active role in reviving the Indian Ocean Rim Association and the Indian Ocean Naval Symposium (IONS), as well as in promoting BIMSTEC. It is also a founding member of the Indian Ocean Rim Association (IORA).

At the tactical level, India has been focusing a lot on building its naval capabilities, operations, interoperability, capacity building in other states, building maritime domain awareness, and Humanitarian Assistance and disaster relief (Jaishankar, 2019b).

Operations

Since 2017, the Navy has been carrying out and increasing its mission-based deployments in the region from the Persian Gulf to the Malacca Strait by deploying warships on a 24x7 basis to deal with eventualities like disaster relief, maritime terrorism, or piracy (Pandit, 2017). This means that there are between 12 and 14 destroyers, frigates, corvettes, and long-distance patrol vessels, backed by the naval satellite Rukmini (GSAT 7) and daily sorties by the Poseidon 8I maritime patrol aircraft at any point of time (Pandit, 2017). India plans to deploy "mission-ready warships" and aircraft along key SLOCs and choke points like the Malacca and Sunda Straits. This will likely add to the Indian Navy's reputation as the first responder and net security provider in the region.

Indian warships have been escorting both foreign and Indian merchant vessels in the Persian Gulf, partly because of the US president Donald Trump's demand that countries which import hydrocarbons from West Asia should protect their own vessels. In 2016, India deployed a P-8I long-range maritime reconnaissance aircraft to Seychelles for the first time and in March this year, the Indian Coast Guard ship *INS Vijit* visited the Indonesian port of Sabang. In an expansion of its Mission Based Deployments (MBD) in the Indian Ocean Region (IOR), the Navy deployed its P-8I long-range maritime surveillance aircraft for anti-piracy sorties from Salalah in Oman to patrol the Gulf of Aden in June 2019 (Peri, 2019a). The Indian Navy has escorted 3,440 ships, of which 3,027 were foreign and 413 were Indian, and its Navy ships also made 414 interventions at sea (Ibid.). So far, the Navy has deployed 73 ships on anti-piracy patrols (Ibid.). Also, under the neighbourhood first policy, the Navy undertakes Joint Exclusive Economic Zone (EEZ) surveillance with Maldives, Seychelles, and Mauritius and Coordinated Patrols (CORPAT) with Bangladesh, Myanmar, Thailand, and Indonesia (Ibid.). It has an agreement that allows it access to facilities in Oman and in Indonesia as well as a maritime agreement with Singapore.

Interoperability

In 2018, India and the US signed the Communications, Compatibility, Security Agreement (COMCASA) to increase interoperability by giving India access to sensitive communication equipment and codes. It has signed a similar agreement with France. India has been holding joint exercises with several countries to deepen military cooperation and interoperability. In December 2018, the Indian and Japanese air forces held the "Shinyuu-Maitri 18" exercises; in April 2019, India and Australia completed the third round of the India-Australia biennial maritime defence exercise Ausindex, and in September, the Malabar naval exercises, which includes India, Japan, and the US, took place; in the first week of November, India and Indonesia held the Samudra Shakti naval exercises, and in November 2019, India and the US completed a nine-day tri-service joint exercise. The 37th edition of Corpat Indo-Indonesia was held. Exercise Varuna was held with France. In 2020, the Malabar exercises were held between the naval services of India, Japan, and the US, with Australia participating for the first time. JIMEX

2021 was held between India and Japan, in which INS Kochi (with sea king MKb42B helicopters), MiG 29K fighters, guided missile frigate INS TEG, a P8I shore-based maritime reconnaissance aircraft took part, along with Japanese helicopter carrier Kaga and guided missile destroyer Murasame. In 2020, both the countries had signed an "Acquisition and Cross servicing agreement" that would allow them to exchange supplies and services during exercises. The 4th edition of AUSINDEX, which was held in 2021, was the most elaborate military exercise. In 2019 itself, it had included anti-submarine operations. In a historic Mutual Logistics Support Agreement that was signed between the two countries in 2020, meant that these countries have allowed each other access to military bases. In 2021, the US sent a carrier strike group to participate in a two-day exercise in the Eastern Indian Ocean in which the Indian Air Force had taken part for the first time. This is in addition to the many exercises held in the past and ones planned for the future.

Capabilities

India has been quietly building up its naval capabilities, focusing on the Andaman and Nicobar Islands, including building extended runways in the Nicobar Islands to aid P-8i landings. India has also enhanced its submarine basing facilities. The importance of the Andamans to India's security as it protects the East Coast and secures control over the Bay of Bengal, is again something which K.M. Panikkar had pointed out (Panikkar, 1945: 93). New Delhi has further "negotiated agreements with Mauritius and Seychelles for the development of two islands, Agalega and Assumption Island respectively, although negotiations have often been difficult and have faced local political opposition" (Jaishankar, 2019a: 18). These are both widely believed to be military facilities. In 2018, the Indian Navy's Boeing P-8i Long Range Maritime Reconnaissance Anti-Submarine Warfare aircraft made its maiden landing at Car Nicobar, and in 2019, India inaugurated its fourth air base and the third naval air facility, the *INS Kohassa*, in the Andamans.

Capacity Building

India has been helping its partners build their civilian and defence capabilities. With the Maldives, India is finalising agreements to lease a Dornier aircraft, bringing the Maldives under India's coastal radar chain network and a broad-based humanitarian assistance and disaster relief (HADR) exercise (Peri, 2019b). India has signed an agreement with Bangladesh, which will allow India to install surveillance radar along its coast on the Bay of Bengal. India has been increasing aid to its partners in the Indian Ocean like Mauritius and Seychelles and announced a $12 million grant to the 12

India-Pacific Islands Developing States (PSIDS). It has helped build infrastructure projects like the Sittwe port in Myanmar and the Metro Express and ENT Hospital in Mauritius and a container port in Chabhahar, Iran. It has also given patrol vessels to Sri Lanka and Mauritius and aircraft to Seychelles and also trained officers from several countries (Jaishankar, 2019a: 18). In addition to this, India's sale of the Brahmos supersonic cruise missile systems to the Philippines makes India's commitment to the region much more explicit.

Maritime Domain Awareness

India launched an Information Management and Analysis Centre (IMAC) in Gurgaon. In 2018, the Indian Navy established its Information Fusion Centre (IFC) meant to collaborate with different partners to increase maritime domain awareness and to share information, especially on commercial shipping. It has signed agreements with several countries to share information about civilian and military shipping and maritime awareness agreements with Sri Lanka and the Maldives. "The use and export of Indian coastal radar systems, including to Myanmar, and the leveraging of Indian satellite capabilities have also added to India's MDA capabilities" (Ibid.).

HADR

In 2015, during the Yemeni crisis, India helped rescue its own citizens and more than 550 foreigners trapped in Yemen. In March 2019, New Delhi extended support to help Mozambique deal with the aftermath of Cyclone *Idai*.

Domestically, India has been focusing on improving its ports and building new ones through the *Sagarmala* project.

Challenges

The biggest challenge for India in achieving its goals in the Indo-Pacific is the lack of definitional clarity or definitional consensus about what the Indo-Pacific actually is. There are varying interpretations in different countries of what the Indo-Pacific stands for. Prime Minister Modi in his speech at the Shangri La dialogue described it as stretching "from the shores of Africa to that of the Americas" (Modi, 2018). It is clear from this definition that New Delhi sees the Indo-Pacific as a theatre which encompasses East Asia as well as the Middle East. India is concerned about China's growing naval capabilities and presence in the Eastern Indian Ocean and wants to secure its strategic interests in the Straits of Malacca, Sunda, and Lombok (Rej and Mukherjee, 2018). It could even consider maintaining a forward presence in the South China Sea and combine its efforts with the Quad in other parts of the Western Pacific Ocean (Ibid.). However, the waters towards its West or the Western Indian Ocean are of equal importance to it as India gets around 70 percent of its oil and gas supplies from the Middle East and because of the over seven million strong Indian diaspora in the region. Moreover, China is also almost as dependent on the Middle East for its energy supplies and has strong economic relations with the countries of the Middle East. This explains the Indian Navy's Maritime Security Strategy document's focus on the Western Indian Ocean. In fact, the document clearly states that "the Arabian Sea, Bay of Bengal, Andaman Sea, and their littoral regions"; "the Persian Gulf and its littoral", "the Gulf of Oman, Gulf of Aden, Red Sea, and their littoral regions", "South-West Indian Ocean, including IOR island nations therein and East Coast of Africa littoral regions" and "the choke points leading to, from and across the Indian Ocean" are India's primary areas of maritime interest (Indian Navy, 2015). Interestingly, the document mentions the "South-East Indian Ocean, including sea routes to the Pacific Ocean and littoral regions in vicinity" and "South and East China Seas, Western Pacific Ocean, and their littoral regions", among others, as secondary maritime interests (Ibid.). For the US, however, the Western Indian Ocean does not seem to be important to its conception of the Indo-Pacific. The US National Security Strategy document defines it as extending from the west coast of the United States to the west coast of India or as Admiral Harry Harris said, "from Hollywood to Bollywood". The Middle East continues to come under the US' Central Command (CENTCOM) rather than Indo Pacific Command, perhaps because many of these countries were part of the CENTO earlier. This could be a problem because the Middle East is where India and the US have had the most differences, whether it is the US action in Libya, Syria or its continuing attacks on Iran, a country which is crucial for India. It is the same region which hosts a hostile Pakistan which continues to have good relations with the US. It does not seem like the US understands how crucial India's relations with the Indian Ocean Rim countries are for India. Moreover, Trump's legacy has left India worried about how much it can depend on the US if the Republicans again come to power and how much of the burden it will have to shoulder. It is uncertain if the US has the will, resources, or strength to prop up an India-centric security framework in the region as it is also distracted by the war in Ukraine.

Tokyo, on the other hand, sees the Indo-Pacific as a much broader canvas extending across the two oceans and two continents (Asia and Africa). As for Australia, it refers to the maritime and littoral regions that span the two oceans. However, it is difficult to guess how far Australia would be willing to be involved in military problems in East Asia. Thus, there are variations in definitions depending on each actor and their own geographic positioning in the huge spread of the two oceans, and this lack of congruence about the definition is going to be the biggest challenge for India and it can create problems in operating together in some situations.

The second challenge is that Tokyo, New Delhi, Washington, and Canberra do not seem to have identical levels of strategic awareness and military capabilities in the Indian Ocean. They should therefore develop practical strategic cooperation by promoting habits of cooperation, coordinating, and jointly adopting policies and strategies.

The third challenge again is related to China. Most of India's close partners in its Indo-Pacific strategy, whether it is the members of the Quad or the IOR nations or ASEAN, all have stronger economic ties with China than with India. This could turn out to be a problem, particularly if China decides to play hardball. The example of how the Quad frittered out in 2008 after Australia under Kevin Rudd left it to cater to Chinese sensitivities must remain in the minds of Indian strategists as well as academics. So, the possibility of cooperation on the Indo-Pacific being held hostage to domestic politics in these countries and to China's concerns cannot be dismissed.

The fourth challenge is that of India's own capability and capacities. It is not certain how much India will be able to invest in developing its naval power and in its partner countries given the economic situation in India, at a time when there are so many competing pressures on the budget, particularly in the light of the impact of the COVID-19 pandemic on the Indian economy. It is also not certain if the US will go back to isolationism or whether Japan and Australia will be interested in investing military and economic power to support India.

The fifth challenge is to convince partners in the Indo-Pacific region that India is sufficiently invested in the region and is there for the long haul. This has become a little difficult with India not signing the RCEP. While the domestic reasons for not joining the RCEP were valid, it would be interesting to see if this will affect the way the region views India's credibility and if it will damage the Indian economy in the long run as it could make India uncompetitive and close it out of the Asian market. An economically weak India will not be of interest or use to any of its partners.

The sixth challenge is the "slowness" caused by red tape in India's bureaucracy as, for example, even for simple policies on shipping, decisions go through the MEA and then to national security before finally going to the Ministry of Shipping (Pascal, 2021). An understaffed MEA adds to the problem.

Finally, overemphasising the Indo-Pacific runs the risk of antagonising China since it sees the Indo-Pacific essentially as a strategy to contain it. While the US and Australia are physically distant from China, India, Japan, and their other partners being geographically close to China need to be more nuanced in their pronouncements about the Indo-Pacific. While it is true that modern technology has made distance a non-factor in war, geography still matters, particularly since India shares a long border with China. The US needs to understand this dilemma that New Delhi faces.

Conclusion

Undoubtedly, the idea of the Indo-Pacific has increased India's centrality in regional and global geopolitics; all the major powers recognise India's importance in the region and seek to court it (except for China). It has also paved the path for New Delhi to emerge again as a maritime power. But much of the debate on the Indo-Pacific in India has focused on Indo-US relations and what impact it could have on India's strategic autonomy. Should India follow the lead of the US in the Indo-Pacific or work out its own strategies and policies? Though initially, India seemed to have played the role of a follower of the US in the Indo-Pacific, in recent times, it has begun asserting itself. In fact, the Quad's recent emphasis on vaccines and supply chains was mostly due to gentle nudging by New Delhi. Similarly, despite the Indo-Pacific and despite immense pressure from the US, India has gone ahead with its decision to buy S400s from Russia and has in fact refused to sanction Russia or condemn its invasion of Ukraine. This proves that India's strategic autonomy remains intact notwithstanding the convergence of interests with the US in the Indo-Pacific.

In New Delhi's policy towards the Indo-Pacific, one can see elements of both realism and liberalism. The realist urge to counter or balance China can be seen in all the strategies and tactics that India has adopted, including the Quad, military exercises, as well as in enhanced partnerships with the major powers as well as regional players, etc. The liberal stance can be seen in its repeated references, mimicking the US and sometimes together with it, to a "free, open, secure and prosperous Indo-Pacific region", "freedom of navigation" and a "rules-based order".

In conclusion, the Indo-Pacific is likely to witness a lot of strategic turbulence in the form of new alliances forming and old alliances splitting, and a lot of great power rivalry. India will be right in the middle of it all, playing a vital role in balancing the region and ensuring the stability of the region as a key security provider. India's growth as a power and its rivalry with China ensures that it will remain an inevitable presence in the region, one which no power can afford to ignore. So, Indian foreign policy is in for a lot of interesting times, which could bring both opportunities and challenges. The key for India would be to remain realistic about its goals, keeping in mind its own as well as its partners' will and capabilities and changing regional and global geopolitical configurations.

References

Brewster, D. (2014). Beyond the 'String of Pearls': Is There Really a Sino-Indian Security Dilemma in the Indian Ocean?. *Journal of the Indian Ocean Region*, *10*(2), 133–149. https://doi.org/10.1080/19480881.2014.922350

Brewster, D. (2015). An Indian Ocean Dilemma: Sino-Indian Rivalry and China's Strategic Vulnerability in the Indian Ocean. *Journal of the Indian Ocean Region*, *11*(1), 48–59. https://doi.org/10.1080/19480881.2014.994822

Indian Navy. (2015). Ensuring Secure Seas: Indian Maritime Security Strategy. Retrieved from https://www.indiannavy.nic.in/sites/default/files/Indian_Maritime_Security_Strategy_Document_25Jan16.pdf

Singh, Kritika. (2024). Sailing towards Success

Jaishankar, D. (2018). The Real Significance of the Quad. Retrieved from https://www.aspistrategist.org.au/the-real-significance-of-the-quad/

Jaishankar, D. (2019a). *Acting East: India in the Indo-Pacific*. Delhi: Brookings Institution India Center.

Jaishankar, D. (2019b). Retrieved from https://twitter.com/d_jaishankar/status/1199127899846184962

Kim, J., Yu, J., and French, E. (2020). How COVID-19 Will Reshape Indo-Pacific Security. Retrieved from https://thediplomat.com/2020/07/how-covid-19-will-reshape-indo-pacific-security/

Kovind, R. N. (2017). Speech by the Hon'ble President of India Shri Ram Nath Kovind on the Occasion of Presentation of the President's Colour to the Submarine Arm of the Indian Navy. https://pib.gov.in/PressReleaseIframePage.aspx?PRID=1512042

Kuo, M. (2018). The Origin of 'Indo-Pacific' as Geopolitical Construct: Insights from Gurpreet Khurana. Retrieved from https://thediplomat.com/2018/01/the-origin-of-indo-pacific-as-geopolitical-construct/

MEA. (2020). Indo-Pacific Division Briefs. https://mea.gov.in/Portal/ForeignRelation/Indo_Feb_07_2020.pdf

Modi, N. (2018). Prime Minister's Keynote Address at Shangri La Dialogue. Retrieved from https://www.mea.gov.in/SpeechesStatements.htm?dtl/29943/Prime+Ministers+Keynote+Address+at+Shangri+La+Dialogue+June+01+2018

Modi, N. (2019). Address by Prime Minister at the Inaugural Ceremony of the 16th India-ASEAN Summit. Retrieved from https://www.mea.gov.in/Speeches-Statements.htm?dtl/31996/Address_by_Prime_Minister_at_the_inaugural_ceremony_of_the_16th_IndiaASEAN_Summit

Mohan, R. (2013). *Samudra Manthan: Sino-Indian Rivalry in the Indo Pacific*. New Delhi: Oxford University Press.

Nehru, J. (1985). *The Discovery of India*. New Delhi: Oxford University Press.

Oak, N. C. (2019). India's Place in the Altering Indo-Pacific Construct. Retrieved from https://www.orfonline.org/expert-speak/indias-place-in-the-altering-indo-pacific-construct-47863/

Pandit, R. (2017). Eye on China, India Expands Naval Footprint. Retrieved from https://timesofindia.indiatimes.com/india/india-expands-naval-footprint-in-indian-ocean-as-a-net-security-provider-with-an-eye-on-china/articleshow/61210011.cms

Panikkar, K. M. (1945). *India and the Indian Ocean: An Essay on the Influence of Sea Power on Indian History*. London: George Allen & Unwin Ltd.

Pascal, C. (2021). Indo-Pacific Strategies, Perceptions and Partnerships: The View from Seven Countries. Retrieved from https://www.chathamhouse.org/2021/03/indo-pacific-strategies-perceptions-and-partnerships/05-india-and-indo-pacific

Peri, D. (2019a). Indian Navy Steps Up Anti-Piracy Patrol. *The Hindu*, 2 June.

Peri, D. (2019b). India, Maldives to Take Forward Defence Ties. *The Hindu*, 21 October.

Rej, A. and Mukherjee, T. (2018). Whither India in the Indo-Pacific?. Retrieved from https://www.ispionline.it/it/pubblicazione/whither-india-indo-pacific-20688

Sempa, F. P. (2015). Karl Haushofer and the Rise of the Monsoon Countries. Retrieved from https://thediplomat.com/2015/03/karl-haushofer-and-the-rise-of-the-monsoon-countries/

Sibal, K. (2019). Why India Shuffled the Quad Deck. Retrieved from https://www.dailyo.in/politics/quad-dialogue-india-china-relations-india-china-ties-narendra-modi-shinzo-abe/story/1/32069.html

10

INDO-PACIFIC

Australian Middle Power Ambitions and Dilemmas

Madhusudhan. B

The Indo-Pacific, particularly the regions in and around the East Indian Ocean, South China Sea, and Western Pacific Ocean, has been of great significance of strategic interest to various nations, including the US, India, and China. The strategic significance of the Indo-Pacific region has gained momentum since 2010. The fundamental manifestations of the Indo-Pacific comprise securing sea levels of communications, freedom of navigation, maintaining an open and rule-based order, abiding by international law, open dialogue and discussions, and enhancing regional development by involving in infrastructure and connectivity projects (Prasad, 2018). The region has been dominated by the US for a long time, and of late, the US hegemony has been questioned by a number of challenges, including the growing Chinese assertion in the region. China's flourishing economy, raising military spending, and outstripping its interests to a wider area are crucial parts of the changing geopolitical landscape. China has started asserting certain maritime claims in the region. The issues of maritime territory, resource sharing, and historic and nationalistic aspects pose a challenge to China's relations with key neighbours such as Japan, Vietnam, and the Philippines. By 2020 and 2050, China intends to finalise its fighter jet programme and strengthen the widening of the blue water navy, which will impart the country the capacity to operate in second island chains that contain Japanese-held Bonin islands and the US-held Northern Marianas, Guam, Palau, and Carolines (Bakrie, 2013). The relations between India and China have been aggravated on account of the continuing border issues and the growing naval presence of China in the Indian Ocean. India, especially after PM Narendra Modi assumed power, has reaffirmed its commitment to engage aggressively in the policy postures of the 2014 "Act East Policy" a modified version of

DOI: 10.4324/9781003479307-12

the 1990s "Look East Policy". One of the cardinal policy postures of the "Act East Policy" is to intensify India's ties with ASEAN and the Asia-Pacific region. The US strategy in combating the growing Chinese presence in the region is also significant. The Obama administration's response to the Indo-Pacific was centred on India as its major thrust. This particular policy position had led to soaring US–India ties during his administration (Pitakdumrongkit, 2019: 3). This has further manifested in the form of an annual strategic dialogue to a strategic and commercial dialogue in 2015 as a platform to discuss bilateral relations at the highest political level was a case in point (Mistray, 2016). However, the Trump administration's perception of the Indo-Pacific is in a different modulation. Trump has used the term in a national document as the US National Security Strategy (NSS), and his Indo-Pacific policy has been designed in the light of a rising and revisionist China (Grossman, 2018). The policy was devised under the premise that the US and China are engrossed in a power disputation. The stimulation for the Trump administration to act more aggressively in the Indo-Pacific could be attributed to the administration's perception that the US and China are currently in a strategic competition and if unchecked could be disastrous for US interests. National Defence Strategy (NDS), 2018 maintains that "China is leveraging military modernization, influence operations, and predatory economics to coerce neighboring countries to reorder the Indo-Pacific to their advantage" (National Defence Strategy, 2018: 2). Similarly, the US NSS contends that "China seeks to replace the United States in the Indo-Pacific region, expand the reaches of its state driven economic model, and reorder the region in its favor" (US White House Office, 2017:25). In response to these developments in the Indo-Pacific, the regional powers are gradually strengthening their military capabilities and also have shown an inclination towards closer relations with the US. In the event of China emerging successful in its strategic intervention in the Indo Pacific region, the US would try to prevent such a situation, as also with many countries in Indo-Pacific Asia such as Japan, India, South Korea, Indonesia, Vietnam, and Australia. Against this backdrop, the responses of Australia as a Middle power of the region are significant. Australia has responded to the regional developments. Canberra believes that the Indian Ocean is a significant trade route and economic interdependence with China poses a real challenge. The focus is on the "rule-based order" which is gaining currency both in Australia and internationally, implying a shared community by all countries to conduct their activities in accordance with agreed rules that evolve over time, such as international law, regional security arrangements, trade agreements, immigration protocols, and cultural arrangements. There are also certain concerns and opportunities that Australia finds significant. The major concerns of Australia are the decreasing US presence in the region owing to the estrangement under the Trump Administration and also the rising potency of China. In short, the idea of the "Indo-Pacific" seems to be an attempt to manage and adjust Australia's relationships with China and the US without sacrificing their national interests. The chapter seeks to bring out the under-pinnings of "Indo-Pacific" strategies of middle powers with a special focus on Australia.

Theoretical Approach

The theoretical position of the chapter could be placed in constructivism in international relations. Alexander Wendt contended that even when interna-tional politics is socially constructed, these structures encompass material resources (Wendt, 1995: 73). Hence, Australia's perception of the Indo-Pacific as the new regional architecture could be evaluated in terms of its material and ideational realities. Various theoretical positions have emerged in the context of middle power assertions. Scholars, especially liberalist and realist traditions, have reduced the role of middle powers to an alliance of great powers. However, constructivism provides a critical evaluation. This is owing to their agency in both the international and regional arenas; middle powers have effectively created an accurate identity that serves as the basis to explain their behaviour; such behaviour entails a tendency towards mul-tilateralism (Hijar-Chiapa, 2020: 82)

Australian Perception on Indo-Pacific

While Australians view the "Indo-Pacific" as a significant strategic arena, it is crucial to trace out the undercurrents of Australian policy postures. It has to be seen in the context of the US perception of China and the emerg-ing presence of India in the region. The term Indo-Pacific has been taken up by Australia very recently in an assertive manner, albeit it was debated in Australian circles way back in the 1960s. The Australian diplomats and foreign policy experts argue that the Asia-Pacific is no longer relevant today and gradually the centre of attention is shifting from the Asia-Pacific to the Indo-Pacific. However, the strategy of the Indo-Pacific does not emanate from leaders of the US or Australia but rather it had been coined by the then Japanese Prime Minister Shinzo Abe. He had talked about the Indo-Pacific in the Indian Parliament in 2007, arguing "Confluence of the two Seas". The Japanese view of the Indo-Pacific has been shaped by the Sino-Japanese competition, particularly in the economic front, which led to a situation as to who would take up the issue of Asia's regional integration. Chinese influ-ence in ASEAN was manifested in 1997 when the ASEAN +3 meeting was held, in which ASEAN member states had invited Korea, Japan, and the PRC to participate in a talk on the Asian financial crisis. Diplomats in Japan had made many attempts to enlarge the groupings to include Australia, New Zealand, and India, but these were futile attempts. Therefore, the Australian perception and assessment of the Indo-Pacific, especially in the early stages, was influenced by the Sino-Japanese competition, in which both constitute two different models and systems. In fact, Australia was apprehensive about the growing complexity of relations between China and Japan.

It is also significant that Australia's as well as India's role has been stressed upon by various scholars. The question of Indo-Pacific has been in the lexicon of Australian foreign policy for about two decades. However, during the last decade, more and more attention has been given by Canberra to the Indo-Pacific rather than the Asia-Pacific. This has been attributed primarily to the fact that "Indo-Pacific" could be a bridge to the "US" or "Asia" binary which has become a cardinal foreign policy debate of Australian foreign policy since the end of the cold war (Satake, 2011:87–114). It was John Howard's administration that gave importance to this region by referring to the Cold War concept of 'Asia Pacific' and its extended areas from the Indian Ocean to the Pacific Ocean as the 'wider Asia Pacific region (Defence White Paper, 2000). Kevin Rudd administration gave further impetus to this region in a high-profile manner (2009, Defence White Paper). The Julia Gillard Labour government which came into power after the Rudd government had abandoned the Asia-Pacific focus of Australia and stressed a wider realm of Indo-Pacific. The shift in perception from Asia-Pacific to Indo-Pacific had been reinforced by the subsequent coalition governments headed by Tony Abbot, Malcolm Turnbull, and the present Prime Minister Scott Morrison. The 2016 Defence White Paper and 2017 Foreign Policy White Paper brought out by the coalition government conceptualise the India-Pacific as an arena where the United States and China cooperate and compete as the most powerful players, and Australia recognises this arena as significant in terms of its diplomacy and security (Australian Government Department of Defence, 2016, Australian Government, 2017).

In addition to that, Australia has long been encountering a dilemma in its foreign policy pertaining to the adoption of "Asian facing policy" and "US facing policy". And the Indo-Pacific is best suited for Australia to adopt a balanced approach which is inclusive of both realms of policy postures. In January 2013, the official National Security Strategy Document mentioned that "while the Asia-Pacific has been primarily Australia's strategic and economic frame of reference over recent decades…. the term Indo-Pacific" has emerged recently (Australian Government, 2013). Kim Beazley, the former leader of the Labour Party and Australia's ambassador to the US, argued that the Indo-Pacific region is a critical path of the global commons – with the US, India, and China will active there" (Beazley, 2012: 50–52). Australian High Commissioner to India Peter Varghese comments that

> today it makes more sense to think of the Indo-Pacific rather than Asia Pacific, as the crucible Australian security …. this new construct of the

Indo-Pacific connects the Indian and Pacific oceans, thereby underlining the crucial role that the maritime environment is likely to play in our future strategic and defence planning. The Indo-Pacific represents the centre of gravity of Australia's strategic and economic interests.

(IPCS Special Report, 2012)

Long coast lines in the East facing the Pacific and, in the West, facing the Indian Ocean generate "Australia's unique geography as a continent bridging Pacific Ocean and Indian Ocean .... for this country the idea of Indo-Pacific is here to stay" (Medcalf et al, 2011). Another academic raises the hope that "Australia offers a huge politically stable, reliable as well as technically capable, bridge between the Indian Ocean and the Western Pacific" (Gilber, 2012:11–19) and also between the US and India. This has enabled the emergence of a trilateral India-Australia-US grouping.

Australia has assimilated with the idea of the Indo-Pacific as it has analysed the geo-political architecture of the area in terms of rising India and China and the US rebalance and "pivot" back to the Pacific. This embrace was consequently also in the sense of Australia shaping its policies, disposition of forces, and strategic agreements in the Indo-Pacific logic (Scott, 2013:1–24).

The above discussion reveals that the Australian perception of the Indo-Pacific has been influenced by two important factors – one being the traditional alliance with the US and the other is an apprehension over the growing dimensions of China's economic and military power. The US dimension of the Indo-Pacific has been a traditional one which persuaded Australia to think in terms of Asia-Pacific earlier and later Indo-Pacific. The US has been a close ally of Australia and an economic partner as well. One of the current underpinnings of US-Australian ties is the rising China. The US perceives China as a threat and a competitor to US interests in the region and Australia regards it as a bulwark against Chinese assertion in the Indo-Pacific, South China Sea, and the whole of Southeast Asia. These two dimensions have forced Australia to adopt three policy postures which can be termed as three pillars: US as a close ally, China as a threat and competitor, and assertion of Australia as a middle power.

US Factor in Australian Strategy in Indo-Pacific

The Australian approach towards the US is invariably consistent and positive. This alliance enjoys vibrant support across the mainstream political spectrum and the broader public (Medcalf, 2018). Some of the Australian official documents bring out the gravity of this relationship. This is particularly true of US-Australian defence relations. Discussion of the Australian-US defence relationship fundamentally focuses on military cooperation and interoperability, but the relationship continues to be founded upon higher order issues such as shared values and interests . This approach of shared interests includes the strategically crucial area of the Indo-Pacific. From the Australian perspective, chief among these interests is the need for a stable Asia-Pacific that allows to maintain its security and economic prosperity (Australian Parliament House, 2006).

From the US perspective as well, the Indo-Pacific is cardinal in various ways. One of the reasons for granting serious attention to the Indo-Pacific is emerging and asserting China in various ways, especially militarily and economically. China's enhancing confidence in asserting itself regionally and internationally, combined with longstanding apprehensions about whether the US has the capacity and commitment to remain the region's dominant actor, is leading the US allies and partners to adjust their strategic position. One of the reliable allies in the Indo-Pacific for the US is Australia. Australia is a major defence partner for the US and an important source of stability in the region. The current strength of the US-Australia defence relations and multilateral connections is manifested by the July 2019 Talisman Sabre military exercise that included 34,000 personnel from the US and Australia, as well as embedded troops from Canada, Japan, New Zealand, and the United Kingdom, and observers from India and South Korea (US Indo-Pacific Command, 2019). However, the US-Australia relations are viewed with a sense of apprehension in Australia when Donald Trump assumed office in the US. However, the Australian response towards the Australia-New Zealand and United States alliance remains positive. It is also significant to evaluate some of the studies on the US-Australian relations that have been conducted recently. One of the studies reveals that the US "no longer enjoys military primacy in the Indo-Pacific and its capacity to uphold a favourable balance of power is increasingly uncertain". It also points out that "A strategy of collective defense is fast becoming necessary as a way of offsetting shortfalls in America's regional military power and holding the line against rising Chinese strength" (Townshend et al., 2019). The 2019, the Australian-US Ministerial Consultations (AUSMIN) "emphasized the need for an increasingly networked structure of alliances and partnerships to maintain an Indo-Pacific that is secure, open, inclusive and rule based" (Minister for Foreign Affairs, 2019). The US-Australian ties are still vigorous and proactive despite the tendency on the part of the former to engage in a low-profile manner in the Indo-Pacific. Therefore, the Indo-Pacific notion of Australia has its justification as a concept of "closed and depended ally" that is the US.

Australian Perception of China and the Indo-Pacific

In 2013, China announced the Belt and Road Initiative (BRI), a key strategy aimed at establishing a network of transport, port, aviation, and energy-related infrastructure across the world. Later, China ventured into two significant projects: the China-Pakistan Economic Corridor (CPEC) and the China-Myanmar Economic Corridor (CMEC). These projects have long-term implications in the Indo-Pacific region. These projects are viewed with suspicion by the US and its partners.

The Australian perception of China revolves around numerous factors, some of which are contradictory and complex. Canberra has long been maintaining strong ties with China with a twin strategy of boosting economic ties and even monitoring Chinese projects as part of security interventions. Australia has frequently raised its anxiety over China's enhanced interference in the South China Sea. Australia's persistent concern has been China's interference with the former's internal affairs. Its 2017 Foreign Policy White Paper clearly cautions China against interfering in Australia's internal affairs and institutions without being excessively confrontational (Department of Foreign Affairs and Trade, 2017).

The economic aspect of Australian and Chinese relations needs some focus. The traditional export markets of Australian products, especially minerals, were initially located in Britain, and later in Japan from the 1970s to 2000. But it shifted to China by 2009 as China had emerged as a top export market of Australia, especially iron ore. China is currently the largest export market of Australia, a trading partner, and also a large foreign investor. Bilateral trade reached US$106.15 billion in 2016, accounting for about 22.7 percent of Australia's total trade (Medcalf, 2018). Of late, the economic ties have grown to great heights and outgrowing into new areas such as agriculture, tourism, and education. Australian defence experts and strategists have started to feel that there is an ever-increasing threat from China, particularly in the Northern seas of Australia.

The Australian calculations in the South China Sea are also crucial factors that influence Australian strategy in the Indo-Pacific. However, the Australian calculation of the South China Sea encounters twin challenges. First, the US pressure on Australia to conduct Freedom of Navigation Operations in support of the UN Convention of the Law of the Sea in 2016. Second is the fact that China is not agreeing to a South China Sea Code of Conduct, which is detrimental to Australian interests.

However, in the midst of vibrant economic relations, there have been certain negative aspects that impair the relations with Australia. In 2017, Australian public opinion was critical of China's human rights record. During 2008 to 2010, the Australian attitude towards China underwent substantial changes, manifested by higher anxiety. The South China Sea dispute is another bone of contention between Australia and China, with implications for the Indo-Pacific. The South China Sea is highly relevant to the Indo-Pacific notion, and Australia has clear interests at stake here (Douglas, 2019). Medcalf also remarks that "Australian policymakers recognize the sea lines of communication through Southeast Asia, including the South China Sea, as the core of the Indo-Pacific" (Medcalf, 2016:9). Since 2002, tensions have escalated in the South China Sea pertaining to the sea lines. The tensions developed as a result of Chinese encroachments and interventions in the South China Sea, as well as intrusions into the Spratly Islands and Parcel Islands. China has also made claims on areas exclusively belonging to the Philippines and Vietnam. The Chinese claims over the South China Sea have rejuvenated Australian foreign policy positions based on a middle power perspective. These developments have also led to a more rigorous US-Australian relationship in the defence sector. There have been several close encounters between US and Chinese military ships and aircraft operating in these waters (Hijar-Chiapa, 2020). These encounters can be attributed to the American insistence on the "free and open Indo-Pacific Strategy" (FOIP). Despite positive movements from the US, Australia has not responded enthusiastically. The Australian perception is more focused on a rules-based order. This does not mean that Australia has shown lukewarm interest in the South China Sea. Of late, Australia has enhanced its "operation gateway" maritime patrols, which began in the 1980s and are performed by Australian Navy P-3 Orion maritime aircraft (Hijar-Chiapa, 2020).

The COVID-19 pandemic has created a strain in the bilateral ties between Australia and China. Australia has turned out to be a target for Chinese aggression since Australia insisted on the need for and the importance of conducting an independent inquiry into the origins of COVID-19 (Hurst, 2020). This has been a serious concern for China as Beijing has been Australia's largest trading partner, which accounts for 7% of Australian Gross Domestic Product (GDP) and 36% of total exports (Vijaya, 2021). This is in addition to the huge number of tourists and students who make their way to Australia.

The Middle Power Assertions and Engagements of Australia

In fact, Australia is now in a critical juncture of its policy as far as the notion of Indo-Pacific is concerned. As the Australian policy and proximity with the US have been wavering especially during the Trump Administration, despite the US and Australian ties in defence and trade surging in a big manner, Australia's position to act independently and also act more aggressively with several nations in the Indo-Pacific, South Asia, and Southeast Asia seems to be significant.

Similarly, the Chinese threat and involvement in the region stretching from South Asia to the Pacific seems to be critical for Australia. Australia is now keen on developing ties with middle powers in the region to tackle the Chinese menace without disturbing the trade ties with China. In this particular juncture, an evaluation of its relations with the middle powers of the region is crucial.

Canberra is keen on nurturing its relations with many of the multilateral institutions of the Indo-Pacific, which includes the East Asia Summit (EAS) and the ASEAN Defence Ministers Meeting Plus Eight (ADDM+). Australia was an early proponent of the notion of "connecting the spokes" in a hub-and-spoke strategy by building a web of security cooperation among the US allies and partners in Asia, both bilaterally and trilaterally (Medcalf, 2018). Australia also desires to improve relations with numerous regional players such as Japan, Singapore, Indonesia, Vietnam, and the Republic of Korea, etc.

Japan and Canberra are laying strong foundations for their relations. Both nations have committed to the rule-based order. The Australian-Japan declaration remains vibrant and solid with a commitment to an annual "2+ 2 Dialogue" to discuss mutual strategic concerns between their respective defence and foreign ministers (Medcalf, 2018). The renewed Australian-Japanese ties are justified owing to a vacillating US policy and an ever-increasing threat from China.

The Australian-Indian relations have also reached a significant phase. The Indian Ocean links India to near and extended neighbourhoods in both eastern and western parts of Asia, Africa, and Oceania. The Look East Policy has initiated India's engagements with the Asia-Pacific for more than 20 years, resulting in strengthening India's institutional, economic, and security relations with the region. The initial objective of the policy was to strengthen India's economic interactions with Southeast Asia. Later, it has assumed the dimension of engaging with Northeast Asia and Australia. Under Prime Minister Modi, the Indian government, has renewed its interest in the region. The objective of the 2014 Act East Policy was to promote economic cooperation, greater cultural ties, and develop strategic relations among ASEAN countries (Ministry of External Affairs, 2017). India's Act East policy is, in fact, an extension of the Look East policy with a more assertive posture in multiple arenas such as countering the Chinese rise and assertiveness, addressing the inadequacies of the security order, and an awareness of India's growing capabilities. The overall justification for the Act East policy includes securing the Indian Ocean through maritime domain awareness, naval operations and capabilities, infrastructure, and capacity building. It is also significant for India to have meaningful interactions with Southeast Asia through institutional integration, military relations, commerce, and connectivity. As part of the Act East policy, strategic relations and balancing of powers with the US, Japan, Australia, and others (Russia, France, UK, etc.) are also significant. When it comes to managing relations with China, several issues are involved such as bilateral security, regional security (Belt and Road Initiative), and bilateral trade and economics.

Australian and Indian Strategies in Indo-Pacific

Australia and India consider the Indo-Pacific a significant arena cutting across various middle level powers. For Australia, India occupies a crucial position within the Indo-Pacific. The Indo-Pacific occupies a strategic position and acts as a link between the Indian Ocean and the Pacific. This is one reason why today it makes more sense to think of the Indo-Pacific, rather than East Asia or even Asia-Pacific, as the crucible Australian security. This broader definition brings India into Asia's strategic matrix. It connects the Indian and Pacific oceans, thereby underlining the crucial role that the maritime environment is likely to play in our future strategic and defence planning. It reinforces India's role as a strategic partner for Australia, and it brings in the big Asian economies of Japan, Korea, Indonesia, and Vietnam as well as the diplomatic and trade weight of ASEAN (Varghese, 2012).

There are good prospects for India and Australia strategies in Indo-Pacific. These two democracies may be dissimilar in their physical and economic structures, including in their economic development, demography, and diplomatic traditions (Medcalf and Raja Mohan, 2014:16). Both the nations have joined together in various issues in the last decade on issues of maritime security, counter-terrorism, and regional order not dominated by any one power. They have overcome a Cold War history of mistrust and mutual indifference, surmounted differences over uranium exports, built economic and social links, and now are poised for a deeper defence relationship, including regular naval exercises and high-level dialogue (Medcalf and Raja Mohan, 2014:16).

From a broader perspective, the convergence of Indian and Australian interests in Southeast Asia is seen as the strategies they intend to develop in the Indo-Pacific region. Southeast Asia lies at the conjunction of these oceans.

In the context of distancing with the US and China, Australia is keen on strengthening its cooperation network with Indo-Pacific countries other than the US and China. India is one such power in the region that it considers for network diplomacy. In 2012, the Gillard government decided to permit uranium exports to India. In 2017, the first India-Australia 2+2 Foreign and Defence Secretaries' Dialogue was held. It discussed future security cooperation between the two countries and initiated the Japan-Australia-India-Indonesia trilateral frameworks. Besides, the first Australia-India naval exercise AUSINDEX with a thrust on anti-submarine warfare was held off the coast of Australia in 2018.

Despite the progress in cooperation in various sectors, the divergence of interests is emerging in certain areas. Despite Australian interest, India is not keen on the Royal Australian Navy participating in the Japan-US-India joint exercise "Malabar". It reflects India's unwillingness to accept Australia's tilt towards the US ally club.

158 Madhusudhan B.

In addition to Japan and India, Australia has intensified its relations with other players including Singapore and Indonesia. In these engagements, it is reasonable to assume shared concerns about China – and a desire to build regional resilience in the face of uncertain US engagement – are motivating factors (Medcalf, 2018).

Quad and Trilateral Strategies

Canberra was keen on establishing Australia-US-Japan trilateral dialogue developed in the 2000s. This particular arrangement has been refined into a movement against Chinese assertion and favours a rule-based regional order. A similar kind of endeavour was initiated involving Australia-India-Japan in a trilateral dialogue in 2015. When the four democracies joined together to form a quadrilateral security arrangement in 2007 to include the US, India, and Japan, Canberra was an initial supporter (Medcalf, 2018). The Quad concept, after its initial failure, has been revived back in 2017. In the first in the office, the Trump Administration warmed quickly to the Quad concept, and in August 2017, US Secretary of State Rex Tillerson discussed its revival with the foreign ministers of Australia and Japan on the sidelines of an ASEAN Summit in Manila (Smith, 2020). An assessment of the Quad and its revivals shows that Australia has an abiding interest in preventing its neighbourhood from becoming an arena of Chinese domination and a history of strategic collaboration with the US (Smith, 2020: 8).

Australia's Pacific Step-up – a neighbourhood approach to engagement, is considered to be one of its cardinal foreign policy priorities. Both the Pacific Step-up and Quad provide direction to Australian foreign policy. In the Quad framework, Australia has embarked on various partnerships and consultations. The Australian-US Ministerial consultations carried out in July 2020 promoted intensified collaboration between the two countries in granting financial assistance to Pacific Island states. The US granted Australia $118 million to tide over the COVID-19 crisis. Both the nations have also agreed to support and contribute to the Pacific Islands Forum (Pankaj, 2021). In addition to that the two countries have made strategies to invest in qualitatively enhanced infrastructure projects for Pacific Island states.

The COVID-19 pandemic has initiated significant actions from Australia. Canberra has spent $1.44 billion for development assistance for COVID-19 economic recovery 2020–21 (Vijaya, 2021). As part of the Japan-Australia Economic Partnership, Japanese foreign direct investments have gone up significantly and have taken efforts to connect the partnerships to Australia's Pacific Set-up programme. Hence, it augments collaboration between Australia, Japan, and the US in realising common Pacific goals. Besides, the three-nation collaboration, another endeavour in the arena of Supply Chain Resilience Initiative (SCRI) was initiated by Australia, Japan, and India.

The SCRI was initiated to bring about sustained growth in the Indo-Pacific region without relying on China for the supply chain.

India-Australia bilateral relations are often termed as the weakest link compared to other bilateral and trilateral relations in the Quad (Jaishankar, 2020). However, there has been remarkable progress in bilateral relations during 2020. Project Sagarmala and Project Mausam are significant measures and initiatives within the Act East Policy (Vijaya, 2021). Australia has shown keen interest in these projects. The defence partnerships between the two countries have also been enhanced by way of signing crucial agreements with regard to equal access to military bases. India's trade interactions with Australia have improved significantly accounting for $45.5 billion (John, 2022) between the two countries.

The Quad architecture has expanded to a wider platform, which goes beyond the theatre of its engagement. The ongoing conflict between Russia and Ukraine has led to a situation where the Quad leaders interact virtually to discuss the crisis in March 2022. In subsequent reactions as well, the Quad members, particularly the US, Australia, and Japan have severely criticised severely Russia's invasion of Ukraine. In this context, India's stance is significant, as New Delhi has taken a neutral posture. Despite reassurances on the part of the Modi government, India's position clearly manifests its long-term and short term political, economic, and security issues (Panda, 2022). The Quad imparts a space for strategic autonomy for member countries and at the same time, they are free to express their realpolitik needs. Australian responses bear testimony to that line of thinking.

The New Australian Leadership and the Indo-Pacific Strategy

The new Prime Minister, Anthony Albanese, has assumed power in May 2022. After one year of assuming power, Prime Minister Albanese visited India in March, 2023, and a reciprocal visit of the Indian Prime Minister took place in May 2023. During Albanese's visit to India, a joint statement was released by both countries. The joint statement has reaffirmed multifaceted cooperation in a plethora of domains, which include trade, investment, climate change, science and technology, energy, and security cooperation.

At this particular juncture, the Indo-Pacific has gained serious momentum. Various statements made by Prime Ministers in the joint statement have demonstrated the strategies that both countries are adopting, which have long-term implications in the Indo-Pacific realm. The crucial among them are the enhancement of the India-Australia Comprehensive Strategic Partnership and the hosting of Malabar exercises by Australia in 2023. In the regional and multilateral cooperation arena, both Canberra and New Delhi have renewed their commitment to contribute to an open, inclusive, stable, and prosperous Indo-Pacific where sovereignty and territorial integrity are respected (High Commission of India, 2023). Further, the Prime Ministers reiterated the significance of exercising rights and freedom in all oceans and seas in accordance with the UN Convention on the Laws of the Sea (UNCLOS). There has also been a resolution to solidify cooperation through the Quad, which would realise a region that is free, open, inclusive, and resilient.

The joint statement discerns the fact that maturity has been regained in the relationship between India and Australia. Maritime exchanges have now become regular exercises fuelled by a shared sense of strategic convergence of interest in the Indo-Pacific domain (Pant, 2023).

AUKUS: A Shift in Indo-Pacific Strategy?

AUKUS was formed in September 2021 as a trilateral security arrangement between Australia, the UK, and the US. AUKUS is primarily a military and technological advancement pact, enabling Australia to procure nuclear-powered submarines which remarkably intensifies Australia's deterrence capability in the context of the rising threat of Chinese naval power.

Scholars have opined that AUKUS might erode the significance of the Quad. In reality, AUKUS is essential for the fulfilment of the Quad on account of several reasons. Firstly, when it was announced, AUKUS leaders reiterated their commitment to sustaining partnerships with the Quad, ASEAN, and other allies in Europe to counter Chinese aggression. The second aspect is that AUKUS is established on the same principles similar to that of the Quad – ensuring freedom, shared prosperity, and IPCS observing the rule of law. Thirdly, the crisscrossing nature of relationships makes the region so dynamic that more countries tend to become part of the Quad arrangement to dissuade China.

Conclusion

The Indo-Pacific region has assumed greater significance today due to the interplay of various nations with different geopolitical interests. The focus has now shifted from Asia-Pacific to Indo-Pacific. Today, the notion of Indo-Pacific has been debated by academics and policymakers in a heated way. However, the concept has its origins in the 1960s. Australian foreign policy has long been characterised by a binary view of the US and Asia-Pacific. It has long been projected as either US-centred or Asia-Pacific centred. However, various kinds of developments have emerged in the region for the last two decades, especially from 2008 onwards. This has been attributed to multiple factors, which include global economic crisis and the subsequent emergence of China as a growing power in the region. Along with these developments, the US role in the Pacific and East Asia evokes apprehensions among various middle players in the region, especially Australia. This is despite the fact that the US still remains the largest trading partner of Australia and a defence partner as well. The crucial question that emerges is whether the US could provide security protection or not. At the same time, the largest market for Australian iron ore is China and Australia has shown its anxiety over Chinese intrusion in South China. Recent developments in the event of the Ukraine war have opened up strategic autonomy for Quad members, taking into consideration the national interest of each member in the Quad. Meanwhile, India and Australia have taken proactive engagements in the Indo-Pacific, especially in the defence and security domains.

In this complex kind of relation in the region, Australia tends to adopt the policy of Indo-Pacific because it encompasses a wider area involving a number of middle powers. The perception of the Indo-Pacific poses a challenge to Australia as Canberra is at a crossroad of its foreign policy postures. The Indo-Pacific reality has forced Australia to adopt a pragmatic position by aligning with several of the middle players in the region. Quad and trilateral dialogues are manifestations of that endeavour.

References

Defence White Paper (2000). *Defence 2000: Our Future Defence Force*. Retrieved from https://www.defence.gov.au/about/strategic-planning/defence-white-paper.

Defence White Paper (2009). *Defending Australia in the Asia Pacific Century: Force 2030. Downloaded* from https://www.defence.gov.au/about/strategic-planning/defence-white-paper .

Australian Government Department of Defence (2016). *2016 Defence Industry Policy Statement*. Downloaded from https://www.defence.gov.au/about/strategic-planning/defence-white-paper

Australian Government (2017). *2017 Foreign Policy White Paper*. Retrieved from https://www.dfat.gov.au/sites/default/files/2017-foreign-policy-white-paper.pdf

Bakrie, Connie Rahakundini (2013). US Pivot: The Future of Indo-Pacific Region (Part1 of 2). *The Jakarta Post*. September 13, 2013. Retrieved from https://www.thejakartapost.com/news/2013/09/12/us-pivot-the-future-indo-pacific-region-part-1-2.html

Beazley, Kim (2012). Australia in the Indo-Pacific Century. *Policy: A Journal of Public Policy and Ideas*, Vol. 28(3),pp.50-52.

Department of Foreign Affairs and Trade (2017). *2017 Foreign Policy White Paper: Opportunity, Security, Strength*. Canberra: Common Wealth of Australia. Downloaded from https://www.dfat.gov.au/publications/minisite/2017-foreign-policy-white-paper/fpwhitepaper/pdf/2017-foreign-policy-white-paper.pdf

Douglas, Guilfoyle (2019). The Rule of Law and Maritime Security: Understanding Lawfare in South China Sea. *International Affairs*, 95, no. 5, pp.999–1017. DOI: https://doi.org/10.1093/ia/iiz141

Pankaj, Eershika (2021). *Australia's Pacific Step-up and the Quad*. Australian Naval Institute. Retrieved from https://www.lowyinstitute.org/the-interpreter/australia-s-pacific-step-quad

Gilber, H. (2012). Australia's Geo-Political Strategy and the Defence Budgeting. *Quadrant nline*. Retrieved from: https://quadrant.org.au/magazine/2012/06/australia-s-geo-political-strategy-and-the-defence-budget/

162 Madhusudhan B.

Australian Government (2013). *Strong and Secure-A Strategy for Australia's National Interest.* Canberra: Australian Government. Retrieved from https://apo.org.au/sites/default/files/resource-files/2013-01/apo-nid33996.pdf

Grossman, Marc (2018). *Emerging Strategies for the Indo-Pacific.* Yale Global Online, April 3, 2018. Retrieved from https://yaleglobal.yale.edu/content/energizing-straegies-indo-pacific.

High Commission of India (2023). *1st India-Australia Annual Summit: Joint Statement (March 10, 2023).* . High Commission of India, Canberra, Australia. Retrieved from https://www.hcicanberra.gov.in/news_letter_detail/?id=100.

Hijar-Chiapa, Miguel Alejandro (2020). Australia and the Construction of Indo-Pacific 1. In Ash Rossiter & Brendon J. Cannon (Eds.), *Conflict and the Cooperation in the Indo-Pacific: New Geopolitical Realities.* London: Routledge, pp. 78-90.

Hurst, Daniel (2020). Australia Insists WHO Inquiry into COVID Origin Must be Robust, Despite China Tensions. *The Guardian.* Retrieved from https://www.theguardian.com/.

IPCS (2012) *Australia and India in the Asian Century, Address by H.E. Peter Varghese AO, High Commissioner of Australia to India.* IPCS Special Report, No. 127, May 2012. Retrieved from https://www.ipcs.org/issue_briefs/issue_brief_pdf/SR127-AustraliaandIndiaintheAsianCentury.pdf.

Jaishankar, Druva (2020). *The Australia-India Strategic Partnership: Accelerating Security Cooperation in the Indo-Pacific.* Lowy Institute. Retrieved from https://www.lowyinstitute.org/.

John, S. (2022, October 10). India gathering pace: Australian Speaker. *The Hindu.* Retrieved from: https://www.thehindu.com/news/international/trade-and-security-ties-between-india-and-australia-are-gathering-pace-speaker-milton-dick/article67404371.ece

Medcalf, Rory (2016). Rules and Balance and Lifelines: An Australian Perspective on South China Sea. *Asia Policy,* 21, pp. 6-13.

Medcalf, Rory (2018). Australia. In J. M Smith (Ed.), *Asia's Quest for Balance, China's Rise and Balancing in Indo-Pacific.* London: Rowman & LittleField.

Medcalf, Rory & Raja Mohan, C. (2014). *Responding to Indo-Pacific Rivalry: Australia, India and Middle Powers Coalitions.* Lowy Institute for International Policy. Retrieved from: https://www.files.ethz.ch/isn/182718/responding_to_indo-pacific_rivalry_0.pdf

Medcalf, Rory, Heinrichs, Raoul, & Jones, Jones (2011). *Crisis and Confidence: Major Powers and Maritime Security in Indo-Pacific Asia.* Sydney: Lowy Institute for International Policy. View online: https://nla.gov.au/nla.obj-318043773/view

Ministry of External Affairs (2017). *Question No. 26 Act East Policy. Answer by Minister of State in the Ministry of External Affairs, Rajya Sabha, February 02, 2017.* Retrieved from https://www.mea.gov.in/rajya-sabha.htm?dtl/27982/question+no26+act+east+policy

Minister for Foreign Affairs (2019). *Joint Statement Australia-US Ministerial Consultations (AUSMIN) 2019,* August 4, 2019. Retrieved from: https://www.foreignminister.gov.au/minister/marise-payne/media-release/joint-statement-australia-us-ministerial-consultations-ausmin-2019.

Mistray, Dinshaw (2016). *Aligning Unevenly: India and the United States.* Policy Studies no. 74. Honolulu: East-West Center. Retrieved from http://www.eastwestcenter.org/system/tdf/private/ps074.pdffile=14type=node4id=35623.

National Defense Strategy (NDS) (2018). *Summary of the 2018 National Defense Strategy of the United States of America: Sharpening the American Military's Competitive Edge.* Department of Defense, January 19, 2018. Retrieved from https://dod.defense.gov/Portals/1/Documents/Pubs/2018-National-Defense-Strategy-Summary.pdf

US White House Office (2017). *National Security Strategy of the United States of America*, December 01, 2017, The White House. Retrieved from https://trumpwhitehouse.archives.gov/wp-content/uploads/2017/12/NSS-Final-12-18-2017-0905.pdf

Pant, Harsh V. (2023). "Australia's Bold Moves Present Opportunities for India to Capitalise on Indo-Pacific Strategic Convergence". *Observer Research Foundation*, March 13, 2023. Retrieved from https://www.orfonline.org/research/australias-bold-moves-present-opportunities-for-india

Panda, Jagannath (2022). Quad Divided Over Ukraine, United in the Indo-Pacific? *The National Interest*, March 18, 2022. . Retrieved from https://nationalinterest.org/feature/quad-divided-over-ukraine-united-indo-pacific-201243

Australian Parliament House (2006). *Australia's Defence Relations with United States. Inquiry Report*. House of Representatives. Joint Standing Committee on Foreign Affairs Defence and Trade. Downloaded from https://www.aph.gov.au/Parliamentary_Business/Committees/House_of_representatives_Committees?url=jfadt/usrelations/report/fullreport.pdf

Pitakdumrongkit, Kaewkamol Karen (2019). *The Impact of the Trump Administration's Indo-Pacific Strategy on Regional Economic Governance*. Policy Studies 79. 978-0-86638-287-8 (print) and 978-0-86638-286-1 (electronic) Hawai: East West Center.

Prasad, Nidhi (2018). *India's Foray into the Indo-Pacific: Embracing Ambiguity through Strategic Autonomy*. Retrieved from https://www.ide.go.jp/library/Japanese/P/Download/Report/2018/pdf2_40_011_ch07.pdf.

Satake, Tomohiko (2011). The Origin of Trilateralism? The US-Japan- Australia Security Relations of the 1990s. *International Relations of Asia–Pacific*, (https://www.jstor.org/stable/26159402) Vol. No. 11(1), pp. 87-114.

Scott, David (2013). Australia's Embrace of the 'Indo-Pacific': New Term, New Region, New Strategy?. https://doi.org/10.1093/irap/Ict009.

Smith, Jeff M. (2020). *The Quad 2.0: A Foundation for a Free and Open Indo-Pacific*. Asian Study Center.

Townshend, Ashley, Thomas-Noone, Brendan, & Steward, Matilda (2019). *Averting Crisis: American Strategy, Military Spending and Collective Defence in the Indo-Pacific*. https://united-states-studies-centre.s3.amazonaws.com/uploads/32c/cd3/8dd/32ccd38ddb0ead934d743d487bd6080c01dc950a/Averting-crisis-American-strategy-military-spending-and-collective-defence-in-the-Indo-Pacific.pdf Sydney: United Studies Centre at the University of Sydney.

US Indo-Pacific Command (2019). *Talisman Sabre 2019, Largest Ever Bilateral Defense Exercise in Australia Opens*, July 9, 2019. Retrieved from https://www.pacom.mil/Media/News/News-Article-View/Article/1899433/talisman-sabre-2019-largest-ever-bilateral-defense-exercise-in-australia-opens/.

Vijaya, P. (2021 Winter). Australia's Role in the Quad and Its Crumbling Ties with China. *Journal of Indo-Pacific Affairs*, pp. 136-144. Retrieved from https://media.defense.gov/2021/Dec/12/2002907693/-1/-1/1/JIPA%20-%20VIJAYA.PDF

Wendt, Alexander (1995). Constructing International Politics. *International Security*, Vol. 20(1), pp. 71-81. DOI: https://doi.org/10.2307/2539217

SECTION C

Key ASEAN Nation States and Vulnerable Neighbours of China

11

MALAYSIA'S RESPONSES TO THE INDO-PACIFIC

Between Trepidations and Aspirations

Ivy Kwek

Malaysia is a country that has been historically placed at geopolitical cross-roads. With the South China Sea in between its two landmasses and the Malacca straits to its West, Malaysia is strategically located on important sea lines of communication (SLOCs) that links the East to the West, and is also home to rich resources. For that reason, Malaysia, along with Southeast Asia, is often the centre of power contestations. Since the 15th century, the then-Malacca sultanate with its strategic location commanded an important entrepot for trades from East to West, eventually becoming a target of colonisation by the Western Powers – first the Portuguese, the Dutch, and the British. Today, the Malacca Strait sees more than 30 percent of global seaborne trade pass through, and is considered one of the choke points on the global sea route (Reuters, 2010). Keeping the region safe hence is crucial to safeguard global supply chains.

Positioning Malaysia in the wider region has changed with the development of global politics. Many different names have been given in the past to this region, which is now commonly known as "Southeast Asia" and its neighbour, "Northeast Asia". This ranges from the colonial iteration of "Far East", to "Asia" and subsequently "Asia-Pacific" which denotes the US dominance across Pacific oceans. The "Indo-Pacific", while some argued is not a new concept, was the latest to join the bandwagon of lexicons.

Whereas the term "Asia-Pacific" was conceptualised as a region that links the US with East Asia, cementing the US's dominance in the region, the Indo-Pacific concept envisions a greater linkage between the Indian and the Pacific Ocean. It includes India, one of the fastest growing countries in the world, and the South Asian region and was pioneered by the Japanese Prime

DOI: 10.4324/9781003479307-14

Minister Shinzo Abe, who started the conceptualisation in his speech about the "Confluence of Two Seas" back in 2007.

Ten years later, the term gained a different connotation when the Trump administration of the US introduced the "Free and Open Indo-Pacific" in its 2017 National Security Strategy (US White House, 2017; and US Department of Defense, 2019). The same document also characterised China as its strategic competitor, a notion that has received bipartisan support. While the new Biden administration has moderated its approach, it remains tough on China and US-China strategic competition continues to intensify.

Forming the backbone of the Indo-Pacific framework is the Quad, an "alliance" of four countries – the US, Japan, Australia, India. Even though the Quad grouping can trace its root to the 2004 Acheh Tsunami, its prominence has fluctuated until its reconvening in 2017 recently. The new-found enthusiasm for strategic cooperation between the four democracies that has a "shared vision for a free and open Indo-Pacific", as well as the adoption of the Indo-Pacific by more countries such as the UK, France, Germany, the Netherlands and South Korea, has shown that the Indo-Pacific construct is gaining acceptance as the geopolitical reality of the region. Of particular concern to these countries is China's increasingly assertive behaviours in the South China Sea, as well as the expansion of China's influence via the Belt and Road Initiative to a region with great geostrategic values.

Interestingly, Southeast Asia, which is geographically central in the Indo-Pacific, is much less vocal against these behaviours. Despite having territorial disputes with China – Beijing claims sovereignty over more than 90 percent of the South China Sea via its "nine-dash line", which cuts into the EEZs of Vietnam, the Philippines, Malaysia, Brunei, and Indonesia – Southeast Asian countries opted for "quiet diplomacy" in resolving conflicts. Equally, Malaysia's response towards the Indo-Pacific has been muted, or lukewarm at best. While it does not reject it, it has not made any official statement in support of it either.

To date, the closest document that can reflect Malaysia's stance on Indo-Pacific would be the ASEAN Outlook on the Indo-Pacific (AOIP), which was spearheaded by Indonesia but supported by all member states including Malaysia. The AOIP was written in 2019 and has been lauded as a proactive move on ASEAN's part to define the values of Indo-Pacific and assert ASEAN's centrality in the region.

Essentially, Malaysia viewed this regional construct as a great power game, and prefers to thread carefully before any endorsement. However, as the Indo-Pacific concept gains prominence, it warrants greater deliberations as to how Malaysia would respond to the changing geopolitical dynamics within the region.

The purpose of the chapter is to provide an overview of Malaysia's position in the Indo-Pacific from a geographical perspective as well as the Malaysian perspective of the Indo-Pacific Strategy and its reservations towards it. Further, it compares of Malaysia's responses to the US-led Indo-Pacific Economic Framework and to the Chinese-led Belt and Road Initiative. The third section will explore the existing multilayered bilateral, mini-lateral, and multilateral relations Malaysia maintain with key countries in Indo-Pacific despite its lack of overt endorsement of the terminology. Finally, the chapter concludes by proposing the way forward to make the Indo-Pacific region more inclusive, and the role Malaysia can play as a "bridging lynch-pin" in the region.

Malaysia's Position in the Indo-Pacific "Region" and Malaysia's Perspective of the Indo-Pacific "Strategy"

The Indo-Pacific construct connects the Pacific Ocean and Indian Ocean, and encompasses more than 35 countries, with India on one end and the US on another. It comprises both developed and developing countries, democratic and non-democratic systems, and small nations like Fiji and Laos and big powers like China and Russia alike. The major inclusion of Indo-Pacific, as compared to Asia-Pacific, is India and South Asia (US State Department, 2019).

Malaysia is strategically located in the middle of the Indo-Pacific region, in the middle of the South China Sea, which links the Pacific Ocean, and the Malacca Straits, which lead up to the Bay of Bengal and subsequently the Indian Ocean. It is one of the busiest sea routes in the world and important sea lines of communication (SLOCs), carrying a third of global shipping, with some USD3.37 trillion of trade estimated to have passed in 2016 (CSIS, 2021).

At 32.7 million population, a GDP size of RM1791.4billion (USD386.45billion) and 330,621 km^2 of land, Malaysia is a medium-sized country with a great geographical endowment (Malaysia Department of Statistic, 2023). While the post-Independence Malaysia has a pro-West incli nation, in the 1970s it shifted its foreign policy orientation to non-aligned during the Cold War period. Diplomatically, Malaysia has maintained good relations with many countries in the Indo-Pacific region. Despite not having any formal defence alliance, Malaysia maintained good defence cooperation with many regional countries, and is a member of the Five Power Defence Agreement (FPDA) which includes the United Kingdom, Australia, Singapore, and New Zealand.

Malaysia's geographical advantage lies not only in that it is situated between two ocean regions, it also enjoys a land connectivity to the rest of continental Asia and Europe. Indeed, in its latest 2019 Defense White Paper, it described itself as a "Maritime Nation with continental roots", and emphasised the need to beef up maritime security in defending the national interest from external threats. The White Paper also declared Malaysia's potential as a "bridging linchpin" between the Pacific and Indian Oceans

– short of using the "Indo-Pacific" term explicitly. Further, it stated that it can play "an interrelated role of 'bridging, building, and binding' that… add values and options for countries in two regions: Asia Pacific and Indian Ocean" (Ministry of Defence, Malaysia, 2020)

In that regard, the Indo-Pacific vision fits well into Malaysia's vision of herself, and accurately highlighted the importance of the maritime domain. Nevertheless, a distinction ought to be made between discussing "Indo-Pacific" as a region, and as a strategy. While it seems geographically feasible, the term "Indo-Pacific" is perceived by Malaysia as loaded with political motivation. Given the intensity of great power competition between the US and China, the Indo-Pacific and the Quad are seen as a containment strategy towards China. Anwar Ibrahim, Malaysia's 10th Prime Minister who assumed power in November 2022, said in his first major foreign policy speech that the intensifying major power rivalry "has led to the emergence of new mini-lateral groupings across the board", which "could be cast as exclusive and exclusionary in nature". He expressed concerns that countries in Southeast Asia and the Asia-Pacific are only offered a binary choice, and warned against unfettered competition in the region. Further, he vowed to leverage on Malaysia's good relations with both the US and China to promote a stronger rules and norms-based order (Ibrahim, 2023).

These remarks aptly explain Malaysia's reservations in embracing the Indo-Pacific strategy. Malaysia does not want to be seen as siding with any superpowers and resists choosing sides especially with the heightened great power rivalry currently playing out. It is consistent with Malaysia's usual non-aligned, hedging approach, which reflects the insecurity of a small state (Kuik, 2020). Since it is clear that the Indo-Pacific vision is not embraced by China (环球时报, 2021), and any endorsement of the Indo-Pacific might be seen as following the tune of the US. There are a few considerations that drive Malaysia to be reluctant:

Firstly, for small states like Malaysia, maintaining peace and stability will be the priority. While the US presence is welcomed in the region, countries like Malaysia would not want to be embroiled in a proxy war between the US and China. US categorisation of China as a strategic competitor has not helped to diffuse the concern, but reinforced the belief that the Indo-Pacific Strategy's real agenda is to stymie China's rise. If that is true, throwing their support behind the Indo-Pacific strategy would amount to siding with the US in the current climate of tense big-power competition.

Secondly, the region's changing dynamics has expedited the development of the Indo-Pacific as a centerstage for power competition. Whereas some Quad member countries have been careful not to overplay their hand and risk antagonising China in the past, recent developments might have pushed the countries closer towards the Quad. Likewise, Southeast Asia will weigh on the cost-benefit analysis between the perceived China's "threat" and getting pushback from China. There is also fear that the Quad will turn into an Asian NATO, hence over-securitising the region with destabilising effect (Heydarian, 2021). The initial reaction towards the announcement of AUKUS by Southeast Asian countries clearly demonstrated this concern (Djalal, 2021).

Thirdly, Southeast Asia has developmental needs to be fulfilled. Compared to BRI, which is mainly an infrastructure programme and backed by investments, the Indo-Pacific strategy and the Quad alliances has thus far remained more rhetorical and security-focused. Kuik (2008) argued that a small state's strategy towards a rising power is "motivated more by an internal process of regime legitimation in which the ruling elite evaluate – and then utilize – the opportunities and challenges of the rising power for their ultimate goal of consolidating their authority to govern". This also depends on the "ordering of the elite's legitimisation bases of the day" – whether it is more prosperity-maximising, or security-seeking. Because the "threat" is more perceived than actual at the moment; while the "opportunities" is more actual, it can be argued that the Malaysian policy elites are inclined to play down the security risks *vis-a-vis* China.

Fourth, not only is China an important economic trading partner and foreign investor for many Southeast Asian countries, including Malaysia, but geographically speaking China will always be a giant neighbour. Southeast Asia Southeast Asia refuses to be a theatre of conflict between the superpowers and reserve some scepticism towards the West. This is particularly telling in Malaysia, who has a huge Muslim population who hold huge enmity towards the US's Middle East policy, particularly on the issue of Palestine.

As such, even though Southeast Asia's foreign policy responses seem inconsistent or even "subservient" to China, it is on a deeper level a careful calculation to navigate great power relations to its best interests by hedging and resisting to choose. The pragmatism practised by the Malaysian foreign policy establishment also meant that it is willing to forego their differences or disagreements on certain occasions when dealing with great powers, in cognisant of the power asymmetry in the relations.

Even though relations with China have not been easy over the South China Sea dispute, Malaysia and China go a long way historically. In the 1970s, Malaysia began to normalise relations with China, shifting away from its pro-West stance since its independence in 1957. This shift was partly induced by the British retreat from the Suez Canal in 1967 and the US withdrawal from Indochina under the Guam doctrine in 1969, where Malaysia realised that they could no longer merely rely on the Western powers for its security (Kuik, 2021). Despite the communist insurgency still taking place in the country, Malaysia was the first ASEAN member to establish diplomatic relations with China in 1974 and played an instrumental role in getting China into the ASEAN architecture, when the first ASEAN-China Summit was held in Kuala Lumpur in 1997.

Equally, Malaysia and other Southeast Asian countries recognised the US as a regional power in Southeast Asia. The anxiety over China's increasing influence in the South China Sea has grown, as China began the militarisation of the islands *circa* 2012, as well as the frequent intrusions in the Exclusive Economic Zone (EEZ) of the Southeast Asian nation as far south as Natuna Islands, which are claimed by Indonesia. Such increasingly aggressive actions that directly challenge the sovereignty of the littoral states have driven maritime Southeast Asia to foster greater cooperation with the US and partners. To a certain extent, maritime Southeast Asia has hitherto seen the US as an insurance for peace and stability against Chinese aggression, even when they feel hard pressed to proclaim. Malaysia has good bilateral relations with the US, and is a beneficiary of the Maritime Security Initiative, which allocated USD 425 million for a five-year period from 2015 to 2020 to Indonesia, Malaysia, and the Philippines.

There is no doubt that a consistent US presence is key to check on China's actions in the South China Sea, but it must be done with tact in order to not risk escalation. Former Defence Minister Mohamed Sabu's off-the-cuff characterisation of "When two elephants fight, the grass suffers" at the Shangri-la Dialogue in 2019 has quite adequately reflected the Malaysian psyche (Rithaudeen, 2019). Malaysia and other Southeast Asian countries have been performing a delicate, balancing act, to manage the risks of escalations and protect its own interests.

The Contestations between Indo-Pacific Economic Framework and Belt and Road Initiative

Competing with Indo-Pacific to envision the region is the Belt and Road Initiative driven by China. The BRI, a USD 1 trillion flagship project of China promoted by President Xi Jinping, aims to connect East Asia to Western Europe via a land belt and Chinese coastal cities to Africa and the Mediterranean via a maritime road. Essentially, the BRI will link Asia with Europe and foster greater integration between the two regions. More than 130 countries and 29 international organisations have either signed memoranda of understanding (MoUs) or expressed interest in the BRI, with all Southeast Asian states having done so (Sophie Boisseau du Rocher, 2020). Malaysia is one of the key countries in the BRI – in 2018, Malaysia is estimated to receive USD 98 billion in capital inflows from BRI-related projects (Yan, 2018).

Acting on feedbacks from the region that the US need to become a more serious economic contender in the region, the Indo-Pacific Economic Framework was announced in May 2022, with 14 countries taking part in it including Malaysia. Together, the participating countries formed 40 percent of the global GDP. Given that the US has not rejoined the Comprehensive and Progressive Agreement for Trans-Pacific Partnership (CPTPP), nor part of the China-dominated Regional Comprehensive Economic Partnership (RCEP), the IPEF will be instrumental in filling the vacuum and reintegrating the US into the regional economic framework. However, it should be noted that IPEF is not a free trade agreement, but rather a framework to set rules and standards (Menon, 2023).

Malaysia is cognisant of the strategic value attached to both IPEF and the BRI and have expressed no difficulty in participating in both. Instead of seeing BRI as a grand design of China to infringe on their sovereignty, the infrastructure development and greater connectivity brought by Chinese capitals are welcome. At the same time, Malaysia is not oblivious to the cost or the risks of debt traps. In the case of Malaysia, the East Coast Rail Link (ECRL), which aims to become a land bridge between the Kuantan Port and Port Klang to circumvent the heavy traffic at the Malacca Straits, was briefly terminated in 2018 due to cost concerns, and revised to MYR74.96 billion (USD16.17billion), MYR11.01 billion less than its initial amount of MYR85.97billion (USD18.55billion) (Chung, 2023).

Likewise, Malaysia has welcomed the IPEF as a good platform to engage with the US in negotiating a new set of trade rules which will determine the competitiveness of Malaysian companies, and as an avenue for the U.S. to help more companies developing countries to comply with international rules while gaining better market access (NHK World, 2023).

Under Biden's leadership, the Quad has also been further institutionalised with the first Quad summit held in 2021. The grouping has toned down the anti-China rhetoric while at the same time offered a more positive agenda of common interests to Southeast Asia including on vaccine cooperation, climate change, and green energy (White House, 2023). While the implementation of these programmes remains to be seen, this provides a good window of opportunity for Malaysia and Southeast Asia to strengthen cooperation with the US and its allies.

The Role of ASEAN and Other Middle Powers in the Indo-Pacific

Other middle powers, particularly among the Quad members, have put forward different iterations of the Indo-Pacific vision that are more inclusive. Such an ambivalent nature of "Indo-Pacific" gives more room for smaller states to shape the outlook on the region, and middle powers play crucial roles in boosting Southeast Asia's and Malaysia's confidence and trust on the Indo-Pacific Strategy. Below is a short description of the key strategic cooperation between Malaysia and other middle powers in the Indo-Pacific.

Japan

Japan has attempted to define their own version of FOIP which is more inclusive in nature. Instead of calling it a strategy, Japan opted for the word "vision" (Soeya, 2020). In its FOIP articulation, Japan sees ASEAN as a "hinge between Asia and Africa" (Ministry of Foreign Affairs, Japan). It stressed cooperation between shared principles and has tried to distinguish their economic diplomacy from that of the Chinese investment through the articulation of the Principles for Quality Infrastructure Investment, which was established in 2015 and looks to provide a 30 percent increase in infrastructure investment, accounting for approximately USD110 billion, until 2020 (Ministry of Foreign Affairs, Japan, 2015).

Japan sees Malaysia as a "strategic lynchpin for greater connectivity, between the Pacific and Indian Oceans" (David, 2020). Malaysia and Japan have had a very close relationship as a result of the "Look East Policy" implemented by former PM Mahathir in the 1980s. Malaysia also cooperated with Japan on the safety of navigation in Malacca Straits and has received two patrol vessels from Japan (Permal, 2017).

Australia

Australia has been a key driver of the adoption of the Indo-Pacific concept, being the first country to use the term "Indo-Pacific" in its Defence White Paper in 2013. In its 2017 Foreign Policy White Paper dedicated an entire chapter to discuss *a stable and prosperous Indo-Pacific*, which reaffirms that competition for influence in Southeast Asia is sharpening (Government of Australia, 2017).

Australia and Malaysia have strong defence ties, both being members of the Five Powers Defence Arrangement (FPDA) along with Singapore, New Zealand and the United Kingdom, which turned 50 this year. While it is not a binding treaty, it nevertheless commits the member country to help in the event that Malaysia and Singapore are attacked (Parliament of Australia, 2007). Regular exercises are held under the ambit of FPDA. The Headquarter Integrated Area Defence System (HQIADS), the permanently manned element of FPDA in Butterworth, Malaysia is headed by an Australian Air Vice-Marshal. Malaysia and Australia also signed a Strategic Partnership in 2015 and administer a Malaysia-Australia Joint Defence Programme (DFAT Australia, 2015). In April 2020, Australia frigate HMAS Parramatta joined three US warships in South China Sea following the presence of Chinese survey ship Haiyang Dizhi 8 in Malaysian waters (Latif, 2020).

India

India's Prime Minister has stated that India views the region as "a multipolar Asia in a multipolar world". He has also stressed that his vision for the Indo-Pacific region is "inclusive" as is "not directed at anyone". (Siddiqui, 2019). India turned its "Look East Policy" to "Act East Policy" in 2014, which focuses on 3Cs – Commerce, Culture, Connectivity – signalling resolve to step up its engagement with Southeast Asia (Chand, 2014). In tandem of that, India's new maritime strategy also expanded to the Western and Southwestern Pacific Oceans (Kuo, 2018).

The defence relations between Malaysia and India have grown steadily since the signing of the MoU on Defence Cooperation in 1993. The Royal Malaysian Navy and Malaysian Maritime Enforcement Agency has a close working relationship with the Indian Navy and Coast Guards, particularly in monitoring the movement of ships from Andaman Sea into Straits of Malacca (MEA India, 2017). Malaysia held three joint exercises – Udara Shakti, Samudara Laksamana and Harimau Shakti – with India in 2022 (Abdullah, 2023).

Taiwan and South Korea

Both Taiwan and South Korea have launched the "New Southbound Policy" and the "New Southern Policy", respectively, in 2016 and 2017, both considered a flagship foreign policy under the Tsai Ing Wen's and then-Moon Jae-In's administration. This dual "Southern pivot" from East Asia also signalled the importance and the centrality of Southeast Asia and ASEAN in the Indo-Pacific region. Even though not officially included in the Quad, Taiwan has expressed its support to the Indo-Pacific framework. In December 2022, the new Yoon Seok-Yul administration, South Korea published its first "Strategy for a Free, Peaceful, and Prosperous Indo-Pacific Region", expanding South Korea's foreign policy horizon into the wider region (Kim, 2023). During the East Asia Summit in 2019, President Moon also gave a nod to AOIP and said that Korea endorsed "principles of ASEAN Centrality, openness, inclusivity, transparency and respect for international law", with special mentions of cooperation on connectivity and maritime affairs (MFA Republic of Korea, 2019). Malaysia is listed as an important partner in both Taiwan and South Korea's policies. Despite not having formal diplomatic ties, Taiwan has become the eighth largest FDI source for Malaysia in 2022 (TECO Malaysia, 2023).

Europe and the United Kingdom

The European Union has also published a "Strategy for Cooperation in the Indo-Pacific" in April 2021 (Council of the European Union, 2021). Of the

EU countries, France (Ministry of Armed Forces, France, 2018; Ministry of Europe and Foreign Affairs, France, 2021), Germany (Federal Government of Germany, 2020), and the Netherlands (Government of the Netherlands, 2020) have respectively their own Indo-Pacific strategy and increasingly raise concerns about stability and freedom of navigation in the South China Sea. The United Kingdom has also adopted the term in its latest Integrated Review in March 2021 (HM Government of the United Kingdom, 2021).

Malaysia also has good defence relations with the United Kingdom, France, and Germany. Being a former protectorate, Malaysia's defence relation with the UK is long-standing – starting with the Anglo-Malayan Defence Arrangement (AMDA) which later evolved into the FPDA. The historical ties were further cemented in 1998, when both countries signed an MoU on defence cooperation including bilateral military exercises, capability and capacity building, and training of personnel, as well as defence science, technology, and industry. In 2021, the two countries established the Malaysia-UK Strategic Dialogue (FCDO UK, 2022). Likewise, Malaysia has a robust partnership with France and Germany, particularly on defence science, technology and industry as well as personnel exchanges.

ASEAN

ASEAN published the ASEAN Outlook on Indo-Pacific (AOIP) in 2019. The AOIP states that it "envisages ASEAN Centrality as the underlying principle for promoting cooperation in the Indo-Pacific region, with ASEAN-led mechanisms, such as the East Asia Summit (EAS), as platforms for dialogue and implementation of the Indo–Pacific cooperation, while preserving their formats". It also claims that it is "intended to be inclusive in terms of ideas and proposals" and that "ASEAN also needs to continue being an **honest broker** within the strategic environment of competing interests".

Rather than an endorsement to the Indo-Pacific, it should be seen as an attempt to provide an alternative iteration of the term and to reclaim the geopolitical narrative amid the strategic rivalry between China and the United States" (Tyler, 2019). Nevertheless, it gave the concept a nod by stating that "Asia-Pacific and the Indian Oceans are amongst the most dynamic in the world as well as centers of economic growth for decades... As a result, these regions continue to experience geopolitical and geostrategic shifts". It continues to state that "these shifts present opportunities as well as challenges" and that "the rise of material powers, i.e., economic and military, requires avoiding the deepening of mistrust, miscalculation, and patterns of behavior based on a zero-sum game".

Malaysia was the founding member of ASEAN. Other than the ASEAN-led security mechanisms, notably ASEAN Defence Ministerial Meeting (ADMM) and ADMM-plus, East Asia Summit and ASEAN Regional

Forum, Malaysia is also involved in various minilateral cooperation with fellow ASEAN countries, most notably the Malacca Straits Patrol (MSP) and the Eye-in-the-Sky Initiative with Singapore, Indonesia, and Thailand, the Trilateral Cooperative Arrangement (TCA) with Philippines and Indonesia in the Sulu and Sulawesi Seas (MINDEF Malaysia, 2020).

Conclusion: The Way Forward

The Indo-Pacific has expanded the geopolitical theatre by merging the two ocean regions, and more adequately emphasised the maritime aspect of the current geo-security reality, as compared to Asia-Pacific. While the Indo-Pacific construct makes sense for the region, the political undertones and the tense relations between US and China have made it hard for Malaysia and Southeast Asia countries to embrace the lexicon officially.

As such, articulating an inclusive Indo-Pacific, where ASEAN-led mechanisms will continue to be utilised as the regional architecture and ASEAN centrality respected, is imperative in seeking Southeast Asian's buy in. Southeast Asia countries will also take a cue from China's attitude and the development of relations between the US and China under the Biden administration. As with any geopolitical scenario, nothing is constant. SEA will continue to observe the development by evaluating the Quad's impact to the region, and at the same time assess the threats of China and calculate its cost and benefits.

The role of middle powers in iterating alternative visions of Indo-Pacific that is less of a zero-sum game by the great powers will also be instrumental. As demonstrated, they do not necessarily share the US' interpretation of Indo-Pacific and also prefer a less confrontational, more inclusive Indo-Pacific. Downplaying the anti-China rhetoric and striking a more constructive tone would help to create more acceptance from Malaysia and other ASEAN member states. Engagement should not be a binary choice for smaller states in the Indo-Pacific.

Rather than responding passively and reactively to great power competition in the region, Malaysia has an important role to play and must indeed formulate a clear strategy to respond to all possibilities. Moving forward, Malaysia should play a more active role in the Indo-Pacific region, cementing its role as a "bridging linchpin" for the region. Malaysia's strategic location has not only made it a "linchpin" in regional security, but also an ideal destination for business, thereby crucial in improving connectivity and supply chain resilience in the region. As illustrated by the preceding section, Malaysia has had strong existing relations with Indo-Pacific countries, which can form the basis to more multilateral cooperation in the Indo-Pacific. Precisely because of the low-profile approach, Malaysia is also well placed to be a "bridge" between different Indo-Pacific powers.

178 Ivy Kwek

Similarly, ASEAN's role must also not be overlooked. ASEAN has exhibited the ability to gather various powers including the US, the Quad countries, China and Russia within its mechanism. Yet, ASEAN's role should not be a passive one, and its real prowess will be tested when faced with tricky issues in the region, particularly the post-military coup situation in Myanmar and an increasingly destabilising situation over the Taiwan Straits.

As the name is increasingly normalised, Malaysia and Southeast Asian urgently needs to find a way to work with both the US and China and avoid the Indo-Pacific becoming a battleground for supremacy, so that the competing regional constructs will be able to accommodate, if not complement each other. Singapore's Prime Minister Lee Hsien Loong has summarised the Southeast Asian sentiment when he said that, "Southeast Asian countries, including Singapore, are especially concerned, as they live at the intersection of the interests of various major powers and must avoid being caught in the middle or forced into invidious choices". The way out would be for the two powers to "work out a modus vivendi that will be competitive in some areas without allowing rivalry to poison cooperation in others" (Lee, 2020).

Whether or not Malaysia will warm up to the term in the near future remains to be seen, but it is clear that Malaysia can no longer passively observe the evolving geopolitical dynamics in the Indo-Pacific, but strive to demonstrate its ability to "build, bridge and bind" with other powers for the stability and prosperity of the region.

References

Adrian David, 2020. Malaysia Lynchpin for Indo-Pacific Connectivity. *New Straits Times.* https://www.nst.com.my/news/nation/2020/02/569672/malaysia-lynchpin-indo-pacific-connectivity

Council of the European Union, 2021. Council Conclusions on an EU Strategy for the Indo-Pacific. https://data.consilium.europa.eu/doc/document/ST-7914-2021-INIT/en/pdf

CSIS, 2021. How Much Trade Transits the South China Sea?. *China Power Project. Center for Strategic and International Studies* https://chinapower.csis.org/much-trade-transits-south-china-sea/?utm_content=buffer2dfa4&utm_medium=social&utm_source=twitter.com&utm_campaign=buffer .

Department of Foreign Affairs and Trade, Australia, 2015. *Joint Declaration of Strategic Partnership, Malaysia.* https://www.dfat.gov.au/geo/malaysia/Pages/joint-declaration-of-strategic-partnership#:~:text=In%20declaring%20a%20strategic%20partnership,strengthen%20further%20the%20bilateral%20relationship

Dino Patti Djalal, 2021. ASEAN Responses to AUKUS Security Dynamic. *East Asia Forum.* https://www.eastasiaforum.org/2021/11/28/asean-responses-to-aukus-security-dynamic/

Ellen Kim, 2023. Assessment of South Korea's New Indo-Pacific Strategy. *Center for Strategic and International Studies.* https://www.csis.org/analysis/assessment-south-koreas-new-indo-pacific-strategy

Faiz Abdullah, 2023. Malaysia's Role in the Emerging Indo-Pacific Order. *Institute of Strategic & International Studies Malaysia.*

Federal Government of Germany, 2020. *Policy Guidelines for the Indo-Pacific Region. Germany—Europe—Asia: Shaping the 21st Century Together.* https://rangun.diplo.de/blob/2380824/a27b62057f2d2675ce2bbfc5be01099a/policy-guidelines-summary-data.pdf

Foreign, Commonwealth & Development Office, United Kingdom, 2022. Malaysia-United Kingdom Strategic Dialogue – Feb 2022. https://www.gov.uk/government/publications/uk-malaysia-strategic-dialogue-2022/malaysia-united-kingdom-strategic-dialogue-february-2022#defence-security-and-serious-organised-crime

Government of Australia, 2017. *2017 Foreign Policy White Paper.* https://www.dfat.gov.au/publications/minisite/2017-foreign-policy-white-paper/fpwhitepaper/pdf/2017-foreign-policy-white-paper.pdf

Government of the Netherlands, 2020. *Indo-Pacific: Guidelines for Strengthening Dutch and EU Cooperation with Partners in Asia.* https://www.government.nl/documents/publications/2020/11/13/indo-pacific-guidelines

Hailey Chung, 2023. New Government to Proceed with ECRL Project at RM74.96 bil, Says PM. *The Edge Malaysia.* https://theedgemalaysia.com/article/ecrl-project-proceed-cost-reduced-rm1101b-says-pm-anwar

Her Majesty's Government of the United Kingdom, 2021. *Global Britain in a Competitive Age – The Integrated Review of Security, Defence, Development and Foreign Policy.* https://assets.publishing.service.gov.uk/government/uploads/system/uploads/attachment_data/file/975077/Global_Britain_in_a_Competitive_Age-_the_Integrated_Review_of_Security__Defence__Development_and_Foreign_Policy.pdf

环球时报, 2021. 美解密"印太战略"要与印度等国合作制衡中国? 外交部: 十分荒谬. 环球时报. https://world.huanqiu.com/article/41Wj9rhqzBd

Human Siddiqui, 2019. India's Concept of Indo-Pacific is Inclusive and Across Oceans. *Ministry of External Affairs, India.* https://mea.gov.in/articles-in-indian-media.htm?dtl/32015/Indias_concept_of_IndoPacific_is_inclusive_and_across_oceans

Ibrahim, 2023. Keynote Address by the Prime Minister of Malaysia at the 36th Asia-Pacific Roundtable. https://www.pmo.gov.my/2023/08/keynote-address-by-yab-dato-sri-anwar-ibrahim-prime-minister-of-malaysia-at-the-36th-asia-pacific-roundtable-apr/

Jayant Menon, 2023. What can Malaysia Expect from IPEF? *ISEAS-Yusof Ishak Institute, Singapore.* https://www.iseas.edu.sg/articles-commentaries/iseas-perspective/2023-64-what-can-malaysia-expect-from-ipef-by-jayant-menon/

Jinny Yan, 2018. The Belt and Road Initiative in Southeast Asia. In *China's Belt and Road Initiative (BRI) and Southeast Asia.* CIMB ASEAN Research Institute (CARI). https://www.lse.ac.uk/ideas/Assets/Documents/reports/LSE-IDEAS-China-SEA-BRI.pdf

Kuik Cheng Chwee, 2008. The Essence of Hedging: Malaysia and Singapore's Response to a Rising China. *Contemporary Southeast Asia*, Vol. 30, No. 2, pp. 159–185. ISEAS – Yusof Ishak Institute. https://www.jstor.org/stable/41220503

Kuik Cheng Chwee, 2020. Hedging in Post Pandemic Asia: What, How and Why. *The Asan Forum.* http://www.theasanforum.org/hedging-in-post-pandemic-asia-what-how-and-why/?dat=

Kuik Cheng Chwee, 2021. Malaysia's Fluctuating Engagement with China's Belt and Road Initiative: Leveraging Asymmetry, Legitimizing Authority. *Asian Perspective*, Vol. 45, No. 2, pp. 421–444. Johns Hopkins University Press. https://muse.jhu.edu/article/787859

Lee Hsien Loong, 2020. The Endangered Asian Century. *The Foreign Affairs*. https://www.foreignaffairs.com/articles/asia/2020-06-04/lee-hsien-loong-endangered-asian-century

Malaysia Department of Statistics, 2023. *Current Population Estimates, Malaysia, 2023*. https://www.dosm.gov.my/portal-main/release-content/current-population-estimates-malaysia----2023

Malaysia Department of Statistics, 2023. *Gross Domestic Product 2015–2022*. https://www.dosm.gov.my/portal-main/release-content/0ac27ca0-ee08-11ed-96d5-1866daa77ef9

Malaysia Ministry of Defence, 2020. *2019 Defence White Paper: A Secure, Sovereign and Prosperous Malaysia*. http://www.mod.gov.my/images/mindef/article/kpp/Defense%20White%20Paper.pdf

Manish Chand, 2014. Act East: India's ASEAN Journey. *Ministry of External Affairs, India*. https://www.mea.gov.in/in-focus-article.htm?24216/Act+East+Indias+ASEAN+Journey

Melissa Conley Tyler, 2019. The Indo-Pacific is the New Asia. *The Interpreter, Lowy Institute*. https://www.lowyinstitute.org/the-interpreter/indo-pacific-new-asia

Mercy A. Kuo, 2018. The Origin of 'Indo-Pacific' as Geopolitical Construct. *The Diplomat*. https://thediplomat.com/2018/01/the-origin-of-indo-pacific-as-geopolitical-construct/

Ministry of Armed Forces, France, 2018. *France and Security in the Indo-Pacific*. https://franceintheus.org/IMG/pdf/France_and_Security_in_the_Indo-Pacific_-_2019.pdf

Ministry of Europe and Foreign Affairs, France, 2021. *France's Partnership in the Indo-Pacific*. https://www.diplomatie.gouv.fr/en/country-files/asia-and-oceania/the-indo-pacific-region-a-priority-for-france/

Ministry of External Affairs, India, 2017. *India-Malaysia Bilateral Relations*. https://mea.gov.in/Portal/ForeignRelation/Malaysia_August_2017.pdf

Ministry of Foreign Affairs, Japan. *Free and Open Indo-Pacific: Basic Concepts*. https://www.mofa.go.jp/files/000430632.pdf

Ministry of Foreign Affairs, Japan. 2015. *Announcement of "Partnership for Quality Infrastructure: Investment for Asia's Future*. https://www.mofa.go.jp/policy/oda/page18_000076.html

Ministry of Foreign Affairs, Republic of Korea, 2019. *Opening Remarks by President Moon Jae-in at 14th East Asia Summit*. https://www.mofa.go.kr/eng/brd/m_5674/view.do?seq=319976

NHK World, 2023. Navigating Neutrality: How Malaysia Sustains Ties with Two Competing Superpowers. https://www3.nhk.or.jp/nhkworld/en/news/backstories/2496/

Parliament of Australia, 2007. Inquiry into Australia's Relationship with Malaysia, Chapter 3: Security and Defence Ties. *Joint Standing Committee on Foreign Affairs Defence and Trade*. https://www.aph.gov.au/Parliamentary_Business/Committees/Joint/Completed_Inquiries/jfadt/malaysia/report/chapter3#def

Raggie Jessy Rithaudeen, 2019. *When Elephant Fight, the Grass Will Suffer – YB Mat Sabu*. https://twitter.com/RaggieJessy/status/1135586348067303424

Reuters, 2010. *Factbox – Malacca Strait is a Strategic 'Chokepoint'*. https://www.reuters.com/article/idUSTRE62335X/.

Richard Javad Heydarian, 2021. The Quad: An "Asian NATO" against China?. *China-US Focus*. https://www.chinausfocus.com/peace-security/the-quad-an-asian-nato-against-china

Rozanna Latif, 2020. Australia Joins U.S. Ships in South China Sea Amid Rising Tension. *Reuters*. https://www.reuters.com/article/us-china-security

-malaysia/australia-joins-u-s-ships-in-south-china-sea-amid-rising-tension
-idUSKCN2240FS

Sophie Boisseau du Rocher, 2020. The Belt and Road: China's 'Community of Desitny' for Southeast Asia? *Asie.Vision, No. 113. IFRI.* https://www.ifri.org/sites/default/files/atoms/files/boisseau_bri_community_destiny_2020.pdf

Sumathy Permal, 2017. Japan-Malaysia Cooperation in the New Security Landscape of the Indo-Pacific. *Maritime Awareness Project.* http://maritimeawarenessproject.org/2017/11/01/japan-malaysia-cooperation-in-the-new-security-landscape-of-the-indo-pacific/

Taiwan Economic and Cultural Office (TECO) in Malaysia, 2023. Wistron – A Shining Example of Taiwan's Successful Investments in Malaysia! https://www.roc-taiwan.org/my_en/post/9287.html#:~:text=James%20Chang%20said%20that%20Taiwanese,8th%20largest%20investor%20in%20Malaysia.

U.S. Congressional Research Service, 2022. *Biden Administration Plans for an Indo-Pacific Economic Framework.*

U.S. Department of Defense, 2019. *The Indo-Pacific Strategy Report. June 01, 2019.* https://media.defense.gov/2019/Jul/01/2002152311/-1/-1/1/DEPARTMENT-OF-DEFENSE-INDO-PACIFIC-STRATEGY-REPORT-2019.PDF

US State Department, 2019. *A Free and Open Indo-Pacific: Advancing a Shared Vision. November 04, 2019.*

US White House, 2017. *National Security Strategy of the United States of America. December 1, 2017.* . https://trumpwhitehouse.archives.gov/wp-content/uploads/2017/12/NSS-Final-12-18-2017-0905.pdf

U.S. White House, 2023. Quad Leaders' Joint Statement. https://www.whitehouse.gov/briefing-room/statements-releases/2023/05/20/quad-leaders-joint-statement/

Yoshihide Soeya, 2020. Japan and the Indo-Pacific: From Strategy to Vision. *The Strategist, Australia Strategic Policy Institute.* https://www.aspistrategist.org.au/japan-and-the-indo-pacific-from-strategy-to-vision/

12

SINGAPORE'S STRATEGY IN THE INDO-PACIFIC

Vignesh Ram

Singapore's success story has become a classic case study about a nation's development in post-colonial Asia. Singapore continues to hold several developmental distinctions in Asia and around the world, including being the second-best place to do business in the world and number one in Asia. Despite its small size, Singapore has been able to leverage its position in the region and with major and great powers as a result of a carefully calibrated strategy, which has helped it maintain its economic and diplomatic independence. The success of the "Singapore model" of development inspired other countries, including China, which developed and modelled some of its first free trade areas on Singapore.

Several factors have contributed to the success. Tough foreign policy choices have led to increased friction at times with its larger neighbours. This has been tactfully dealt with in the form of cooperation within the established regional mechanisms as well as extra-regional states. Singapore, due to its geopolitical compulsions, has maintained a positive approach in engaging major powers such as the US in the region as compared to Indonesia and Malaysia, which have maintained relations with the West largely at arm's length. Hence, it can be said that the maturation of the regional mechanisms in Southeast Asia, mainly through the Association of Southeast Asian Nations (ASEAN), has been able to help build a closer consensus on regional issues.

Singapore's dynamic approach has fascinated several analysts who have tried to understand the ability of a state with no natural resources to wield a long-ranging influence in the world as well as regional affairs. Rightfully, this behaviour which is attributed to smaller countries has been termed as

DOI: 10.4324/9781003479307-15

"punching above its weight". The foreign policy of small states is often an overlooked area in the largely realist dominated international relations literature. However, with the changing dynamics of regional equations, the role of multilateral groupings has been able to play a key role in the changing decentralised regional architecture of the multipolar world.

In this context, with the emergence of the Indo-Pacific conceptualisation, there has been rising speculation on the role of groupings such as ASEAN, which comprises smaller and medium states closely linked to the global trading architecture. In the Indo-Pacific era, as major power competition intensifies, Singapore finds itself in yet another regional transition of power. Hence, it is important to understand the strategy of the nation-state as it will have ramifications for regional geopolitics as well as business interests. In this context, the paper sets out to analyse Singapore's foreign policy from different theoretical perspectives and lays out the foreign policy perspective. The chapter then moves on to assess Singapore's security calculus and factors leading to the development of unique perspectives on the Indo-Pacific. Finally, the chapter assesses Singapore's position among the great power politics of the Indo-Pacific.

Deciphering Singapore's Foreign Policy Calculus

The chapter has attempted to decipher and understand the prevailing conditions to which Singapore's foreign policy has adapted. Several leaders and foreign policy decision makers in the Singaporean context have aligned to the perspective of Singapore being a realist state (Leifer, 2000) in which core tenets of policy including territorial integrity, sovereignty, and survival are emphasised in elite policy outreach. Small states are often considered in the traditional realist parlance as actors insignificant in affecting the direction of international relations and are merely considered as aligning their interests to those of dominant or major powers. A cursory study of the city states' foreign policy behaviour demonstrates much more dynamism than the mere description of a theoretical lens. Singapore's early foreign policy behaviour demonstrates a need for survival, as demonstrated by moves made by the nation state to adopt measures to streamline its foreign policy in tune with its interests, which at times went contrary to its neighbours' foreign policy outlook. Domestic calculations and ideological signalling prompted "anti-communist" narratives, which also were instrumental in pushing Singapore closer to the ideological spectrum of the "west".

Early adoptions of economic models also signalled trade-friendly and export promotion initiatives as opposed to import substitution models. Hence, Singapore's outlook was more modelled on having a strong foreign policy perspective by forming strategic alliances (even if it meant having an opposing stand in the region and with its neighbours) and building a cohesive society with the state building welfare and openness to trade. The often-contradicting nature of defining Singapore through one theoretical lens has been encapsulated by some as "Abridged Realism". The author has argued that Singaporean realism is only a partial demonstration of realist orthodoxy and that its realism is framed by liberal prefixes in the sense that future value-adding possibilities are generated as a map for the Global City collaborating with and persuading the major powers and regional states of developing faith in win-win cooperation (Chong, 2006). This view of a varied perspective breaking away from the traditional core realist understanding is also highlighted by other experts who note that given the city states' liberal institutionalism and constructivist approaches there is an opportunity. It is contended that the emphasis on Singapore's foreign economic policy and its national security approach, in the broader sense of the term, is dictated by the liberal framework of globalisation rather than the mercantilist notion of self-reliance and autarchy, which would be closer to realism. Similarly, its approaches to building a culture of socialisation and development of dialogue through ASEAN and other regional institutions can be more tuned to social constructivist ideas (Acharya, 2007).

It could be well assessed that Singapore's foreign policy is multi-dimensional and multi-layered to protect its foreign policy security and trade interests. The increasing stature of the city-state in global trade has led to increased threats of global risk, which have been balanced by its building of networks to buffer the fallout of these risks. This includes balancing the presence of local vulnerability by building closer ties or promoting US presence in the region. The early notion of vulnerability has transcended into increased challenges for the city-state to negotiate (Heng, 2013). One instance of using multi-level strategies to balance its interests can be seen with Singapore's backing for the US rebalance strategy. In assessing the major foreign policy thrust, it has been argued that the policy was a demonstration of support for America's forward presence and belief in the importance of America's strategic guarantee to the Asia-Pacific region. This support for the US policy not only provided Singapore heft in the regional politics but also allowed it to use these relations as one of the bedrock for its cooperation (Tan, 2016). Another important narrative on Singapore's approaches to building a multi-layered relationship is on its integration with the larger regional frameworks such as ASEAN. This, in turn, is also driven by its core identity principle of self-preservation and vulnerability.

Hence, eminent historians of Southeast Asia have noted that "Singapore's leaders have consistently approached the matter of foreign policy from the perspective of a small state obliged to cope with a world that was potentially hostile and without a common government" (Leifer, 2000). This challenge has also been highlighted by several analysts who have tried to go beyond the mandate of realist theories and study the external relations of

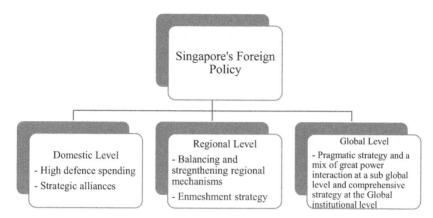

FIGURE 12.1 Singapore's Foreign Policy

small states. It is noted that small states do not have the elements of physical power through which they can play this role. However, they are based on the internal determinants (such as political leadership and the variable of perception) and non-physical dimensions of power to play an effective and influential external role (Galal, 2020) (Figure 12.1).

In the contemporary sense, the above-mentioned distillation easily encapsulates Singaporean foreign policy as elucidated by former Singapore Foreign Minister Vivian Balakrishnan. Considering the perennial limitations of geography and size, being a small state, Vivian Balakrishnan states that Singapore's foreign policy has five core principles: 1) a successful and vibrant economy depending on stable politics and a united society, 2) maintaining sovereignty and territorial integrity (military), 3) being friend to all and enemy to none – peace and stability in the immediate neighbourhood and with superpowers and other regional powers, creating their stakes in the success of Singapore. No compromising on national interest, 4) promoting a global world order governed by the rule of law and international norms, and 5) being credible and consistent partner – providing a sense of strategic predictability (Balakrishnan, 2017).

Development, Security, and the Shaping of Singapore's Security Culture and Outlook

Singapore's strategic position did not protect it from the diverse sets of security challenges which existed since its independence and even before. Development and security were intertwined right from the beginning of its separation from Malaysia. Developing a security culture and a global security outlook was important for the development of Singapore's strategic position globally as well as regionally. While not always their neighbours agreed with Singapore's position, in terms of its alignments with other major powers, they did find it useful to bin the various narratives about regional cooperation to bring in more diversity into the regional setting. To understand the interlinkages between defence, security, and development it is important to note the development agenda in place and how they were closely linked with security and foreign policy manoeuvring as a result.

Singapore's first Prime Minister, Lee Kuan Yew, and several initial leaders of Singapore had clearly highlighted the need to look at economics, security, and global challenges impacting every aspect of the city states' existence including its domestic politics. Lee highlighted that "defence and security were indivisible from trade and industry". Years later, he would describe the nexus as two sides of the same question by stating that "you cannot have a strong defence unless you have strong finance, and you cannot have strong defence and finance unless you have a strong, unified, well-educated, and increasingly cohesive society." Hence, promotion of trade was a key objective of Singapore's security.

Throughout the Cold War, Singapore's domestic interests aligned well with US interests in the region and the capitalist mode of development. This was also supported by the decision-making elite in the country who sought to use economic growth and development as the main reasons, i.e., to safeguard domestic political stability and create more strategic relevance for a small state such as Singapore in the international community. Hence, most of the processes including Singapore's relevance and development were closely linked to defence and security. As noted, the first defence against communist subversion is "economic", a point that Lee Kuan Yew also emphasised. Singapore's then finance minister Goh Keng Swee highlighted that "economic development is the most effective inoculation against subversion and revolution". The second line of defence, according to Goh, is police intelligence. The armed forces provide the third and last line of fire (Guan, 2015).

It is then important to understand the Singaporean model of development, a unique potential opportunity presented to the political entity almost by accident. As the following argument will make clear, Singapore's foreign policy and its contemporary policy towards major powers are a result of a carefully calibrated strategy. The "Singapore Model of Development" has been analysed quite a bit, but the variables that make this model, and by its application, Singapore a success story, are important to understand. There were three major elements in this model, i.e., political, economic, and social dynamics and characteristics. The Singapore model, according to some, is the result of a tight grip on the political aspect with the promotion of investor-friendly policies while being open to foreign talent. The emphasis is on the creation of an environment that banks on credibility and the rule of law (Ananta Aspen Centre, 2013).

Nevertheless, as argued elsewhere, the leadership/the ruling elite played a key role in steering this development. As one analysis argues, the quality of governance coupled along with political stability plays a key role in distinguishing Singapore's or, for that matter, the development in economies. It has been argued that political stability is an exogenous variable. Leadership matters in providing political stability, but political stability will not always guarantee or ensure the quality of governance. The quality of governance, the author goes on to argue, emerges from the type of economic system and the political processes in place. Hence, it has been understood that Singapore's global dependence played in disciplining Singapore's single-party government (Lim, 2016). Hence, the role of foreign policy in determining Singapore's acceptance to global policies has been crucial.

Hence, it can be noted that the roots of Singapore's foreign policy alignment had its roots in the need to balance regional, domestic, and international security and developmental considerations. The alignment with the US during most of the Cold War enabled Singapore to benefit from the levels of growth and bring it on par with the Western world. Singapore benefited from technology from the West and Japan and security from the US presence. However, Singapore's foreign policy consistently remained sensitive to neighbouring considerations, which led to the lack of complete immersion with the US-led alliance system. Nevertheless, this development led to more innovation in maintaining its economic position in the region.

As one analysis notes, Singapore realised that it was losing a competitive advantage in its manufacturing sector. The rising costs of production, labour, and land forced the country to rethink its developmental model. Singapore innovated by moving industries to provinces in neighbouring countries. In turn, these countries used Singapore as the springboard for various services whereby Singapore's manufacturing competitiveness was not lost, and it was at the same time able to develop a high level services economy (Stimson, Stough, & Rob, 2006). This became a crucial part of the model of development in neighbouring countries, which was also helpful in certain ways unifying the complementarity in the region. Hence, Singapore's economic policy and its development cannot be separated from its larger foreign policy goals. Therefore, a review of foreign policy and its implications for Singapore's domestic, regional, and global position will help understand its position and stand on the Indo-Pacific.

The Competing Narratives in the Indo-Pacific: Great Power Engagement and Singapore

A primary reading of Southeast Asian history would define Singapore as gifted in terms of geography, if not anything else. Geopolitics was the very reason that the city-state was founded by Sir Stamford Raffles in 1819.

Raffles, in a bid to secure a key port along the trade route between India and China connecting the Indian Ocean and the South China Sea, established Singapore to break the Dutch monopoly in controlling the trade routes (Glendinning, 2013). Not only Singapore but the strategic sea routes which pass through Southeast Asia have continued to retain their strategic significance for global trade. Indeed, sea routes and trade and access to markets remain key reasons for interaction. This elucidates the fact as to why countries in the region have taken the initiative to address concerns about the issue. For instance, Indonesia, with strategic access to its sea lanes, projected a "Maritime Fulcrum" policy while vouching for an "Indo-Pacific Treaty of Friendship and Cooperation". Similarly, Indonesia also latched onto, and was in fact, the first place where China declared the Maritime Silk Route (the second component of the Belt and Road Initiative (BRI). The importance of getting countries in the region on board could not be much clearer.

Apart from the shift from the "Asia-Pacific" to the "Indo-Pacific", China's influence on the Southeast Asian region has been tremendous. Over the years, China's influence within Southeast Asia has been manifested in several key strategic engagements with countries at the regional as well as sub-regional levels. ASEAN has been grappling with several issues putting countries at the mercy of picking sides, which defeats the purpose of a regional mechanism set up under ASEAN to regulate regional ties with extra-regional powers. ASEAN's inability to persuade China to agree to a legally binding code of conduct or regulate or contain China's expansion in the South China Sea and illegal fishing in Southeast Asian waters.

In this context, the role of countries such as Singapore becomes difficult to navigate. Singapore has been facing key challenges in dealing with China under the context of the Belt and Road Initiative. Singapore's Prime Minister Lee Hsien Loong was not invited to the first summit despite being one of the first supporters of the project since its initiation. This was in sharp contrast to Singapore's neighbours where the Heads of State were invited. As one Chinese scholar has opined, "China's decision not to invite the Singaporean leader reflected a growing belief in Beijing that the Lion City sought only economic benefits from China, while 'relying on the US for security'" (Jaipragas, 2017).

The long-standing challenge has altered and tested Singaporean foreign policy in the new emerging Indo-Pacific architecture. While Singapore continues to remain a key player for China and Chinese companies to operate in Southeast Asia (including having one of the largest offshore yuan centres in the world), Singapore has continued to keep away and use ASEAN and regional mechanisms to deal with China's disputes with the Southeast Asian region. It has played a much bigger role in enhancing the US military's position in the region.

In 2015, the US and Singapore agreed to an "enhanced" cooperation agreement, and the US began deploying surveillance aircraft to Singapore around the same time. The US Navy maintains a logistical command unit – Commander, Logistics Group Western Pacific – in Singapore that coordinates warship deployments and logistics in the region. Singapore's Changi Naval Base is one of the few facilities in the world that can accommodate a US aircraft carrier, and Singapore-stationed littoral combat ships (LCSs) have performed patrols in the South China Sea (Congressional Research Service, 2022). The highlight of the US's relations with Singapore was the renewal of the US-Singapore defence pact in 2019, which will give US forces access to Singapore's bases till 2035. It has been noted that this agreement strengthens and indicates Singapore's position as a trusted and important partner in the US strategy in Asia (Sim, 2019). Similarly, the Singapore Navy has been part of the Quadrilateral initiative a few times, indicating its willingness to be co-opted within the larger security framework in the Indo-Pacific region.

Despite its proactive approach, Singapore continues to maintain an independent stance on the Indo-Pacific, especially when signing onto regional statements and official positions on the region or its conceptualisation. The Free and Open Indo-Pacific Concept has been endorsed by all major powers in the region. The powers, including India, the US, Japan, and Australia, had signalled and continue to coordinate their policies. However, the Association of Southeast Asian Nations stayed off from commenting on the issue despite its geopolitical contiguity with the region.

However, despite its reluctance at the close of the 34th ASEAN Summit in Bangkok, leaders from the bloc's member countries issued the "ASEAN Outlook for the Indo-Pacific" document (Association of Southeast Asian Nations, 2019). While the agreement was spearheaded by Indonesia, Singapore in its foreign policy outlook opposed any document to be released on the pretext that the concept did not adequately address the centrality of ASEAN to the emerging architecture.

Singapore views the Indo-Pacific construct as an important geopolitical concept that captures the increasing interconnectedness of the Indian and Pacific Oceans, especially given the rise of India and China and the strategic significance of the maritime routes connecting the two oceans. However, it has been very cautious on the approach towards taking affirmed interest or hedging its bets on the Quad-focused military concept. As far back as 2013 when the concept was gaining more currency, Singapore remained on the sidelines and preferred to wait and watch. As some analysts noted, some in Southeast Asia, notably "the Singaporeans, are still much more comfortable with "Asia-Pacific" even though their interests span the two oceans" (Medcalf, 2013). While visibly as the first informal summit of the then emerging "Quad" countries was held on the sidelines of the ASEAN Regional

Forum (ARF) summit in Manila, the joint statement reflected "Asia-Pacific" and avoided the Indo-Pacific reference (Association of Southeast Asian Nations, 2012).

The vision of Singaporean foreign policy vis-à-vis the Indo-Pacific can be encapsulated in Vivian Balakrishnan's statement in 2018. He stated, "Frankly right now, the so-called free and open Indo-Pacific has not yet fleshed out a sufficient level of resolution to answer these questions that I've posed... We never sign on to anything unless we know exactly what it means" (Yong, 2018). While ASEAN did release its vision document to showcase its position, Singaporean foreign policy observers have closely seen this process as a positive sign of growing transparency within ASEAN diplomacy.

The analysis brings a spotlight on Singapore's foreign policy and its core principles as discussed elsewhere in this chapter. As argued in the section on the foreign policy of Singapore in this chapter despite the lack of a consensus or a reshuffle within the regional organisation, Singapore has acted well within its core foreign policy principles. For instance, maintaining the need for a balanced perspective (read: A much more diluted statement) and centrality of ASEAN remains the key approach followed by the country at the domestic and regional level to maintain maximum leverage in dealing with extra regional powers in the region. More importantly, it kept Singapore and its options with China. This effort to balance relations could be seen in the light of separate trade dynamics (in the guise of the Regional Comprehensive Economic Partnership (RCEP) unfolding in the region. While ASEAN centrality was established within the RCEP concept right from the very start.

Furthermore, the policy perspective continues to evolve in the light of changing geopolitical realities. Singapore continues to try to balance between the competing narratives laid out by the US and China in the region. US Defence Secretary Austin's visit to Singapore (along with a visit to Vietnam and the Philippines) in 2021 reflected an accurate prioritisation of US partnerships in Southeast Asia (Poling, 2021). More recently, in a trip to the US, Foreign Minister Balakrishnan once again highlighted Singapore's unique balanced yet nuanced position. On the question of picking sides (between the US and China), he emphasised that Singapore preferred an "overlapping circle of friends" including both the US and China, and Europe and other emerging poles, real stakes in the peace, prosperity, and development of Southeast Asia. However, in a similar vein when asked about India and its position on non-condemnation of Russia on Ukraine, he emphasised that India's position and diversity provided it to work based on its national interest calculations (Ministry of Foreign Affairs Singapore, 2023)

The above arguments capture the essence of the dynamic nature of Singapore's foreign policy and its core still is realist in nature while it uses other tools at the regional and international level to increase its capacity and stakes. Nevertheless, Singapore continues to cautiously tread its position as an attractive investment destination, competitive vis-à-vis its neighbours and internationally. Singapore's neighbours have taken a keen interest in building positions on either side of the spectrum, reflecting a problem for the ASEAN-centric consensus building in the region. It can be understood that Singapore's model of engagement could be beneficial considering its size, resources, and reach in the international system in conjunction with its national interests.

Conclusion

The observers of Southeast Asia have long predicted that the rise of new powers and the challenges and shifts in the geopolitical conceptualisations in Asia will pose the most significant challenge to ASEAN. The Southeast Asian region has been both geopolitically and geographically situated at the centre of a dynamic area with its crucial seaways. While ASEAN members have experienced the benefits of China's trade and the repercussions of its military rise, the revision of the US' position in the region has further complicated the situation. The diversity of opinions within ASEAN stems from the reluctance of regional states to revise their positions despite the changing geopolitical environment.

Singaporean foreign policy, in essence, echoes the fundamental principles laid by its founding fathers. Despite the shifts in the regional climate, Singapore continues to maintain a balanced approach towards extra-regional powers. At the domestic level, Singapore benefits from the security provided by the US presence in the region, while at the regional level, through the utilization of regional mechanisms, Singapore advocates for regional trade agreements. As a precaution against potential misadventures by extra-regional states, it emphasizes the centrality of ASEAN as a by-product of such negotiations. This follows an established principle used by smaller regional countries to involve larger powers as stakeholders, if not partners, in the region's development.

The numero uno priority of Singapore's foreign policy is fundamentally centered on building and maintaining its vibrant economy as well as peace and stability on the domestic front to achieve that goal. In the context of a city-state like Singapore, domestic and foreign policies are closely linkaged, and sometimes, due to various dependencies, foreign policy holds more significance in maintaining order. This core understanding has driven Singapore to develop diverse policies enmeshed and, at most times, is a combination of multiple alignments and strategies at the domestic, regional, and global levels.

As the city-state remains heavily reliant on trade and commerce, it can be understood that any new mega conceptualization needs careful consideration before endorsement. Such decisions will significantly impact the economy of the nation. Hence, Singapore has moved cautiously to align with any notions of the Indo-Pacific with a permanent bearing on its foreign policy. For instance, Singapore has continued to maintain a pragmatic stance on dealing with the various components of the Indo-Pacific architecture but has been at most cautious in showcasing its association with any one side. This has helped the city-state and, as an extension of the region, maintain a favourable consensus on its association with multiple powers while explicitly maintaining its centrality and unique stance on the issue.

Singapore's foreign policy considerations will continue to drive debates within the academic community about its future course. While it has shown dynamism and pragmatism, it has been able to wade through the waters well to date. For, the basic founding principle for Singapore's foreign policy, like other powers, has been maintaining its relevance and survival. Singapore has thrived, and it has done so with a carefully calibrated foreign policy firmly rooted in realism and a dynamic policy with multiple enmeshments at different levels. This has ensured that the "little red dot" has always continued to "punch above its weight".

References

Acharya, A. (2007). *Singapore's Foreign Policy: The Search for Regional Order.* Singapore: World Scientific.

Ananta Aspen Centre. (2013). *Gopinath Pillai: The Singapore Model of Growth & Development*. New Delhi: Ananta Aspen Centre.

Association of Southeast Asian Nations. (2012, July 6). Chairman's Statement 14th ASEAN Regional Forum Manila, 2 August 2007. Retrieved from asean.org :https://asean.org/chairmans-statement-14th-asean-regional-forum-manila-2-au gust-2007/This can be added to the endnotes

Association of Southeast Asian Nations. (2019). *ASEAN Outlook on the Indo-Pacific*. Joint Statement, Jakarta. Jakarta: Association of Southeast Asian Nations.

Balakrishnan, V. (2017, July 17). Full Speech: Five Core Principles of Singapore's Foreign Policy. *The Strait Times.*

Chong, A. (2006). Singapore's Foreign Policy Beliefs as 'Abridged Realism': Pragmatic and Liberal Prefixes in the Foreign Policy Thought of Rajaratnam, Lee, Koh, and Mahbubani. *International Relations of the Asia-Pacific*, 6(6),269–306.

Congressional Research Service. (2022). *U.S.-Singapore Relations*. Washington: Congressional Research Service.

Galal, M. A. (2020). External Behavior of Small States in Light of Theories of International Relations. *Review of Economics and Political Science*, 5(1), 38–56.

Glendinning, V. (2013). *Raffles and the Golden Opportunity*. London: Profile Books.

Guan, A. C. (2015). Singapore's Conception of Security. In B. Desker & A. C. Guan (Eds.), *Perspectives on the Security of Singapore The First 50 Years* (pp. 8–9). Singapore: World Scientfic.

Heng, Y. K. (2013). A Global City in an Age of Global Risks: Singapore's Evolving Discourse on Vulnerability. *Contemporary Southeast Asia*, 35(3), 423–446.

Jaipragas, B. (2017, May 18). What New Silk Road Snub Means for Singapore's Ties with China. *South China Morning Post*.

Leifer, M. (2000). *Singapore's Foreign Policy: Coping with Vulnerability*. London: Routledge.

Lim, L. Y. (2016). *Singapore's Economic Development: Retrospection and Reflections*. Singapore: World Scientific.

Medcalf, R. (2013, October 10). The Indo-Pacific: What's in a Name?. *The American Interest*.

Ministry of Foreign Affairs Singapore. (2023, June 15). Transcript of Minister for Foreign Affairs Dr Vivian Balakrishnan's dialogue at the Council on Foreign Relations. https://www.mfa.gov.sg/Newsroom/Press-Statements-Transcripts-and-Photos/2023/06/20230616transcriptcfr

Poling, G. B. (2021, July 30). Austin Accomplishes Two Missions in Southeast Asia. Retrieved from Center for Strategic and International Studies:https://www.csis.org/analysis/austin-accomplishes-two-missions-southeast-asia

Sim, D. (2019, September 24). Singapore Renews Military Bases Pact with the US amid Deepening Defence Ties with China. *South China Morning Post*.

Stimson, R., Stough, R. R., & Rob, B. H. (2006). *Regional Economic Development: Analysis and Planning Strategy*. New York: Springer Science & Business Media.

Tan, S. S. (2016). Facilitating the US Rebalance: Challenges and Prospects for Singapore as America's Security Partner. *Security Challenges*, 12(3), 20–33.

Yong, C. (2018, May 14). Singapore Not Joining US, Japan-led Free and Open Indo-Pacific for Now: Vivian Balakrishnan. *The Strait Times*.

13

INDONESIA IN THE INDO-PACIFIC

The Rise of a Strategic Geopolitical Power

Vignesh Ram

In the study of geopolitics, history has favoured states that have utilised their geography to their advantage. The transactions between geographically significant states and others have shaped how socio-cultural and socio-economic behavioural patterns have emerged, defining global trade and commerce as well as conflict. Geographically diverse and culturally significant, Indonesia has historically been central to the development of the socio-cultural and socio-political ecosystems in Asia. Indonesia's historical centrality to the trade between the Indian and Pacific Oceans, especially the South China Sea region and East Asia, is well documented in archival research. In the contemporary context, this geopolitically significant nation, which was once blindsided in the early days of Cold War geopolitics, has been rising once again with a revered fervour to command its position among what seems to be a growing great power-led contest.

Indonesia's post-Cold War democratic transition (an ongoing process) to date has played a key role in projecting wider stability and a proactive role in commanding a stable position in the geopolitics of the region. Central to this power projection has been Indonesia's use of its core foundational foreign policy approaches and blending them with more proactive regional diplomacy through the Association of Southeast Asian Nations (ASEAN). ASEAN remains a major facet of Indonesia's foreign policy approach. Nevertheless, ASEAN, with its historical antecedents reflects a mirror onto the powerful role of Indonesia's normative approach within the organisation.

In the emergent regional security scenario, Indonesia has taken a more proactive approach, especially in the past decade, to propel itself as a key Indo-Pacific player, taking advantage of its geographical position. However, Indonesia has mostly adopted a different approach as opposed to other

DOI: 10.4324/9781003479307-16

major proponents driving the debate over the Indo-Pacific. Keeping in line with its approach, Indonesia has mostly preferred an institutional approach driven by a multitude of powers. This approach has stood out as a dynamic option for the future regional architecture in the Indo-Pacific. Nevertheless, in the developing processes in the Indo-Pacific, a lot of permutations and combinations need to be understood.

In the process of understanding the core debates in the Indo-Pacific, the chapter will understand the evolution of Indonesia's foreign policy and its positioning on the Indo-Pacific within this setting. The chapter will also try to assess and analyse the Indonesian proposals on the Indo-Pacific and its receptiveness by other regional and subregional stakeholders. Finally, the chapter will assess the motivations and the scope of Indonesia in the emerging regional security architecture in the Indo-Pacific.

Indonesia's Foreign Policy: Gradual Broadening of the Horizon

In 1953, Mohammed Hatta wrote in the publication "Foreign Policy" providing some clarity on the policy orientation of the new Indonesian state, while collaborating incidents throughout in the arguments, he acknowledged its weak post-colonial position amidst the emerging bipolar rivalry and acknowledged that Indonesia followed a "Free and Independent" foreign policy (Hatta, 1953). Nevertheless, this foreign policy approach played a key role in defining the regional outlook and understanding the prospects of engaging the country in the regional setting. Indonesia's early engagements within the region and efforts by regional and extra-region states highlighted that any regional setting or organisation without Indonesia was not possible in Southeast Asia. Indonesia's foreign policy has always hinged on subtle approaches towards its neighbourhood and the extended Asia-Pacific region. The outlook largely was driven by the New Order government to have a more nuanced approach towards the region. President Suharto would pursue more modest foreign policy goals centred on Indonesia's needs for security, stability, and economic development (Anwar, 2014).

Indonesia's firm entrenchment in ASEAN after it joined as a founding member in 1967 became one of the central tenets of the country's foreign relations. ASEAN is a cornerstone of Indonesia's foreign policy approach to this day. The impact, however, in shaping the regional discourse is a two-way process with Indonesia impacting ASEAN's normative structure and its functioning. The cultural processes have an interesting linkage to indigenous cultural processes in Indonesia. As one of the writing notes, the usage of the traditional cultural practice (consensus building) helps in maintaining good relations with disputing parties which may otherwise be affected, and the other important point it notes is that the dispute can be resolved without any confrontation. More importantly, as the writer notes, the issue is rooted in their (Indonesian) culture (Junwana, 2014:327). The concept of consensus-building is a core principle within ASEAN. Another writing on politics in Indonesia notes that the traditional practice (Muswarayah and Mufakat) has a wide-ranging reach within processes in Parliament in Indonesia, where due to an ever-evolving dynamic democratic setup, reaching consensus is difficult, paving the way for the use of the mechanism (Kawamura, 2013:182–186).

Hence, while analyzing ASEAN within the larger contexts of its early formulation and its adopted style of decision making and consensus building, it is quite evident that there has been an overarching accommodation of dominant cultural practices within the organisation. In a sustained effort to play a role in regulating the conflicts within the organisation, ASEAN member states have preferred to discuss contentious issues behind closed doors. However, there have been instances where ASEAN has faltered due to various instances where there have been accommodations for the regional decision-making processes to be amended.

As one analyst notes in terms of political deliberations, the idea of Mufakat is used widely while a modification is done to the consensus principle in economic matters to integrate the ASEAN-X principle to have more room for bargaining (Anthony, 2005:72–74). These instances highlight the important role of Indonesia and its cultural processes and how ASEAN has adopted and accommodated the practices to coopt the country within its regional framework. Some of the criticisms of this process, however, highlight that the process is slow and incremental thereby taking too much time in sorting important issues. One more criticism of the same amounts to the idea that issues may not be relevant to all members in equal proportion; however, by adopting this process, all members are expected to reach a consensus regardless of their bilateral viewpoints on foreign relations.

The above understanding of normative influences has come to define why several analysts in Southeast Asia claim Indonesia and its approaches as a key aspect of foreign policy in the region. Indonesia emerged from an outlier and non-committal country in the Sukarno era to very much its de facto leader or as some authors on Southeast Asian affairs have put it, its primus inter pares (first among equals) within ASEAN. This displays the importance and the reason why Indonesia has held ASEAN engagement as a central aspect of its foreign policy practice and also as an avenue to project its power. Its need to propel the ASEAN process and maintain it as a cornerstone of its foreign policy endeavours has its merit where it benefits from being able to harness the capabilities of ASEAN to project its power diplomatically and also shields itself from larger irrelevance in a great power dominated geopolitical environment by bringing together a collective approach through ASEAN.

The approach towards ASEAN fits in what one of the New Order foreign ministers, Mochtar Kusumaatmadja, termed as the concentric circle. The policy, as he would highlight in a speech, noted that "Indonesia's foreign policy is always adapted to political dimensions at home, to allow Indonesia to determine its position in facing problems" (Indonesia. Kedutaan Besar (U.S.), 1984:3). While there was a strong focus on developing a focus on its neighbourhood and to an extent the East Asian region, the New Order leadership was also criticised for being "too low profile" and no longer active in foreign affairs, as the 1970s and 1980s were largely spent on domestic economic development. Nevertheless, the criticism started to wane once the New Order began to pursue the principle of bebas-aktif more vigorously by restoring diplomatic ties with China in August 1990, becoming the Chairman of the Non-Aligned Movement for 1992–95, and hosting the Asia-Pacific Economic Cooperation (APEC) summit in November 1994 (Sukma, 1997: 234).

Indonesia's Democratic Transition and Global Foreign Policy Thrust

Indonesia's careful transformation into a stable democracy over a period has been a key driver of a more nuanced foreign policy approach. Nevertheless, as also experts agree, the core principles of Indonesia's foreign policy, including the *Bebas Aktif* (free and active) principle, would be central and non-negotiable central components of the policy (Sukma, 2019). The assertion of Indonesia as a refashioned rising power and a revamp of its foreign policy in the contemporary sense has evolved during the era of the Yudhoyono presidency. Five key focus areas have been highlighted by analysts as contributions to the foreign policy approach: 1) democratic projection, 2) multilateral activism, 3) expanded regionalism, 4) partnership diplomacy and changing contours of great power relationships, and 5) military modernisation (Shekhar, 2018).

The following approaches could be seen in conjunction with a revamp in Indonesia's foreign policy. While external policy changes were driving regional countries to adopt a more proactive stance, especially towards major powers, there was a clear move where regional states, especially in Southeast Asia, had felt the impact of the changing nature of major power relations. While the US proposed its "Rebalance to the Asia-Pacific", China had emerged as a key power exerting its influence and its position in regional organisations such as ASEAN. The emerging decision refocused Indonesia's foreign policy approach to promote a more regional and norms-based alignment to meet its own foreign policy needs and position. Its regional position was cemented by its approaches in dealing with multiple regional crises via ASEAN and its leadership of the organisation.

Indonesia's role in the mediation process in the Thai-Cambodian conflict is to be noted in this regard to safeguard the regional process of conflict resolution. Indonesia, under whose leadership the dispute was occurring among fellow ASEAN members, decided to mediate and hold talks between Cambodia and Thailand. However, even though eventually the countries resorted to solving the issues through international forums such as the ICJ, the facilitation of ASEAN to set up observers under the leadership of ASEAN and the proactive role of Indonesia in setting up the monitoring group was seen as a new step in moving away from shying away from security issues. The fact that the ASEAN Ministers are meeting specifically on the issue of the bilateral dispute between its two Member States and the willingness of the two neighbours to resort to ASEAN support in this time of conflict is a significant step in ASEAN's history of managing disputes (Association of Southeast Asian Nations, 2011).

The role played by Indonesia and as a result, the "chair" of the organisation was very well highlighted. The reconciliation effort was brought about by the proactiveness of the chairing country. The then Secretary-General of ASEAN, Dr. Surin Pitsuwan highlighted, "UNSC's open and official support for conciliation efforts to the ASEAN Chair is a sign that the United Nations has faith in ASEAN to help its member states find amicable regional solutions to bilateral problems such as this" (Association of Southeast Asian Nations, 2011).

Hence, the preservation of a regional power position of ASEAN seemed to be in the best interest of Indonesia in the regional setting. However, as highlighted, the rapidly changing external environment demanded that countries in the region preserve a united position vis-a-vis the emerging regional security architecture. Hence, countries in the region pushed for a multilateral effort maintaining ASEAN centrality as a key tenet of the engagements with extra regional states.

Indonesia's Indo-Pacific Policy: A Natural Foreign Policy Progression towards Rising Power Status

The Indo-Pacific for all practical purposes in its current context is a major power-driven top-down approach narrative. While it emerged as a concept envisioned in parts with the rising convergence between India-Japan, India-US and US-Japan-Australia, the policy has now reached a point where regular albeit non-structured exchanges take place between the countries at the diplomatic and economic levels. The Indo-Pacific as a strategic concept has taken a position as regional geopolitics has altered due to the relations between the US and China as well as China and India.

The changing notions of regional security have left ASEAN nations, which, through their institutional mechanisms, controlled and devised norms of engagement between major powers intending to control the regional environment. The rising uncertainty may provide countries with fewer chances of maintaining a balance of power and relations among major powers and the regional states.

Indonesia's former Foreign Minister Marty Natalegawa was instrumental in devising a structured approach towards channelising the Indonesian position towards the Indo-Pacific. In a speech given at the United Nations, Natalegawa highlighted the regional security environment marked by a *dynamic equilibrium*. He noted that this situation was where preponderant power is absent not by the promotion of bloc politics and often self-fulfilling geopolitical fault lines; rather, a new kind of international relations with its emphasis on common security, common prosperity, and common stability (Permanent Mission of the Republic of Indonesia to the United Nations, 2011). Further, the clarity highlighting the concept and its linkages to the Indo-Pacific was provided by Natalegawa in a speech at the Conference on Indonesia at Washington, DC, in 2013.

> *The word "dynamic" suggests recognition that change is inherent and a constant in the region. It is a natural phenomenon that cannot and should not be artificially resisted. At the same time, "equilibrium" reminds that this state of constant change does not imply an anarchical state of affairs: either due to the unchecked preponderance of a single state, or due to the disorder or uncertainty associated by a multipolar region. Instead, peace and stability in the region ought to be brought about through the promotion of common security, prosperity, and stability. A recognition that security can only be enjoyed sustainably by states if it is viewed as a common good and not one that is obtained at the expense of the other. A dynamic equilibrium thus is marked by an absence of preponderant power not through the rigidity, rivalry, and tensions common to the pursuit of a balance of power model. Instead, through the promotion of a sense of common responsibility in the endeavor to maintain the region's peace and stability.*
>
> *(Natalegawa, An Indonesian perspective on the Indo-Pacific, 2013)*

Indonesia had suggested the first steps in formalising any future interaction over the Indo-Pacific by suggesting an "Indo-Pacific Treaty of Friendship and Cooperation". It envisaged establishing a treaty much in line with the established norms and rules of engagement that have been taking place through ASEAN and its affiliated entities. While this could be a singular effort in enforcing centrality of an organisation with a diverse institutionalisation such as ASEAN, on numerous occasions, Indonesian presidents have highlighted Indonesia's rightful geopolitical positioning in the region straddling the heart of the Indo-Pacific. In one instance, President Yudhoyono highlighted in 2014 that "As Indonesia is both a Pacific Ocean country and an Indian Ocean country, it is in the best interest of Indonesia to bridge the Pacific region with the Indian Ocean" (Fiji Government, 2014).

The incoming administration of President Joko Widodo in 2014 provided a reset in Indonesia's projection as a maritime power and the Indo-Pacific in a much more maritime-naval setting as compared to the previous dispensation which stressed the regional diplomatic nature of possible Indo-Pacific links (Scott, 2019:200). President Jokowi presented the vision of Indonesia's position further at the East Asia Summit. He highlighted that the "Maritime axis" doctrine would have five pillars, namely rebuilding Indonesia's maritime culture, maintaining and managing sea resources with a focus on establishing sovereignty over sea-based food products, prioritising infrastructure and maritime connectivity, maritime diplomacy to end all the sources of conflict at sea, such as fish thefts, violation of sovereignty, territorial disputes, and piracy, and building maritime defence (Widodo, 2014).

As comprehensive as it was, the concept of the Global Maritime Fulcrum (GMF) did entice major powers charting the Indo-Pacific to take notice. However, by the second term of President Jokowi, several analysts saw issues in either the implementation of the grand visioned project or saw the idea as either too naïve or dead. For instance, one analyst notes that the GMF, despite the promise, was caught in Jakarta's notorious bureaucratic challenges and also fell short of devising a centralised agency which could corroborate all projects under focus and execute them, including finding the right finances. The critique further notes that the confusing self-interpretation by each ministry also added to more ambiguity about a coherent policy outlook (Supriyanto, 2017:57–58).

Consequently, as another analyst notes, neither President Jokowi nor Foreign Minister Retno Marsudi mentioned the GMF within the policy space. Further, it is highlighted that despite being a crucial aspect which could have placed Indonesia centrally in the Indo-Pacific, the neglect of the GMF and its abandonment halfway through, placed Indonesia's geopolitical interests in the backseat in favour of idiosyncrasies, bureaucratic inertia, and domestic politics (Laksmana, 2019).

Nevertheless, looking at certain latest developments in 2020, there have been some positive signs of Indonesia's assertion of a stronger posture in the maritime space. Indonesia has taken a stern stance on China's encroachments on the Indonesian Natuna Islands on the southern edges of the South China Sea. Likewise, it has also been taking a strong stance on illegal fishing trawlers in its waters. It has resorted to apprehending and destroying illegal Chinese fishing trawlers in its waters. At the same time, it has strengthened naval cooperation with India to its west and embarked on joint development of Sabang port, which is a geopolitically crucial point in the Indian Ocean Region. The area sits strategically at the mouth of the Strait of Malacca. Indonesia's geographic position and its ability to indulge in generating a favourable view among its ASEAN peers will be the plus point for the "Quad" Indo-Pacific grouping members. This would also gel well with the Indonesian foreign policy outlook.

The Challenges and Opportunities for Indonesia's Foreign Policy in the Indo-Pacific

In the process of evolution of the Indo-Pacific concept, it is prudent to understand the implications for Indonesia and its foreign policy on the various core principles. In the analyses elsewhere in this article, it has been elucidated that two of Indonesia's approaches have been core to its foreign policy. The "Free and Independent" or "Bebas Aktif" approach has been central to dealing with external powers and overtures towards regional states as well. However, in dealing with the Indo-Pacific conceptualisations, this policy has been fused with the ASEAN approach of Indonesia, which has been the other central tenet of Indonesia's foreign policy.

In its approach towards the Indo-Pacific, Indonesia has proposed an institutionalisation approach suitable to its normative culture which is central within ASEAN and familiar ground for countries in Southeast Asia in dealing with extra-regional powers. However, internal challenges in developing a common perspective on the Indo-Pacific have remained a challenge for regional countries. The changing notions of regional security have left ASEAN nations, which, through their institutional mechanisms, controlled and devised norms of engagement between major powers, out of the race to control the regional environment. ASEAN as an organisation did not possess "one vision" of on the Indo-Pacific region. This reason led countries in the region to formulate "a common view" as opposed to "ten different" positions leading to more frictions in the regular coordination of regional policies. Through this exercise, Indonesia's Indo-Pacific vision became a cornerstone of embedding itself in the regional security of the emerging conceptualisation through ASEAN.

In the instance of the adoption of a common Indo-Pacific vision, the challenge in this context was to match a domestic leadership vision with a regional vision centring on ASEAN's norms which have been seen as acceptable to all members who have been part of the organisation. However, it has to be understood that in this perspective, ASEAN members have been able to maintain their foreign policy alignments vis-à-vis other extra regional countries as long as the other countries adhered to regional norms such as acceding to the Treaty of Amity and Cooperation in Southeast Asia (TAC). Nevertheless, the overt signalling which the "Indo-Pacific" security conceptualisation had vis-à-vis the US in terms of alignment pushed some ASEAN members to doubt the neutrality of the vision in balancing US and China ties (Yuniar, 2019). The existing document which was finally adopted emerged to neutralise any major pointed references towards any one country. However, it aligned with ASEAN by placing it centrally within the framework and hence by extension met with placing Indonesia's foreign policy goals in the region in consonance with the Indo-Pacific (Association of Southeast Asian Nations, 2019). Hence, holding together this complex "united position" in the face of changing regional realities will be a challenge for Indonesia.

Similarly, the other challenge for Indonesia within the Indo-Pacific setting would be to project and embed itself in the emerging Indo-Pacific "Quad" driven security structure. While Indonesia has been looking to project its position and say within the emerging Indo-Pacific security architecture, there have been developments among the Quad countries which indicate movement over designing and "institutionalising" the regional security and economic space in the region. There have been consultations on the Economic and Foreign ministerial levels between India, Japan, and the US, on the security front, and there have also been assertions for joint naval exercises among Quad countries (Malabar). There have been movements on the economic front as well, where there have been suggestions to initiate the Supply Chain Resilience Initiative (SCRI). The emerging economic and security calculations have let out the inclusion of Southeast Asian countries, which have a divergent view in terms of how the security and trade environment must be shaped.

While the Quad held its virtual meeting in March, the meeting also invited Vietnam and South Korea to join the meeting in what came to be known as the Quad plus. The Quad plus emerged as a strategic concept of extending maturation of the foundational concept could be one of the avenues where some commonalities can be achieved. However, US officials have indicated that unless there is a formalisation of the Quad at some point in time, the cooperation will remain loose and an "undefined entity" (Lakshman, 2020). This closely echoes Secretary of State Mike Pompeo's statement where he suggested that the "institutionalisation" of the Quad was eventually the goal and it was in line with the "Free and Open Indo-Pacific" concept.

The most recent Quad Summit held in Australia (2023), presented a few opportunities and few threats to the whole process of ASEAN centrality as well as Indonesia's leadership in the region. While Mike Pompeo explicitly highlighted the availability in the future of expanding the Quad on the sidelines of the 2020 summit (Akita & Sugiura, 2020), three years down the line India's Defense Minister explicitly mentioned the objective of India-US collaboration via defense cooperation and multilateral strategic engagements such as the Quad in the region were eyed on countering the 'Chinese aggression' (Ganapathy, 2023). This upcoming dilemma on choosing the Quad versus its own strategic regional positions would be a major challenge. While the "ASEAN Vision on the Indo-Pacific" explicitly highlights ASEAN as the centrepiece of the common emerging vision, the institutionalisation of the Quad with its formulations would contradict the position.

Moreover, the existing regional security and trade architecture that Indonesia endorses through ASEAN has a much more complex network of trade arrangements that are driven by familiar normative structures as opposed to an unknown major power-driven concept that may not have a leading role for regional countries. The RCEP, for instance which is endorsed by ASEAN and Indonesia at present, does not include the US and India (two Quad members) but includes China. Similarly, while ASEAN and China are moving towards a "Code of Conduct" in the South China Sea, other members, especially Quad members, have been posturing directly against China in the form of joint exercises and diplomatic positioning in the region.

Hence, with contrasting positions and visions of the "Indo-Pacific" and the emergent regional security environment, Indonesia would face key challenges in balancing these positions in projecting its foreign policy outlook as a growing middle power. Moreover, with the solidification of the alternative mechanism, Indonesia will also find several challenges in accommodating the position of China vis-à-vis the other nations within the existing ASEAN-led institutional setup. Some analysis has already argued that the existing standalone meetings and the task of institutionalisation have led to the weakening of the ASEAN centrality (Teo, 2020). In the future, due to this setup, there will be a growing challenge for Indonesia in managing diverging positions if ASEAN-centric institutions do not form a core part of the institutionalisation mechanisms which drive the process forward.

This finally raises an important question on the foundations on the Indo-Pacific and the role of individual countries and how they envision their position towards ASEAN. In the most recent and first visit as Prime Minister, Yoshihide Suga chose two ASEAN nations, Vietnam and Indonesia, for his first overseas visit. The conversation that ensued between PM Suga and the Deputy FM of Indonesia mainly revolved around the interpretation of the Indo-Pacific architecture and questions on its inclusiveness (Purba, 2020). Hence, it can be noted that the divergence of views and perspectives about future engagement is quite evident in emerging security debates.

Conclusion

Asia continues to remain in transition, and the emerging regional security environment has been displaying a change from the past towards a more streamlined and delineated region. Amidst this transition, the varied definitions of Indo-Pacific between the "Quad" and "non-Quad" and who will ultimately define the region will depend on the game of narratives and alignments and interests that will be played out in the transactional geopolitical environment. In essence, the diverging viewpoints of inclusivity vs exclusivity will come to be the central focal point of the future Indo-Pacific architecture.

The countries in the Southeast Asian region who are all members of the ASEAN have played a key role in shaping the regional security and trade narrative by impressing "ASEAN centrality" as a concept which they have now codified and have made as a basis to ensure "compliance for cooperation". The methodology has thus far worked in ensuring stable regional relations albeit with a lot of compromises and back-channel negotiations which have come to define the style of ASEAN-led processes. Nevertheless, the de facto leader of ASEAN, Indonesia, which has provided the basic normative framework in the organisation and its style of functioning, has been pushing a more wide-ranging concept of the Indo-Pacific much in line with preserving the unanimous regional position and also to avoid external interference in regional agenda setting.

The dilemma faced in Indonesia's foreign policy in confining to the emerging agreement stems from the foundational foreign policy structures which restrict the country from swerving too much towards either side. While this is positive in a regulated and stable environment, it could prove costly when the regional security architecture is changing gears and moving towards creating an alternative and more robust but albeit exclusive system. The inability to retune its foreign policy endeavours such as the Global Maritime Fulcrum to be more effective in addressing issues, Indonesia and as an extension the rest of Southeast Asia will find itself excluded from the emerging regional calculations. Hence, as broad as it has been envisioned the ASEAN Outlook on the Indo-Pacific which in essence was driven by a distillation of ideas by Indonesia might need closer coordination with the Quad countries to streamline policies.

The ability to bridge the Indian and the Pacific Oceans and its geographical expanses along the key waterways of the region makes Indonesia a valuable partner and a key player in the strategy of the Indo-Pacific. Its recent but stunted proactivity may be the only reason why its policy appeal fails to touch base with the existing dispensation of the Quad as a whole. While it is almost certain that China's growing regional presence has been close to impossible for Southeast Asian countries to resist either individually or collectively through ASEAN, the imbalance in pushing the regional narrative and the centrality of the organisation thereof may not be appealing for most countries to sign up for while designing the new Indo-Pacific architecture. However, the importance of the countries to the trade and strategy will not diminish. Even though most of the Quad countries have accepted "ASEAN centrality" a parallel major power institutionalisation may be on the cards.

The scope for Indonesia to manoeuvre in the emerging Indo-Pacific dialogue would be to push its efforts in signalling and posturing beyond the diplomatic structures and towards suggesting innovative ideas to co-opt the existing Quad framework to synchronise with ASEAN-led institutions. If at all possible, that any country can pull it off, it would be Indonesia. While worries do arise about ASEAN centrality, the unity of ASEAN has been tested time and again by rising Chinese belligerence. The need to compromise every time due to various tactics adopted at the regional level by China has proven to be costly for the region. It has been Indonesia's constant efforts in restoring ASEAN's position after each fallout. Nevertheless, the predictable permutations and combinations may soon change with the inability of ASEAN being at the region's driver's seat. The Indonesian position, in this case, may very well work towards driving ASEAN in a more suitable direction of a 'dynamic balance' in sync with the Quad, which would bring about positive gains for the whole region.

Eventually, the need for a Quad plus and an expansion of the envisioned institutional mechanism would have to include a few ASEAN member states to project a more holistic approach in revising the security and trade architecture. Indonesia's push to join the league and position itself as the leader of ASEAN, which it has cultivated over a point of time, will play a key role. The thought itself raises multiple questions about the proactivity of Indonesia's foreign policy and whether it, like other nations, will mark a change in its approach signalling yet another sea change in the geopolitics of Asia.

In the emerging scenario, the Indo-Pacific presents itself as an opportunity and a threat to Indonesia. In the space of opportunity, it can showcase its leadership skills in bringing a closer meeting point in the distinct approaches between ASEAN and other nations in the regional setup. The threat remains in the form of irrelevance, increased regional friction, and the continual need for picking sides in the emerging Cold War. In this context, the old Indonesian saying will suffice in providing the regional scenario: *Gajah berkelahi dengan gajah, pelanduk mati di tengah* (Elephants fight, mousedeer stampede to death in the middle). If the scene looks to signal the latter proposition as the position of the ASEAN countries in the emerging scenario, then the former seems the best probability for Indonesia to spearhead and the rest of Southeast Asia to support to propel the region forward into the Indo-Pacific century.

References

Akita, H., & Sugiura, E. (2020, October 6). Pompeo Aims to 'Institutionalize' Quad Ties to Counter China. *Nikkei Asia.*

Anthony, M. C. (2005). *Regional Security in Southeast Asia: Beyond the ASEAN Way.* Singapore: Institute of Southeast Asian Studies.

Anwar, D. F. (2014, February 4). *Indonesia's Foreign Relations: Policy Shaped by the Ideal of 'Dynamic Equilibrium'.* East Asia Forum. Canberra: ANU Press.

Association of Southeast Asian Nations. (2019, June 23). ASEAN Outlook on the Indo-Pacific. Association of Southeast Asian Nations (ASEAN). Retrieved from asean.org: https://asean.org/storage/2019/06/ASEAN-Outlook-on-the-Indo -Pacific_FINAL_22062019.pdf

Association of Southeast Asian Nations. (2011, February 21). Historic Firsts: ASEAN Efforts on Cambodian-Thai Conflict Endorsed by UNSC. Retrieved from asean.org: https://asean.org/historic-firsts-asean-efforts-on-cambodian-thai-conflict-endorsed-by-unsc/

Fiji Government. (2014, June 19). Keynote Address at the Second Summit of the Pacific Islands Development Forum. His Excellency Prof. Dr. Susilo Bambang Yudhoyono President of the Republic of Indonesia – Keynote Address at the Second Summit of the Pacific Islands Development Forum. Nadi: Fiji Government.

Ganapathy,N. (2023, November 12). India defence minister raises eyebrows saying India, US agree on countering 'Chinese aggression'. *The Strait Times*. Retrieved from https://www.straitstimes.com/asia/south-asia/india-defence-minister-raises-eyebrows-saying-india-us-agree-on-countering-chinese-aggression

Hatta, M. (1953). Indonesia's Foreign Policy. *Foreign Affairs, 31*, 441–452.

Indonesia. Kedutaan Besar (U.S.). (1984, October 1). Mochtar on Indonesia's Foreign Policy. *Indonesia News and Views*, p. 3.

Junwana, H. (2014). Courts in Indonesia: A Mix of Western and Local Character. In Y. Jiunn-rong & W.-C. Chang (Eds.), *Asian Courts in Context* (p. 327). London: Cambridge University Press.

Kawamura, K. (2013). President Restrained: Effects of Parliamentary Rule and Coalition Government on Indonesian Presidentialism. In Y. Kasuya (Ed.), *Presidents, Assemblies and Policymaking in Asia*. UK: Palgrave Macmillan.

Laksmana, E. (2019, November 8). *Indonesia's "Global Maritime Fulcrum": A Post-Mortem Analysis*. AMTI Update. Washington: AMTI and CSIS.

Lakshman, S. (2020, October 20). Quad Should Eventually Become Formalised, Says Top U.S. Official. *The Hindu*.

Natalegawa, M. (2013, May 20). *An Indonesian Perspective on the Indo-Pacific*. Washington, DC: CSIS.

Permanent Mission of the Republic of Indonesia to the United Nations. (2011). Statement by H.E. DR. R. M. Marty M. Natalegawa Minister for Foreign Affairs Republic of Indonesia at the General Debate of the 66th Session of the United Nations General Assembly. New York: Permanent Mission of the Republic of Indonesia to the United Nations.

Purba, K. (2020, October 19). PM Suga's Indo-Pacific Initiative is Alarming for RI and Region. *The Jakarta Post*.

Scott, D. (2019). Indonesia Grapples with the Indo-Pacific: Outreach, Strategic Discourse, and Diplomacy. *Journal of Current Southeast Asian Affairs, 38*. 194-200.

Shekhar, V. (2018). *Indonesia's Foreign Policy and Grand Strategy in the 21st Century: The Rise of and Indo-Pacific Power*. New York: Taylor & Francis.

Sukma, R. (1997). Indonesia's Bebas-Aktif Foreign Policy and the 'Security Agreement' with Australia. *Australian Journal of International Affairs, 234*, 213-241.

Sukma, R. (2019, May 28). Strategic Imperatives of Indonesia's Foreign Policy. *The Jakarta Post*.

Supriyanto, R. A. (2017). The Indian Ocean and Indonesia's Global Maritime Fulcrum: Relevance To ASEAN. In S. Bateman, R. Gamage, & J. Chan (Eds.), *ASEAN and the Indian Ocean: The Key Maritime Links* (pp. 57–58). Singapore: Rajaratnam School of Internataional Studies.

Teo, S. (2020, October 9). What the Quad Meeting Means for ASEAN. *The Diplomat*.

Widodo, J. (2014, November 14). The Seas Should Unite, Not Separate Us. *The Jakarta Post*.

Yuniar, R. W. (2019, June 16). Indonesia Reveals Frustration with Singapore Over Delay in Asean Adopting President Joko Widodo's Indo-Pacific Concept. *South China Morning Post*.

14

VIETNAM IN THE CHANGING STRATEGIC ENVIRONMENT OF INDO-PACIFIC

Aswani R. S.

Indo-Pacific has a shared platform filled with opportunities for promoting social, political, economic, and cultural relations between the littoral nations of the Indian and Pacific Oceans. With such goals in mind, the world has witnessed many successful bilateral and multilateral ties across Asia, which have significantly secured the cooperating countries in this competitive international realm. There are tremendous opportunities in the Indo-Pacific, which is predicted to be the place where the future geopolitical game will be played. Vietnam is strengthening its relations with extra-regional powers through increase in defence cooperation measures, infrastructure development, and strengthening maritime security. Vietnam's perspectives towards security, trade, commerce, cooperation, development, and economy are rooted in its balancing act of China in the Indo pacific (Aswani, 2020). This study aims to understand those prospects and examines how these secure Vietnamese interests against the fast-changing geopolitical situations in the Indo-Pacific. Vietnam is growing as a confident nation in the Indo-Pacific, taking into confidence its neighbours and other important powers in the region. With aims to play an assertive role in the Indo-Pacific, despite the qualms of a tough China, Vietnam is unhesitant to project its interests in China's periphery, and its growing relations with the US and India, is proof for a "new mark in the foreign policy of Vietnam". Vietnam is located at the heart of the Indo-Pacific, the South China Sea disputes derail the existing peaceful equilibrium in the region, and it aims to build a peaceful Indo-Pacific with shared interests.

As a maritime state, located at the geo-strategically significant intersection in the Indo-Pacific, Vietnam is building its economic and political relationships with major powers of the world. Its relationship with ASEAN is quite

DOI: 10.4324/9781003479307-17

fascinating, as it is based on the enormous economic potential of Vietnam as an emerging economy and the balancing act towards China is quite predictable. With the rise of China in Asia, and its expansion in the Indian Ocean Region, the need for a counterbalancing relationship in the Pacific became apparent to India, and thus the Indo-Vietnam relationship became strategic in orientation. Among the ten nations in the Association of Southeast Asian Nations (ASEAN), Vietnam holds an important axis in India's Look-East/Act-East Policy, and their bilateral relationship is much looked upon due to the geo-strategic implications it projects. Vietnam has backed India's attempts to obtain a prominent role in ASEAN as possible counterweights to growing Chinese assertion in the region (Chandran, 2018). Vietnam is also growing as a core partner of India in various sub-regional, regional, and multilateral forums. Immediately after Vietnam was voted as a non-permanent member in the United Nations (UN), it reaffirmed its support for India's bid for a permanent membership in the Security Council of the UN (Asian News International, 2019). US is also growing as a core partner of Vietnam in various sub-regional, regional, and multilateral forums. Bilateral ties between the US and Vietnam have strengthened in recent years; following high-level diplomatic exchanges have witnessed a shared focus on regional security issues, trade, and commerce.

In the 21st century, the game of geopolitics has turned into one that is of balancing and counterbalancing. In the context of this study, Vietnam is viewed as a fulcrum in the whole drama of counterbalancing act to contain Chinese expansion in the Indo-Pacific (Ross, 2006). After sowing seeds for its ambitious plans in the South China Sea, China has expanded in the Indian Ocean Region through its "string of pearls" strategy by building ports and other infrastructure developments in Pakistan, Maldives, Sri Lanka, Bangladesh, and Myanmar (Ashraf, 2017). The Chinese defence expenditure in these countries is increasing with the pretext that these ports and highways need security (Ahmad et.al, 2017). This direct threat to the autonomy of countries in the Indo-Pacific has created security dilemma in the region and has started looking for a possible partner to counter China in its periphery. This quest ended in the possibility of strategic partnerships with Vietnam that can be built on mutual trust and strategy. This counterbalancing strategy is geopolitically good for the peace of the Indo-Pacific as it contains China to its territorial waters.

The objective of this study is to understand Vietnam's policy, interest, and approach to the developments in the Indo-Pacific and to use those prospects to secure its national interests against the fast-changing geopolitical situations in the Indo-Pacific. Vietnam is often known as a "miracle economy", "Asian miracle", etc. due to its rapid growth to a socialist-orientated market economy within a decade after the losses of the Vietnam War. Vietnam is an export powerhouse due to its rise in population, and many Asian countries have seen a haven in Vietnam for investments in manufacturing and textiles. It has grown to become the world's third-largest textile exporter after China and Bangladesh (Chakrabarty, 2019).

Vietnam's "Three Nos" have barred it from strategically cooperating with major powers in the world forever, and it was fiercely implemented in all defence relationships they have committed to. However, it has entered into a comprehensive strategic partnership with China in 2008, India in 2007, and Russia in 2001. However, it is interesting to see that despite multiple discussions on counterbalancing China in the Indo-Pacific, the US has not upgraded its comprehensive partnership of 2013 with Vietnam to a strategic one. It is also interesting to note that India's Vietnam policy has gained momentum ever since both parties signed the "Joint Vision for Peace, Prosperity, and People" in 2020. In this chapter, the foreign policy of Vietnam in general and in the Indo-Pacific is studied by focusing on its relationship with great powers interested in the region, such as China, India, and the US.

China, BRI, and Vietnam

Vietnam has taken a cautious approach in dealing with China's infrastructural development activities in the South China Sea due to the potential geopolitical implications of it, as seen in the Hambantota debt trap. The 2014 oil rig crisis in the South China Sea has led to a series of anti-China sentiments in Vietnam, which despite its explicit willingness to be part of the BRI initiative raises security dilemma in Hanoi. Chinese President Xi Jinping addressed the Vietnamese parliament in 2015 and suggested how China and Vietnam can survive these disruptions and go ahead collaborating on multiple fronts. Vietnam is concerned about the sustainability of many proposed BRI projects, which heavily depend on fossil fuels and outdated inhumane work conditions The public exposure of Chinese debt trap diplomacy measures clearly indicate to Vietnam to be cautious while agreeing to Chinese technology and infrastructural projects in its periphery, from which Vietnam already has bitter experiences. This opens space for geopolitical games in the region, as Vietnam receives funding from other sources such as India, the US, and Japan, which affects the balance of power in the region. Japan's influence in Vietnam is high, especially in the soft power front, as there is people-to-people exchange and trust, which China is highly sceptical about.

Given this scepticism in China's intentions in Vietnam and disdain for the BRI, the likelihood of reliable Vietnam-China relations is not promising in the near future. China has invested in rail lines, bridges, roads, and ports all over Africa and Asia, yet has only pilot projects in Vietnam. The scope for receiving huge loans from the Chinese-dominated AIIB (Asian Infrastructural Investment Bank) helps Vietnam not to not depend on BRI

210   Aswani R. S.

loans, thus escaping the economic and strategic implications of China's debt traps and inadvertently raising BRI implementation challenges to China in Vietnam.

China and Vietnam: Continuity and Challenges in Indo-Pacific

China and Vietnam share a very complex relationship with each other, often crossing philosophical commonality. They both share a similar system of government, yet their border disputes and geopolitical insecurity offer diplomatic tensions between both (Thu, 2020). In Southeast Asian politics, Vietnam was seen as a reluctant participant to counter Chinese expansion; however, in recent times Vietnam is seen balancing power relations in the Indo-Pacific by extending its diplomatic channels to outside powers such as India and the US. This ensures Vietnam can strengthen its soft power with these countries and its sovereignty in the region (Hai, 2021).

In 2020, China and Vietnam celebrated their 70th year anniversary of diplomatic relations between their current political regimes, and promises of camaraderie and cooling off relationships were promised. Yet, the year 2020 began with a major blow to the bilateral relationship between Vietnam and China. This was because of the maritime conflicts around a sunken Vietnamese fishing boat near the Paracel islands and the Chinese missile tests in the South China Sea (Jennings, 2020). Vietnam's "Three Nos" policy of no alliances of military, no reliance on fights with other countries, and no foreign bases on its land, went into a total U-turn with the introduction of the latest white paper of national security policy released by Hanoi (Grossman and Huynh, 2019). Coupled with the scope for "yes" from Vietnam in alliances for balancing the growing Chinese expansion in the Indo-Pacific, Vietnam is heralding the leadership of ASEAN (Stafford, 2020). When looked at together, this provides major scope for Vietnam to decide its impending geostrategic relations in the Indo-Pacific . After twenty years of using the "Three Nos", Vietnam's new white paper on defence has added a new No-No threat of force or use of force in international relations. At the onset, it looks merely as Vietnam is drawn closer towards its original founding values of non-aggression and non-violence, but closely observed, it ensures China that Vietnam will not seek any military escalation in the South China Sea.

Implications of these changes in China-Vietnam relations can help India to counterbalance China in its own periphery. While much talk about the growing ties between India and Vietnam is shown, in the last two years (i.e., 2021 and 2022) we do not see any improvements in the bilateral or multilateral ties between both countries. The last agreement between India and Vietnam was concluded on a virtual summit on 21 December 2020, and the Prime Ministers of both countries adopted the India-Vietnam Joint Vision for

Peace, Prosperity, and People. During the summit, a concrete Plan of Action for the period 2021–2023 for further implementation of the Comprehensive Strategic Partnership was developed. To encourage cooperation between the defence industries of both countries, an agreement for Defence-Industry Cooperation was also adopted at the summit. India also extended a USD5 billion grant assistance to develop an Army Software Park in Nha Trang. An agreement to optimise the UN peacekeeping force was also developed. India and Vietnam had also agreed for mutual assistance on nuclear safety and protection, between the atomic regulatory bodies of both countries. On the non-renewable front, an agreement on petroleum research was concluded, and in the renewable front, an MOU between the Solar Federation of India and Vietnam Clean Energy Association was concluded (MEA, 2021).

The paybacks of these agreements can be seen in the increasing trade relations between India and Vietnam. India and Vietnam are developing their economic and trade relations through the MoU on Economic and Trade Cooperation, signed in March 2018. This cooperation also entails agricultural development ties and the transfer of knowledge and technology. In the year 2000, the bilateral trade between both countries was USD200 million, and it has grown over the years. Vietnam was India's fifteenth largest trading partner in 2021, and India was the tenth largest trading partner for Vietnam. In the year 2018–19, the bilateral trade between both nations stood at USD13.70 billion (World Bank, 2021).

Vietnam has accorded its highest ever partnership title of "Comprehensive strategic cooperative partnership" with China in 2008, and yet had to face the excessive Chinese assertion in the East Sea (South China Sea for Vietnamese). Anti-China sentiments are on the increase in Vietnam in the last few years following China's actions not only in the South China Sea but also its dam construction in the Mekong River that has threatened the livelihoods of millions of people in the lower riverine part of Vietnam. The 10th Ocean Dialogue in Nha Trang, Vietnam discussed the Chinese threats in the South China Sea and their implications on offshore renewables and maritime security of Vietnam and other Southeast Asian countries. Vietnam hosted the 15th South China Sea Conference in October 2023, with the overarching theme of energy at crossroads, which is a direct indicator of Hanoi's gentle push in discourses that call out the Chinese actions in the region to the outside world – it's tender ways of counterbalancing the aggression.

ASEAN Centrality in Indo-Pacific and Vietnam

Though Free and Open Indo-Pacific (FOIP) is a US strategy to contain China in its neighbourhood and to increase its power in Southeast Asia, its effective execution necessitates support and involvement of countries such as

Vietnam. Vietnam constantly aligns its foreign policy to the broader happenings around it, and its proactive measures to actively take part actively in ASEAN display its need to defend its national security interests amidst an increasing Chinese expansion and enthusiasm to advance its social and economic growth (Hiep et al., 2021). Vietnam has always seen multilateral institutions as a necessary platform to gather support for its causes and raise its voice, and ASEAN has offered such a space, rightfully so.

ASEAN is politically very significant in achieving a peaceful, free, and open Indo-Pacific and is a big element in the geopolitics of Asia. ASEAN in recent times is seen building relationships with strategic partners such as the US, China, Japan, Australia, India, and EU and has started arriving at strategic frameworks such as ASEAN+1, ASEAN +3, etc. For ASEAN, the South China Sea disputes are a major trouble, and despite its best efforts, it has not been successful in keeping those conflicts at bay. These disputes are complex due to the geostrategic competition and the territorial sovereignty claims, and due to the lack of an effective conflict resolution mechanism. ASEAN potentially has the ability to manage the regional security issues of the South China, including non-traditional maritime security threats (Hung and Nguyen, 2021). During the 34th ASEAN Summit in Bangkok, the ASEAN Outlook on the Indo-Pacific was released, which states that the members of ASEAN have shared interests in the Indo-Pacific. According to Dung (2019), the ASEAN played a strategic role in the Indo-Pacific, which is not a place for competition, but dialogue and cooperation, ensures shared prosperity, and needs to develop a common regional architecture for maritime security.

Over the last 50 years, ASEAN has achieved a strategic position in global affairs, in enhancing its political position and that of its member countries. In the political game in the Indo-Pacific between China and the US, ASEAN is a key player and is significant for ensuring a peaceful, free, and open Indo-Pacific. While the South China Sea disputes greatly affect ASEAN centrality, all members of ASEAN have equal rights, and bringing them all to the same platform and arriving at the same decision is difficult. This lack of consensus affects the ASEAN centrality, as inter-state disputes remain complex and unresolved (Kien, 2020). Among the ASEAN countries, Vietnam, through its foreign policy, aims not to be a proxy for any extra-regional power; a lesson zealously followed since the Cold War days and avoids big-power competition. Vietnam has developed a foreign policy of multilateralism and non-alignment, which depicts it as a responsible member of the region, and it is emerging as a friendly face to many international bodies. For example, even though the US, historically, had close relationship with the Philippines, while proposing the potentiality of a "Quad plus", US chose Vietnam, presenting its confidence in Vietnam to build a secure strategic counterbalance to China in Indo-Pacific. Quad also aims to build a large network for economic development, and Vietnam's strategic location adds to the possibilities. The Free and Open Indo-Pacific is a US strategy, and Vietnam can become an important element in its expanding economic network due to its long coastline and diplomatic relations with other countries in ASEAN.

Vietnam's response to the Free and Open Indo-Pacific strategy was cold in the beginning as it was very cautious of displeasing China; nonetheless, recent Vietnamese White Paper and diplomatic speeches and press releases affirm its readiness to be a part of the existing defence and security mechanisms in the region. The ASEAN region is increasingly becoming economically, culturally, and politically interconnected (IISD, 2023) and the ecosystem of the Indo-Pacific has different dimensions of policy, politics, and strategy. The norms and viability of the ASEAN way of regionalism framework have space for transnational challenges of countries such as Vietnam in ensuring national security (Acharya, 2009). There is existing competition among the Southeast Asian countries to attract the inflow of Foreign Direct Investments, which allows them opportunities for economic growth and infrastructural development that China, through its BRI has tapped (Ferchen, 2021). Due to this increase in competition in the regional architecture of the Indo-Pacific, Vietnam's position in ASEAN aids it in economic development and improves its relationship with the rest of the world. While the total export and import of ASEAN with the US accounted for USD307.7 billion in 2020, the total export and import of Vietnam with the US accounted for USD92.2 billion. Vietnam has free trade agreements with ASEAN countries, and its major exports are oil, coffee, rice, textiles, and rubber, while its imports are fertilisers, steel, machines, and petroleum products. Eighty percent of Vietnam's trade is with the countries in the Indo-Pacific, depicting the significance of these countries in the geopolitical policies of Vietnam. Even though, economically quite substantial, Vietnam joined ASEAN in 1995 purely for pragmatic reasons of political independence, regime revival, and post-Cold War trappings (Tung, 2007). Until 1986, Vietnamese foreign policy was monopolised and centralised, and Doi Moi, the economic reform policy, revolutionised the leadership transitions through a decentralised foreign policy (Abuza, 1997) (Hiep, 2018). In recent times, Vietnam's foreign policy is rooted in independence, multilateralism, diplomacy, and self-reliance, which helps Vietnam enrich its relationship with other countries in the Indo-Pacific and enhance competition. Vietnam, through its own perception, position, and perspectives, has achieved economic growth and stable relationships in the Indo-Pacific (Thuong & Oanh, 2021).

However, Vietnam's foreign policy has been facing substantial uncertainty in the last decade with the increase in Chinese aggression in its land and sea, followed by the renewed interest of countries such as the US and India in attempts to balance China in the Indo-Pacific. Vietnam has upheld the ASEAN centrality multiple times during the last decade, especially since the new Prime Minister Phuc has assumed office. His first official visit was to China, reassuring the latter of the importance Vietnam accords it in bilateral relations, despite the maritime disputes. China's closer ties with Cambodia, and the latter's repeated obstruction on the joint statements of ASEAN on the South China Sea, is the core concern for Vietnam's Indo-Pacific strategy. Vietnam has shared national interests with Cambodia and the leaping of the Cambodian nationalism has further aggravated Hanoi and continues to haunt its foreign policy initiatives.

US and Vietnam: New Maritime Dimensions

America's vision of Southeast Asia in general and Vietnam in particular has taken many twists and turns, with President Obama's Asia Pivot being the latest strategic initiative towards the Indo-Pacific. While critiques on the intent of this policy initiative have been widely discussed as a counterbalancing strategy of the US to contain the expansionist policies of China, Obama administration had projected it to be a multilateral policy with embedded non-traditional security ambitions, such as HADR (Humanitarian Assistance and Disaster Response). The military activities of China in Western Indian Ocean and Africa created a security dilemma for the US, and building bilateral military and commercial relationships with countries in the Indo-Pacific helps balance the power disparity and ensure regional stability and security. The stability of Asia and the effervescence of this region heavily depend on maintaining this balance of geopolitical power, and it has wide considerations on the strength and growth of the US. Hence, US plays a critical role in diplomatic, economic, and strategic dimensions of Southeast Asia, for which Vietnam acts as a trusted partner.

After the Cold War ended, by 1995, the US and Vietnam established their bilateral relations, and by 2020, both countries celebrated 25 years of the commencement of their diplomatic relations. In the year 2013, the US-Vietnam Comprehensive Partnership was concluded, which helped evolve their partnership into different realms, especially the maritime defence front. The economic ties and cultural ties had also strengthened this relationship and made the partnership comprehensive. Vietnam's ambition to build its economy in terms with UN sustainable development goals is met with technical and scientific help from the US in areas of renewable energy generation, trade competitiveness, biodiversity preservation, and sustainable energy trade. Since 2001, the trade relations between Vietnam and the US had taken dramatic turns, from USD51 million to USD90 billion. The trade has evolved from traditional items of agriculture and textiles to computers, machinery, electronics, which has also increased US investments in the Vietnamese manufacturing sector. Vietnam is also a leading nation in climate change adaptation in the Indo-Pacific, with a vision to respond to coastal environmental challenges such as sea-level rise and marine pollution. The US has concluded remediating dioxin contamination for Danang airport in 2017 and Bien Airbase in 2019, building assistance to Vietnam's vulnerable populations, and taking its promise of comprehensive partnerships forward.

Biden administration's Indo-Pacific strategy names Vietnam as a key strategic partner, ensuing many years of Vietnam's focus on multilateralisation since its reformation policy since 1987. These reforms, known as "*Doi Moi*" were created in Vietnam following years of unification efforts between its Southern and Northern sides and focused on the creation of a socialist-orientated market economy. In areas of diplomacy and commerce, both Vietnam and the US had undergone multiple transformations in the last few decades. China's emergence as a regional hegemon in Asia has altered Vietnam's strategic position in the US's global partnerships. Ever since the Soviet Union left Vietnam's side to join hands with China in 1986, Vietnam has diversified its relationships with great powers, without committing to one great power. Vietnam's overarching foreign policy of *Three Nos* also looms over any possible relationship between both countries. US withdrawal from the Trans-Pacific Partnership (TPP) has indicated that the US is not certain about its commitment to Vietnam, which has raised questions in Hanoi about how the US values Vietnam. How the US will forge closer ties with Vietnam, overlooking the above concerns, needs to be examined in the times to come. It's repeated mention of democracy and democratic ideals in the Indo-Pacific strategy document will only further alienate Vietnam, and any US strategy in this region ought to consider repeated reassurances to Vietnam through maritime security cooperation, defence capabilities, and diplomatic exchanges.

Curious Case of Cam Ranh Bay Naval Base

Widely acclaimed as the "best deep port naval base in whole of Southeast Asia", (Sautin, 2016), Cam Ranh Bay is a treasure that bejewels Vietnam. The presence of an airport adjacent to the port, equipped with access to heavy-weighted transport planes and strategic bombers, further enhances the strategic value of the port. Gateway to dominance in South China Sea, this port was with the French and Japanese during colonial periods. The US had built a naval base over the island during Cold War times, and it served as "a major logistics hub" during the 1970s (Sautin, 2016). After the end of the Vietnam War, despite many efforts from the part of the USSR, Vietnam was not willing to lease out Cam Ranh. However, the Chinese attacks of 1979 changed the tables in favour of the Soviets, and Cam Ranh became the "largest Soviet foreign installation outside of eastern Europe" (Sautin,

2016). After the 20-year lease period, in 2002, the Vietnam government took over the port and modernised it for foreign vessels for repair, refuelling, and docking (Oak, 2018). Vietnam is open to "all foreign powers", diversifying its interests, as all the Western countries cooperating with Vietnam are ultimately in the lookout to this deep-water port that would be a great naval strategic asset for their geopolitical ambitions. Though China, Japan, Russia, and the US is interested in accessing Cam Ranh, to consolidate a strategic international domain for themselves, Vietnam is not likely to give away any access to the port anytime soon, until the situation in the South China Sea deteriorates.

Soft Power Diplomacy

Soft power is a sum of activities undertaken by a nation, through political diplomacy, business investments, cultural exchanges, and charming leadership. Vietnam is entering a realm of global significance, and soft power has a big role to play in taking advantage of new avenues of growth. Vietnam's emergent relations should not merely be seen from a defence perspective, as there is a huge scope of cooperation in the multidimensional sector through which it can grow and contribute to regional peace and prosperity. One common trend seen in global politics recently is the increased relevance of the third sector in foreign relations. Soft power diplomacy has emerged as a strong supplement to strategic partnerships, thus pulling forward people-to-people exchanges and citizen support. Vietnamese festivals are displayed in the US, India, and Europe, and Vietnam has also hosted many international events and film festivals. Cultural centres are opened in Europe to spice up the soft power tactics. In September 2016, India had opened a Cultural Centre to strengthen its cultural presence in Vietnam, on the 45th anniversary of India-Vietnam diplomatic ties. On the inauguration of the centre, the Indian Minister of State for External Affairs described the 2000 years long historical affinity between both nations and reminded the Vietnamese about the need for the safeguarding and advancement of the heritage and values both nations cherish (Diem, 2017) .

Hanoi International Film Festival has become one of the most prestigious film festivals in the world, opening a large platform for countries outside of Southeast Asia to collaborate with Vietnam in the exchange of its art and culture. Cinema is a major soft power; Cinema – Integration and Sustainable Development was the theme of the film festival, and it has offered multiple dimensions of cooperation to all Asian nations. These trends indicate an active people-to-people exchange of culture, art, and language, and with Vietnam as a strategic soft power relationship would be a strong cooperative mechanism that could build trust and connection between nations outside of the Indo-Pacific. Accompanied by the intergovernmental strategic

Vietnam in the Changing Strategic Environment of Indo-Pacific **217**

partnership agreement, such soft power tactics would benefit the cause of a counterbalance, as people's trust is what would take both these democracies forward to achieve a grand strategic geopolitical balancing in Indo-Pacific.

Conclusion

Vietnam is one of the most influential countries in Southeast Asia, whose strategic environment is changing due to China's expansionist policies and opportunities from collaborating with the US, India, and Japan to "contain" China in the region. This reflects in Vietnam's recent foreign policy initiatives and choices to collaborate with reliable partners, in military, cultural, and commercial terms. Vietnam has been cooperating in areas of arms, ammunition, science, technology, energy trade, and training. Vietnam has higher strategic interests in the Indo-Pacific, and this cooperation benefits both parties in the great game of geopolitics. Vietnam has become the beacon light of geopolitical aspirations in Southeast Asia. The changing geopolitical situation in the Indo-Pacific indicates that major powers such as the US, Japan, Russia, and North Korea are shifting their economic focus to this region due to their volatile relations with China, needing to take gain of the current disputes. This affects the peace, security, and stability of not just Southeast Asia but also the Indian Ocean periphery, owing to the increasing dependency on the Indian Ocean for global trade and commerce. To ensure peace in the Indo-Pacific, all countries in the region need to share the common vision of secure seas and borders, and Vietnam has a major role to play in this. A major contention and dilemma-inducing development in the Indo-Pacific is China's Belt and Road and the various debt trap policies of it in the Indo-Pacific, along with environmental degradation and unsustainable practices. This study sheds light into the need for an open and robust security architecture in the Indo-Pacific, and Vietnam can help balance peace and security in the region. The COVID-19 pandemic and great reset of geopolitics that followed indicate that policies on improving bilateral and multilateral relationships with Vietnam should be drafted based on UN Sustainable Development Goals. The policies should also emphasise the exchange of goods and services that can lead to a reduction of greenhouse gases, and both economies becoming carbon neutral by 2050 (Aswani et al., 2021). This sustainable energy trade can include a platform for exchange of information regarding the emissions that were accrued due to trade. Such a scope for quantification and exchange of emission rates helps expand the trade practices more sustainably. Thus, a mechanism that leads to a trusted platform where goods and services are assessed according to a calculation of emissions should be created. This would generate a unique, reliable, and sustainably conscious relation in the Indo-Pacific. The desire of Vietnam to invest in new and renewable energy is seen in their large-scale production of wind energy. This reduces the import of fossil fuels, which in turn reduces the maritime traffic in the Indian Ocean Region (IOR) and the Pacific, reducing the threats imposed on energy security. Vietnam has a successful offshore policy, and the investments in renewables should be encouraging of the smooth transfer of knowledge, technology, and best practices. Such policies should be developed by careful consultation with countries that have excelled in the application of renewable energy technologies. Investments in infrastructure, both hard and soft, can improve the relationship and help form a mega-allied power. The investments in Vietnam face different forms of risks, and sustainable diversification of the energy mix reduces the uncertainties created due to the political volatilities in the Indo-Pacific region.

Vietnam occupies the heart of Southeast Asia and commands the neighbouring countries with different geopolitical interests to move towards an advantageous symmetry of relationship in the South China Sea region. The close examination of bilateral and multilateral relations Vietnam has entered, especially with the US and India, shows the vision of the extra-regional powers in the Indo-Pacific. This study is limited to examining Vietnam in the Indo-Pacific vis-à-vis the counterbalancing relationships. The future research agendas can be through examining the relationship through quantitative terms. Vietnam's commitment to freedom of navigation and establishing peace and stability in the Indo-Pacific is a tool for it to observe the mounting tensions in the South China Sea, due to Chinese claims on islands, and questions on maritime sovereignty claims. Keen observers of the Indo-Pacific declare that Hanoi is not building its strategic partnership with extra-regional powers, in fear of history repeating itself, due to the Cold War drama between the US and USSR. However, the intensifying Chinese assertion in the Indo-Pacific is forcing Vietnam to stretch itself. The 2019 Vietnamese White Paper mentioned the term "Indo-Pacific" for the first time, mentioning how Vietnam is ready to participate in security measures in the Indo-Pacific, a term that the US had coined and promulgated. This indicates the need for Vietnam to ensure a peaceful maritime region in the Indo-Pacific, aligning itself with the US dream of a "peaceful Indo-Pacific".

References

Abuza, Z. (1997). Institutions and actions in Vietnamese foreign policy-making: A research note. *Contemporary Southeast Asia*, 19(3), 309–333. http://doi.org/10.1355/CS19-3E

Acharya, A. (2009). Constructing a security community in Southeast Asia. *ASEAN and the Problem of Regional Order*, Second Edition, 1–322.

Ashraf, J. (2017). String of Pearls and China's emerging strategic culture. Vol 37 (4). 166-181.*Journal of Strategic Studies*.

Asian News International. (2019, June 20). Vietnam reaffirms support for India's permanent membership at UNSC. *India Today*. Retrieved from https://www.indiatoday.in/india/story/vietnam-reaffirms-support-for-india-s-permanent-membership-at-unsc-1552382-2019-06-20

Aswani, Rs. (2020). Non-Traditional maritime security threats in the Indian Ocean Region: Policy alternatives. *Journal of Public Affairs.* Vol. 10, Issue 2. e2456

Aswani, R., Sajith, S., & Bhat, M. Y. (2021). Is geopolitics a threat for offshore wind energy? A case of Indian Ocean Region. *Environmental Science and Pollution Research.* https://doi.org/10.1007/s11356-021-12779-z

Chakrabarty, M. (2019, August 20). India needs to gear up for stronger economic partnership with old ally Vietnam. *Economic Times.* Retrieved from https://economictimes.indiatimes.com/blogs/et-commentary/india-needs-to-gear-up-for-stronger-economic-partnership-with-old-ally-vietnam/

Chandran, N. (2018, March 15). Southeast Asia is increasingly turning to India instead of the US or China. *CNBC.* Retrieved from https://www.cnbc.com/2018/03/15/southeast-asia-increasingly-turns-to-india-instead-of-the-us-or-china.html

Diem, L. (2017, April 27). Indian cultural center opens in Hanoi. *Vietnam Economic Times.* Retrieved from https://vneconomictimes.com/article/society/indian-cultural-center-opens-in-hanoi

Dung, N. V. H. (2019). ASEAN's vision on Indo-Pacific and implications for Vietnam. *Journal of Northeast Asian Studies,* 8, 9–18.

Ferchen, M. (2021). The Two Faces of the China Model: The BRI in Southeast Asia. In F. Schneider (Ed.), Global Perspectives on China's Belt and Road Initiative: Asserting Agency through Regional Connectivity (pp. 245–264). Amsterdam University Press. https://doi.org/10.2307/j.ctv1dc9k7j.13

Grossman, D., & Huynh, D. (2019). Vietnam's defense policy of 'No' quietly saves room for 'Yes' – The Diplomat. *The Diplomat.* https://thediplomat.com/2019/01/vietnams-defense-policy-of-no-quietly-saves-room-for-yes/

Hiep, L. H. (2018). Introduction: The making of Vietnam's foreign policy under doi moi. Ed. Le Hong Hiep, Anton Tsvetov,*Vietnam's Foreign Policy Under Doi Moi,*SEAS – Yusof Ishak Institute3–22.

Hiep, T. X. et al. (2021). Another view of the "Closed-door policy" of the Nguyen Dynasty (Vietnam)with Western countries (1802 – 1858). Cogent Arts & Humanities. Vol 8(1), DOI: 10.1080/23311983.2021.1973648

Hung, N. T and Nguyen, X. C. (2021). Non-traditional Security Complex in the South China Sea: Vietnam's Perspectives and Policy Implications. *Journal Global Policy and Governance.* Vol. 10 (2), pp. 51-72. https://doi.org/10.14666/2194-7759-10-2-004

IISD. (2023). Trends Shaping the ASEAN Region. In ASEAN-IGF Minerals Cooperation: Scoping study on critical minerals supply chains in ASEAN. International Institute for Sustainable Development(IISD). pp. 11-14. Retrieved from http://www.jstor.org/stable/resrep49369.6

Jennings, R. (2020). China, Vietnam try to make amends after stormy start to 2020. VOA. https://www.voanews.com/a/east-asia-pacific_china-vietnam-try-make-amends-after-stormy-start-202/6195334.html

Kien, L.T. (2020), 'Vietnam: The Indo-Pacific Regional Architecture: The Quad, Inclusivity and ASEAN Centrality', in R. Huisken and K. Brett (eds.), CSCAP Regional Security Outlook 2021, Kuala Lumpur: Council for Security Cooperation in the Asia Pacific, pp.49–51. Retrieved from http://www.jstor.org/stable/resrep28672.16

MEA. (2021). Government of India. https://mea.gov.in/

Oak, N. C. (2018, October 6). Cam Ranh port: A lever in Vietnam's naval diplomacy. Observer Research Foundation. Retrieved from https://www.orfonline.org/expert-speak/cam-ranh-port-lever-vietnam-naval-diplomacy/

Ross, R. S. (2006). Balance of power politics and the rise of China: Accommodation and balancing in East Asia. *Security Studies.* https://doi.org/10.1080/09636410601028206

Sautin, Y. (2016, May 8). This Vietnamese base will decide the South China Sea's fate. *The National Interest.* Retrieved from https://nationalinterest.org/feature/vietnamese-base-will-decide-the-south-china-seas-fate-16093

Stafford, A. (2020). Vietnam's strategy: Change, continuity and balance – Encyclopedia Geopolitica. Encyclopedia Geopolitica. https://encyclopediageopolitica.com/2020/03/11/vietnams-strategy-change-continuity-and-balance/

Hai, D. Thanh (2021). Vietnam and China: Ideological bedfellows, strange dreamers. *Journal of Contemporary East Asia Studies,* 10(2), 162–182. https://doi.org/10.1080/24761028.2021.1932018

Thu, H. L. (2020). Rough waters ahead for Vietnam–China relations – Carnegie endowment for international peace. Carnegie Endowment. https://carnegieendowment.org/2020/09/30/rough-waters-ahead-for-vietnam-china-relations-pub-82826

Thuong, N. L. T., & Oanh, N. T. (2021). Vietnam in the Indo-Pacific region: Perception, position and perspectives. *India Quarterly,* 77(2), 129–142. http://doi.org/10.1177/09749284211005036

Tung, N. V. (2007). Vietnam's membership of ASEAN: A constructivist interpretation. *Contemporary Southeast Asia,* 29(3), 483–505. http://doi.org/10.1355/cs29-3f

15

SOUTH KOREA'S APPROACH TO INDO-PACIFIC

Jojin V. John

Over a decade, the Indo-Pacific has emerged as one of the most popular concepts in international relations. As an idea associated with the emergence of a new regional construct, the Indo-Pacific has become an essential factor shaping the foreign policy thinking of countries in the region and around the world. South Korea (hereafter Korea) presents an interesting case in its approach to the Indo-Pacific. Despite having significant stakes and showing interest in the emerging regional order, Korea is yet to embrace the concept in its official foreign policy. Korea's current approach to Indo-Pacific can be defined as "strategic ambiguity", where it engages with the regional process associated with the Indo-Pacific, however, without endorsing the concept.

The Korean approach to Indo-Pacific is not an isolated case but rather represents a situation of strategic dilemma in the foreign policies of several middle and small powers in the region. It is a situation shaped by the ensuing regional great power rivalry between the US and China and their respective visions of regional order (Kliem 2019). For Korea, the dilemma is profound, considering its geopolitical location and its security dependence on the US and its economic partnership with China. In a context where Beijing views the Indo-Pacific as an American-led strategy to contain China and its Belt and Road Initiative (BRI), it will not be easy for Seoul to endorse the concept. Despite Washington's insistence, Korea's ambiguity appears to accommodate Beijing's sensitivity on the matter and maintain a delicate balance between Washington and Beijing. Strategic ambiguity is also intended to enhance autonomy and maximise Seoul's foreign policy leverage without getting caught up in the strategic rivalry between the two for regional dominance (Lee 2019). Korea's ambiguity of the Indo-Pacific is also linked to the

DOI: 10.4324/9781003479307-18

entanglement-abandonment dilemma in Korean foreign policy associated with the US-Korea security alliance (Park 2019).

Though cautious, Korea's approach to the Indo-Pacific regional construct has been evolving. Korea articulated its vision of an emerging regional order under the New Southern Policy (Lee 2019). Echoing its interest in the emerging regional order, Korea also signed an agreement to promote collaboration between the New Southern Policy and the Indo-Pacific strategies of various countries (US Embassy 2019). These developments indicate a change in Korea's perception and approach to Indo-Pacific.

Explaining factors underpinning Korea's ambiguity and changing perception, the chapter evaluates Korea's evolving approach to the Indo-Pacific. The chapter is organised into six thematic sections. Following the introduction, the second section elaborates on conceptual aspects of the Indo-Pacific. The third section discusses the emerging dynamics in Korean foreign policy. In particular, it highlights the dilemma in Korean regional foreign policy in the background of rising US-China strategic competition. The fourth section provides a detailed discussion of the Korean discourse on the Indo-Pacific, highlighting its evolution. The fifth section introduces Korea's "New Southern Policy" as its pivot to the Indo-Pacific. A summary of the main arguments and the prospects of Korea's Indo-Pacific approach is discussed in the concluding section of the chapter.

Indo-Pacific and the New Regional Context

The emergence of the Indo-Pacific concept captures the evolutionary dynamics of international relations in Asia, especially concerning maritime Asia. During the Cold War and until recently, the maritime space was viewed as two separate regions, the Pacific Ocean and the Indian Ocean region. The centrality of the US-led security alliance and the economic dynamism that it helped to build through trans-Pacific linkages provided substance to the Asia-Pacific regional imagination. The economic dynamism of the Asia-Pacific outstripped what was happening in the Indian Ocean region, and the hub and spoke security architecture provided the luxury to ignore the interconnected nature of the two Oceans. However, with the shifting of the economic growth centre from East Asia to Southeast Asia towards the Indian Ocean region and Africa along with reconfiguration of the balance of power in the region, particularly with the rise of China, the emergence of India, repositioning of the US global posture, the emergence of new security challenges in the maritime domain, the linkages between the Indian and the Pacific Ocean regions can no longer be ignored. In essence, what happens in the Pacific will not end there but will have consequences in the Indian Ocean region and vice versa. It's true for politics, economics, security, and other dimensions of international relations.

The emergence of the Indo-Pacific concept, in essence, is simply acknowledging the new regional reality of the integrated nature of the Pacific and the Indian Ocean regions and recognising its immense implications for international relations in the years to come. It is a concept that is still evolving, and the region's institutionalisation is still in its infancy. There is no consensus on its definition except a broad understanding that the idea of two separate strategic spaces was a thing of the past and a historical aberration and a recognition of the strategic importance of the interconnected geographical space. The countries that promote the Indo-Pacific concept differ in their respective approaches (Heiduk and Wacker 2020) and even their descriptions of Indo-Pacific geography differ (Haruko 2020). However, the concept has acquired greater salience in international relations with more countries adopting the Indo-Pacific framework, including Japan, India, Australia, the US, ASEAN, and many European countries. However, even those countries that do not endorse the concept practice an Indo-Pacific strategy. China is the most important country that falls into this category. Perhaps no other state in recent history has invested in its interaction between the Pacific and the Indian Ocean than China. South Korea also has increased its Indo-Pacific presence and attention. The New Southern Policy that focused on strengthening Seoul's relations with India and ASEAN countries and its growing attention to the Indian Ocean and Pacific Islands countries is nothing short of an Indo-Pacific foreign policy in action.

Along with the idea of the Indo-Pacific as strategic geography, the concept anchored a new geopolitical narrative. The idea of the Indo-Pacific had a geopolitical conception since its inception a decade ago; however, the unveiling of Washington's "Free and Open Indo-Pacific" strategy in 2017 was framed as a full-fledged counter-narrative to China's vision of regional order. The Indo-Pacific, since then, is often interpreted as an alternative narrative to the "Rise of China" and Beijing's BRI initiative (Septiari 2019). Washington's endorsement of the concept and the promotion of the "Free and Open Indo-Pacific" vision were intended to refute the narrative of US decline and its disengagement from the region and to upset Beijing's narrative on its irresistible regional ascendency. In doing so, Washington, under President Donald Trump, heightened the rhetoric of the US role in the region, focusing on its military strength (Pugliese 2018).

The American narrative of the Indo-Pacific not only heightened Washington's confrontation with Beijing, focusing on the military, but more importantly, from an ideological perspective. The ideological dimension of the US's Indo-Pacific narrative presented a picture of Washington and its allies in the region as "peaceful, democratic players confronting autocratic and nefarious challengers" (Pugliese 2018). The logic of ideological confrontation in American strategic thinking is demonstrated in the 2017 US National Security Strategy, which describes what is happening in the Indo-Pacific as a "geopolitical competition between free and repressive visions of world order" (White House 2017). As a clear indication of heightening the confrontation with China, the Trump administration not only engaged in a long-drawn trade war but also criticised its infrastructure projects as *debt-trap diplomacy*, called Beijing a *new imperial power* and *revisionist power,* and blamed for its use of *"sharp power"* in meddling with domestic political affairs in the US (Solomon 2018; Pence 2018; White House 2017). COVID-19 pandemic further intensified the geopolitical narrative of the Indo-Pacific with growing confrontation between Washington and Beijing on multiple fronts and the institutionalisation of many US-led minilateral forums, including the Quad. Under new President Joe Biden, the US attempts to revitalise Washington's alliances and partnerships in Asia. The formation of AUKUS and the announcement of Washington's Indo-Pacific strategy clearly recognised the "China threat" as one of the primary reasons for Washington's intensifying focus in the region. Together with China's "Wolf Warrior" diplomacy, it added heft to the narrative of the Indo-Pacific as a geopolitical narrative.

Korean Strategic Outlook in a Changing Regional Context

Korean foreign policy in the 21st century has undergone a profound transformation. Traditionally, it focused on Korean Peninsula affairs and managing bilateral relations with four regional powers: the US, China, Russia, and Japan (Lee 2011). However, a narrow-focused foreign policy that served Korea well in the past is increasingly becoming incompatible for two reasons. First, Korea's strategic interest has expanded beyond the Korean Peninsula with its emergence as a middle power (John 2014). Meanwhile, Seoul has also been under pressure to make adjustments in its foreign policy in response to the changing strategic environment, mainly in the context of the rise of China and the US-China strategic competition.

The foreign policy challenges that Korea is facing in the context of structural transformation are not unique; many small and middle powers in Asia are also dealing with a similar situation. However, compared to other countries in the region, the Korean dilemma is acute given its geographic and strategic location in Northeast Asia and its dependence on the US for security and a strong economic partnership with China. Strong alliance relations with the US are needed more than ever before in the face of North Korea's rising missile and nuclear weapons capability. China today is Korea's most important economic partner, accounting for about one-quarter of its total trade and the top investment destination. Seoul also recognises the importance of maintaining good relations with China to resolve the North Korean nuclear problem and the issue of unification (Min 2016).

During the last three decades, Korea has successfully strengthened its economic, social, and political engagement with Beijing while maintaining its security alliance with Washington. The congenial relationship between Beijing and Washington has been an important factor that has helped foster Korea-China relations. However, the escalating strategic competition between the US and China constrains Korea's room for manoeuvring and autonomy. The recent escalation of China-US competition in trade and technology, in addition to the pervasive security competition, has further exacerbated Korea's strategic dilemma. According to a recent survey, Koreans see the economic and technological rivalry as the biggest challenge for Korea's foreign policy (54.3 percent) rather than their military competition (48.0 percent) or unstable inter-Korean relations (49.8 percent) (Lee Sook 2019).

Korea's ability to maintain a balanced foreign policy between Beijing and Washington has come under severe stress, amplifying its strategic dilemma. The THADD controversy is a case in point about how Korea has become the focal point of strategic competition between the US and China (John 2018). Similar situations of strategic dilemma in Korean foreign policy were evident on issues like the South China Sea, Asian Infrastructure Development Bank, Belt and Road Initiative, and Huawei (Moon and Boo 2017).

Maintaining a delicate balance between Washington and Beijing has been a running theme in Korean foreign policy for some time. Since his inauguration in 2017, President Moon Jae-in had openly said that he is pursuing balanced diplomacy. Highlighting the importance of balanced diplomacy, Moon said

> The relationship with China has become more important not only in terms of economic cooperation but also for strategic cooperation for the peaceful resolution of the North Korean nuclear issue. That is why I am pursuing balanced diplomacy with the US as well as China.
>
> *(Moon 2017)*

President Moon's balanced diplomacy in many respect is the continuation of President Park Guen-hye's *gyunhyong oigyo* (balanced or alignment diplomacy) which was focused on fine-tuning the two wheels of Korean foreign policy, alliance with Washington and Comprehensive Strategic Partnership with Beijing (Moon and Boo 2015).

Along with balanced diplomacy, Seoul also adopted regional multilateralism and diplomatic diversification as measures to address its foreign policy challenge emerging from regional great power competition. In this regard, President Moon's "Northeast Asia Plus Community of Responsibility (NAPCOR)" constitutes Korea's multilateral and diversification strategy (Kim 2017). The Northeast Asia Plus vision of President Moon is, in some respects, the continuation of previous President Park Guen-hye's Northeast

Asia Peace and Cooperation Initiative (Lee 2014). There are three components to NAPCOR: Northeast Asia Peace and Cooperation Initiative (NAPCI), New Northern Policy (NNP), and New Southern Policy (NSP). While the main focus of Moon's government's regional multilateralism is focusing on Northeast Asia, the "plus" dimension of the NAPCOR extends the scope to Eurasia through NNP, and Southeast Asia and the Indian Ocean region through NSP. Lately, the Moon administration has been giving more emphasis on NSP in a context where NAPCI and NNP are held up due to a lack of progress in the Korean Peninsula peace process (Lee 2019a).

Korea and Indo-Pacific: Evolving Dynamics

The region under the purview of the Indo-Pacific is the pathway for 30 per cent of Korea's exports, around 90 per cent of its oil and gas supplies, and has substantial Korean investments. Korea has been proactively engaged in the discourse of regional order mainly through ASEAN-centric regional institutions and reaching out to countries beyond East Asia. The introduction of the New Southern Policy in 2017 to strengthen Korea's relations with ASEAN and India has articulated Korea's growing interest in the Indo-Pacific region. To enhance its position in the Indian Ocean region, Korea became a sectoral partner of the Indian Ocean Rim Association (IORA) in 2018. Korea, since 2009, has been participating in overseas anti-piracy missions cooperating with the Combined Task Force 151, a task force operated by the US-led multinational naval partnership. In 2012, Korea also joined the India-China-Japan coordinated naval patrols and escort missions in the Gulf of Aden. The decision of Korea to build a blue-water navy, capable of operating in far seas, coinciding with its regional outreach, indicates Seoul's growing ambition of its role in maritime issues (Harris 2018).

Though the discourse of Indo-Pacific has been around for some time, Korea started paying serious attention to the concept only after Washington announced its "Free and Open Indo-Pacific Strategy" in 2017 (Kim 2018). During his visit to Korea in November 2017, President Trump stated that Washington sees the US-Korea alliance as "the linchpin of security, stability, and prosperity in the Indo-Pacific region" (White House 2017a). President Trump's invitation to join the Indo-Pacific strategy put Seoul in a difficult situation. Cross messaging and confusion created in response to Indo-Pacific indicate Seoul's strategic dilemma. The foreign ministry and the Presidential office were at odds in their response to President Trump's call for Korea to join Washington's Indo-Pacific strategy. While the foreign ministry welcomed the Indo-Pacific, the Presidential Office was indifferent in its response. The Presidential office later dismissed the idea, arguing that Korea sees little benefit from the Indo-Pacific strategy. In its explanation for rejecting the idea, the Korean Presidential office noted that it was President

Trump who "highlighted that the United States-Republic of Korea alliance remains a linchpin for security, stability, and prosperity in the Indo-Pacific", not President Moon (Kim 2018).

The main reason for Seoul's indifference to the Indo-Pacific in general and the US's Indo-Pacific proposal was its perception as a strategy to contain China (Kim 2018). With the release of the US National Security Strategy in December 2017, which categorically represented China and Russia as revisionist powers and its recognition that the growing competition between free and repressive visions of the future international order is the most consequential challenge for Washington's foreign policy, reinforced Korea's perception of FOIPS as a China containment strategy (Hankyoreh 2019; Lee 2018). In this regard, the Korean strategic commentators associated Indo-Pacific mainly with the Quadrilateral involving the US, Japan, India, and Australia, a consultative mechanism commonly known as the QUAD, to the extent of interpreting it as a US-led security arrangement to counter the rise of China and its Belt and Road Initiative (BRI) (Seol 2019). The timing was also very critical. Washington's Indo-Pacific proposal came at an instance when Seoul was making an effort to patch up its relations with China which was deteriorated due to the THAAD controversy (John 2018).

Another important aspect of Korea's indifference to Washington's Indo-Pacific proposal and the subsequent ambiguity is to do with the entanglement-abandonment dilemma in Korean foreign policy associated with the US-Korea security alliance (Kim and Cha 2016). Korea views that the US efforts to expand the scope of the ROK-US alliance to include the Indo-Pacific are not in the best interest of Korea, as it could lead to entanglement, meaning Korea could be entrapped in a conflict that the US might engage in the region. However, rejection of the US proposal brings up the problem of abandonment. In the context of North Korea's growing asymmetric military capability, the end of the alliance would be detrimental to Seoul's national security.

Despite its initial apprehension of the Indo-Pacific as a US-led containment strategy, Korea began taking an interest in the Indo-Pacific concept and appreciating the multiple narratives of the Indo-Pacific. India-Korea joint vision adopted during the visit of President Moon to India in July 2018 highlighted Korea's growing interest in the Indo-Pacific discourse. India and Korea adopted a shared vision for "a peaceful, stable, secure, free, open, inclusive and rules-based region" for the first time, indicating a growing convergence between India's Act East Policy and Korea's NSP. The bilateral vision for regional peace recognised the link between prosperity and security, thus underlining the significance of "freedom of navigation, overflight and unimpeded lawful commerce" (MEA 2018). It also highlighted the principles of "peaceful resolution of conflicts through dialogue, underlying the centrality of sovereignty and territorial integrity, in accordance with the universally-recognised principles of international law" (MEA 2018). In its outlook, the India-Korea shared vision for regional order strikes a similar chord with India's vision for the Indo-Pacific, though without mentioning the "Indo-Pacific" expression. However, it stated that Korea "took note of India's inclusive and cooperative vision for the Indo-Pacific region" (MEA 2018).

Korea also welcomed the ASEAN outlook of Indo-Pacific, which was announced in June 2019. President Moon, during the Korea-ASEAN commemorative summit, said Korea "welcomes the 'ASEAN Outlook on the Indo-Pacific' announced by the ASEAN countries ... and we will join in regional cooperation based on ASEAN Centrality" (Moon 2019). The joint statement issued at the Summit and Moon's remarks seem to indicate that Seoul is openly espousing the "ASEAN Outlook (ASEAN 2019). In the joint statement issued at the ASEAN-Korea commemorative summit, they agreed to work together to "contribute to enhancing regional and international peace, security, stability, prosperity and partnership through the ASEAN-ROK Strategic Partnership which supports sub-regional, regional and multilateral cooperation in order to realise mutual benefits for our people" (ASEAN 2019).

"New Southern Policy": Korea's Indo-Pacific Pivot

After a year of contemplation, Seoul has promoted the New Southern Policy (NSP) as Korea's approach to the emerging regional order and claimed to complement the FOIPS of the US and BRI of China. In this regard, Korean Foreign Minister Kang Kyung-wha said that Seoul is

> promoting a new policy to strengthen our relations with our southern neighbors – ASEAN, India, Pakistan, Sri Lanka. There are other competing, ... initiatives in this area – the Indo-Pacific Initiative, the One Belt and Road Initiative – and it's good that we have these initiatives because it underscores the centrality of this region, the centrality of ASEAN, but we must ensure that these initiatives are promoted in a way that's complementary, that preserves the openness, the inclusivity and the transparency, and very much in line with established international norms.
> *(Kang 2018)*

Minister Kang also recognised the existence of multiple versions of the Indo-Pacific; however, she underlined that the principles "openness, inclusivity and transparency is what drives all of these initiatives". A senior official of the Korean foreign ministry further laid out the Korean vision of regional order, highlighting three important points. First, it promotes the idea of open regionalism as the basis of the Indo-Pacific regional order. In this regard, Seoul would support "an open, transparent and inclusive regional architecture, where all the players live in harmony for peace and prosperity while respecting each other and abiding by international laws." The second principle of Korea's vision of regional order focuses on the promotion of "multilateral norms and institutions". The third element suggests that the "future regional architectures should be built upon the existing institutional resources". In this regard, Seoul stands for the full utilisation of "ASEAN-led multilateral institutions, such as ARF, ADMM+ and EAS ... In particular, EAS, whose membership includes 18 nations in the Indo-Pacific, can be a solid platform on which we can build open and multilateral regional architectures" (Cho 2018).

Promoting NSP as a regional initiative, Korea began engaging with the US Indo-Pacific strategy, indicating an attempt to find common ground between FOIPS and NSP. During his Summit with President Donald Trump in June 2019, Korean President Moon Jae-in stated, "Under the regional cooperation principles of openness, inclusiveness and transparency, we have agreed to put forth harmonious cooperation between Korea's New Southern Policy and the US' Indo-Pacific Strategy" (Moon 2019a). Following up on the lead taken by the two leaders, a joint document issued in November 2017 stated,

> The Republic of Korea and the United States are working together to create a safe, prosperous, and dynamic future for the Indo-Pacific region through cooperation between the Republic of Korea's New Southern Policy and the United States' Indo-Pacific Strategy based on the principles of openness, inclusiveness, transparency, respect for international norms, and ASEAN centrality.
>
> *(US Embassy, Seoul 2019)*

The document outlined the regional cooperation between NSP and FOIPS in three categories: prosperity (energy, infrastructure, development loans, and the digital economy), people (good governance and civic society), and peace (Mekong region-water management and Pacific Island countries-climate change). During the 4th ROK-US Economic Dialogue in November 2019, infrastructure, energy, and digital technology were discussed as potential areas of cooperation (State Department, 2019). The release of a joint document in November 2019 on regional cooperation provided a blueprint for Korea-US regional partnership (US Embassy, Seoul 2019). The discussions on collaboration between FOIP and NSP between the senior officials of the two countries in 2021 were focused on seven areas, including vaccine health cooperation, cooperation to improve ASEAN connectivity, response to climate change and green growth, ASEAN digital transition cooperation, water resource management in the Mekong region, cooperation in strengthening maritime capacity in the region, and people-to-people exchanges with young people (MOFA 2021).

References to the Indo-Pacific also increased significantly at the May 2021 Korea-US summit. The expression Indo-Pacific, which appeared only once at the Korea-US summit in November 2017, appeared five times in the joint statement of the May 2021 summit. In particular, the two leaders said,

> The importance of the ROK-U.S. relationship goes far beyond the Korean Peninsula and is based on our shared values and our respective approaches to the Indo-Pacific region. We are committed to working together to link Korea's New Southern Policy with the free and open Indo-Pacific initiative of the United States, and to work together to create a safe, prosperous and dynamic region for both countries.
>
> *(Cheongwade 2021)*

Korea has also shown interest in engaging with the Indo-Pacific strategy of Australia. During the second Korea-Australia 2+2 Dialogue in December 2019, Seoul agreed to find synergy between the "New Southern Policy" and Australia's "Indo-Pacific Strategy" "based on the principles of openness, inclusiveness, transparency, and respect for international norms" (DOD Australia 2019). As a first step towards regional partnership, Seoul and Canberra signed an agreement on regional development cooperation during the 2+2 Dialogue. During the first Korea-Australia cooperation on ASEAN in February 2021, the two sides discussed cooperation in four areas, including vaccines and health, water management in the Mekong region, support for ASEAN's post-COVID-19 economic recovery, and regional connectivity. It also stipulated bilateral cooperation in the promotion of maritime security (MOFA 2021a).

During President Moon Jae-in's trip to Australia in December 2021, South Korea and Australia upgraded their bilateral relations to a "Comprehensive Strategic Partnership" has seen more cooperation on Indo-Pacific (Yonhap 2021). In the Joint Declaration of Comprehensive Strategic Partnership, the expression Indo-Pacific appears eight times more than in the US-ROK summit statement. According to the joint statement, the Korea-Australia partnership,

> contribute[s] to our common vision of an open, inclusive and prosperous Indo-Pacific region... [t]he security of Australia and the ROK is tied to the stability, openness, and prosperity of the Indo-Pacific and a rules-based international order that protects the rights and sovereignty of states regardless of size or power....Australia and the ROK recognize that the stability of the Indo-Pacific depends on adherence to international law in the maritime domain, including in the South China Sea.
>
> *(DFAT Australia 2021)*

In addition, at the 2021 Korea-US and Korea-Australia summit, specific cooperation with the US and Australia regarding supply chain stability was discussed. Efforts have been made with the US to strengthen supply chain stability and strengthen partnerships, mainly in the semiconductor sector. For example, in December 2021, the Korean Ministry of Trade, Industry and Energy held a "Korea-US Semiconductor Partnership Dialogue" with the US Department of Commerce (Korea JooAng Daily 2021). At the summit meeting with Australia in December, an agreement was reached on strengthening the supply chain in a complementary form that combines Korea's strong manufacturing sector with Australia's resources (Yonhap 2021a).

Immediately after the outbreak of COVID-19 in 2020, South Korea has also been participating in regional multilateral efforts to respond to infectious diseases, which many analysts referred to as QUAD Plus (Smith 2020). It was a series of video-conferences between senior officials of the US, Japan, India, Australia, New Zealand, South Korea, and Vietnam initiated by the US side and meant to start an initiative to share best practices and collaborate and synergise actions against COVID-19. Though the initiative was started to exchange notes on the COVID pandemic, supply chain issues, and climate change are also being discussed at a later stage. However, Seoul was very apprehensive about being associated with QUAD. Korean Foreign Minister Kang Kyung-wha rejected the idea that the seven-country health security coordination meeting was an enlarged form of QUAD. In this regard, she said, "We don't think anything that automatically shuts out, and is exclusive of, the interests of others is a good idea". On QUAD, Minister Kang said, "If that's a structured alliance, we will certainly think very hard whether it serves our security interests" (Kang 2020).

While Korea has come a long way from its initial indifference to the Indo-Pacific, its approach remains ambiguous. Seoul has not yet officially announced an Indo-Pacific strategy, nor has it ever announced a separate position on the Indo-Pacific region Korea's Indo Pacific engagement through NSP remains mainly bilateral mainly and has been apprehensive about multilateral/minilateral cooperation initiatives underway in the Indo-Pacific. Even though Korea has taken initiatives to find common ground with the US and Australia's Indo-Pacific strategy, the scope of the cooperation is limited to ASEAN regions. It is also interesting to note that areas with traditional security or military or strategic implications are excluded, and the focus is on softer and less politically sensitive areas such as non-traditional security, human security, and the economy.

Conclusion

Notwithstanding this evolution, Seoul continues to maintain ambiguity on the Indo-Pacific concept. This ambiguity can be seen as the absence of articulation of its position or as an endorsement of the concept. Seoul continues to define the region as the Asia-Pacific. Korea's attempt to maintain distance from the Indo-Pacific concept is equally reflected in its cautious approach towards US-led minilateral dialogue formats in the region, including QUAD or QUAD Plus and initiatives like the Economic Prosperity Network, Clean Network Initiative, among others. Though it appears superficial and semantic at first glance, the matter is fraught with severe geopolitical implications from a Korean perspective. Korea's approach of strategic ambiguity towards the Indo-Pacific reflects its sensitivity towards geopolitical developments in the region. Though Korea values the US-ROK alliance as the centrepiece of its security, Seoul's dilemma stems from the perception that the Indo-Pacific is a US-led geopolitical vision designed to contain China. Seoul's ambiguity on the Indo-Pacific attempts to maintain a delicate balance between its relations with the US and China and avoid getting entangled in the strategic competition between the two. In the context of intensifying Sino-US regional rivalry, the promotion of the "New Southern Policy (NSP)" as Korea's regional policy is an attempt to maintain autonomy and promote its image as an independent regional actor. In doing so, Seoul attempts to find a middle ground between the US and China to take advantage of the regional opportunities while reducing the impact of great power geopolitical rivalry. It also provides a certain amount of flexibility to Korea in maintaining its approach of "strategic ambiguity" of selective engagement without endorsing the Indo-Pacific concept.

References

ASEAN (2019, November 26). *ASEAN-Republic of Korea Joint Vision Statement for Peace, Prosperity and Partnership.* Retrieved from https://asean.org/asean-republic-korea-joint-vision-statement-peace-prosperity-partnership/

Cheongwade (2021, May 22). *Korea-US Summit Joint Statement.* Retrieved from https://www1.president.go.kr/articles/10346

Cho, Byung-jae. (2018, September 4). *Speech by KNDA Chancellor at Minister's Panel II of the Third Indian Ocean Conference.* Retrieved from https://tinyurl.com/5xwk6jme

DOD Australia (2019, December 12). *Australia-Republic of Korea Foreign and Defence Ministers' 2+2 Meeting 2019 Joint Statement.* Retrieved from https://www.minister.defence.gov.au/minister/lreynolds/statements/australia-republic-korea-foreign-and-defence-ministers-22-meeting-2019

Hankyoreh (2019, November 19). *S. Korea Needs to Consider its Own National Interests Ahead of the US.* Retrieved from english.hani.co.kr/arti/english_edition/e_international/917637.html.

Harris, Bryan. (2018, October 19). South Korea Plans Blue-Water Naval Fleet. *Financial Times.* Retrieved from https://www.ft.com/content/b598f570-d34c-11e8-a9f2-7574db66bcd5

Haruko, Wada. (2020, March 16). *The "Indo-Pacific" Concept Geographical Adjustments And Their Implications.* Retrieved from https://www.rsis.edu.sg/wp-content/uploads/2020/03/WP326.pdf

Heiduk, Felix and Wacker, Gudrun. (2020). *From Asia-Pacific to Indo-Pacific: Significance, Implementation and Challenges.* Retrieved from https://www.swp -berlin.org/publications/products/research_papers/2020RP09_IndoPacific.pdf

John, Jojin. (2014). Becoming and Being A Middle Power: Exploring A New Dimension Of South Korea's Foreign Policy. *China Report,* 50(4), 325–341.

John, Jojin. (2018, May 2). *Towards a "New Normal": Explaining Developments in South Korea- China Relations.* Retrieved from https://icwa.in/pdfs/IB/2014/DevSouthKoreaChinaIB27022018.pdf

Korea JoogAng Daily (2021, December 9). *Korea, U.S. Launch New Dialogue on Semiconductor Partnership.* Retrieved from https://koreajoongangdaily.joins .com/2021/12/09/business/tech/semiconductor-US-Korea/20211209182241330 .html

Kang, Kyung-wha. (2018, September 17). *Session on Asia's Geopolitical Outlook at the WEF on ASEAN.* Retrieved from https://tinyurl.com/2d4hb4wh

Kang, Kyung-wha. (2020, September 25). *FM Reacts Negatively about Joining U.S.-led 'Quad' Alliance.* Retrieved from https://en.yna.co.kr/view/AEN2020 0925008900325

Kim, Ellen and Cha, Victor. (2016). Between a Rock and a Hard Place: South Korea's Strategic Dilemmas with China and the United States. *Asia Policy,* 21, 101–121.

Kim, Jaechun. (2018, April 27). *South Korea's Free and Open Indo-Pacific Dilemma.* Retrieved from https://thediplomat.com/2018/05/south-koreas-free -and-open-indo-pacific-dilemma/

Kim, Joon Hyung. (2017, November 2). *The Moon Administration's Multilateral Regional Diplomacy An Initiative of Northeast Asia Plus Community of Responsibility.* Retrieved from http://www.kida.re.kr/cmm/viewBoardImageFile .do?idx=23519

Kliem, Frederick. (2019, August 6). *ASEAN's Indo-Pacific Dilemma: Where To From Here?.* Retrieved from https://www.rsis.edu.sg/rsis-publication/cms/aseans -indo-pacific-dilemma-where-to-from-here/#.XktsFGgzaM8

Lee, Chung Min. (2011). Coping with Giants: South Korea's Responses to China's and India's Rise. In Tellis, Ashley (Ed.), *Strategic Asia 2011–12* (pp. 161–192). Washington, DC: National Bureau of Asian Research.

Lee, Dae Woo. (2018, July 26). *U.S. Indo-Pacific Strategy.* Retrieved from http:// www.sejong.org/boad/1/egofiledn.php?conf_seq=3&bd_seq=4410&file_seq =11288

Lee, Jaehyon. (2019a, June 21). *Korea's New Southern Policy. Motivations of 'Peace Cooperation' and Implications for the Korean Peninsula.* Retrieved from en.as aninst.org/contents/tag/northeast-asia-plus-community/

Lee, Jeong-ho. (2019, July 7). South Korea's US-China Dilemma Deepens with Support for America's Indo-Pacific Strategy. *South China Morning Post.* Retrieved from https://www.scmp.com/news/china/diplomacy/article/3017509/ south-koreas-us-china-dilemma-deepens-support-americas-indo

Lee, Sang-Hyun. (2014, December 15). *The Northeast Asia Peace and Cooperation Initiative (NAPCI): A Vision toward Sustainable Peace and Cooperation in Northeast Asia.* Retrieved from www.theasanforum.org/the-northeast-asia -peace-and-cooperation-initiative-napci-a-vision-toward-sustainable-peace-and -cooperation-in-northeast-asia/

Lee, Sook Jong. (2019, November 26). *ROK-US Cooperation in an Era of US-China Strategic Competition.* Retrieved from http://www.eai.or.kr/main/english/ publication_01_view.asp?intSeq=10351&board=eng_report&keyword_option= &keyword=&more=

MEA (2018, July 10). *India and Republic of Korea: A Vision for People, Prosperity, Peace and our Future.* Retrieved from www.mea.gov.in/bilateral-documents.htm

?dtl/30041/India_and_Republic_of_Korea_A_Vision_for_People_Prosperity
_Peace_and_our_Future

Min, Ye. (2016). Understanding the Economics–Politics Nexus in South Korea–China Relations. *Journal of Asian and African Studies*, 51(1), 97–118.

MOFA (2021a, February 15). *Korea-Australia ASEAN Policy Dialogue*. Retrieved from https://www.mofa.go.kr/www/brd/m_4080/view.do?seq=370962

MOFA (2021, May 13). *Held the Korea-US ASEAN Policy Dialogue*. Retrieved from https://www.mofa.go.kr/www/brd/m_4080/view.do?seq=371175

Moon, C.-I. and Boo, S. C. (2015). Korean Foreign Policy: Park Geun Hye Looks at China and North Korea. In Inoguchi, T. (Ed.), *Japan and Korea Politics: Alone and Apart from Each Other* (pp. 221–248). New York: Palgrave.

Moon, C.-I. and Boo, S. (2017). Coping with China's Rise. *Asian Journal of Comparative Politics*, 2(1), 3–23.

Moon, Jae-in (2017, November 3). *Cooperation with the US, Japan Important to Deal with Tension with Pyongyang: South Korea's Moon*. Retrieved from https://www.channelnewsasia.com/news/asia/cooperation-with-the-us-japan-important-to-deal-with-tension-9373348

Moon, Jae-in (2019, November 28). *South Korea's Support of the ASEAN Outlook on the Indo-Pacific*. Retrieved from english.hani.co.kr/arti/english_edition/e_edi torial/918905.html

Moon, Jae-in (2019a, June 30). *Opening Remarks by President Moon Jae-in at Joint Press Conference Following Korea-U.S. Summit'*. https://tinyurl.com /3m33e5w4

DFAT Australia (2021, December 13). *Australia-ROK Comprehensive Strategic Partnership*. Retrieved from https://www.dfat.gov.au/geo/republic-of-korea/republic-korea-south-korea/australia-republic-korea-comprehensive-strategic-partnership

Park, Cheol Hee. (2019, March 26). *South Korea is a Hesitant, but Friendly, U.S. Ally in the Indo-Pacific*. Retrieved from https://www.cfr.org/blog/south-korea-hesitant-friendly-us-ally-indo-pacific

Pence, Mike. (2018, October 4). *Vice President Mike Pence's Remarks on the Administration's Policy Towards China*. Retrieved from https://www.hudson .org/events/1610-vice-president-mike-pence-s-remarks-on-the-administration-s-policy-towards-china102018

Pugliese, Giulio. (2018, March 29). *The Military Dimension of the "Free and Open Indo-Pacific"*. Retrieved from https://www.chinausfocus.com/peace-security/the-military-dimension-of-the-free-and-open-indo-pacific

Seol, In-Hyo. (2019). *Trump's Administration Indo-Pacific Strategy*. Retrieved from http://www.kida.re.kr/cmm/viewBoardImageFile.do?idx=26600

Septiari, Dian. (2019, April 30). US Indo-Pacific Concept Best Alternative to China's BRI: Washington Official. *The Jakarta Post*. Retrieved from https://www .thejakartapost.com/news/2019/04/30/us-indo-pacific-concept-best-alternative-china-s-bri-washington-official.html

Smith, Jeff. (2020, March 30). *How America is Leading the "Quad Plus" Group of Seven Countries in Fighting the Coronavirus*. Retrieved from https://www .heritage.org/global-politics/commentary/how-america-leading-the-quad-plus-group-7-countries-fighting-the

Solomon, Salem. (2018, December 19). As US 'Debt-Trap Diplomacy' Rhetoric Heats Up, China-Africa Relations Hold Fast. *Reuters*. Retrieved from https:// www.voanews.com/africa/us-debt-trap-diplomacy-rhetoric-heats-china-africa-relations-hold-fast

US Embassy (2019, November 02). *The Republic of Korea and the United States Working Together to Promote Cooperation between the New Southern Policy and the Indo-Pacific Strategy, Joint factsheet issued by US and ROK*. Retrieved from https://kr.usembassy.gov/110219-joint-fact-sheet-by-the-united-states-and-the-republic-of-korea-on-cooperation-between-the-new-southern-policy-and-the-indo-pacific-strategy/

US Embassy, Seoul (2019, November 2). *U.S. & ROK Issue a Joint Factsheet on their Regional Cooperation Efforts*. Retrieved from https://kr.usembassy.gov/110219-joint-fact-sheet-by-the-united-states-and-the-republic-of-korea-on-cooperation-between-the-new-southern-policy-and-the-indo-pacific-strategy/

White House (2017, November 17). *National Security Strategy of the United States of America*. Retrieved from https://www.whitehouse.gov/wp-content/uploads/2017/12/NSS-Final-12-18-2017-0905.pdf

White House (2017a, November 8). *President Donald J. Trump's Visit to the Republic of Korea*. Retrieved from https://www.whitehouse.gov/briefings-statements/president-donald-j-trumps-visit-republic-korea/

Yonhap (2021, December 14). *Moon, Morrison Pledge Cooperation in Security, Pandemic Response*. Retrieved from https://en.yna.co.kr/view/AEN20211214002200315

Yonhap (2021a, December 14). *Moon Says S. Korea-Australia Cooperation to Strengthen Supply Chains*. Retrieved from https://en.yna.co.kr/view/AEN20211214004652315

16

TAIWAN IN THE INDO-PACIFIC

Suresh K.

As a geopolitical construct, stretching from the West Coast of the US to the Western shore of India, the Indo-Pacific has become the centre of world politics due to the increasing economic development and the competing claims made by various actors on the global commons. Different governments have officially emphasised the concept in the region, such as Australia, India, Japan, the US, Indonesia, and Singapore. Even though regional actors have different interpretations of the concept of the Indo-Pacific, it mainly denotes the emergence of an economic, geopolitical, and security system. It also signifies the increasing importance of two Asian nations, China and India. The geographical combination also signifies the importance of energy security and maritime security with regional security.

Indo-Pacific is a host to the world's most populous countries, various great and middle-level powers, abundant natural resources, and a hub of primary industrial production. In the maritime connectivity chain linking Europe with Asia, Taiwan acts as an essential linking point of vital sea lanes in the Indo-Pacific (Katoch, 2015). Its strategic positioning and proximity to the South China Sea, where most commercial activities are taking place, underpin the role of Taiwan in the region and its dependence on sea trade. Taiwan's geographical location allows it to deploy radar and sensors to understand the developments in the surrounding areas of the South China Sea. Moreover, Taiwan has a capable array coast guard, naval, and air forces that enable it to conduct joint freedom of navigation operations for all parties in the region. This position and assets would be of great advantage to the Indo-Pacific littoral states to protect their interest by enforcing the principle of international law. The region has thus become a critical geostrategic and economic area of all powers, including the US, China, Japan, Russia,

DOI: 10.4324/9781003479307-19

Australia, and India. Therefore, Taiwan can also contribute significantly to the maritime trade and commercial cooperation in building peace and stability across the Indo-Pacific (Panda, 2016).

The Strategic Significance of Indo-Pacific

The rise of China as a significant economic, political, and military power has been one of the significant features of the Indo-Pacific region. China increasingly depends on maritime shipment through the Indo-Pacific as an energy scarce state. China considers the Pacific region a window of economic opportunities due to the abundant supply of natural resources, a market for Chinese exports, and a hub for tourism joint ventures. Therefore, China considers the region strategically significant and thus engaged in building military presence and power projections in the Indian Ocean. Now China has enormous potential to compete militarily with the US and use military technologies that could, over time, tilt the traditional US military advantages to its side. Its economic miracle has also enabled most Asian economies to diversify their trade partnership exclusively confined to the US and the West (Beeson, 2009). Moreover, its military modernisation, coupled with a relative decline in the US military power vis-a-vis China's military buildup, has given China the impression that it can fill any power vacuum created in the region by the distracted US. It has not only accelerated its military modernisation programmes by increasing its defence budgets, but it has also increased its territorial claims in the South and the East China Sea. It has also increased its naval presence in the Indian Ocean region. The conventional interpretations of international maritime laws suit Chinese immediate strategic and national interests. Beijing's territorial claims are expressed through its UN-submitted 9-dashed line map, its 2014–2015 building expeditions, dredging and filling to create human made islands in disputed areas of the South China Sea, as well as claims against the Japanese Senkaku Islands and the establishment of an Air Defence Identification Zone (ADIZ) in the East China Sea. All these measures are supported by aggressive military, maritime security, and coast guard actions in both the South and East China Seas. These activities had jolted Japan, Vietnam, and the Philippines and have signalled China's aggressive intentions to the US (Ahlawat and Smith, 2016). In 2009, the PLA navies directly confronted American surveillance ships in the Chinese Exclusive Economic Zone on the ground of territorial infringement.

China's increasing assertiveness in the Indo-Pacific is manifested through its economic dominance in the Belt and Road Initiative (BRI), also known as One Belt One Road. The ambitious US$1 trillion investment project aimed at creating a wide network of infrastructure across Central Asia, the Middle East, and South-East and South Asia (Brian et al., 2017). The BRI, however, has certain strategic objectives. Through this initiative, China has been trying to expand its political influence, encouraging its industrialists and financial institutions to invest and loan, securing necessary resources from abroad, and exporting excess products to other countries (Kitaoka, 2019). Therefore, China does not consider itself a Pacific Power alone but is trying to reach westward to the Indian Ocean Region. China has determined to use IOR as a geopolitical space for advancing its vital economic objectives, including energy security (Singh, 2016). In order to maintain its position in the Indo-Pacific Region, China has also increased its relations with South Asian states like Sri Lanka, Bangladesh, Maldives, and Pakistan. The increasing assertiveness of China in the South China Sea and its selective approval towards international norms reveals that China can accept the present international order only to the extent that it suits Chinese interests (Pant and Das, 2018). As a result, China's new assertiveness stems primarily from four related developments. Firstly, Beijing's increasing realisation that the balance of power is shifting in its favour. Secondly, China's national interests include maritime security in the nearby Seas and trade routes. Thirdly, China considers its military power to extend its maritime interests. Finally, a favourable sentiment from the population at large (Yahuda, 2013).

Despite the vast opportunities offered by a free and open regional and international system, China has always tried to upset the system by challenging the values of a rule-based order. The People's Republic of China (PRC) is now robustly challenging the leadership position of the US, Australia, and New Zealand in the Pacific Islands by providing aid to gain political clout (Roy, 2019). Therefore, China's assertiveness in the maritime domain will continue due to its emphasis on anti-access/area denial (A2/AD) strategy and its firm belief that such a strategy has been effective in accomplishing its objectives (Mastro, 2018).

The increasing assertiveness of China has witnessed a balancing act from other actors in the region. The US has a keen interest in maintaining its influence in the Indo-Pacific region. The US, with its regional partners like Japan and Australia, has become significant partner in this regional security system. Thus, with China's rise and its increasing influence in the region, other partners, including India, are developing a regional security system based on equality and prosperity under an open Indo-Pacific strategy (Soong, 2018). The US may actively promote economic development and security cooperation with Japan, Australia, and India to create an open Indo-Pacific region with Taiwan as an active partner. They also provide extensive support for Pacific island states to increase their economic development and quality of governance and provide extensive military assistance that enables them to have strategic leverage over these states. In the maritime domain of the Indo-Pacific, the US and its partners consider Taiwan sensitive to the politics of the region and thus plays a more significant role in humanitarian and disaster relief operations. Taiwan has a well-trained military with advanced helicopters and naval vessels, which can be incorporated into the US plans to help with disaster relief throughout the region. Moreover, strong US support would allow Taiwan to gain access to naval bases in other countries. Thus, Washington could help Taiwan assist the US and its regional partners in securing overall peace and stability in the region.

The increasing assertiveness of China in the Indo-Pacific region is also manifested in its relations with Taiwan. The political, ideological, and historical origins of mistrust resulted in stifling the development of cross-strait relations. These cross-strait tensions did impact Taiwan's global economic and trade exchanges. The difference between the two countries dates back to the Cold War period when the UN General Assembly gave Taiwan the seat allotted to PRC. This resulted in both countries subsequently in winning over the maximum number of diplomatic friends to their side. In this respect, Taiwan considers that retaining even a few diplomatic allies, even small and medium powers, can have a determining role in Taiwan's international legitimacy. However, at the same time, the cross-strait tensions were used by the Chinese to limit Taiwan's economic expansion in the region by designing its exclusion from various negotiations on regional collaboration, forcing Taiwan's economic integration with mainland China, and undermining its autonomy (Yelery, 2016). China has been continuously exerting its pressure on Indo-Pacific countries to switch its recognition to PRC. Among the 17 countries that officially recognise ROC, six are from the Pacific Islands. Kiribati, Marshall Islands, Nauru, Palau, Solomon Islands, and Tuvalu are the countries that officially recognised ROC. However, China is trying to buy off Taiwan's diplomatic partners worldwide and has substantially increased its aid to the Pacific states to cultivate more considerable influence. China's policy has become more pronounced when China has become more powerful and spent a massive amount of money as assistance to those states that support its cause. Beijing spends about ten times more than Taipei's financial aid to the Pacific islands. Since 2016, about five countries have switched their recognition from ROC to PRC. China recently used its economic leverage to turn Palau, which has diplomatic relations with Taiwan and gets an annual stimulus grant of $10 million from Taiwan. China has also pressured its diplomatic partners Fiji and Papua New Guinea to restrict even their unofficial relations with Taiwan. As a result, in 2017, Fiji revoked its 20 years of diplomatic relations by closing its representative office in Taiwan. Papua New Guinea followed the same path by renaming its representative office from Trade Mission of the Republic of China to Taipei Economic and Cultural Office. This chequebook diplomacy between the two countries has negatively influenced the region's development. It has also resulted in a substantial financial loss for both countries as the negotiations and payoff are often secret and competitive. Taiwan, for example, lost

240 Suresh K.

$30 million in 2006 when talks with Papua New Guinea fell through, and international brokers pocketed the money).

The US, India, and Japan in the Indo-Pacific

The US considers China as the biggest peer competitor in the Indo-Pacific. Therefore, Washington actively sought partners to ally with the US in the Indo-Pacific region. Japan and Australia are two reliable allies in the Indo-Pacific. The US strongly advocated that a healthy and vibrant Taiwan is essential to maintain peace and security in the Indo-Pacific and advance its region's interest. Such a strategy can effectively prevent China from becoming a full-fledged maritime power, despite China's increasing military balance (Graham, 2019). The US and Taiwanese governments converge on common ground like democracy, human rights, and the rule of law. The increasing competition and conflict between the US and China in economic, trade, military, and technological fields strengthen Taiwan's geostrategic position. The US has been persuading Taiwan to maintain its sphere of influence through economic assistance, security guarantee, trade, and technological assistance. The US has expressed its commitment and willingness to strengthen its long-standing military relationship and develop a strong defence network with Taiwan and its partners. The Trump administration approved a $1.4 billion arms sale to Taiwan in June 2017. Earlier, President Barak Obama had approved $10 billion for Taiwan's defence needs. China has been much more adamant and even used its economic, security, and political power to dissuade Taiwan from actively engaging and building relations with outside powers, particularly the US. The US National Security Strategy 2017 emphasised Taiwan's legitimate defence needs and deter coercion. It also believes that a peaceful settlement is essential for the future of Taiwan, which should be based on the interest of the Taiwanese people. But at the same time, neither the US nor its partners are willing to engage in direct balancing against China.

In early 2018, the Foreign Affairs Committee of the United States passed two legislations, the Taiwan Travel Act and a bill to include Taiwan in the World Health Organisation (WHO), to strengthen the US-Taiwan partnership. While the former encouraged the visit between the US and Taiwan at the diplomatic and people-to-people levels, the latter aimed to counter any attempt to undermine Taiwan's inclusion in the WHO. The US also strengthened its defence partnership with Taiwan. The National Defence Authorisation Act (NDAA), passed in December 2017, provided US arms to Taiwan. The US also invited Taiwanese military forces to participate in the Red Flag exercise and the advanced aerial combat training drill and exchanges. The US concluded a US$1.4 billion arms sale package to Taiwan in 2017, which included technical assistance for the development of early warning radar, anti-radiation missiles, torpedoes, and missile components. The US justifies these defence partnerships based on the Taiwan Relations Act, which provided the necessary support for Taiwan to maintain its self-defence capability. The US expressed its willingness to support Taiwan and its identity as an independent nation through all these measures. However, the US has paid little attention to the role of Taiwan in the Indo-Pacific region. Countries like Japan and Australia also follow a similar approach towards Taiwan. The increasing support by the US, both in the ideological and security spheres, naturally invites severe punishment from China. Thus, the competition between the US and China will naturally harm the interest of Taiwan in the region.

India also has a very significant stake in the maritime security architecture of the Indo-Pacific. Three factors have motivated India to play a vital role in the Indo-Pacific. Firstly, in recent years, India's rapid economic growth has highlighted its critical role in enabling "good order at sea". The growing energy demand has made India connect with the Indo-Pacific region more comprehensively to ensure the region's maritime security. The World Economic Outlook 2015, presented by the International Energy Agency, projects that the energy demand for India will dramatically increase from 2014 to 2040. When India relies exclusively on energy imports, freedom of navigation of the Indo-Pacific will have to be assured. Therefore, the Indian navy will concentrate more on the Indo-Pacific region. India's objective is to maintain maritime dominance to counter China's expansionism in the Indian Ocean (Sakuja and Khurana, 2016). Secondly, India's maritime policy has been driven by an active leadership role replacing its traditional continental focus. Finally, the Indian navy's expanding capabilities can effectively meet its foreign policy goals (Gopal, 2017). All these factors, coupled with the increasing assertiveness of China, have led to a progressively increasing role of India in the Indo-Pacific security architecture.

Being a littoral state, India can play a significant role in the Indo-Pacific. The Look East Policy of 1990 seeks to expand India's engagement with South East and East Asia. When renamed the Look East Policy as Act East Policy, greater emphasis was given to strengthening India's strategic partnership with the Indo-Pacific region. Around 55 percent of India's trade in the Indo-Pacific transits through the South China Sea. India also reaffirmed its commitment to protecting the Sea lanes of Communications of the Indian Ocean through a shared commitment to peace and security, collective responsibility, and shared goals. The Concept of SAGAR – Security and Growth for All in the Region – unveiled by the Prime Minister of India, Narendra Modi in 2015 emphasised cooperation and development of all powers in the Indo-Pacific. Therefore, as India is looking more to the East in terms of the Act East Policy for security and economic cooperation, it has widened its security stake with regional countries, especially in sharing a maritime interest.

In protecting the SLOCs, India seeks cooperation with maritime powers like the US, Japan, Australia, and Indonesia (Terita and Perwita, 2018). India has welcomed the concept of free and open Indo-Pacific as proposed by the US and increased maritime cooperation with Japan. India's primary concern is the increasing influence of China in the Indian Ocean. The Act East Policy also indicates India's willingness to counterbalance China's growing influence in the Indo-Pacific. The bilateral naval exercise between the US and India has become a trilateral forum with the induction of Japan as a permanent member in 2015 (Garge, 2017). Thus, due to its geostrategic compulsions, India engages in strategic balancing with China though actively engaging with the US, without any formal strategic or security alliances.

India also considers Taiwan as an active partner to advance its interest in the region. The relations between India and Taiwan have made substantial progress due to their shared interests in multiple areas ranging from bilateral to multilateral areas. The NDA government, which came to power in 2014, has unveiled a set of policy initiatives to do business in India. It includes measures such as reducing the administrative and procedural requirements for the starting and running of business enterprises. The "Make in India" initiative has also emphasised changing India's approach towards the manufacturing sector. It encouraged foreign enterprises and domestic companies to increase India's investment and production facilities. In this respect, India considers its Act East Policy has an important place in the Go South Policy of Taiwan. India has a greater attraction towards Taiwan's long-standing expertise in physical infrastructure development. India looks towards Taiwan as a partner in fulfilling the vacuum in hardware technologies and combines it with its specialised knowledge in space science and services. With the increasing profile of India as a rising and progressive economy, there will be increasing investment from Taiwan. Similarly, the economic slowdown in Taiwan for the past several years will naturally encourage Taipei to greater economic engagement with India, with whom it has a complimentary economic interest. Moreover, India considers Taiwan a vital partner in India's approach towards the South China Sea, where joint exploration of resources and commercial activities are India's key priorities.

Japan has also played an essential role in the emerging Indo-Pacific region. Being the third-largest economy globally and a strong military power, Japan has increased its geopolitical clout beyond its territorial jurisdiction (Chellaney, 2018). Due to the geostrategic location and the changing geopolitics of the Indo-Pacific, Japan has been creating close links with like-minded partners to counter China's rise. Japan's Free and Open Indo-Pacific (FOIP) strategy converges with the strategy of other major and middle-level powers in the region. Thus, by emphasising a rule-based order, Japan has recognised the role of law and norms in dealing with the question of instability and conflicts in the maritime domain of the Indo-Pacific region (Nagy,

2019). Japan has nurtured its relationship with the US, Australia, India, the Philippines, and Vietnam. Japan has placed Taiwan as a strategic partner in its long-term objective to deal with an increasingly assertive China. It considers Taiwan's defence and security as one of the foremost foreign policy priorities. Japan is ready to work with Washington and like-minded states to check any potential Chinese aggression against Taiwan. On 16 March 2021, the US and Japanese defence ministers agreed to work together in the event of a direct military confrontation between China and Taiwan. Japan emphasised that trilateral relations between Japan, the US, and Taiwan are essential for the stable development of cross-strait relations. Japan also considered democratic Taiwan a critical partner and an important ally with which Tokyo shares fundamental values. Japan's Government continued its formal membership in the Taiwan-led Global Cooperation and Training Framework (GCTF).

A close examination of the policies pursued by major powers in the region shows that all the states in the region have their purposes or objectives in mind, ranging from short-term to medium-term and long-term strategic interests. There is an ongoing power competition between China, the US, and their respective partners. China has become one of the undisputed leaders of the region, both in military and economic terms. The military modernisation programmes, economic and security policies, and the One Belt One Road (OBOR) were designed to establish China's primacy in the Indo-Pacific region. The US and its regional partners like Japan, Australia, and Taiwan are also attempting to establish their dominance in the Indo-Pacific region. Therefore, the Maritime Silk Road Initiative, the Act East Policy, and the Rebalance to Asia are part of the big power competition for influence in Indo-pacific (Liu, 2016). This big power competition has a significant role in their policy towards Taiwan. Moreover, their policy also determines the existence of Taiwan as a sovereign nation and stop any forcible acquisition by China.

Taiwan in the Indo-Pacific

In terms of geography, Taiwan is a small country, i.e. the territory of Taiwan is 35,980 square kilometres. Taiwan faces the Western Pacific and the South China Sea in one direction and the Chinese mainland across the Taiwan Strait in the other. This geographical location underpins the geopolitical significance of the Indo-Pacific (Scott, 2019). The population of Taiwan is 23 million, similar to Australia or Haryana state or 52 times smaller than India. Although Taiwan is a full-fledged sovereign state, most international organisations in which the People's Republic of China participates refuse to grant membership to Taiwan or merely consider it a non-state actor. Only 22 small Central American, African, and Pacific Countries recognise the ROC diplomatically

(Singh, 2016). The rest of the states maintain their relationship through their representative offices and institutions. However, at the same time, this should not undermine Taiwan's positive features also. Taiwan is the 22nd most prominent country in terms of economy. It is a middle-power with a sizable population, a prosperous economy, a strong military, and a sizable foreign reserve (Jacob, 2016). Its high-tech industry also plays a crucial role in the global economy. The Taiwan Strait has also added significance to Taiwan in the Indo-Pacific region. It's a Pacific tributary that runs between Taiwan and mainland China, linking the East and South China Seas. It is a gateway used for maritime trade by nearly all the important ports in North East. Due to its geographical closeness to most Asian nations, the Strait is significant to the world maritime trade. The Strait is also important due to the increasing conflicts attached to it. Therefore, despite the improving cross-strait relations, the Strait risks instability and conflicts in Asia.

Taiwan plays a vital role in the emerging Indo-Pacific construct. It is located at the intersection of most East Asian nations. It is a meeting ground of the South China Sea's shipping lanes, 100 metres off the coast of China, 200 metres from the Philippines towards the South, 900 miles from Vietnam, under 100 miles from the Spratly Islands, and 1000 miles from Japan's homeland. Thus the geostrategic position of Taiwan and its coast guard, naval, and air force assets enable it to impact the emerging power play in the Indo-Pacific region. Its concern for protecting national autonomy motivated Taiwan's activity in the region. Being a small country lying at the periphery of an aggressive and assertive China and its limitation in having an advanced weapons system, Taiwan has emphasised cultivating goodwill with other governments by sharing its expertise in agriculture and healthcare. Through these engagements, Taiwan tries to demonstrate itself as an international actor and thereby ensure the international community's support in dissuading any attempt by the PRC to attack and invade the island unilaterally. Moreover, by aiding the developing world, Taiwan tries to maintain its official relations with those states that are willing to recognise the identity of Taiwan as a sovereign state. Though not a part of the Quad dialogue of the US, Japan, Australia, and India, Taiwan, due to its geostrategic location, will play a significant role in the future of the Indo-Pacific construct. The Indo-Pacific thus provides a common platform for Taiwan and like-minded states to address some of their domestic and foreign policy challenges.

Taiwan now faces many security challenges in the political, economic, diplomatic, and military areas. Due to the covert and overt systematic Chinese influence in and around the Indo-Pacific region, Taiwan has been subject to intense international isolation. Thus, Taiwan finds it more challenging to achieve meaningful participation in international organisations and defend its agenda abroad. Even Taiwan's friends and supporters are reluctant to intimidate China (Famularo, 2009). The relations between the People's

Republic of China and Taiwan have witnessed turbulences with the election of Tsai Ing-Wen of the Democratic People's Party as the president of Taiwan. Tsai refused to endorse the 1992 Consensus and the alternative proposal placed had been rejected against the One China Policy advocated by the PRC. Since then, Beijing has increased its pressure on Taiwan through measures like suspending the cross-strait dialogues, conducting informal consultations with local KMT-led governments, restructuring tourism, blocking. Taiwan was also restricted from participation in international forums like the WHO, WHA, and the ICAO, persuading the diplomatic allies of Taiwan to switch their recognition to PRC, increasing military exercises and patrols in the territorial waters adjacent to Taiwan.

China has never renounced military force against Taiwan and continues developing and deploying the advanced military capabilities needed for a potential military campaign (Department of Defence, 2019). These policies have a long-term impact on Taiwan's security and interests. Taiwan's military modernisation has stagnated over the past two decades, and the total spending on military development and modernisation has declined dramatically since the 1990s. However, the Tsai administration has proposed raising the military budget by 20 percent by 2025. However, this increase will not affect the primary picture of a highly resource-constrained military facing a rapidly modernising adversary across the Strait (Templeman, 2018). Moreover, Taiwan's long-term security planning has been impacted by its inability to attract youth to take up a career in the military. Even though the intensity of cooperation between China and Taiwan has increased, Beijing has not been reluctant to deploy force for shifting the military balance to its advantage. China has been deeply concerned about the growing relationship of Taiwan with the US, India, and Japan and who have their purposes or objectives ranging from short-term to medium-term and long-term strategic calculations. Therefore, Taiwan follows a realistic foreign policy, neither balancing China nor bandwagon the US. It has to follow a multi-vectored foreign policy based on its national interest. It should engage not only the US and China but with all the members of the international community, including the littoral states, to get maximum support for its legitimate claims. In this respect, the New South Bound Policy has a significant role in designing Taiwan's foreign policy for the 21st century.

The New Southbound Policy and the Changing Geopolitics of the Indo-Pacific

The New Southbound Policy (NSP), started in 2016 by President Tsai Ing-Wen, has brought about significant changes in Taiwanese foreign policy. For building a comprehensive partnership with ASEAN, South Asia, Australia, and New Zealand, the New Southbound Policy has attempted to reposition Taiwan's role in Asia and the Indian subcontinent through multiple social and business links based on equality and reciprocity, thus sustaining its current position (Chen and Chattaraj, 2017). It was adopted in 2016 after China proposed the OBOR in 2013. China's Maritime Silk Road geographically covers all ASEAN and South Asian countries. Beyond economic and trade links, the NSP emphasised developing multiple strategic linkages with Southeast and South Asian nations. These nations play an important role in regional integration through developing supply chains and production bases and developing Taiwan as a global logistic hub (Bell, 2019). The NSP consists of 18 countries, including ASEAN members, plus South Asian States, Australia, and New Zealand. The new policy has four pillars: 1) resource sharing and development; 2) collaboration in trade; 3) the development of institutional linkages; and 4) interpersonal contacts (Hsiao and Killy, 2019). Thus NSP and OBOR are two competing initiatives aimed at extracting resources and attention from the countries belonging to the Indo-Pacific region (Hsu, 2017).

The rejuvenated Go South Policy was initiated in 1994 under President Lee Tung-hui to encourage the business community to go south under enhanced policy coordination and resources. The Go South Policy also encouraged Taiwan to extract the benefits of the investment flow to develop trade diplomacy and negotiate bilateral agreements with Southeast Asian countries to encourage investment and other forms of economic engagement. Between the 1990s and 2000, the Go South Policy has radically changed to include several strategic goals beyond various economic calculations. Taiwan has also decided to redirect its investment away from China by placing Southeast Asian economies as a significant destination for trade and investment. It also tried to enhance bilateral trade with Malaysia, Singapore, the Philippines, Thailand, and Indonesia. Thus, for the first time, Taiwan placed Southeast Asia vis-a-vis the US, Japan, and Europe. Moreover, for the first time, India was placed in the policy. Later, the policy was reoriented towards market determination, and it intended to create a more innovative economy. These regional exchanges helped to promote and ensure stability and peace, which work in unison with the US concept of a free and open Indo-Pacific region.

The New Southbound Policy also has a similar objective. The policy aimed at increasing the socio-cultural, economic, and technological development of Taiwan while developing effective relations with China (Glaser et al., 2018). Besides domestic collaboration, the NSP aimed to make Taiwan less dependent on a single market and improve its scope and diversity of cooperation with like-minded powers at global and regional (Yang, 2017). In 2016, among the 15 trading partners of Taiwan, nine were from the Indo-Pacific region. The NSP seeks to increase trade with South Asian economies, increase FDI, and encourage soft-power diplomacy through tourism and education. While Taiwan's business community recognises the potential of South and Southeast Asia as a production base and market, it also maintains strong ties to mainland China (Black, 2019). The New Southbound Policy has already initiated cooperation in agricultural development, industrial innovation, entrepreneurial initiatives, and Overseas Development Assistance.

Moreover, under the auspices of the Taiwan-ASEAN Exchange Foundation, Taiwan began to give opportunities to young leaders from other countries to study in Taiwan. Many Indian students were offered the opportunity to study at various technical colleges. The NSP is also significant for Taiwan's regional integration and connectivity. It would be advantageous for the US and its partners, including Taiwan, to share the values and principles of a free and open Indo-Pacific. Essentially, Taiwan's attempt to forge closer economic ties with other countries in Southeast Asia, Australia, and South Asia is a form of balancing vis-à-vis Beijing (Scott, 2019). Therefore, the NSP, with its regional exchanges and collaboration, converges with the US and Japanese policy of a Free and Open Indo-Pacific. By aligning with FOIP, Taiwan will be represented at various multilateral and international forums and thus preserve its identity and sovereignty. However, there is also an increasing possibility that Taiwan will be used as a bargaining chip for US counterbalances against China (Hong and Pauley, 2018). While Taiwan upgrades its economic engagement and people-to-people ties with the US, Japan, and India, it can also work with other like-minded countries to promote increased connectivity standards consistent with international law and prudent financing (Hsiao and An, 2018). In conclusion, the US Free and Open Indo-Pacific, Japan's Arc of Freedom and Prosperity, India's Act East Policy, and Taiwan's New Southbound Policy converge on creating a web of partnerships based on the shared values of equality and freedom. They are also working in unison to address the common goals and challenges in the region. Thus, through its Indo-Pacific strategy, Taiwan has been increasing its position in the Indian Ocean and the Pacific Ocean by working with other nations in terms of trade, investment, and infrastructural development and thus ensuring freedom of navigation in the Indo-Pacific region.

Conclusion

Today, the Indo-Pacific is increasingly confronted with a more confident and assertive China that is unilaterally undertaking a set of policies to secure its political, economic, and security interests. Most of the countries in the region are directly or indirectly affected by China's activities at various levels. Among these countries, Taiwan considers China a great threat to its interests and the interests of the whole region. There is also a pattern in the relationship of countries with China and Taiwan. Most of them maintain diplomatic relations with the PRC while engaging with Taiwan in other matters. There is a broader convergence of interest between the US, Japan, Australia, and India in the Indo-Pacific region. Their interest coincides with Taiwan's interest in undertaking a collaborative approach to regional security efforts. Despite China's increasing pressure to deliberately exclude

248 Suresh K.

Taiwan from various international fora, sever ties with diplomatic allies, and isolate it from various regional trade blocs, Taiwan has never stopped contributing to a world where liberal international order and universal values have a significant role. Thus, through the New Southbound Policy, Taiwan is attempting to effectively balance China and ensure the support of all members of the region for maintaining peace and stability in the Indo-Pacific.

References

Ahlawat, Dalbir and Smith, Fred C. (2016), "Indo-Pacific Region: Evolving Strategic Contours", in D. Gopal and D. Ahlawat (eds.), *Indo-Pacific: Emerging Powers, Evolving Regions and Global Governance*, Delhi: Aakar Books.

Beeson, Mark (2009), "East Asian Regionalism and the End of the Asia-Pacific: After American Hegemony", *Asia Pacific Journal* 7 (2), pp. 1–19.

Bell, Corey (2019), "Why Taiwan's New Southbound Policy Should Steer Clear of American Geopolitik", *Taiwan Insights*, 27 November.

Black, Lindsay (2019), "Evaluating Taiwan's New Southbound Policy Going South or Going Sour?", *Asian Survey* 59 (2), pp. 246–271.

Brian, Crowley Lee, Majumdar, Shuvalov and Donough, David Mc (2017), "Responding to China's Rise: Japan and India as Champions for the Rule of Law in the Indo-Pacific", *Observer Research Foundation Occasional Papers*, no. 120, pp. 1–22.

Chellaney, Brahma (2018), "A Concert of Democracies in the Indo-Pacific Region", *Japan Times*, 14 November.

Chen, Mumin and Chattaraj, Saheli (2017), "New Southbound Policy in India and South Asia", *Prospect Journal* 18, pp. 35–62.

Famularo, Julia M. (2009), "The Taiwan Quadrennial Defence Review: Implications for the US –Taiwan Relations", *Project 2049 Institute*, 22 June, pp. 1–16.

Garge, Ramanand (2017), "Maritime Outreach as Part of India's Act East Policy", *Australian Journal of Maritime and Ocean Affairs* 9 (3), pp. 150–167.

Glaser, Bonnie S., Kennedy, Scott, Mitchell, Derek and Funaiole, Matthew P. (2018), *The New Southbound Policy: Deepening Taiwan's Regional Integration*, Washington, DC: Centre for Strategic and International Studies.

Gopal, Prakash (2017), "Maritime Security in the Indo-Pacific: The Role of the US and Its Allies", *Maritime Affairs: Journal of the National Maritime Foundation of India* 13 (1), pp. 27–40.

Graham, Euan (2019), "Reflections on Taiwan's Strange Centre Periphery Status in the Indo-Pacific", 3 April [oneline]. Available at https://taiwaninsight.org/2019/04/03/reflections-on-taiwans-strange-centre-periphery-status-in-the-Indo-Pacific/.

Hong, Chen Sheng and Pauley, Logan (2018), "Taiwan's New Southbound Policy Meets the US Free and Open Indo-Pacific Strategy", *The Diplomat*, 28 June.

Hsiao, Russell and An, David (2018), "Taiwan is Ready to Serve as an Indo-Pacific Partner", *The National Interest*, 4 January.

Hsiao, Russell and Borsoi-Killy, Marzia (2019), "Taiwan's New Southbound Policy in the US Free and Open Indo-Pacific", *Asia Pacific Bulletin*, 10 April.

Hsu, Tsun-tzu Kristy (2017), "A Review of Taiwan's Old and New Go South Policy: An Economic Perspective", *Prospect Journal* 18, pp. 63–87.

Sakhuja, V. and Khurana, G.S. (2016), Maritime Perspectives 2015, National Maritime Foundation: New Delhi [online]. Available at https://maritimeindia.org /View %20Profile /Maritime %20Perspective %2015 .pdf

Jacob, Jabin T. (2016), "Taiwan –India Relations: Constrained or Self Constraining", in Jagannath P. Pande (ed.), *India-Taiwan Relations in Asia and Beyond: The Future*, New Delhi: Pentagon Press.

Katoch, Prakash (2015), "Taiwan-why Shy Full Relations", 4 December [online]. Available at http://www.indiadefencerevie.com/news/Taiwan-wh-shy-full relations.

Kitaoka, Shinichi (2019), "Vision for a Free and Open Indo-Pacific", *Asia-Pacific Review* 26 (1), pp. 7–17.

Liu, Fu-Kuo (2016), "Maritime Security and the Indo-Pacific Security Link: The Strategic Reorientation of India and Taiwan", in Jagannath P. Panda (ed.), *India-Taiwan Relations in Asia and Beyond*, New Delhi: Pentagon Press.

Mastro, Oriana Skylar (2018), "Why Chinese Assertiveness is Here to Stay", *The Washington Quarterly* 37 (4), pp. 151–170.

Nagy, Stephen R. (2019), "A Key Role for Japan in the Indo-Pacific", *Japantimes*, 7 April.

Panda, Jagannath P. (2016), "India and Taiwan: Potential Regional Partners", in Jaganath P. Panda (ed.), *IndiaTaiwan Relations in Asia and Beyond: The Future*, New Delhi: Pentagon Press.

Pant, Harsh V. and Das, Pushan (2018), "China's Military Rise and the Indian Challenge", in Pushan Das and Harsh V. Pant, *Defence Primer: An Indian Military in Transformation*, New Delhi: Observer Researcher Foundation.

Roy, Denny (2019), "Taiwan's Potential role in the Free and Open Indo-Pacific Strategy: Convergence in the South Pacific", The National Bureau of Asian Research Special Report 77, pp. 1–14.

Scott, David (2019), "Taiwan's Pivot to the Indo-Pacific", *Asia Pacific Review* 26 (1), pp. 29–57.

Singh, Antara Ghosal (2016), "India, China and the US: Strategic Convergence in the Indo-Pacific", *Journal of Indian Ocean Region* 12 (2), pp. 161–167.

Soong, Hseik-When (2018), "US Strategy of a Free and Open Indo-Pacific: A Perspective of Taiwan", *Prospect Journal*, no. 19, pp. 9–28.

Templeman, Kharis (2018), "Taiwan's Place in the Evolving Security Environment of East Asia", *A Workshop Report by the Taiwan Democracy and Security Project*, Stanford University, pp. 1–27.

Tertia, Joseph and Perwita, Anak Agung Banyu (2018), "Maritime Security in Indo-Pacific: Issues, Challenges and Prospects", *Jurnal Ilmiah Hubungan Internasional* 14 (1), pp. 77–95.

The Department of Defence, United States of America (2019), "Indo-Pacific Strategy Report: Preparedness, Partnership, and Promoting a Networked Region", 1 June [online]. Available at https://www.defense.gov/News/Releases/Release/Article /1863396/dod-releases-indo-pacific-strategy-report/.

Yahuda, Michael (2013), "China's New Assertiveness in the South China Sea", *Journal of Contemporary China* 22 (81), pp. 446–459.

Yang, Alan H. (2017), "Strategic Appraisal of Taiwan's New People-Centered Southbound Policy: The 4 Rs Approach", *Prospect Journal* 18, pp. 1–34.

Yelery, Aravind (2016), "India-Taiwan Economic Relations and the China Factor: Prospect of Synergies and Challenges for Rapid Economic Integration", in Jagannath P. Pande (ed.), *India-Taiwan Relations in Asia and Beyond: The Future*, New Delhi: Pentagon Press.

17

CONCLUSION

Joyce Sabina Lobo and Josukutty C. A.

The geopolitics being played out in the Indo-Pacific are new to the region given the involvement of both the internal and external players. This is significantly so in the context of the rise of China as the preeminent power and the relative decline of the extant superpower – the US. Historically, countries in the region, major and minor, have not been caught mired in the matrix of power competition and balancing between the big powers as witnessed today. This is the first time in history that the countries of the Indo-Pacific region are faced with a situation to take sides between an Asian power – China, and the US, a Western power within Asian and most specifically the Indo-Pacific region. Even during the Cold War, though there was big power rivalry, it had not seen the current level of competition and confrontation in the Asian theatre with a great number of stakeholders. The key driver of geopolitics in the region is the intense rivalry between the extant great power (Waltz, 1993; Mearsheimer, 2001), the US and the emerging power China. Most of the countries are in a tricky situation whether to take sides either with the US or China and to what extent. The traditional allies of the US in the Indo-Pacific – Australia, Japan, South Korea – prefer the US security guarantees to meet the threat posed by China. At the same time, sticking to the Asian tradition, some of these middle powers and littoral states seek to keep away from intense big power rivalries to evade insecurity and war. India's policies of multi-alignment, inclusiveness and strategic autonomy are indicative of its aversion to bloc politics and all out confrontation in the Indo-Pacific.

The economic rise of countries like China and India, being figured in the high tables of global politics, and the anxiety it causes to the US, are fundamental to the developments in the Indo-pacific. China has been consistently

DOI: 10.4324/9781003479307-20

investing massive resources in projects like the Belt and Road Initiative (BRI) to make it economically and financially indispensable for trade and development in the region. Beijing has effectively utilised the reliance of other countries on the Chinese economy for political gains and has blocked many others from turning hostile in the new geopolitics. The rise of China was seen as a great opportunity by the countries in the region for lucrative economic cooperation with it. China is an indisputable power in the Indo-Pacific, and its strategic interests lie in safeguarding national unity and territorial integrity; ensuring the safety and security of energy and trade sea lines of communication; and maintaining stable strategic space in the Indo-Pacific, which are in no way threatening to others, asserts Huo Wenle in his chapter. One of the important points that Wenle makes is that China is the only major power to have not completed its reunification process. And hence indirectly, its territorial claims are justified, adding more to the security concerns of the Indo-Pacific region. The economic might of China began to be interpreted and felt in terms of political might through mega projects like BRI with duality of economic and political objectives, China's territorial expansion, and assertive engagements with neighbours in terrestrial and oceanic boundaries. The COVID-19 pandemic and the rather defeatist withdrawal of the US from Afghanistan and the aggressiveness of China in its conduct have only accelerated the new geopolitics of the Indo-Pacific.

Russia finds it very convenient to support China's claims over its spheres of influence. Moscow has carved out its Greater Eurasian partnership and therefore believes that it should be the leading pole within the Eurasian region and act as a link between Europe and the Asia-Pacific. The greater isolation of Russia since the Ukraine war has made Moscow to pivot towards the East, specifically the Indo-Pacific countries. The dangers of this pivot include Russia's growing relations with nuclear North Korea and how responsible it would be in terms of its desperate needs for war supplies. On a positive note, this pivot to the East has reinforced Russia's long-term strategy to bolster economic growth and development in the Russian Far East. Hence, the US and its allies will have not one challenger but two – Russia and China, along with North Korea – as rivals in the Indo-Pacific region. The rivalry here is in terms of balance of interests. Cooperation by Russia with partners in the Indo-Pacific region is largely for trade, especially in the energy sector, and for importing technology and high-end goods. With regard to Siberia and the Far East, the search for partners also includes investments.

The US, as the relatively declining power, came out with schemes to sustain its primacy by balancing against China with the help of traditional and newly cropped allies. Both nations today use realist means to justify their ends of power projection – the US by stifling the rise of China as a regional power within the Indo-Pacific and China by exerting undue influences on neighbouring states (Brunei, Indonesia, Malaysia, the Philippines, Taiwan, and Vietnam) through territorial claims in the South China Sea. Hence, China's rejection of the Indo-Pacific concept as being anti-Chinese and a threat to overall interests.

For the US, the Indo-Pacific is not just an oceanic route for free navigation or a safe zone free from non-traditional security challenges, but a "priority theatre" by calling itself a Pacific nation emphasising its bond with several nations of the region as enunciated by Nanda Kishore in the chapter on the discussion of the interest and strategies of the US. Most of the schemes enunciated by the US to deal with the new geopolitics in the Indo-Pacific have an underlying anti-China angle. The primary purpose of Quad, as pointed out by Surendra Kumar, is containing China, though many non-conventional security concerns are also part of the scheme in which other Quad members – India, Australia, and Japan – have committed at different levels. The central concern of Quad is to mitigate the perceived security threats arising from the rise of China. At the same time, they focus on essentially liberal norms of "free and open Indo-Pacific", "rules-based order", respect for sovereignty, and freedom of navigation. The fact that there is no agreement among the Quad members on many challenges that confront them points to the strategic dilemma they face. Simultaneous alternative schemes and engagements with the middle powers such as India, Japan, and Australia outside the US reflect their urge for diverse means to protect and promote their interests. This shows that states within the Quad strengthen their military capabilities, especially the rivals US-China (Waltz, 1979; and Mearsheimer, 2010). This added with the fact that there is a dilemma amongst the stakeholders, especially in security terms (Jervis, 1978) knowing the fact that the Indo-Pacific region hosts six of the world's nuclear weapon states, leads to escalation of offensive cum defensive arms.

Given the fact that other nations within the Quad, the middle powers within the ASEAN, and vulnerable states like Taiwan and South Korea have hesitations of direct confrontations between the US and China in the Indo-Pacific region, render open space for alternative schemes (Medcalf & Mohan, 2014). Moreover, these countries, such as Russia, understand that confronting the West or its spheres of influence leads to access denial to advanced technologies. Ionin (2015) terms this as "technological colonialism".

However, due to the historical past and the one's position of leading the Eastern camp during the Cold War, Russia has postured that it would establish itself as an independent power. This has unfolded in its policy towards Ukraine. Though economically and in terms of advanced technology, it has its limitations, it is still a military power to reckon with. The political and economic systems of Russia and China are compatible with similar ideologies of establishing their hegemony over their "spheres of influence". Hence, in this mosaic of the Indo-Pacific region, their partnership will bring an symmetry to the understanding of the region contrary to the one held by the US, Quad, ASEAN, and alliance partners.

Other nations of the Quad, the middle powers, ASEAN member states, and vulnerable states within the region, while aligning with the US in containing China have exhibited a propensity in their bilateral and multilateral actions to balance the rivalry of the two great powers and protect their interests and ensure peace and stability in the region (Keohane, 1984; Oye, 1986; Grieco, 1990). ASEAN members such as Brunei, Indonesia, Malaysia, the Philippines, and Vietnam have China as one of their top trading partners despite the latter making territorial claims. Therefore, most of these states have adopted liberal economic investment, infrastructure and development, human security measures for a peaceful, orderly, and stable Indo-Pacific. Fighting the non-conventional challenges of piracy, terrorism, climate change, energy security, and pandemic and ensuring technology cooperation for achieving better results through liberal cooperative means.

Apart from the scenario of big power rivalry and associated balancing, most of the countries in the region have their own positions and diverse and distinct interests to protect. India's interests in the Indo-Pacific include a favourable balance of power in the region, to protect and promote its trade and to emerge as a great power and to be able to project power abroad. Though not explicitly stated, containment of China is an important concern integrated into these objectives. India aims to achieve these goals through the Quad, Act East Policy and bilateral and multilateral engagements in an inclusive framework with the countries in the region. India's relationship with Japan and Australia, ASEAN and other littorals are designed to achieve these goals.

The Australian and Japanese approach to the Indo-Pacific is largely influenced by their traditional alliance with the US, and therefore containment of China is an important aspect of their relations through the Quad and defence and security understanding with the US. The September 2021 establishment of the trilateral security pact that is the AUKUS between Australia, the UK, and the US appears to be a renewal of the Cold War pact giving form to new Cold War. Shankari Sundaraman points to a play of great rivalry as the ingredients of Cold War like blocs at systemic level with mechanisms of economic power is clearly missing in the present context. She most importantly points out the fact that communist China's socialist market economy brings greater economic integration. Therefore countries like Australia like other stakeholders maintain strong beneficial economic relationship with other countries in the region emphasising the norms of free and open trade in a liberal context. Hence, elements of new Cold War appear in the form of tensions in several spheres, although the economic relationships write off this notion. However, the great power rivalry unfolds in the Indo-Pacific region like power contestations. Countries such as Malaysia are uncomfortable in accepting, as Ivy Kwek points out, the Indo-Pacific as a strategy and therefore siding with any of these rival powers. This stance of Malaysia echoes the positions of other similar smaller nations like Singapore or South Korea. Malaysia perceives the Indo-Pacific concept as part of the ploy for strategic competition between the US and its allies on one side, and China on the other and therefore is very cautious to avoid angering any of the big powers.

South Korea is a classic case of a strategic dilemma in accommodating the sensitivities of both China and the US and maintaining a delicate balance between the two. This strategic ambiguity is also intended to enhance autonomy and maximise Seoul's foreign policy leverage without getting caught up in the strategic rivalry between the two for regional dominance. Therefore, South Korea has vacillated between its security concerns by aligning with the US and at the same time trying to take advantage of the economic connectivity with China and hence has not endorsed the Indo-Pacific concept through any specific policy.

Singapore has maintained a consistently pragmatic stance on dealing with the various components of the Indo-Pacific architecture but has been utmost cautious in showcasing its association with any one side. This has helped the city-state to maintain a favourable consensus on its association with multiple powers while explicitly maintaining its centrality.

Indonesia's approach to the Indo-Pacific has been a fusion of its "Free and Independent" or "Bebas Aktif" approach that has been central to dealing with external powers and the ASEAN-centred institutional-normative approach. But this clashes with the security signalling of the Quad and Indonesia's urge for mutually beneficial economic relations with China.

Vietnam has openly opposed China's expansionist policies in the region. From a strategic perspective, Vietnam is willing to ally with extra-regional powers to become a major ally in its grand game to counter China's rise, especially in South China Sea. At the same time, Vietnam has explored the possibilities of economic cooperation with other countries in the region.

Taiwan, being a country under the US security cover, maintains strong relationship with countries of the Indo-Pacific, endorsing the idea of freedom of navigation for the benefit of all countries based on international law. What adds to the security dilemma of Taiwan is its strong economic and cultural ties with mainland China, while balancing US-China rivalry under the threat of a takeover by China. With Russia setting the example of territorial encroachment based on the past history in states such as Georgia and Ukraine, China might feel emboldened to invade Taiwan. The Russia-Ukraine crisis will have its effects on the Indo-Pacific region and its politics.

Significantly, countries with an anti-China mode also focus on how they together can progress faster through an inclusive rather than an exclusive policy. India's Indo-Pacific inclusivity approach and emphasis on negotiations, transparency, and evasive balancing; the ASEAN Outlook on the

Indo-Pacific" (AOIP) statement in 2019, which emphasised the "inclusiveness" of regional architecture and regional cooperation over "rivalry"; Japan's FOIP vision and Expanded Partnership for Quality Infrastructure (EPQI) insist on developing regional rules and norms for peace and development; for Australia, bilateral relations with China are crucial for trade and investment; Indonesia's and Malaysia's commitment to economic cooperation with Beijing; and Vietnam and the Philippines, who have direct territorial disputes with China, have strong economic and diplomatic association with China. Some of these countries like India, Japan, and Australia explore the prospects of middle power coalitions as parallel arrangements for mutual benefit and to mitigate the master rivalry of the big powers. The economic and trade ties of most of the countries in the region with China have grown in the recent past in the midst of growing security concerns. These countries want to avoid getting enmeshed in intense China-US rivalry. They opt for freedom and stability in the region through mutually beneficial economic and trade ties, taking advantage of mega projects including BRI. Cooperative engagement between these countries is encouraged to attract large-scale investments. China has skilfully exploited the COVID-19 pandemic to promote its geopolitical objectives. The US withdrawal from Afghanistan, India-China border clashes, diverse opinions in the Quad, formation of the AUKUS, and the Ukraine crisis add credence to realist politics. Therefore, the new dynamics in the region have a combination of both realist and liberal logic and compulsions at work, and the countries in the region explore both realist and liberal options to materialise their goals. Therefore, the region witnesses increasing big power rivalry and balancing at the highest level with doubting allies attached to them who simultaneously follow liberal means to protect their interests and peace and development in the region.

The new geopolitics in the Indo Pacific is cumulative of myriad uncertainties and dilemmas of the players of the region – the big, the middle, and the littorals. Apart from the larger drive of Sino US rivalry, what is equally significant is the dilemma of other powers and their urge to follow alternative bilateral and multilateral relations to protect their interests without inviting the wrath of the big powers. The vacillation and fluctuation visible in the views and approaches of all the players are born out of their fear of unpredictable impacts of the ongoing developments. What is driving the region rudderless is the absence of agreement on normative and institutional mechanisms to ensure security and development. Even if these mechanisms existed, institutions such as the ASEAN have been limited in terms of their centrality and their efforts towards multilateralism by the resuscitation of the Quad, the Quad Plus, AUKUS, and the like.

As pointed out above, the need for a balancing act of containing China while economically engaging with it has its repercussions on the emergence of the New Cold War. Though the US and China along with their respective partners through initiatives such as Quad and BRI, appear as Cold War elements, the ensuing dilemma, ambiguity, and circumspection of the stakeholders on the threat perception of China or the direct reference to China as a threat are absent. The security pact like AUKUS does not include any Asian partners. So far Asia has never experienced, since the Japanese militarism during World War II, the intentions of going for large-scale wars or provoking Cold War-like situations. These have been largely triggered by two events. Firstly, the US posture of openly identifying blatantly China and its rise as both a challenge and a threat to its policy on the Indo-Pacific. Secondly, the Chinese aggression in the South China Sea, its territorial claims, and the skirmishes in which it is involved, along with maritime strategies like BRI, CPEC, and the string of pearls to acquire naval bases. The need for economic cooperation has weakened regional institutional mechanisms like the ASEAN Regional Forum (ARF) to oppose the irredentist claims of China.

What is to be observed is the tendencies of undemocratic countries such as China and Russia, and their irresponsible behaviours have been boosted due to a silenced domestic audience. Both states have challenged the Westphalian system of state sovereignty at least within their respective neighbourhoods. But a fair share of blame should be laid on the US for its official policies and actions through its 2017 National Security Strategy and 2019 Indo-Pacific Strategy Report. These have been crucial in creating a Cold War-like scenario by directly identifying China and Russia as "revisionist" states as causes for the erosion of "values and principles of the ruled based order" (US DoD, 2019). The most damaging effect of the 2019 policy was the dissection of the ASEAN states as "friends", "potential friends", and "unfriendly states" which Shankari Sundararaman refers to as "salami slicing" that negates the very role of ASEAN. ASEAN since the end of the Cold War has moved towards embracing multilateralism with external players like China, Japan, India, Australia, New Zealand, etc., with the underlying principle of non-interference in any member state's internal affairs. Even the interstate disputes and territorial claims within the ASEAN members have not come in the way of tearing the institution asunder or diluting its real intentions. Moreover, ASEAN members along with the stakeholders of the Indo-Pacific region feel the need to stifle any promotion of the US-China rivalry playing out in the region that may lead to proxy wars or to take sides. This leads to the prevention of the crystallisation of a pure form of military pact or security organisation within the region that is driven by the Asian states.

What is observed in these myriad perceptions of the stakeholders on the Indo-Pacific is that while strong economic integration and trade cooperation exist, it weakens the regional responses to security pact/cooperation measures such as Quad. The strong move towards such security mechanisms is more pronounced among external players like the US, the UK, Australia, or France who are ironically part of the Cold War structures. Any balancing that is observed emerges from the remnants of the Cold War structure, and the recent example is the AUKUS. What emerges as Quad Plus is nothing but the liberal conception of the Indo-Pacific at play, with members like South Korea cooperating on grounds of countering pandemic COVID-19-related economic and public health concerns.

That is why nations focus on country-specific views and positions with room for multiple opportunities, which in turn adds to ambiguities and insecurities of the region. Therefore, the new dynamics in the Indo-Pacific need to be analysed through a vast spectrum that includes realism and liberalism. The countries are exploring both realist and liberal options for a stable and peaceful order in the region. But the leading framework of analysis is realist in nature as both big powers engage in realist balancing. But individual countries exploit liberal means to protect their interests and peace and development in the region. Thus, the template of the new dynamics in the Indo-Pacific is a combination of realist balancing and liberal mechanisms working side by side as enunciated by different countries. The focus on country-wise perspectives in the context of the big power rivalry adopted for the book captures the entirety of developments from a realist template with liberal insights superimposed on it.

References

Grieco, Joseph. (1990). *Cooperation among Nations*, Ithaca, NY: Cornell University Press.

Ionin, A. (2015, January/March). "A Technological Alliance: New Ways to Respond to Strategic Challenges", *Russia in Global Affairs*, 1. https://eng .globalaffairs.ru/articles/a-technological-alliance-new-ways-to-respond-to -strategic-challenges/

Jervis, Robert. (1978). "Cooperation under the Security Dilemma", *World Politics*, 30 (2), pp. 167–214.

Keohane, Robert. (1984). *After Hegemony*, Princeton: Princeton University Press.

Mearsheimer, J. John. (2010). "The Gathering Storm: China's Challenge to US Power in Asia", *The Chinese Journal of International Politics*, Vol 3 pp. 381–396. https://www.mearsheimer.com/wp-content/uploads/2019/06/The-Gathering -Storm-Chinas-Challenge-to-US-Power-in-Asia.pdf

Mearsheimer, John. (2001). *The Tragedy of Great Power Politics*, W.W Norton, New York.

Medcalf, R., & Mohan, R. C. (2014). "Responding to Indo – Pacific rivalry: Australia, India and Middle Power Coalitions". Lowy Institute for International Policy. https://www.lowyinstitute.org/publications/responding-indo-pacific -rivalry-australia-india-and-middle-power-coalitions

Oye, Kenneth A. (ed.). (1986). *Cooperation under Anarchy*, Princeton: Princeton University Press.

US DoD. (2019). "Indo-Pacific Strategy Report, Preparedness, Partnerships and Promoting a Networked Region". https://media.defense.gov/2019/Jul/01/2002152311/-1/-1/1/DEPARTMENT-OF-DEFENSE-INDO-PACIFIC-STRATEGY-REPORT-2019.PDF

Waltz, Kenneth N. (1979). *Theory of International Politics*, Reading, Massachusetts: Addision Wesley.

Waltz, Kenneth N. (1993). "The Emerging Structure of International Politics", *International Security*, 18 (2), pp. 44–79.

INDEX

Abbot, Tony 151
ABM treaty 92
Act East policy 24, 25, 139–140, 148–149, 156, 159, 227, 253
Afro-Asian unity movement 17
Air Defence Identification Zone (ADIZ) 22, 237
Albanese, Anthony 159
Allison, Graham 104
Anglo-Malayan Defence Arrangement (AMDA) 176
anti-access/area denial (A2/AD) strategy 238
anti-China strategy 113
Ashwani R. S. 13
Asia Infrastructure Investment Bank (AIIB) 60
Asia Pacific Economic Cooperation (APEC) 18, 38, 52, 94, 108, 118, 124, 198
Asia-Pacific Region (APR) 92, 94
Asia Pivot strategy 103
Association of Southeast Asian Nations (ASEAN) 6, 16, 17, 37, 94, 112, 150, 157, 182, 188, 195, 197, 208; ASEAN Defence Ministerial Meeting (ADMM)176; ASEAN Defence Ministers Meeting Plus Eight (ADDM+)156; ASEAN Expanded Maritime Forum (AEMF)

40; ASEAN Outlook for the Indo-Pacific (AOIP) 13, 45, 168; ASEAN Regional Forum (ARF) 35, 40, 256; and Middle Powers 174–176
AUKUS (Australia, the UK, the US) 63–64, 137
Australia 4–6, 9, 37, 61, 94, 112, 114, 149–152, 158, 174; Australian foreign policy 151; IPR 150–152; relationship with India 110
Australia, in Indo-Pacific Region (IPR): AUKUS 160; Australian Diplomacy 157–158; Australian-Indian relations 156; Australian perception on 150–152; Australia's relationships with China 150; military cooperation and interoperability 152–153; New Australian Leadership 159–160; Quad and trilateral strategies 158–159; security and economic prosperity 153; US-Australia defence relations 153; US factors in 152–153

Balakrishnan, Vivian 185, 190
Baldino, Daniel 111, 112
Bangladesh 51, 55, 63, 82, 95, 141, 142, 207–209, 238
Beazley, Kim 151
Belt Road Initiative (BRI) 4, 6, 8–10, 17, 18, 24, 42, 74, 79, 84, 95, 98,

260 Index

106, 125, 153, 168, 188, 225, 227, 237, 251
Biden, Joe 22, 75, 92, 93, 224
bilateral security 156
bilateral trade 95, 154
Bordachev, Timofei 98
Brazil, Russia, India, China and South Africa (BRICS) 94
Build Back Better World (B3W) plan 6
Bullock, Richard 36
Bush, George 53, 93

Cambodia 27, 36, 42, 43, 83, 95, 199, 214
Campbell, Kurt 20
Carr, Andrew 111
Chen Bangyu 76
Cheney, Dick 49
Chen Shuibian 19
China 6; and BRI 209–210; China ASEAN Free Trade Agreement 42; China-Japan relations 83; China-Philippines relations 83; China-US rivalry 9; Chinese loans 43; continuity and challenges in 210–211; Russian-Chinese relations 93; US investments in 36
China, in Indo-Pacific Region: China-Japan relations 83; China-Philippines relations 83; crude oil and natural gas consumption 78; geo-economic and geopolitical developments 73; geographic range 74; geo-security, geo-economy, and geopolitical interests 72; indisputable stakeholder in 72; Malacca Dilemma 78; maritime rights 80; maritime security and cooperation 80; national security and sustainable development 78; nuclear/conventional submarines 81; piracy and maritime terrorism 78; politics, diplomacy, and military approaches 74; regional cooperation initiatives 73; safeguarding national sovereignty and territorial integrity 84; security issues 76; territorial and maritime disputes 77; territorial integrity 80
China-ASEAN Summit 82
China-Myanmar Economic Corridor (CMEC) 154
China-Pakistan Economic Corridor (CPEC) 81, 154

Clean Network Initiative 235
climate change 76, 113
Clinton, Hillary 11, 19, 37, 107
Code of Conduct in the South China Sea (COC) 82
cold war politics: ASEAN multilateralism in 38–42; China's relations with regional states 42–44; economic integration 34, 36; India-ASEAN Convergences 44–45; regional cooperation 34; security dilemma 35; state-driven economic model 36; US-China Rivalry and multilateralism 36–38
Combined Task Force 150 226
Committee on Foreign Investment in the United States (CFIUS) 126
Commonwealth of Independent States (CIS) 94
Communications, Compatibility, Security Agreement (COMCASA) 141
Communist International 17
Comprehensive and Progressive Agreement for Trans-pacific Partnership (CPTPP) 173
Comprehensive National Power (CNP) 105
constructivism 10, 12, 40, 109, 111, 150
counter-proliferation 76
counter-terrorism 50, 65, 76, 157
COVID-19 6, 8, 9, 13, 36, 45, 113, 137, 139, 146, 155, 217, 224, 251, 257
Cui Tiankai 72
cultural diversity 82, 90

Danilevskii, Nikolai 90
Declaration on the Code of Conduct (DoC) 42
Delyagin, Mikhail 91
Deng Xiaoping 105
Diamond, Larry 112
Diaoyu Island 80
Doklam crisis 135, 136
Doyle, Michael 9
Dugin, Aleksandr 91
Duterte, Rodrigo 83

East Asia Summit (EAS) 40, 51, 94, 118, 134, 156
East China Sea 6, 57, 59, 74, 77, 80, 94, 95, 99, 124, 130, 144, 237

Index 261

East Coast Rail Link (ECRL) 171
Eastern Economic Forum (EEF) 97
economic development 3, 11, 73, 84, 97, 128, 157, 186, 196, 198, 212, 213, 236, 238
economic globalisation 75, 82
economic integration 10, 18, 34, 36, 42, 75, 94, 130, 131, 256
Economic Prosperity Network 235
Eurasian Economic Union (EAEU) 94
Eurasian Union 91
Europe 175–176
Exclusive Economic Zone (EEZ) 172
Expanded Partnership for Quality Infrastructure (EPQI) 9, 255

Five Power Defence Agreement (FPDA)169, 174
foreign direct investments 126, 158, 213
foreign policy 3, 94, 146, 151, 154; 2017 Foreign Policy White Paper 151, 154; Australian foreign policy 151; Bebas-Aktif Foreign Policy 198; Indian foreign policy 146; Indonesia 196–199; Singapore 183–185, 191; South Korea 224
Forum for India-Pacific Island Cooperation (FIPIC) 140
France 27, 55, 64, 104, 110, 113; with Malaysia relations 176; in Quad countries 41
Free and open Indo-Pacific (FOIP) 12, 36, 108, 118–119, 123–128, 145, 155, 211, 213
free trade agreement (FTA) 51, 95, 213
Fumio Kishida 58, 84, 121
Fursov, Andrei 91

geo-politics, of Indo-Pacific: Australia's role 25; France 27; India's role 23–26; role of Japan 22–23
Global Maritime Fulcrum (GMF) 45, 201, 206
Global Security Initiative (GSI) 8, 62
Gorbachev, Mikail 90
Go South Policy 242, 249
Greater Eurasian Partnership (GEP) 94
Gross Domestic Product (GDP) 5
Guam doctrine 171
Guen-hye 225

Haiyang Dizhi 27, 174
Hambantota port 81

Haushofer, Karl 3, 115, 134
Headquarter Integrated Area Defence System (HQIADS) 174
Hong Lei 62
Howard, John 151
Hu Jintao 78, 82, 106
Humanitarian Assistance and Disaster Response (HADR) 143, 214
Hun Sen 43
Huo Wenle 11, 251

Ibrahim, Anwar 170
identities 111
imperial Japan 4
India 175; India-Australia Comprehensive Strategic Partnership 159; India-France relations 110; Indian foreign policy 146; Indian Maritime strategy 137; Indian warships 141
India, in Indo-Pacific Region 5, 9, 35, 44, 61, 109–110, 150; Act East Policy 139–140; AUKUS 139; capabilities 142; capacity building 142–143; challenges 143–146; division 140; domestic tranquillity and growth rates 137; economic and political influence 137; HADR 143; Indian shipping industry 137; India-US relations 138; interoperability 141–142; maritime domain awareness 143; operations 140–141; Quad 138–139; regionalism 140; role of seas 135
Indian Ocean Naval Symposium (IONS) 140
Indian Ocean Rim Association (IORA) 140, 226
Indonesia, in Indo-Pacific Region 9, 44, 256; Bebas-Aktif Foreign Policy 198; foreign policy 196–199; institutional approach 196; post-Cold War democratic transition 195
Indo-Pacific Economic Framework for Prosperity (IPEF) 6
Indo-Pacific Oceans Initiative 25, 109
Indo-Pacific Partnership for Maritime Domain Awareness (IPMDA) 6
Indo-Pacific Region (IPR): Australia in see Australia, in Indo-Pacific Region; China in see China, in Indo-Pacific Region; economic and political influence 134; geo-politics see Geo-politics, of Indo-Pacific Region; India-China border issues 148; India

262 Index

in *see* India, in Indo-Pacific Region; Indonesia *see* Indonesia, in Indo-Pacific Region; Japan in *see* Japan, in Indo-Pacific Region; Malaysia *see* Malaysia, in Indo-Pacific Region; regional development 148; Russia in *see* Russia, in Indo-Pacific Region; Singapore *see* Singapore, in Indo-Pacific Region; Sino-Japanese competition 150; South Korea *see* South Korea, of Indo-Pacific Region; strategic significance of 148; Taiwan *see* Taiwan, in Indo-Pacific Region; Trump administration for 37; US, in *see* US, in Indo-Pacific Region; Vietnam *see* Vietnam, in Indo-Pacific Region
Indo-Pacific Strategy 6, 22, 108, 256
Information Management and Analysis Centre (IMAC) 143
"INFRA" 110
INS Airavat incident 24
International Monetary Fund (IMF) 43

Jaishankar, S. 25
Japan 5, 9, 22, 94, 109, 174; and Canberra relations 156
Japan, in Indo-Pacific Region: Free and Open Indo-Pacific 123–128; geo-strategic interests in 122–123; and Quad 128–131
Jiang Zemin 106
John, Jojin V. 13
Joint Coast Guard Committee on Maritime Cooperation 83
Joint Declaration of Comprehensive Strategic Partnership 230

Kang Kyung-wha 228, 234
Kaplan, Robert 103
Khurana, Gurpreet S. 24, 71, 134
Kishore, Nanda 12, 252
Kjellen, Rudolf 3
Kondapalli, Srikanth 10
Korea-China relations 225
Korea-US summit 230
Kovind, Ram Nath 137
Kuik Cheng Chwee 171
Kumar, Anil xiii, 12
Kumar, Surendra 11
Kurlantzick, Joshua 114
Kusumaatmadja, Mochtar 198
Kwek, Ivy 254

Laksmana, Evan 41
Lee Hsien Loong 64, 178
Leifer, Michael 35
Leont'ev, Konstantin 90
Liang Fang 74
liberalism 7, 9, 146, 257
Li Keqiang 83, 124
Lobo, Joyce S. 11
Look East Policy 24–25, 120, 149, 156, 174, 175, 241
Lukin, Alexander 90

Mackinder, Halford J. 3
Madhusudhan B. 12
Mahan, Alfred Thayer 3
Malacca Straits Patrol (MSP) 177
Malaysia, in Indo-Pacific Region 5, 9, 44; ASEAN and Middle Powers 174–176; geographical advantage 169; IPEF and BRI 171; peace and stability 170; Quad alliances 170–171
Maldives 95, 141, 142, 207, 238
Mao Zedong 17
Maritime exchanges 160
Maritime Security Initiative 172
Maritime Silk Road (MSR) initiative 6, 8, 42, 81
Marsudi, Retno 201
May-lee Chai 106
Medcalf, Rory 35, 85, 104
memoranda of understanding (MoUs) 172
Ministry for Development of the Russian Far East (MINVR) 97
Modi, Narendra 25, 44, 61–62, 84, 109–110, 120, 148, 156
Moon Jae-in 229, 230
Morganthau, Hans J. 3
multilateralism 39, 44
multipolarisation 82
multipolarity 93–94
Mutual Logistics Support Agreement 142
Mutually Assured Destruction (MAD) 104

Natalegawa, Marty 200
National Defence Strategy (NDS) 149
National Development Bank (NDB) 60
National Missile Defence 92

National Security Strategy (NSS) 79, 149, 256
NATO 92, 139
Nazi Germany 4
neo-liberal institutionalism 109, 111
neo-realism 109
New Southern Policy (NSP) 13, 226, 228, 249
New Zealand 37, 63, 94, 150
ninth World Peace Forum 73
non-aligned movement 17

Obama, Barack 53, 107, 113, 119
One Belt One Road initiative (OBOR) 120
One China Policy 245

Pakistan 17, 24, 57, 61, 81, 82, 95, 144, 207, 238
Panarin, Alexander 91
Panikkar, K.M. 135
Papua New Guinea 239
Parcel Islands 155
Partnership for Quality Infrastructure (PQI) 6, 120
Pelosi, Nancy 79
People's Republic of China (PRC) 238
Permanent Court of Arbitration (PCA) 42
Philippines 5, 9, 94
Pillsbury, Michael 105
Pitsuwan, Surin 40, 199
Principles for Quality Infrastructure Investment 174
Purushothaman, Uma 12

Quadrilateral Security Dialogue (QUAD) 6, 41, 113, 171, 227, 255, 257; AUKUS 63–64; Australia in 53–54; China in 5, 51–52, 60–63; India in 49, 54–55, 61–62; Japan in 49, 54, 128–131; Quad 1.0 11, 49, decline of 52–55; Quad 2.0 11, 55–56, 59, 62–63; Quad Plus 63; regional forums 52; revival of 56–59; shared security objectives 50–51; shared values 50; US-India bilateral exercises 50

Ram, Vignesh 13
Ratzel, Friedrich 3
realism 9, 109
Regional Comprehensive Economic Partnership (RCEP) 28

regional cooperation 9, 11, 34, 39, 72, 73, 186, 228, 255
regional economic integration 18, 75, 131
regionalism 34, 40, 197
regional security 13, 40, 41, 44, 45, 60, 104, 139, 156, 177, 196, 200, 202–204, 208
Rice, Condoleezza 19
4th ROK-US Economic Dialogue 229
Rudd, Kevin 52, 151
Russia, in Indo-Pacific Region (IPR) 11, 35; Eurasia 90–93; multipolarity 90–94; Russian Far East (RFE) 96–98; Sino-Russian relations 90
Russian-Chinese relations 93
Russian Far East (RFE) 89, 96, 98
Russia-Ukraine war 14, 60, 113

Savitskii, Peter 90
sea lines of communication (SLOCs) 137, 169
Sea routes, control of 3
security threats 5, 123, 130, 252
Shanghai Cooperation Organisation (SCO) 94
Shinzo Abe 19, 22, 49, 55, 56, 57, 61, 71, 72, 83, 111, 119, 123, 124, 128, 134, 150, 168
Shringla, Harsh Vardhan 64
Singapore, in Indo-Pacific Region 6, 13, 256; ASEAN Regional Forum (ARF) summit 190; foreign policy 183–185, 191; Free and Open Indo-Pacific Concept 189; geopolitical compulsions 182; Quad-focused military concept 189; regional geopolitics 183; sea routes and trade 188; security culture and outlook 185–187; trade and commerce 191; US-Singapore defence pact 189
Singh, Manmohan 24, 49
Sino-Indian relationship 74, 84
Sino-Japanese competition 150–151
Sino-Myanmar Oil and Natural Gas Pipelines 81
Sino-Russian relations 35, 96
social informationisation 82
socialisation 35, 184
soft power 216–217
South China Sea 23, 37, 41, 92, 94, 123, 154, 155, 168, 171, 211
Southeast Asia 39

264 Index

Southeast Asia Nuclear Weapons Free
  Zone (SEANWFZ) 39
South Korea, of Indo-Pacific Region 6,
  63, 94, 175, 256; economic dynamism
  222; foreign policy 224; geopolitical
  location 221; New Southern Policy
  223; region's institutionalisation 223;
  strategic ambiguity 221
Soviet Union 4, 17, 36, 105, 215
Special Commemorative Summit 44
Spratly Islands 155
Spykman, Nicholas 3
Sri Lanka 51, 55, 82, 95, 136, 143, 207,
  208, 228, 238
stakeholders 4–8, 10–12, 72, 136, 138,
  191, 196, 250, 256
Strakhov, Nikolai 90
Strategic Defense Initiative (SDI) 92
Suez Canal 171
Suga, Yoshihide 203
Sundaraman, Shankari 10, 253
Supply Chain Resilience Initiative
  (SCRI) 159, 203
Surendra Kumar, S. Y. 11
Suresh, K. 14
sustainable development 45, 78, 82,
  113, 214
sustainable development goals
  (SDGs)122, 214, 217

Tagore, Rabindranath 17
Taipei Act 77
Taiwan, in Indo-Pacific Region 6, 14,
  175, 256; geographical location
  236; geostrategic position of
  244; international organisations
  244; military development
  and modernisation 248; New
  Southbound Policy and geopolitics
  245–248; strategic significance of
  238–240; US, India, and Japan
  240–245
Taiwan Independence Movement 77
Taro Aso 123
THADD controversy 225
Thai-Cambodian conflict 199
Thailand 5, 94
Third Indo-China war 42
Trade tariffs 114
Trans-Pacific Partnership (TPP)
  75, 215
Treaty of Amity and Cooperation
  (TAC) 39

Trilateral Cooperative Arrangement
  (TCA) 177
Trubetskoi, N. M. 90
Trump, Donald 20, 71, 92, 93, 104, 107,
  113–114, 134, 153, 223, 224, 229
Turnbull, Malcolm 151

Ukraine war 251
UN Convention on the Laws of the Sea
  (UNCLOS)154, 160
UN General Assembly 239
United Kingdom 27, 153, 175–176
United Nations Convention on the Law
  of the Seas (UNCLOS) 42–43, 45, 60
United States 9; US-Australian relations
  152; US-China Trade War 36; US
  Department of Defense Strategic
  Guidance 2012 6; US National
  Security Strategy 223, 227; US
  non-profit Freedom House 112; US
  rebalance strategy 184; US-Vietnam
  Comprehensive Partnership 214
United States National Defence
  Education Act 17
United States National Security
  Strategy 37
US, in Indo-Pacific Region: interests
  and strategy 107–113; leaders
  and diplomats 104; limitations
  of strategy 113–115; US-China
  relations 104–107
US-China relations: economic
  interdependence 105; harmonious
  society and the scientific concept of
  development 107; trading partner 18;
  western markets 107

Varghese, Peter 151
Vietnam, in Indo-Pacific Region 9,
  63, 256; ASEAN Centrality in
  211–214; Cam Ranh Bay Naval Base
  215–216; China 209–211; economic
  and political relationships 207;
  geopolitics 207; in manufacturing
  and textiles 208; soft power
  diplomacy 216–217; and US 214–215
Vietnam war 36
VIth Tokyo International Conference
  on African Development (TICAD
  VI) 121

Wang Lina 75
Wang Yi 21, 62, 72, 73

Wei Hong 76
Wendt, Alexander 151
Widodo, Joko 201
Winberg Chai 106
Wong, Alex N. 20
World War II 256
Wu Huaizhong 75

Xie Guiping 74
Xi Jinping 28, 62, 81–84, 119, 172, 209

Yasuo Fukuda 123
Ye Hailin 75
Yukio Hotoyama 124

Zhang Jiadong 75
Zhang Jun 120
Zheng He 106
Zhu Cuiping 75
Zoellick, Robert 52
Zone of Peace, Freedom, and Neutrality (ZOPFAN) 39

Taylor & Francis eBooks

www.taylorfrancis.com

A single destination for eBooks from Taylor & Francis with increased functionality and an improved user experience to meet the needs of our customers.

90,000+ eBooks of award-winning academic content in Humanities, Social Science, Science, Technology, Engineering, and Medical written by a global network of editors and authors.

TAYLOR & FRANCIS EBOOKS OFFERS:

- A streamlined experience for our library customers
- A single point of discovery for all of our eBook content
- Improved search and discovery of content at both book and chapter level

REQUEST A FREE TRIAL
support@taylorfrancis.com

Printed and bound by CPI Group (UK) Ltd, Croydon, CR0 4YY
01/12/2024
01797780-0016